Future-proofing

Future-proofing

Making Practice-Based IT Design Sustainable

CARLA SIMONE
INA WAGNER
CLAUDIA MÜLLER
ANNE WEIBERT
VOLKER WULF

OXFORD
UNIVERSITY PRESS

OXFORD
UNIVERSITY PRESS

Great Clarendon Street, Oxford, OX2 6DP,
United Kingdom

Oxford University Press is a department of the University of Oxford.
It furthers the University's objective of excellence in research, scholarship,
and education by publishing worldwide. Oxford is a registered trade mark of
Oxford University Press in the UK and in certain other countries

Published in the United States of America by Oxford University Press
198 Madison Avenue, New York, NY 10016, United States of America

British Library Cataloguing in Publication Data
Data available

Library of Congress Control Number: 2021941944

ISBN 978–0–19–886250–5

DOI: 10.1093/oso/9780198862505.001.0001

Printed and bound by
CPI Group (UK) Ltd, Croydon, CR0 4YY

Foreword

Sustainability is crucial for the future of our societies. From a computing perspective, the challenge is to design IT artifacts that contribute to improving people's work and everyday life in a sustainable way, thereby also contributing to social and ecological sustainability. To this end, we have developed a research approach that explores the design of innovative IT artifacts with a view to their appropriation in practice.

Research engagements, be they located in academia or in industries, are typically project-based and equipped with resources for only a limited period of time. From a sustainability point of view, the question of how to make these projects and their socio-technical results future-proof in practice arises.

This is the topic of this book. Although the participatory design (PD) and the computer-supported cooperative work (CSCW) research communities are in principle committed to designing IT artifacts that are useful in practice, few researchers have engaged with the future-proofing of the results of their work. Achieving the appropriation and continuous use of IT artifacts by practitioners who have participated in their design is outside the scope of most funding schemes and requires a long-term engagement that academics may find hard to afford.

The book documents the experiences of a number of research colleagues and describes their efforts to achieve sustainable design results, the difficulties that barred the way, and the strategies they adopted to achieve the goal of sustainability. The analysis of these cases motivated consideration of how to more systematically address and possibly overcome the impediments to sustainability.

The changes that would be necessary to make the main stakeholders—funding agencies, IT professionals, management, and the software industry—more open to creating environments for sustainable innovation are substantial. Implementing them would require the (political) will to move from top-down approaches to technology development, and on to a practice-based methodology. It would also oblige the software industry to fundamentally alter its strategies and business models.

The book can only spell out some of these changes. It would not have been possible without the contributions of our colleagues Konstantin Aal, Margunn Aanestadt, Ellen Balka, Matthias Betz, Nicola Bidwell, Jeanette Blomberg, Nico Castelli, Tommaso Colombino, Johannes Gärtner, Antonietta Grasso, Steve Jackson, Christoph Kotthaus, Myriam Lewkowicz, Thomas Ludwig, Volkmar Pipek, and Martin Stein. We are grateful for their experiences, thoughts, and critical comments.

We gratefully acknowledge the support provided by the Collaborative Research Centre (CRC-1187) 'Media of Cooperation' funded by the German Research Foundation (DFG). We would also like to thank the University of Siegen's School of Media and Information (iSchool) and the International Institute for Socio-Informatics (IISI), Bonn, for enabling this line of research.

Table of Contents

SECTION II. CASE STUDIES

SECTION IV. EPILOGUE

List of Abbreviations

ADE	adverse drugs event
AR	augmented reality
AI	Artificial intelligence
CAD	computer-aided design
CC	Competence Center
CLI	command-line interface
CN	community network
EPSRC	Engineering and Physical Science Council
CRM	customer relationship management
CSIR	Council for Scientific and Industrial Research
CSCW	computer-supported cooperative work
CST	Clinical Systems Transformation
EHR	electronic health record
EM	emergency management
EMDC	Emergency Medical Dispatch Centre
EMR	Electronic medical record
EPR	electronic patient record
ERP	enterprise resource planning
EU	European Union
EUD	end-user development
FIT	Fraunhofer Institute
GIS	geographic information system
GSM	Global System for Mobile Communications
HA	provincial health authority
HCI	human–computer interaction
HIS	hospital information system
ICC	intercultural computer club
ICT	information and communication technologies
ICT4D	information and communication technologies for development
IoT	(Integrated) Internet of Things
II	information infrastructure
IS	information systems
IT	information technology
ML	machine learning
MoH	Ministry of Health
MRP	manufacturing resource planning
NAV	Norwegian Labor and Welfare Administration
NLP	natural language processing

NGO	non-governmental organization
NPC	on-profit cooperative
PCC	Palestinian Child Centre
PD	participatory design
PP	production planning
RFP	request for proposal
RFS	request for service
SLA	service level agreement
SME	small and medium-sized enterprise
TA	tribal authority
TO	Transformation Office
UN	United Nations
USO	university spin-off
VC	videoconferencing

SECTION I
FRAMING THE BOOK

1

Introduction

Research in applied computing today requires researchers to engage deeply with practitioners in order to design innovative information technology (IT) artifacts and understand their appropriation. The quality of IT design is shaped and evaluated through social practice, so questions arise such as: how does an innovative IT artifact enrich users' work and everyday lives, and how does it help organizations and communities to improve their services and performance?

But, what happens when the research project is over? What happens to the artifacts and those practitioners who were engaged in the research endeavour? The sustainability of IT research in practice is also an issue of ethics: the engagement of users in a project should be a worthwhile experience for them.

An abundance of stories about systems that are never used—or are abandoned after a short time—points to an enormous waste of resources, not only in economic terms. Likewise, the time and effort that designers and users put into conceiving, developing, and eventually implementing a system will be wasted if the result turns out to be unsustainable. A crucial insight from these stories is this: the key to the success of IT research lies in its ability to develop systems and applications that can be tailored and further developed by users with a view to augmenting their practices. While the term 'sustainability' is closely connected with a 'green agenda', some researchers also use the notion of *future-proofing*. This more specifically refers to IT design, asking designers to devise and implement actions towards the future: 'If you future-proof something, you design or change it so that it will continue to be useful or successful in the future if the situation changes' (Collins Dictionary, 2018). Using empirical material from leading research groups in Europe, North America, and South Africa, this book examines the strategies that IT researchers develop to make practice engagements sustainable.

Academic IT research and design are often carried out in the context of funded projects, which provide external resources for a limited period. The

Future-proofing. Wulf et al., Oxford University Press.
© Carla Simone, Ina Wagner, Claudia Müller, Anne Weibert, and Volker Wulf (2022).
DOI: 10.1093/oso/9780198862505.003.0001

types of projects the book explores are of this kind: they assume a socio-technical perspective and are oriented towards the design of IT artifacts that are to be appropriated in a real-world context, contributing to individual, community, organizational, and larger societal goals. To achieve these goals, researchers need to collaborate with stakeholders that represent a diversity of skills and practical experiences. A project's need for allies to achieve its goals often complicates the trajectory towards a sustainable design result, as communications between stakeholders may require special effort and perspectives may diverge and even conflict. Under such circumstances, the fact that project time is limited may turn into a major impediment to creating a potentially useful technical artifact. When a project ends, the stakeholders collaborating in it face some questions: how can its positive outcomes survive and maintain their usefulness when the consortium dissolves? What is the impact on the target users, who may have had positive experiences during a project, appreciated its results, and would like to rely on them in the future? *Future-proofing*, here, can be summarized as 'how the project outcomes can be sustained and made useful in the long term'.

Research that demonstrates how the collaboration of multiple stakeholders in developing an IT-based solution may lead to a sustainable outcome, and that discusses the 'dissipating forces' that may make this difficult, is scarce. This book seeks to bridge this research gap by developing a socio-technical perspective that looks beyond individual projects to cases in fields as diverse as healthcare, firefighting and emergency management, manufacturing in small and medium-sized enterprises (SMEs), IT service provision, information and communications technology for development, and learning across cultures. In distinguishing between individual projects and broader cases, we suggest that in order to move IT design towards long-term sustainability, researchers may have to look beyond a single project as a unit of activity and try to build support for a more continuous engagement with a research issue, community, and/or organization. Most of the examples assembled in this book are of this nature.

The literature offers a number of sensitizing concepts (Blumer, 1954) that help harvest the experiences of future-oriented projects, such as appropriation work, learning, technological flexibility, the type of innovation a project strives for, and ownership. The book uses examples from a variety of projects and cases to refine and elaborate these concepts, demonstrating how they may help to capture aspects of sustainable IT design and provide insights into a set of 'big questions', including:

- How to assume responsibility towards the user community but also build alliances with key actors that may help ensure the scalability and/or transferability of research outcomes to future users;
- How to resolve the tensions between the push for technological innovation and the need to ethically commit to improving users' work/lives in substantial ways;
- How to share ownership of a project and prepare the grounds for handing over the project results to a user community/organization;
- How to design technologies that are flexible and adaptable, and hence can be adapted to local needs and organizational changes;
- How to take care of the material aspects of technologies such as working with resources that are accessible (and if possible renewable) and taking care of maintenance and repair already in design.

With this overarching and long-term perspective, sustainability and future-proofing are conceptualized as complex issues. In laying out and investigating this complexity, the book assumes a comparative perspective on the projects/cases. Hence, one of its central contributions is methodological—that is, how to compare the conditions, strategies, and outcomes of a set of rather diverse case studies, identifying differences and similarities.

1.1 The notion of sustainability

The United Nations' (UN's) Brundtland Report took a broad view on sustainable development in 1987, defining it to be 'development that meets the needs of the present without compromising the ability of future generations to meet their own needs' (p. 37). The discourse that evolved from there finds sustainability to be strongly connoted with a 'green' agenda and has developed from the original ecological concern to include the economic and social dimensions of human interventions, attracting the attention of researchers from different application domains. Recent TED (Technology, Entertainment, and Design) talks on sustainability by design (TED, 2020) have asked how we as builders and creators can 'build thoughtfully, without waste'. Thoughtful building, it appears, requires careful consideration of multiple details, including material and economic aspects but also social practices, individual and community values, and not least matters of time, to achieve innovative results. In 2015, the UN's member states agreed on the Sustainable Development Goals (SDGs) incorporating 17 objectives with the aim of joining forces against poverty and social inequality and achieving sustainable economic growth. IT is seen as a major driver as well as a measure for ensuring socially just transitions (Tjoa and Tjoa, 2016).

Human–computer interaction (HCI) research has taken up the term 'sustainability' in a discourse that emphasizes the role of IT in encouraging lifestyles that account for the environment (e.g. persuasive technologies), support ambient awareness, or help reduce 'resource wastage and pollution, especially due to the rapid obsolescence of current technologies' (Di Salvo et al., 2010: 1979). IT-based systems and applications have an important but ancillary role, providing tools 'to collect, elaborate and share the (huge amount of) data pertinent to each application domain for the sake of sustainability' (Meurer et al., 2018: 498).

The term sustainability is also used in discussions of whether an IT-based solution lives on and has an impact, although its strong connotations with 'green IT' create potential misunderstandings. Still, it is difficult to avoid a widely used term that relates to taking care of the implications of human interventions. Altman (1995) provides a good argument as to why it makes sense to refer to sustainability in fields other than ecology: 'Researchers involved in community work must face the challenging problem of planning for the time when the research and development phase of a program is completed' (p. 527). In discussing health interventions, he defines sustainability as:

> the infrastructure that remains after a research project ends. Sustainability includes consideration of *interventions* that are maintained, *organizations* that modify their actions as a result of participating in research, and *individuals* who, through the research process, gain knowledge and skills that are used in other life domains.
>
> (Altman, 1995: 527)

This is also the idea behind sustainable IT design: to ensure that the outcomes of a project live on, making a difference for the people, communities, and/or organizations that have participated in their development and/or for whom they have been designed. Sustainable design here defines 'an act of choosing among or informing choices of future ways of being' (Blevis, 2007: 505). This discourse was continued and enriched early on—for example, by Mann et al. (2008), who argued for the integration of education for sustainability into computing education; Wakkary and Tannenbaum (2009), who pointed at 'the creative and sustainable ways people appropriate and adapt designed artifacts' (p. 365) in everyday life; or Blevis (2007), who emphasized the actions of professional designers to foster sustainability. Recent research has further elaborated on the interplay of material and digital, economic and ecological, and individual and community aspects for achieving sustainability (e.g. Cerratto-Pargman and Joshi, 2015; Pantidi et al., 2015; Purvis et al., 2019).

The book builds on and further develops these networked lines of discourse. Looking at a diversity of case studies from a comparative perspective allows us to advance our understanding of the conditions and strategies that create future-proof IT artifacts, enabling their appropriation to continue beyond the time span of a project. This continuity has two tightly intertwined dimensions: (1) the technical maintainability and flexibility of the IT artifact, and (2) the consolidation of the social practices that develop through appropriation work and learning and the ability to maintain the reflective development of these practices. To achieve this continuity, it is important to acknowledge that the starting points of the involved stakeholders with regard to agency, knowledge, skills, networks, and other resources may vary considerably. Future-proofing in both dimensions requires resources and capabilities that were made available by external sources during the lifetime of a project but may fall short after its end. Finally, the term future-proofing also indicates that research oriented towards an IT-supported exploration of problems and opportunities in the real world needs a wider framing.

1.2 Practice-based computing

A set of basic conditions is required for sustainability to become an aim and issue in a project:

- Recognizing the front-end employees as knowledge workers; consequently, focusing on their work practices as a basic way to understand the context of any initiative;
- Valuing the differences of perspectives, interests, values, and knowledge that emerge from the study of the context;
- Consequently, conceiving the technology as a way to manage the resulting complexity;
- And having the ethical mission to empower the users and improve their working conditions in the given organizational or community setting.

This approach is associated with the participatory design community, computer-supported cooperative work (CSCW) research, and the 'ethnographic turn' (e.g. Randall, 2018) that advocated observational studies of (work) practices. Starting with a series of seminal studies of cooperative work in, for example, control room environments (Hughes et al., 1992; Heath and Luff, 1992), print shops (Bowers et al., 1995), law offices (Blomberg et al., 1996), and hospitals (e.g. Berg, 1999), CSCW research has built up an impressive collection of case studies with a view to designing computer support. Participatory design, which started in the 1980s, seeks to include users in all design decisions. Although some participatory design projects are more oriented towards creative and explorative design experiences, the tradition of aiming at sustainable changes in a community or organization continues, as can be seen, for example, in projects in fields as varied as education (e.g. Bødker et al., 2017), healthcare (e.g. Simonsen and Hertzum, 2012; Balka et al., 2018), and community development (e.g. Haskel and Graham, 2016; Ssozi-Mugarura et al., 2017).

This research tradition has lately been extended by the idea of practice-based computing (Wulf et al., 2011; Kuutti and Bannon, 2014; Wulf et al., 2015, 2018). Using ethnographic research in combination with participatory design techniques as a starting point, practice-based computing moves a step further by concentrating more systematically on how to actively support appropriation of an IT artifact beyond the context and time frame of a particular research project and how to ensure that the artifact and practices can evolve over time:

> [...] in any complex environment it is clear that IT artifacts should be designed with an understanding of the variability of practices in potential fields of application and their temporal evolution in mind. We believe that even small differences in social practices may, although not always, require differently designed IT artifacts in their support. So, techniques that support local appropriation practices [...] and those that enable local actors to tailor IT artifacts to differences in the supported practices, need to be investigated and applied.
>
> (Wulf et al., 2018: 10)

One aspect of this shift in attention towards the time after project completion is the need to reconsider the role of the researcher when the design results have been 'handed over' to a user organization or community. The research team may move from observers and designers to new roles as facilitators and technology consultants. As 'strangers' to the organization or community, they may become more entangled with their inner workings but also have less of a voice than before.

Looking beyond a specific project includes developing sensitivities to the real-world contexts that are supposed to benefit from a design result. Wulf et al. (2015) point towards the importance of developing tools to acquire, document, and transfer insight from one project or 'design case study' (p. 119) to another, and also to 'provide actors (researchers, practitioners, designers) with opportunities for self-reflection and learning' (Wulf et al., 2018: 11). Taking a long-term perspective on research and the sustainability of its outcomes seriously has far-reaching implications for the academic culture in which the researchers are embedded.

1.3 The case study perspective

Projects are the most fine-grained and relevant instruments to engage in innovative research, as they provide researchers with the necessary human and technical resources. Projects allow researchers to operate within (international) consortia that combine the experiences and competences of different kinds of stakeholders—such as leading-edge research partners, industrial companies, public and private institutions—and different kinds of users of the projects envisioned outcomes.

IT design projects that operate under the conditions of funded research have to reconcile conflicting social worlds—the worlds of researchers, participating practitioners, and other stakeholders. They have to struggle with the constraints that stem from funding schemes and the structural aspects of a project, including temporal framing, which often make it difficult to create the space to implement a robust design result and observe real use over a longer period. The conditions under which IT projects operate vary widely, depending on the field of activity, the funding scheme, and the project partners. Conditions for doing research also vary between academia and industrial research centres. In the IT sector, research activities are intrinsically linked with the business processes of their clients, irrespective of their specific domain. However, researchers in this context also need to align their research activities with the leading-edge research conducted within academia and public research institutions.

This book seeks to capture the sense of variety outlined above. It does so by considering a wide range of projects. Hence, in preparing the book the authors have carried out a series of in-depth interviews with a number of well-known researchers that are sensitive to the topic of sustainability. These researchers have generously contributed their experiences to the book and have reflected on how to achieve lasting effects in the target setting. These interviews focused on the practices of preparing a project proposal, looking for resources, aligning the perspectives, skills, and goals of different stakeholders, the researchers' experiences with different issues during and after the project, and their strategies for addressing these.

Data collection started with different project lines—all committed to practice-based computing—which have been developed by a core group working at the University of Siegen in Germany. They include projects on bringing Industry 4.0 to SMEs (Thomas Ludwig, Christoph Kotthaus), projects in the domain of firefighting (Matthias Betz) as well as emergency and crisis management (Volkmar Pipek), and an initiative to develop computer clubs as places for computational and cross-cultural learning in several countries (Konstantin Aal, Anne Weibert). Starting from there, we sought to widen the number of fields of activity and research contexts, including the experiences of research groups in Europe, North America, and South Africa. The selection of these projects was based on several partially overlapping criteria: the accessibility of first-hand information about the project characteristics and dynamics; the diversity of the fields of activity that are the target of these projects; and the inclusion of experiences acquired in academic research as well as in industrial research centres.

The book project grew over time due to the varied and insightful contributions made by our colleagues:

- Ellen Balka (Simon Fraser University, Canada) about scaling up a successfully implemented healthcare application to be used province-wide;
- Myriam Lewkowicz (University of Technology of Troyes, France) about a series of projects in support of telecare in the French context;
- Margunn Aanestad (University of Oslo, Norway) about efforts at building large-scale information infrastructures in healthcare, as well as a set of projects adopting off-the-shelf technologies, also in healthcare;
- Carla Simone (University of Milano-Bicocca, Italy) about her long-term experiences with designing a flexible, tailorable solution for an electronic patient record (EPR) in an Italian hospital;
- Nicola Bidwell (The International University of Management, Windhoek, Namibia) about her experiences with bringing affordable IT to a rural community in South Africa as well as fieldwork on community networks in several countries;
- Steve Jackson (Cornell University, United States) about his work in developing countries on cultures of maintenance and repair;

- Antonietta Grasso, Tommaso Colombino (formerly XEROX, Grenoble, now Naver Labs), and Jeanette Blomberg (IBM Research—Almaden, United States) about their experiences with research projects in industrial contexts;
- Martin Stein and Nico Castelli (University of Siegen) and Johannes Gärtner (formerly Vienna University of Technology, now *XIMES*) about their experiences with building a spin-off as a specific sustainability strategy.

These researchers assumed different roles in these projects. In most cases, they were directly involved in practice-based research, combining ethnographic studies with a participatory approach to IT design. Some researchers primarily conducted ethnographic work accompanying projects over a longer period, and some acted not only as IT designers but also as entrepreneurs.

1.4 Comparing 'elsewheres'

The comparative approach the book takes requires special consideration. It begs the question of how to compare case studies from different fields of activity that operated under different conditions. The approach we have chosen focuses on the set of sensitizing concepts we use to guide the analysis of the cases, limiting the large numbers of aspects under which the project trajectories and their outcomes may be described and compared. Our aim was to enrich the concepts through a diversity of examples that illustrate, for instance, the important role of ownership in the appropriation of an IT artifact, the influence of different types of innovation on long-term sustainability, or different paths to achieving technological flexibility in support of future use. At the same time, while taking account of the particular characteristics of each field of activity, these have not been subject to a systematic comparison.

The main focus of the book is on practice-based projects that have been carried out by university-based researchers in collaboration with industrial partners and user organizations, with a strong design component. Most of the examples we have included correspond to this characterization. However, we also included other types of projects or initiatives that were valuable for improving our understanding of sustainability, a move that from our perspective enriched the comparative work we have undertaken.

Commercial IT service providers are part of an important domain in which design projects are carried out in non-academic conditions. Funding, resourcing, and reporting are in the hands of management. Research in these companies is often coupled with the ambition to develop a sustainable service or product that may be sold to their clients. However, we did not look at purely technical projects but at initiatives that had a strong practice-based component that could anchor the emerging design in the practices of users within the company—not always with success.

The university spin-offs (USOs) we included represent a rather small sample of the very different types of spin-offs. They grew out of practice-based initiatives in a university context and exemplify one way of extending project work of many years into the future for many years. They do this by transferring a technology or idea to other contexts which offer the possibility of evolving it. It was interesting to see how much the quality of the product or service these spin-offs offer depends on the continuing strong link of their founders with academia.

Finally, we included a number of observational studies, as they provided access to specific types of projects or fields of activity that are usually not within the reach of participatory designers entering the organization (with some exceptions). The observational studies complement the research field in important ways, as they have been performed from a practice-based perspective.

We think of these rather diverse examples as 'elsewheres' (Robinson, 2016), as they refer to different fields of activities, target organizations or communities, and types of users, but also regimes/conditions under which research takes place.

1.5 Structure of the book

Future-proofing takes place in a complex space. This view sets the tone for the book's organization around case studies, which are conceived and described as taking place in a multidimensional conceptual space (as illustrated in Chapter 2) covering appropriation work and technological flexibility, as well as the multiple facets that come together to lay the ground for sustainable technologies and practices.

Given the number of projects and different contexts, to do them justice and provide enough detail, we had to dedicate separate chapters to each of the cases. Each of these chapters also offers a first-level analysis of the project trajectories and draws some conclusions. Hence, each of the case study chapters forms a stand-alone entity.

Chapter 11 is an analysis chapter that looks broadly at the projects and fields of activity to find commonalities and differences and extract key themes and insights. Finally, the conclusions illustrated in Chapter 12 are dedicated to *future-proofing*, looking into the future and formulating some recommendations.

The Epilogue presents a collection of statements of some of the researchers that contributed to the book—Nicola Bidwell, Ellen Balka, Myriam Lewkowicz, and Margunn Aanestad. They each provide a personal narrative of the projects/cases they have been working on, while also spelling out their own perspective on how to achieve sustainable results in research.

2

Sustainability: The conceptual space

When aiming at future-proofing IT-based solutions in practice, a number of partially interlinked factors have to be considered: the local context, the repertoire of technologies that may prove useful in this context and their adaptability, funding conditions, the possibility of bringing important stakeholders on board, and planning for what happens after the project ends from an early stage. Future-proofing needs to be conceptualized as a process that takes place in a multidimensional space.

The research literature offers different openings and contributions to understanding sustainability in the sense of future-proofing, which can be grouped according to sets of concepts (Figure 2.1). These 'sensitizing concepts' (Blumer, 1954) offer inspiration and guidance 'in approaching empirical instances' (p. 7)—that is, in describing and analysing projects and cases. While the original concepts prove useful, the case study material helps to further substantiate and sharpen them, bringing out nuances and connections.

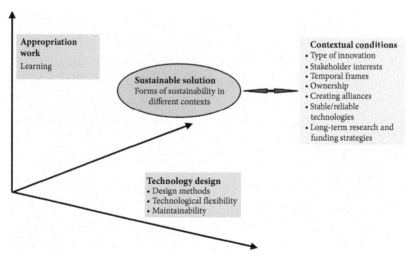

Fig. 2.1 Overview of concepts

Future-proofing. Wulf et al., Oxford University Press.
© Carla Simone, Ina Wagner, Claudia Müller, Anne Weibert, and Volker Wulf (2022).
DOI: 10.1093/oso/9780198862505.003.0002

Fundamental to the long-term sustainability of IT-based solutions is their 'appropriation': how users and hosting organizations and/or communities can learn to make the IT artifacts 'work' in practice. Appropriation of an IT-based solution can be supported through technology design which relates its features to existing and possibly new procedures and work practices and offers sufficient technological flexibility (Dourish, 2003; Pipek and Wulf, 2009; Stevens and Pipek, 2018).

Long-term sustainability is influenced by 'contextual conditions' during and after the design of the socio-technical solution. These conditions refer to a multiplicity of issues that need to be considered when designing for sustainability. In particular, they direct attention to the characteristics of the context in which a project operates, which influence how and to what extent sustainability may be achieved. Finally, and in relation to that, the notion of 'forms of sustainability' expresses the many ways in which a project may aim at and achieve the sustainability of its outcomes: it is a sort of measure of a project's impacts within and beyond its original context.

2.1 Appropriation work

Different authors use the term 'appropriation' in slightly different ways to refer to the types of work designers, (local) experts, and users have to perform to conceive an IT artifact and embed it in a particular context, make it work, and benefit from its use. They have also introduced additional concepts to highlight particular aspects of the appropriation processes they observed.

We use the term 'appropriation work' to emphasize the continuous effort that appropriation requires and to highlight that it can have different outcomes depending on the kind of learning that has occurred. In all studies concerning the sustainability of project outcomes, learning is a key concern. Learning, and how to organize it, is a complex issue in itself.

2.1.1 The different foci of appropriation work

With respect to the context of the home, media and culture studies use the term 'domestication' to describe the work of integrating digital technologies with people's daily routines (e.g. Silverstone and Haddon, 1996). According to Haddon (2003), the process of domestication involves a series of activities. Once a technology has been acquired, there are then the processes of developing the above noted under-standings about 'appropriate' usage (e.g. about how much TV to watch, what to use a PC for)—understandings which can themselves be challenged. There are the processes of fitting the ICTs into routines or creating new ones. And there are the processes by which usage of technologies spreads both among household members (which may mean lending out a personal phone to oth-ers) and in terms of what the technology is used for (e.g. from emergency use of the mobile to its role in organising logistics.

(p. 3)

Hence, domestication entails a series of activities, such as understanding the 'appropriate' usage of a technology, adapting it to existing practices, and en-gaging in changing these practices as new possibilities open up. In work organizations, fitting a technology into work practices often requires actors to resolve rather complex organizational and logistical issues in order to be able to exploit their potential. Each of the following foci provides insights into how sustainable a solution may be in the long term and how it may evolve over time:

- The (work) practices in place and how these might need to be changed for users to benefit from a design solution;
- Technology and its adaptation to the requirements of a specific context;
- The organization that may need to change for users to be able to appro-priate a design solution.

One of the earliest CSCW studies of appropriation work (even though the au-thors do not refer to this concept) is Bowers et al. (1995), which observed how the introduction of a new workflow management system in a print shop in-terrupted the 'smooth flow of work', and how the workers' efforts to adapt the system required 're-working the order of the shopfloor'. They note

how the system could be criticised for not allowing flexible mappings from processes to operators, for not specifically supporting 'run-time' re-allocations, for not recognising ad hoc collaborative arrangements, and for adding to the work that people have to do.

(p. 65)

They also provide a highly detailed account of the actual work needed to make the system function, a system that is unsustainable in the long term, as it does not respond to the questions the workers have to put to themselves while working:

> Workflow from within accomplishes the smooth flow of work through methods which are internal to the work. To do printwork competently requires that, on receipt of a job, an operator is able to orient to matters such as: Is this job properly for me? Should it be done next? How urgent is it? To whom should I pass it when I am done?
>
> (p. 63)

A study of the work required to make a technology (a wireless call system) fit the environment of a newly built hospital wing (Balka and Wagner, 2006) provides an additional perspective, highlighting the need to configure space–technology relations to make a technology work in practice. As the U-shape of the new hospital wing made establishing contact with patients in their rooms more difficult for the nurses, the hospital introduced wireless handsets to help them determine which wing a given audible alarm was coming from. Although the wireless handsets made responding to patient calls easier, they interrupted the practice of visually assessing a patient's needs and status before responding. Moreover, small details such as the placement of the main phone console, wireless handsets, battery chargers mattered, in that they affected the flow of work. Space–technology relations also played a large role in PD projects with the Mankosi community in South Africa (Bidwell, 2013b). The design solution for providing solar charging stations for mobile phones in collaboration with people living in this community of several villages builds on ingrained walking habits (see Chapter 8).

The other key focus when studying appropriation work is the technology itself and the efforts required to make it work properly and reliably. In a study of user-initiated innovation in 'Wireless Leiden', Verhaegh et al. (2016) describe the various kinds of work that went into making the network function in users' homes. This involved, for example, 'aligning intermediary actors, developing black boxed solutions for connecting to the Wi-Fi network, effectively delegating many technicalities to pre-configured devices' (p. 204). It also involved sometimes complex maintenance and repair work, with the result that the work 'on individual artifacts became part of iterative cycles of improving design, based on the feedback of individual, locally situated solutions into the collective, thus enabling artifacts to become more robust and more resilient to forces of resistance' (p. 208).

An early study of the effort involved in making a technical solution work in a complex organization was in relation to *POLITeam*, a cooperative software development project which was deployed and further developed in three steps by several government administrations in Germany. Pipek and Wulf (1999) studied the complete lifecycle of the groupware application in the public sector, from its implementation and use to its removal. 'Congruency in use' (Prinz et al., 1998) with the wider organization was achieved with the third version of the software:

> The main requirement for the third version was the integration of the POLITeam system with the organization specific IT infrastructure. This abolished the situation of the POLITeam users as being on an 'island' within the organization. To enable the use of the POLITeam system along hierarchical lines, new functions were included that focused on the specific requirements of managerial users.
>
> (p. 376)

When the groupware system was removed, mainly due to management failures but also because of outdated technology, the researchers observed that, surprisingly, some of the new patterns of collaboration survived. Although it requires some purely technical work, adapting the technology and further developing it is inextricably linked with developing the practices around it. In this case, the technology was not sustainable in the long run, but some of the practices and the learning that came from it remained (Pipek and Wulf, 1999).

Finally, there is the focus on the organizational changes required in order to integrate a technology. One of the earliest works to emphasize the organizational aspects of appropriation was Orlikowski's study of the adoption of *Lotus Notes*, where she argued: 'If people have a poor or inappropriate understanding of the unique and different features of a new technology they may resist using it, or may not integrate it appropriately into their work practices' (Orlikowski, 1992: 364). She also sought to understand how *Lotus Notes* was used to enable organizational changes over time, highlighting a distinction between changes that were 'anticipated, emergent, and opportunity-based' (Orlikowski and Hofman, 1997). One of the main arguments of this study was 'that where the premises underlying the groupware technology (shared effort, cooperation, collaboration) are counter-cultural to an organization's structural properties (competitive and individualistic culture, rigid hierarchy, etc.), the technology will be unlikely to facilitate collective use and value' (Orlikowski, 1992: 362).

2.1.2 'Weak' versus 'strong' forms of appropriation

One of the key arguments in the debate about appropriation is that it is a process that goes beyond the mere 'adoption' of a technological artifact:

> [...] the term appropriation stresses the option of the appropriator to go beyond the rules and ideas that have been originally associated with the thing that is being appropriated. With regard to technologies, this stresses the options of technology users to go beyond the intentions that technology designers associated with a technology or a technological artefact.
>
> (Pipek, 2005: 30)

This is also stressed by Carroll (2004), who maintains that appropriating, or 'taking into possession', is 'more fundamental than configuring a packaged system prior to implementation or tailoring it to individual users' needs' (p. 3). Stevens and Pipek (2018) suggest the term appropriation be used for describing 'orderly use' of a system, seeing appropriation as being:

> constituted in the interplay of technology development and situated appropriation work, where the outcomes have to be understood as practical inquiry or as infrastructuring. In contrast to technological determinism orderly use is not seen as being caused by external factors but is a product of creative actions dealing with the demands and opportunities of the situation at hand.
>
> (p. 171)

In the same vein, in their research on users appropriating 3D printers Ludwig et al. (2014) emphasize that appropriation goes 'deeper than [...] customization or tailoring of software in that it can encompass fundamental changes in practice and embraces the possibility of users adopting and using the technology in ways not anticipated by its designer' (p. 2). This reflects the experience of what Robinson and Bannon (1991) have described as 'the differences between premeditated support for work, and the facilitation of unanticipated use' (p. 231). Among the examples of unanticipated use that were discussed in the 1990s were systems such as the 'information lens' (Mackay, 1990) and particular office coordination tools (Bullen and Bennett, 1990). The notion of 'unanticipated use' points to the new practices users develop when facing particular problems.

By distinguishing between weak ('just' using a system, customizing it) and strong forms of appropriation, Bossen and Dalsgaard (2005) describe the introduction of a particular *Knowledge Repository* in a software company, which met low acceptance by users 'despite managerial support, extensive training and ongoing refinements of features and user interface' (p. 102). At the same time, and independently of these efforts, some skilled users constructed a series of 'parasitic systems' on top of the system that turned out to be sustainable (and, in the end, were tolerated by the organization), since they were easier to launch, with a simpler interface, and met the knowledge-sharing needs of users in a better way than the original design. Hence, Bossen and Dalsgaard argue, weak appropriation may make a system more useful 'by making it malleable in response to contingencies on the use context', whereas strong appropriation may either be indicative of the fact that a system 'has great potential for supporting work' or 'occur as a way of creating alternatives to inappropriate systems' (p. 105).

Fieldwork by Schmidt and Kaavé (1991) on manufacturing resource planning (MRP) in a Danish company producing specialized optical equipment highlighted another form of strong appropriation: that of flanking the new system with old practices. When the company changed to a 'just in time', order-driven strategy, the MRP system continued to be used for certain purposes. The workers found that it gave them a valuable overview of the whole work process, letting them see, for instance, whether parts they would need shortly were scheduled.

2.1.3 Appropriation work requires learning

Studying the introduction of a new robotized production line in a bakery, Hoeve and Lieuwenhuis (2006) point to the different levels of learning required to make a new technology work, also arguing that these have strong social implications, since

> not only the nature of the work routines changed, but also the roles changed. The position of individuals in the bakery was no longer related to craftsmanship. Craft bakers lost their craft status and had to regain a position based on their ability to work with the technology. Not all the former experts were able to maintain a high position in the working communities' hierarchy. Much younger novices who were able to quickly pick up the requirements of the new technology outstripped some former experts.
>
> (p. 182)

Hence, learning how to appropriate a technology and develop new work practices also requires learning how to respond to the social and personal implications of change.

Honkaniemi et al. (2014) studied innovation-related learning at a work-place level in a project with front-line hospital support service workers. They were interested in fostering the 'kind of future-orientated learning that may challenge prevailing work patterns' (p. 312). They argue that 'without an or-ganizational support system in place to facilitate idea creation, or to sort out, decide and integrate ideas as continuous organizational routine, innovation processes will function inefficiently' (p. 326). The authors also took numerous practical issues into account to address these issues. For example, they devel-oped a set of interventions that included broadening 'the purpose of service work in a wider context and timescale than previously' (p. 313); hence, al-lowing the participating employees to develop a broader view of their work that would help them develop new perspectives is crucial. They also probed different evaluation methods and their contribution to collective learning, em-phasizing the usefulness of 'developmental evaluation as a practice to co-create and transfer ideas into use' (p. 314).

The learning that is fundamental to appropriation work can come in dif-ferent forms. Innovation-related learning in the case of hospital workers is what Ellström (2001) has termed 'developmental' or innovative, with a focus on 'the creation of new practices and solutions' (p. 427). A related concept is expansive learning (Engeström, 2001), which on the individual level is about acquiring new skills and competences and 'as a collective process [...] refers to the establishing, reproduction or transformation of action systems where new tools, rules, routines, and division of labour find their place within the activity system' (Stevens and Pipek, 2018: 144).

However, not all learning that underlies appropriation processes is develop-mental or expansive. Ellström (2001) contrasts developmental learning with adaptive forms that happen when users integrate a new technology in cur-rent practices without necessarily evolving them or adding new functionalities. This is what Orlikowski and Hofman (1997) describe as the 'value of ongoing learning and change in practice' (p. 17) in an organization. In many cases, appropriation work is based on 'learning from ongoing use, responding to un-expected developments' (p. 30), or what we term 'learning-in-practice', while sometimes also 'allowing further innovation and adaptation of both the tech-nology and the organization', which comes close to expansive learning. The distinction between these two forms of learning, although fluid, corresponds to the difference between weak and strong appropriation processes.

With an even more challenging long-term perspective on organizational learning, Andreu and Ciborra (1996) proposed the term 'capability develop-ment', which is based on a learning loop between resources (including IT) and work practices. Mastering a new technology by developing the practice of using it is a first step in any company's internalization of resources. The second step involves 'generalizing work practices and putting them in a wider context that defines *how* they work' so that they become capabilities, conveying 'what an organization is *capable* of doing if properly triggered' (p. 115). While Andreu and Ciborra (1996) do not use the term sustainability, their understanding of organizational learning draws attention to the processes that reach beyond inventing and stabilizing new practices, eventually enabling an organization to develop entirely new capabilities.

'Digital sovereignty' is a concept that was introduced by Baacke (1996) in the context of media research. It expresses the relationship between learning and appropriation on a more general level. It distinguishes three levels of digital competences: the ability to operate digital technologies (use competence); the ability to adapt digital technologies to individual needs and to use them in a creative way (adaptation/design competence); and the ability to orientate oneself in the landscape of new technologies, assessing their individual, social, and societal value and usefulness, and appropriate (or reject) them (orientation competence). 'Digital sovereignty' as a goal applies to individuals but also to communities. It resonates with the work of Carroll and Rosson (2007), who stress the importance of 'creating a self-directed and sustainable process of continuous learning' within communities (p. 258).

These different concepts—learning-in-practice, expansive learning, capability development, and digital sovereignty—are useful for thinking about appropriation and other moves towards sustainability in different fields of activity and contexts.

2.1.4 The role of facilitators in fostering appropriation

A shared characteristic of practice-based projects that succeed in bringing a design result into a real-world context is that their researchers, who are 'strangers' to the community or organizations, may assume new roles as facilitators and technology consultants. This is what Farooq et al. (2007) observed in the *Civic Nexus* project:

In some cases we adopted more passive roles where we simply observe community settings, and in others we adopted more active roles where we co-constructed joint activities with our community partners. As such, it became difficult at times to gauge the level of our influence on community practices.

(p. 11)

Trigg and Bødker (1994) described how they were used to help with technical problems as they arose, as well as as a 'sparring partner'—'someone who
could bring to the discussion a more thorough understanding of technical
constraints and possibilities' (p. 52).

Some studies look into the role of particular technology-affine individuals in processes of technology learning. Well known are the 'gardeners' and
'gurus' that Gantt and Nardi (1992) identified in their study of computer-aided
design (CAD) users. Quiñones (2014) takes up these findings in a study of the
use of a learning management system at a university; he considers gardeners as catalysts of change, and shepherds as those who help others to cultivate
practices around a technology. He observed that 'successful transitions and
learning happened only where there were colleagues who were invested in the
process of shepherding' (p. 313).

2.2 Technological flexibility

Aiming at the sustainability of design-based solution imposes conditions on
both the design method and the nature of the technology that is being developed. The design or selection of the IT artifacts needs to be anchored in a
detailed knowledge of the differentiation and dynamics of the local practices
that it seeks to support. Moreover, the IT artifacts have to offer their users
the possibility to adapt and evolve their functionalities. Alternatively, IT artifacts may offer interpretative flexibility (Doherty et al., 2006) by means of
generic functionalities, and thus support evolving local practices (Stevens and
Pipek, 2018). However, there are many challenges and open questions that
make achieving these goals difficult.

2.2.1 Design method

Research and design work done in the tradition of PD has the anchoring of
technology in people's lives as its main concern. This is done by a process of
'mutual learning' between users and professional designers and ideally involving users in all design decisions—from generating design ideas to concretizing
them in a series of prototypes—with a view to integrating them in the use
context, hence making them sustainable in the long run (e.g. Bratteteig and
Wagner, 2016). However, many PD projects stop at the mock-up or prototype
level, lacking the resources—and often also the necessary commitment from

the participating user organizations—to take steps towards a technology that can be integrated in a real-life context.

Approaches to overcome this barrier suggest that the trajectory to an implementable and possibly also sustainable design solution has to be systematically developed. The design case study approach (Stevens et al., 2018), which is deeply rooted in PD, is based on three overlapping, interleaving, and recursive activities: context study, design study, and appropriation study. These sets of activities have to be planned from the beginning and kept in focus. Moreover,

> quality criteria for design case studies must relate to their different foci and activities: the study of social practices, the IT design (including the design process and designed IT artefact), and the appropriation of the IT artefact in use. These aspects require adequate documentation and analysis to facilitate knowledge gains.
>
> (p. 34)

Documentation has a key role in the design case study approach. It contributes to developing a knowledge base that offers the research community examples and pathways towards sustainable design results.

Simonsen and Hertzum (2012) have formulated a strategy for 'sustained PD' which rests on the integration of design and development with organizational implementation. Using the example of an EPR that was developed and implemented in a participatory process in a Danish hospital, they point to the importance of being able to observe relevant changes in work practices, emphasizing the need to evaluate real use of a system after a longer period 'to allow system errors to be corrected, users to gain proficiency, work practices to stabilize, use situations to reach their true level of heterogeneity, emergent and opportunity-based changes to develop, and long-term outcomes to emerge' (p. 14). One of the challenges, of course, is that the participating user organization is committed to this approach. Another challenge is methodological: '*how to conduct realistic large-scale PD experiments* to evaluate prototype systems during real work' (p. 14).

The 'pilot implementation' of a national electronic Pregnancy Record (ePR) in Denmark described by Bansler and Havn (2010) suggests a similar approach. Here, the emphasis is on the space for learning and redesign early implementation offers, thereby increasing the chances of a system being appropriated. 'Bootstrapping' is a strategy proposed by Hanseth and Aanestad (2003) with respect to the introduction of large-scale systems, such as a telemedicine network. It refers to 'a design process taking as its starting point the challenge of enrolling the first users and then drawing upon the existing base of users and technology as a resource to extend the network' (p. 386). The aim is to improve the technology step by step, 'making it easier for users to overcome barriers' (p. 390).

While some of the projects described in this book successfully shape a research trajectory that leads to a sustainable result, many meet barriers that are difficult—if not impossible—to overcome, such as resistance by management or impediments resulting from the characteristics of a field of activity.

2.2.2 Tailorable and malleable technologies

Users have an active role in the appropriation of IT-based solutions—in integrating them into their current practices and (possibly) in defining new ones. In the early 1990s, the term 'tailorability' of systems was used (e.g. Trigg and Bødker, 1994) to express the quality of a system that users can adapt to their needs. Since then, the issue of tailorability (or configurability) has remained 'on the table', as designing systems that can be modified by users without the burdensome and costly intervention of IT experts sometimes poses formidable conceptual challenges. The chances of success depend on the nature and complexity of the technologies but also on continuous learning in the target communities or organizations, which enables users to 'take over' once a new piece of technology has been installed.

The possibility of designing a technology that users can act on, possibly with the help of domain experts and IT professionals, was described decades ago by Henderson and Kyng (1991) in terms of: choosing between predefined alternatives; constructing new artifacts from existing pieces; and reprogramming the artifact. This seminal idea stimulated a research stream traditionally referred to as 'end user development' (Lieberman et al., 2006, Paternò and Wulf, 2017), which proposes different strategies for achieving user involvement for the purpose of sustainability. The initial goal was challenging and no immediate answer was found, as discussed by Dourish (2003), who drew attention to the characteristics of a technology that is to be implemented in an organization. He argues that 'appropriation relies on flexibility in both practice and technology, and in particular, flexibility in the way in which the technology can be mapped onto user needs' (p. 467). The questions he asks are: 'what features of technological design support appropriation? And so, how could systems be designed in order to accommodate, support and encourage the process of appropriation?' (p. 467).

Under the heading of 'end-user development', a variety of highly flexible IT designs have been developed for the purpose of enabling long-term appropriation (and sustainability) from a technical point of view. For example, Fischer et al. (2017) suggest, among other things, that developers: underdesign for emergent behaviour; share control with users; reach out and converse with other people in real time while they are using the system; combine the design with other tools and systems they use regularly (p. 89). A cornerstone of these and other efforts is the close cooperation of designers with users.

Another approach takes the perspective of a more specific, although generally relevant, kind of application. Cabitza and Simone (2017), whose work we will refer to later, have developed a system to support administrative documentation in hospitals, with building blocks and an editing environment that allow users to define forms and rules and make annotations. The system supports appropriation through 'the presence of different levels of abstraction at which end users can construct, modify and use the combination of the basic building blocks' (p. 147), as well as the domain-dependent language that helps users 'in identifying and expressing the mechanisms supporting their work practices' (p. 149). The authors make a clear distinction between a platform that is targeted to the end user and the underlying technical infrastructure. This is in line with what Lee and Schmidt (2018) propose:

One can also talk about 'infrastructure' in a broader sense of a technical structure in operation, that is, as providing some service, giving support, etc. 'Infrastructure' in this broader sense thus basically means the same as 'socio-technical system', in that any talk about a technical structure in operation presumes the competent organized practices of its operation and maintenance.

(p. 207)

Looking back at a long line of research on this topic, Simone (2018) argues for design for malleability, examining the issues that prevent designers from realizing this goal. She uses the 'Excel spreadsheet', a case that goes back to observations that had already been made earlier (see, e.g., Nardi and Miller, 1991), in the context of a larger discussion about system tailorability to illustrate what malleability means. A spreadsheet is commonly used as a 'shadow tool' (Handel and Poltrock, 2011) that lives 'in the shadow' of big, official systems that are often too prescriptive and hence too difficult to adapt, because it may serve different purposes. Malleability requires the same flexibility but in addition asks for 'a better spreadsheet', Simone (2018) argues. This could be an open platform that offers basic building blocks and composition rules which end users can apply to build and modify their tools in a more agile way at 'the semantic level of work practices, which includes articulation work' (p. 143), since this is the level where users can envision and implement changes.

From this complex and extensive debate, a picture emerges. While any design that is to be used in an organization has to take into account 'the installed base' (Aanestad et al., 2017b), at the same time it has to provide a technology that is 'evolvable'—that is, tailorable and open to technological evolution to be extended and further developed in use (Pipek et al., 2008). This must all be achieved despite the more restricted role of designers (Cabitza and Simone, 2017), and possibly starting with a limited set of functionalities and practices around them (Aanestad and Hanseth, 2003).

While most of this work concerns complex technical artifacts that are meant to support work in organizations, ensuring tailorability is also a concern in contexts of everyday life where users may have limited IT skills and little experience with digital devices. For example, Ballegaard et al. (2006) define 'evolvability' as a basic requirement for technologies for elderly people, arguing that very old people in particular take a lot of time to get used to technologies, and only when deeply familiar with them will they accept new functionalities and think of new ways of doing things. Studying old people's practices of remembering which medication to take, Palen and Aaløkke (2006) argue that designs should reflect the characteristics of the context and the people they are to support, and hence be as tailorable as these.

> Homes and their supporting information systems are tailorable and open to improvement, enabling residents to iteratively perfect placement of medications and steps in their routines, to adapt to the inclusion of new medications, and to optimize the placement of some things vis-à-vis the optimization of others.
>
> (p. 85)

This provides a useful 'rule of thumb' for designers to follow when aiming at sustainable systems. It also draws attention to the importance to the local context and the people they design for. The different terms that are used in the debate about technological flexibility—tailorability, configurability, malleability, or evolvability—have slightly different connotations, while expressing a basic precondition for a technology to be sustainable in the long term.

Finally, technical flexibility can be reached by abandoning the use of an existing system and replacing it with a new application (see Wulf, 1999).

2.2.3 Interpretative flexibility

Interpretative flexibility is an alternative to future-proofing IT artifacts in support of evolving social practices. This term has been introduced by Pinch and Bijker (1987) to express the idea that technological artifacts are constructed and interpreted culturally, with the consequence that they may represent different things to different actors. Email tools or text messengers are typical examples of tools that offer interpretative flexibility. They rather generically support different modes of communication and are appropriated in a vast variety of contexts supporting a diversity of different practices. In these cases, the users do not tailor the artifact itself but rather develop their way of using it without modifying the functionality. This implies that the system at hand does not prescribe a particular use practice but instead allows multiple ones (Wulf, 1999; Stevens and Pipek, 2018).

However, when technical flexibility is lacking, users often try to muddle through the missing technical options by agreeing upon certain social protocols which are based on the existing functionality (Wulf, 1999). This is also emphasized by Doherty et al. (2006), who point to the importance of also understanding 'how a system's technical characteristics might limit its ability to be interpreted flexibly' (p. 569).

The term 'interpretative flexibility' is particularly useful in discussion of projects that do not develop IT artifacts from scratch but rather introduce off-the-shelf technologies in their fields of application. In these cases, technical flexibility cannot be specifically designed into the artifacts; to encourage future-proofing, interpretative flexibility could be an implicit core criterion for their selection.

2.2.4 Appropriation support

With respect to complex systems, Pipek and Wulf (2009) have made an important contribution towards designing for appropriation (hence ensuring sustainability in the longer term) by defining some of the ways of supporting what they refer to as 'infrastructuring'. Apart from 'building highly flexible systems', these are: articulation support, historicity support (e.g. 'documenting earlier configuration decisions, or providing retrievable storage of configuration and usage descriptions'), observation support, exploration support, and explanation support ('explains reasons for application behavior, fully automated support vs. user-user or user-expert-communication') (pp. 467–8). Hence, the idea is to provide functionalities that help end users adapt a technology to the ways in which they are already working.

In this vein, Stevens et al. (2018) have taken a step further, suggesting the development of 'appropriation infrastructures' that support the design of flexible technologies:

> The key idea of this approach is to embed tailoring and collaboration means within the context of use, supporting reflective, expansive learning when in a breakdown situation with the artifact present at hand. As the breakdown situation typically is not detached from the underlying infrastructure, the key idea is to provide channels in this situation to connect to other stakeholders like peers and colleagues, sysadmins, and help desk personnel, as well as developers and user communities.
>
> (Stevens and Pipek, 2018: 168)

Based on fieldwork on how users handle problems with 3D printers, one of the projects we will discuss later by Ludwig et al. (2014) provides an intuitive example of such support. Their observations confirm the importance of sharing experiences and stories within networks of users in situations in which identifying, understanding, and locating the sources of a problem are difficult. Following the idea of 'sociable technologies', they propose to add tools and visualizations in three dimensions, providing information about 'their inner workings, about their current state, as well as about their component and behavioural structure'; the 'socio-material context; e.g. location and surroundings, environmental data like room temperature, maintenance or user/usage data'; and 'the task/process context (e.g. technologies used to build/prepare printed models, position in a production chain or process, purpose and goal of machine usage)' (p. 843)

The debate on how to design technologies in ways that make them open to adaptation, customization, and redesign is ongoing. It is essential for understanding how the specific design outcome of an IT research project can be made sustainable in the long run.

2.3 Creating the conditions for sustainable technologies and practices

Sustainability requires studying *the conditions within and beyond a research project* which allow a design result to be appropriated, maintained, and eventually further developed. Research communities, notably those interested in community development and/or community-based health programmes, have studied the conditions required for sustainability from this broader perspective. From these and other studies, we have identified several key issues to address.

During the project lifetime, among the main issues to account for are: the types of innovation that the funding agency and the participating stakeholders are looking for; potentially conflicting stakeholder interests and perspectives; and the different temporal orientations that come to bear on a project. There are a series of post-project issues that also need consideration: the need to transfer ownership to the hosting institution or community, which includes ensuring longer-term financial sustainability; how to build social and/or organizational structures supporting a continuous appropriation process in the community or organization; and how to provide the conditions for the technology to work smoothly and reliably. The literature also discusses some of the conditions for achieving the sustainability of research lines beyond a single stand-alone project, as well as proposing 'academic entrepreneurship' as a path to long-term sustainability of IT-based solutions.

It is not easy to maintain a distinction between what is important to achieve before and during a project, and what is important to achieve after its completion, since on principle achieving a sustainable design result has to be envisioned from the planning stages onwards. A long-term perspective on sustainability implies that post-completion issues have to be addressed within the project's lifetime. Hence, many of the points of attention—stakeholder perspectives, diverse temporalities, learning and capacity-building—are not only relevant before and during a project. They need to be maintained with consideration for future possibilities and challenges.

An important additional insight is that the process of technology appropriation may evolve over time in a non-linear trajectory. Based on a longitudinal study of an educational software, Mendoza et al. (2007) observed 'multiple windows of opportunity' to improve technology use—that is, 'multiple plateaus of temporary stabilization' that alternate with steady use of the technology and possibly with phases of technology rejection for contingent motivations. They argue that 'it is important that we understand reasons for stabilization and its timing in longer term use of a technology, thereby supporting adaptation as a process of appropriation and avoiding stagnation or even rejection of a technology' (p. 196) and that, we would add, this understanding becomes part of the technology design.

2.3.1 Types of innovation

A practice-based approach to the development of IT technologies aims at socio-technical innovation. Funding schemes may make pursuing this goal difficult, creating pressure to produce artifacts that are 'leading edge' or innovative from a purely technical perspective. What innovation means is not uniquely defined (Anderson et al., 2004). Interpretations vary from originality—that is, a non-existent technological solution and/or an organizational/social arrangement that has not yet been probed—to the adoption of a more consolidated solution in a novel setting or application domain. A simple distinction is the one between 'design-driven' and 'user-driven innovation' (Verganti, 2008).

Following a path of design-driven innovation often makes a project less sensitive to the issue of sustainability, since its focus is either on technical novelty as such or on a more general, possibly marketable solution. The situation gets more complicated when the funder and/or the research consortium plan to evaluate the technical artifact in a use context. In such cases, we would argue, a technically innovative artifact cannot be seen in isolation from the use context in which it is supposed to be implemented. In contrast to a practice-based approach, however, the work needed to integrate a solution into the work environment or the everyday lives of participants is relegated to the background (Meurer et al., 2018). Funding schemes for these types of projects often do not cover the invisible work that is critical to sustainability, such as relationship-building and alignment work with project partners or time-consuming learning activities. Since these activities need to be carried out to be able to evaluate the artifact, a project team may be forced to find the necessary resources aside from the officially funded ones or look for additional external resources. This observation is shared by Karasti et al. (2010) with respect to an information infrastructure project that originally had been mainly focused on technical tools (which 'proved largely unusable at the sites' (p. 393)):

> In general there ensued a large amount of ill-defined, unanticipated work at all levels—from conceptual design to financial support—that was added to the normal workload with minimal new resources provided for planning or for development.
>
> (p. 393)

Hence, in projects that aim at technological innovation, the solution cannot be seen in isolation from the workplace or everyday situation in which the technical artifact is supposed to be embedded, when sustainability becomes a desirable goal or even a necessity, as in the case Karasti et al. describe.

User-driven innovation builds on a socio-technical perspective on innovation. There are different notions of how to define and achieve user-driven innovation. Von Hippel (2005) advocates a 'lead-user' approach to innovation which builds on the ability of expert users to innovate products and services themselves by basically modifying, adapting, or 'hacking' existing solutions. His idea of innovation is strongly directed at market opportunities. A much wider notion of user-driven innovation has been proposed by Buur and Matthews (2008), who seek to extend the PD approach by integrating a concern for business opportunities. Their example is a project that involved workers in a wastewater plant in developing and enacting ideas for changing their work environment. They also developed product ideas and refined them in cooperation with process operators and engineers from the participating company. In the same vein, Dittrich et al. (2014) used the term 'situated innovation' to indicate the 'epistemic, open-ended' (p. 30) nature of PD practice. This notion accounts for the fact that in PD, innovation—"change", "imagination" and sharp breaks with established ways of doing things' (p. 44)—is deeply rooted in users' practices and codesigned with them.

In general, a PD approach is better equipped for types of innovation that may not be considered 'original' from a technical point of view but may foster the development of new practices, facilitate organizational change, and/or help communities to learn. A concept that relates to these goals is 'transformation design' (Burns, 2006). Hillgren et al. (2011) use it to argue in favour of a slow, incremental prototyping process that allows participants in a socio-technical innovation project to evolve the necessary new capacities to use its outcomes and explore the more long-term possibilities that it offers.

The projects we discuss in this book provide examples that go beyond the simple distinction between design-driven and user-driven, identifying different configurations of the technical and the social at different levels of complexity.

2.3.2 Stakeholder interests and perspectives

The participation of multiple stakeholders is common to many IT research design projects that seek to make a difference in the real world. In such a project the worlds of researchers, practitioners (users), other institutional actors, and industry meet, representing different, potentially conflicting interests as well as the power to make these interests prevail.

Strauss's 'social worlds/arenas' theory (1978, 1979) captures some aspects of this phenomenon, as it draws attention not just to the individuals that participate in a project but to their relationships with collectives that they 'bring with them'. An arena is the 'place' where social worlds meet for particular purposes. Strauss has discussed these concepts primarily in relation to organizations which he sees as being rooted in different social worlds and as participating in 'politicized arenas—of various sizes and types—characterized by discussion, debate, positional manoeuvring, and inevitably also by negotiation among the participants' (Strauss, 1979: 351). We can extend these notions to projects which are often portrayed as temporary organizations, asking:

> What are the patterns of collective commitment and salient social worlds operating here? [...] What are the commitments of a given world? How do its participants believe they should go about fulfilling them? What actions have been taken in the past and are anticipated in the future?
>
> (Clarke, 1991: 136)

Within a project, actors from different social worlds meet, have to communicate their views, and agree on a common goal and workplan. While some stakeholders may already have forged relationships in previous projects or other shared activities, others are complete newcomers to a consortium and/or particular research programme. Altman (1995) discusses the sometimes difficult relationships between researchers and communities that are to do with conflicting priorities and goals, issues of ownership and control, and different time orientations. While some stakeholders may have an interest in a sustainable design outcome, others may not—and their ideas about sustainability may differ widely.

Aligning the perspectives and skills of all stakeholders so that they are able to coordinate their efforts poses a big challenge in an IT research design project. The notion of alignment work goes back to Strauss (1988), who defined interactional alignment as 'the process by which workers fit together their respective work-related actions'. Bietz (2010) extends this notion to describe the work that is 'necessary to create enough compatibility between entities so that the relationship can be productive' (p. 253). These entities may be organizational units, external stakeholders, policies, or collaborating specialists. Hillgren et al. (2011) use the term 'infrastructuring' for this process, which they describe as

> a continuous process of building relations with diverse actors and by a flexible allotment of time and resources. This more organic approach facilitates the

emergence of possibilities along the way and new design opportunities can evolve through a continuous matchmaking process.

(p. 180)

A particular aspect of different stakeholders working collaboratively in a project is their relationships to their own social worlds outside the project. Pedersen (2007) has made this point when observing that stakeholders are not just project participants but bring their 'constituencies' with them to the project. He perceives this as a basic conflict, arguing:

> it seems implausible that the dual obligation of participatory design participants to negotiate internal differences—while at the same attempting to instigate and manage a new difference between present and future—should not somehow strain their external relationships to a lesser or greater extent.
>
> (p. 125)

The significance of participants' ties to the world outside a project is acknowledged also by Bødker et al. (2017). They point towards the networks that the different stakeholders bring into a project as an important resource for action:

> They connect the project with arenas outside the project [...] and provide an infrastructure for disseminating results and ideas beyond the project. In terms of politics, these networks are also significant in terms of understanding how certain stakeholders in a project may gain leverage or positions of power.
>
> (p. 251)

The case studies allow us to shed light on the roles that different actors—researchers, funding agencies, management or community leaders, and IT professionals—assume in the projects, their interests and strategies, and how this influences the sustainability of the project outcomes.

2.3.3 Temporal frames

Time and temporality, although recognized as salient aspects of project work and important research issues, have not received much attention. With respect to PD, Saad-Sulonen et al. (2018) have proposed a distinction between project-based and future-oriented temporality. They suggest viewing projects through five 'temporal lenses'—'the phasic, momentary, retrospective, prospective and long-term lenses' (p. 7). They emphasize the importance of the long-term view, which 'provides an understanding of design as processual, where the customary boundaries between design, use, implementation, maintenance, redesign, and repair become blurred' (p. 9). The long-term view reaches beyond the project's lifetime: it also includes the past—the specific constellations that led to a particular project, and it has to account for the timelines and planning cycles of the stakeholders that commit themselves to implementing the design outcomes. Hence, we can think of an IT research design project as having different temporalities that intersect and are possibly in conflict:

- The project timelines in terms of project duration milestones and reviews;
- The different temporalities of the participating stakeholders;
- The future-ended temporality that includes work beyond the end of a project.

However, project timelines often orient participants towards the short term, directing them towards a closure at the end. As a consequence, some of the activities that are key to sustainability may not even come into view. So a typical project duration of two to four years is often too short for an IT design effort to fully come to fruition and reach the stage of 'real use'. Also, technological flexibility as a basic requirement may be hard to achieve within the short term of a single project. There seems to be a fundamental conflict between the ambition and/or necessity of having a product 'finalized in time' and a more open temporal orientation that allows for sustainable development.

Another issue that may create problems in a project is the different temporalities of the participating stakeholders. With respect to community development, Altman (1995) stresses the different time orientations of researchers and community organizations, underlining the need to be sensitive to these differences. Karasti et al. (2010) point towards the need to take account of the 'diverse temporalities of all the involved actors (e.g. scientists, information technology specialists, informatics researchers, data specialists, communities, funding agencies)' (p. 387). These studies also look at the potential conflicts that the different involved temporalities of the implicated actors may produce. Karasti et al. (2010) distinguish between the more short-term concerns of developers who need to accomplish particular goals within 'project time' and the longer-term perspective needed to build and maintain an infrastructure. They state:

> There is a mismatch between developers' project time and information managers' infrastructure time with regard to the duration of a relevant long-term

temporal scale. For developers, a project timeframe of approximately three to five years represents long-term, whereas for information managers the long-term relates to an overarching concern for the long-term of ecological science and legacy datasets as well as expectations of data reuse and new technological solutions by future generations.

(Karasti et al., 2010: 401)

Ribes and Finholt (2009) have used Stuart Brand's notion of 'the long now' to express the need for linking short-term design challenges to promote sustainable development.

A long-term perspective also raises ethical issues that are to do with the need to maintain and nourish relationships over a long period, to welcome new members, and to build trust that survives difficult situations. An impressive example of the challenges faced is found in a long-term collaboration project between a Rwandan non-governmental organization (NGO) and a US university research group focused on recovery from conflict in post-genocide Rwanda. Reflecting on what they call 'multi-lifespan design', Yoo et al. (2018) raise a series of questions: 'How is trust built and sustained over longer-time periods among designers and research partners? How are new members assimilated? How does the research partnership accommodate the growth of individuals and organizations?' (p. 280). Weibert et al. (2017) discuss a similar issue in relation to the cross-cultural learning processes in a computer club (Chapter 7).

2.3.4 Transfer of ownership

A key to sustainability, according to Altman (1995), is the shift of ownership and control from the researchers to the community or user organization. This implies that the community or organization participates in the development of the research protocols and assumes responsibility for the design result. Merkel et al. (2004) use the expression 'seeding ownership', arguing: 'In terms of promoting sustainability, we must see community groups as owners of the projects, not designers' (p. 7). In PD projects, users are considered co-owners of the design solution from the very beginning. But in these cases, the transfer is often also gradual, with full ownership only being reached at the point when a user organization or community takes over the IT artifact for implementation, adaptation, and further development.

There is a strong link between ownership and appropriation. Ownership means the power to take decisions over the long term. Indeed, the cases we discuss show that the people in a position to shape the appropriation work and the associated learning make a difference. Are the final users of a technology in this position, and do they have the skills and resources, the researchers to create the conditions for appropriation and learning, or a management team that provides resources and directs the appropriation in a direction it deems useful?

Trust plays a major role in research partnerships and their relations to participants, communities, and government agencies. In particular, successful projects in sensitive contexts invest in measures to establish credibility and trustworthiness. This was a key issue in projects as vastly different as peace-keeping in post-genocide Rwanda (Yoo et al., 2018), installing a rural Wi-Fi network in South Africa (Moreno et al., 2013), and working with elderly people in Germany (Meurer et al., 2018). The transfer of ownership is an important step in this process of trust-building.

Analysing several digital inclusion projects in India, South Africa, and Brazil, Madon et al. (2009) point towards processes of institutionalization as crucial to sustainability. This perspective reaches beyond ownership, which may only be temporary. In many cases, it may be important to pay heed to the institutional contexts in which IT projects are embedded, as was the case in a successful example from South Africa:

> What has been achieved at Siyabuswa has been of great value to the local community. The training facility is owned and operated by members of the community and provides highly valued services to a broad spectrum of community members. Many of the graduates have found computer-related employment. Some are exploiting their newly acquired skills, and their activities show all the signs of developing into small businesses. The facility is self-sustaining and does not receive outside funding. After 8 years of continued, albeit slow, growth, the facility and what it stands for has become an accepted fact within the Siyabuswa community.
>
> (p. 100)

They also show that seeking government support can be a mixed blessing. While it may be crucial to espouse the government's approach to social inclusion and development, a project may also become trapped in conflicts between its own mission and the interests of different political factions. The same holds for the involvement of businesses that may compromise the priorities of the project and its participants.

An important aspect of ownership and institutionalization is a commitment to ensure the financial sustainability of a project outcome in the long term:

> [...] communities must be equipped organizationally, politically, and financially to handle ownership and control of interventions. In some instances, communities may not be interested in or have adequate resources (staff or financial) to assume responsibility. In the absence of a community structure or commitment to assume ownership, interventions are unlikely to be sustained.
>
> (Altman, 1995: 528)

Looking at the sustainability of health programmes, Shediac-Rizkallah and Bone (1998) stress the visibility of a project in the community, an extended funding period, and financial sustainability as key to ensuring a long-term perspective for an initiative:

> What are the sources of funds for the program (internal, external, a mixture)? What are the community's local resources? Can the community afford the program (e.g. is it able to pay maintenance and recurrent costs)? How much are community members willing/able to pay for services? What strategies are in place to facilitate gradual financial self-sufficiency?
>
> (p. 99)

Factors concerning the broader environment include 'market forces impinging on an organization, legislation affecting the program, support from external community leaders, and the availability of funding and other resources as inputs to the program' (Scheirer, 2005: 325).

Hence, ensuring financial sustainability may have to be addressed by a project consortium at the beginning of a collaboration. Often, IT-related innovations cannot finance themselves unless special funding is provided, with approaches varying depending on whether it is to be used in public or private organizations. Moreover, an internet connection or mobile phone services, as well as the costs of maintaining a lab and/or repairing devices, may be unaffordable for members of a poor community. This may require a project's stakeholders to develop alternative models of financing, such as the ones described by Jackson et al. (2012):

> To deal with this problem, the Computers for Kavango initiative has introduced a model whereby unemployed youth in communities are trained in basic maintenance and repair of computers. In exchange for maintaining the

labs, the youth are allowed to make use of the computers for income generating small to medium-sized business enterprises, ranging from photo printing to basic typing and document services (including personal resumes).

(p. 113)

Transfer of ownership, although key to a project's success in having a long-term influence, needs to be well thought out and eventually backed up with special measures that make technology use affordable and take steps such as 'getting symbolic acceptance by the community, stimulating valuable social activity in relevant social groups, generating linkage to viable revenue streams, and enrolling government support' (Madon et al., 2009: 95).

2.3.5 Creating alliances

Bringing a design solution that has been developed within a project to fruition in an organization or community is not possible without mobilizing the support of key actors, who have to be 'interested', as well as accepting and willing to provide resources. This is why creating alliances is crucial. It requires, among other things, cultivation of the 'art of interessement', which Akrich et al. (2002) deem crucial for any innovation, arguing:

> Since the outcome of a project depends on the alliances which it allows for and the interests which it mobilises, no criteria, no algorithm, can ensure success a priori. Rather than speak of the rationality of decisions, we need to speak of the aggregation of interests which decisions are capable or incapable of producing. Innovation is the art of interesting an increasing number of allies who will make you stronger and stronger.
>
> (p. 205)

We can make a distinction between short-term alliances and building longer-term support structures. Short-term alliances are needed for place-making for a practice-based project in a particular context. They include key actors in the user organization, as well as other actors that may exert influence and/or may be affected by the results of a project. Bødker et al. (2017) use the notion of 'knotworks' (Engeström et al., 1999) to describe constellations of actors that come together temporarily for a common concern, as well as the more enduring networks that participatory processes tie into. In their view, supporting the tying of knots and forming new personal and political relationships among participants are key to the sustainability of a project outcome. This is supported by Bossen et al. (2010), who conclude that 'PD initiatives have the potential to be sustained through the relationships that stretch across organizations and project groups' (p. 148).

At a certain point it may be crucial to engage a wider set of stakeholders. In the case of the FabLab@school.dk project (Bødker et al., 2017), this meant expanding beyond a single project 'to also include a public hearing with parents, national stakeholders, and other interested parties' (p. 262), eventually influencing policy-makers. Bødker et al. (2017) think of these 'backstage' design activities—building support structures that in the long term bring the outcomes of a project to fruition in other contexts—as 'participatory infrastructuring'.

Building a community of practice (Lave and Wenger, 1991) or a community of interest (Fischer, 2001) is a more far-reaching strategy of creating alliances to bring about innovation or achieve sustainability. Swan et al. (2002) use the notion 'community of practice' to describe how managers in a pharmaceutical company succeeded in creating a network that developed a radical innovation for the treatment of prostate cancer. They contend that innovation is 'a political act, taking place within a network of partisan interactions' (p. 7), highlighting the political nature of activities that bring about change in communities and organizations. Obendorf et al. (2009) present a case in which they worked for an extended period on the development of an online learning system, developing a set of methods for building a community of interest. Fischer et al. (2001) use this concept to characterize 'heterogeneous design groups' that join forces for a common purpose that requires a long-term commitment. For self-managing communities, such as users of 3D printing, Ludwig et al. (2014) recommend establishing a social network 'possibly also including stakeholders responsible for machinery maintenance/development' (p. 9).

Although creating alliances in view of sustainability as a core project activity has not been systematically addressed in the research literature, the examples demonstrate its importance, following the call of Bødker et al. (2017) 'for a focus on the longitudinal network of activities in which people and technologies, in the widest sense of the term, are brought together and changed' (p. 265).

2.3.6 Making the technology work reliably

The outcomes of IT research design projects with limited duration are often not sufficiently mature to be installed in a real-world context. But even when the technology is at a stage where it can be implemented, practitioners may need a space for learning as well as continuing technical support. Hence, organizations and/or communities have to engage in capacity building, as described, for example, by Carroll and Rosson (2007), who have documented different forms of learning in a community, such as learning of IT skills; organizational learning (which 'included the broader problem of finding, evaluating, and installing open source software' (p. 254)); and technology learning, including the ability to develop 'strategies for determining how to "choose" among tools' (p. 255).

The question of how to establish more permanent support structures for the daily problems people—whether working in an organization or living at home—may have with IT-based artifacts has only recently attracted attention. With respect to IT projects involving elderly people, Meurer et al. (2018) describe how continuous learning and technology support may be difficult to ensure when there is no community or organization that takes on this responsibility after a project ends. Hyysalo (2004) argues that design for the elderly 'often entails the meeting of two different worlds, one of young male high-tech professionals and one of elderly people and elderly care' (p. 23). Using the example of a seemingly simple security device that was introduced into care situations, he describes observing how most elderly users did not know 'how to determine if the device still worked. In practice, to keep a Wrist-care device up and running reliably, somebody had to check regularly the condition of the Wrist-device and how it was actually worn, and to perform test-alarms' (p. 28). He thinks that the transition between the two worlds has to be better taken care of.

Apart from capacity building, maintenance and repair work is needed to keep a technology functioning through breakdowns and failure. Studies show how to ensure this in different contexts. Orr's (1986) ethnography of the work of photocopier repair technicians is well known; in it, he highlights their use of 'anecdotal experience in the co-operative building of a diagnostic understanding of a broken copier' (p. 62). Henke (1999) has pointed out the importance of improvisation in maintenance and repair work. He also stresses the invisibility of much of the repair work going on in workplaces. In a study of repair technicians in different types of organizations, Barley (1996) remarks on the ambivalence of organizations towards them: 'most computer users implied that computer technicians should be handy helpers who appeared on a moment's notice, resolved problems without delay, and disappeared as quickly as they came' (p. 429). While these ethnographies study the work of repair technicians, the 'Wireless Leiden' project by Verhaegh et al. (2016) looked at the work done by volunteers:

In order for the hybrid collective as a whole to be able to withstand forces of resistance over time, connections between its constituting elements need to be continuously monitored, maintained and if broken, reconnected. Technology needs to be taken care of. Without care, every technology will fall victim to deterioration.

(p. 207)

They found that, as there was a lack of resources for this type of work, strategies were developed for delegating tasks and responsibilities to home users. In Leiden, individual citizens—'virtuoso volunteers'—took care of the network. Being able to resolve complex maintenance problems presented an important source of satisfaction and recognition for them:

Volunteers thrive on the intellectual challenge of finding a creative solution to tough problems, especially when repair work leads to redesign. In order to fix something, an actor has to think up, design and implement a new solution.

(p. 108)

Developing countries grapple with particular difficulties. Rey-Moreno et al. (2013) see low cost, ease of use, and maintainability as prerequisites for technologies to survive in developing countries. This research confirms that one important condition for an IT-based solution to be sustainable is that they are taken care of—maintained, repaired, updated, etc. More generally, as Graham and Thrift (2007) argue, the effort that goes into making technology work smoothly is often undervalued, not recognized, and made invisible, arguing 'that the way in which maintenance and repair is officially represented in most bureaucracies as subordinate hides this work from view, for example in worksheets that cannot acknowledge this knowledge' (p. 4).

2.3.7 Long-term measures to ensure the sustainability of research lines and research outcomes

Given the problems of achieving a design outcome that is sustainable in the future within the framework of a funded project with limited duration, researchers seek to create the conditions for working in a more long-term perspective using different strategies.

One of these strategies is to make the experiences of practice-based research available to other researchers and future projects. Stevens et al. (2018) suggest the construction of what they call *e-Portfolios*—that is, 'digitalized collections of design case studies' that support a long-lasting memory of the design experiences, in terms of both raw data and (documental) artifacts produced and used during design. Such collections could include the perspective of sustainability by paying specific attention to design practices that aim at the sustainability of the design outcomes. Dalsgaard and Halskov (2012) present and discuss a tool designed to support design documentation, emphasizing its usefulness not only for 'shared reflection and discussion in on-going projects' but also for 'scaffolding longitudinal and cross-projects studies' (p. 428). In their work with users in different contexts over a period of ten years, Oberndorf et al. (2009) made use of 'commented case studies' that 'make this face-to-face interaction persistent, providing a written documentation of distributed use experiences and design decisions' (p. 58).

While these examples suggest ways of preserving and sharing knowledge that support building a long-term research line, Huybrechts et al. (2018) propose 'scripting' as a technique that helps sustain long-term engagement with a community after a project comes to an end. Based on work in two living labs, they experimented with different forms and/or stages of 'scripting' that proceeded from 'personal scripts' written by individuals about how they coped with issues, to shared 'community scripts' about 'how to self-organise in the making of both personal and community scripts for the future after the designer leaves her/his project' (p. 19). These examples point at possibilities of supporting a collective process of reflection and learning that, while analysing the course of individual projects, aims at gaining more general insights into practices and strategies suited to achieving sustainable outcomes.

The concept of the 'living lab', which Ehn et al. (2014) define as a kind of participatory laboratory 'in the wild', has been developed with a view to sustainability. The idea behind it is to provide a context and resources for use and redesign that an individual project may have difficulties in establishing. On the basis of three projects in different domains (home entertainment, energy monitoring, and ageing at home), Ogonowski et al. (2018) developed the PRAXLABS framework to reflect on and implement elements of sustainable design in living lab situations. It includes intensive stakeholder and end-user participation and fosters long-term orientation in IT design projects. It supports the transfer of experiences and technologies developed in one context to other, similar contexts, possibly through the involvement of companies sharing the same mission—for example, those seeking to sustain women in the IT workforce (Ahmadi et al., 2020).

Another path towards long-term sustainability is academic entrepreneurship in the form of university spin-offs. According to Nicolaou and Birley

(2003), a university spin-off involves the transfer of a technology from an academic institution into a new company whose founding members may include the inventor academic(s) who may or may not continue their affiliation with the academic institution. Creating spin-offs as a strategy of commercially exploiting some knowledge, technology, or research results is described in numerous publications. However, as Gläser and Laudel (2016) observe, 'although attempts by the state to create and direct research capacities for the support of public policy goals have increased significantly, the impact of these attempts on the dynamics of knowledge production has received comparatively little attention' (p. 129). Moreover, there is little empirical research on how IT design research projects with an interest in achieving practically useful, sustainable outcomes use academic entrepreneurship as a strategy.

2.4 Forms of sustainability

The 'future-proofing' perspective looks beyond the moment when a design outcome has been appropriated by users in the context for which it has been designed, asking 'what happens next and in the near future?' Can the learning and the benefits from the technical artifact in terms of new practices, new ways of organizing, and new opportunities for doing things be maintained? Can these achievements be transferred to other projects and contexts, offering new paths?

Based on a number of PD projects with school children, Iversen and Dindler (2014) propose a set of distinctions between forms of sustainability that is useful in understanding that there are different ways of achieving a sustainable project outcome (Figure 2.2): *maintaining* relates to activities that seek to support the integration of what has been developed into existing practices (inevitably changing them to some extent); *scaling* refers to efforts at bringing an IT artifact and the insights related to it to a larger group of users inside an organization or beyond it; *replicating* is a form of sustainability 'where the initiative, in the form of an idea, system, or way of working, remains relatively stable, but the context of this initiative is changed from one context to another' (p. 158); *evolving* means that what has been developed serves 'as a springboard' for further development and even new ideas. Iversen and Dindler suggest

> that these forms are to be thought of as ideal types that do not exist in their pure forms, but may serve as lenses through which we can inspect PD projects, and begin to understand how sustainability is pursued and achieved.

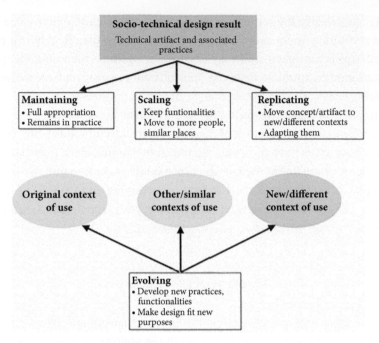

Fig. 2.2 Levels of sustainability

Moreover, they are not mutually exclusive—often, they are accumulative, in the sense that any form presupposes the prior one. These four forms of sustainability may be distinguished by looking at two parameters: the context in which the initiative is sustained, and the extent to which the initiative remains stable or is further developed once the project ends.

(p. 156)

Scaling as a form of sustainability has been observed and also actively promoted in different contexts. Ribes (2014) uses the concept in the context of doing an ethnography of scalar devices, such as a research infrastructure that may be geographically distributed, but also in the sense of 'scaling up' as part of the development of infrastructures that are scalable ('can support growth'), extensible ('can expand into new capacities'), and modular (p. 9). In the example of research infrastructure, scaling is 'about the number and qualities of people involved in projects' (p. 9)—or what Ribes calls 'organizational scaling'. It ensures that researchers that are located in different institutions around the world can share data and techniques. Sahay and Walsham (2006), using the example of implementing health information systems in India, add to this perspective by arguing that scaling is not just about numbers (i.e. how many users adopt it) and size, but 'refers to the processes and embedded practices by which hetero-geneous networks around the technology are spread, enhanced, scoped, and enlarged. Thus, scaling concerns aspects of geography, software architecture, people, processes, infrastructure, technical support, and political support' (p. 188).

Scaling may be driven by more practical concerns in cases where local interventions may need to be part of a larger network to be robust. Braa et al. (2004) make an important point about going beyond a successful intervention, distributing it to other sites. Their case is the HISP project—a large initiative to introduce health information systems in developing countries. They propose a shift from local interventions to interventions involving multiple sites, arguing:

This shift has emerged more out of necessity than by design, through the recognition of the relative failure to institutionalize and make changes sustainable. This, the argument goes, is because local interventions need to be part of a larger network to be robust. In short, scalability is a prerequisite 'not a luxury' for sustainability of local action. Establishing networks creates opportunities for sharing of experience, knowledge, technology, and value between the various nodes of the experience.

(p. 341)

Ensuring the scalability and transferability of design outcomes may be used as a strategy to strengthen the theoretical or empirical bases of results and insights. Reflecting on the transferability of their experiences with rural communities in Namibia, Winschiers-Theophilus et al. (2013) argue that

operating within a single context for a longer term, resulting in the mutual learning that is a necessary and desirable consequence, can obscure the transferability and recoverability of the results. Thus 'moving away' becomes a necessity to explore cross-contextual validity for theory building and explicit lessons learned.

(p. 372)

Although it may be critical for a project not just to anchor design results in one organization or community but to replicate or evolve them to serve other settings, this step may be beyond the scope of a single project, since it would imply a connection to other organizations or communities with their own local conditions: the dimension and set-up of the project have to be designed accordingly. As Meurer et al. (2018) have observed, more feasible is the transferability of results across projects that might involve the same participants or have a different set of target users. In the first case, transferability is more the continuity of an experience from a possibly different and broader perspective; in the second case, transferability involves the research team only. What is to be transferred is also variable: it could be a designed IT artifact with particular functionalities, an approach to solving particular issues (such as community-building, health, mobility), or a component of a technological infrastructure.

2.5 Comparing and contrasting the case studies

Working with empirical material from a large number of projects and/or cases in different fields of activity raises a series of methodological challenges that are to do with the need to look across these examples, comparing and contrasting them. The epistemological challenges of comparative studies are a subject of debate and controversy in sociology and anthropology. Comparative work has been accused of being reductionist (when it proceeds 'by coding [the] single factors and establishing cross-case patterns'; Yin, 1981) and of producing overarching generalizations. What seems to be at stake is the singularity of each case and the seemingly inevitable loss of significant context-specific detail when doing a comparative analysis. Recently, perspectives on comparative analysis have changed as new ways of sharing empirical material from different contexts have been developed, inter alia as part of the EU's funding programme for the 2014 to 2020 period (known as Horizon 2020).

Reflecting on comparative studies of social practices, Robert Schmidt (2008) refers to how Max Weber treats comparison in the construction of 'ideal types':

> The analytical relationships established comparatively can lead to discovering elective affinities (Wahlverwandtschaften) among cases and objects as well as unexpected differences, clashes, collisions, mutual exclusions and tensions [...]. As Weber puts it, comparing critically (kritische Vergleichung) does not serve a search for analogies and parallels but rather should be deployed to shed light on the peculiarity (Herausarbeitung der Eigenart) of the cases and objects.
>
> (p. 357)

Weber saw a comparative perspective not as abstracting from the particularities of a social phenomenon or case but as helping reveal them. This viewpoint has been taken up by, for example, Akrich and Rabeharisoa (2016) in what they term an 'auto-ethnography of a European project'. They conclude the following from their analysis of how they approached comparing patient organizations in different countries:

> We neither built a social theory of patients' organisations out of case-based comparison, nor did we celebrate the uniqueness of events which punctuate the history of each organisation. What we did instead was to highlight the existence of common practices amongst patients' organisations, and to examine each organisation through the lenses of these practices. This eventually enabled us to pick out each organisation's specificities, and to deepen understandings on their singular and original way of dealing with their own problems.
>
> (p. 160)

In the literature, different approaches to doing comparative work are discussed. For example, Noblit and Hare (1988) use the term 'meta-ethnography', suggesting a process of translation and transcription of each case material in the light of other cases (Doyle, 2003). Asking how you actually compare something like home care arrangements in different countries without sidestepping the empirical complexities of the practice of caregiving, Lutz (2016) proposes the term 'ethnographic tinkering' to describe how a particular perspective shapes the ethnographic writing process, carefully working with the interrelations between description and analysis.

These are interesting examples of how to practise comparative work. Still, they do not solve the problem that Wulf et al. (2015) formulate for design: the lack 'of a convincing model of how to transfer design-relevant findings from one context to the next' (p. 117). We propose that such an approach to practising comparative work strongly depends on its main purpose. To take some examples from CSCW research: Martin et al. (2007) focused on classification work in different call centres, with the intention of identifying some common themes and, ultimately, informing the design of systems in support of such work; Schmidt et al. (2007) analysed the coordinative artifacts and the practices surrounding them used in different oncology clinics to identify generic 'techniques of writing'; Balka et al. (2008) used empirical material from ethnographic case studies conducted in two countries to create a typology intended to identify possible sources of local variability in healthcare work practices; Betz and Wulf (2018) performed a meta-analysis of three design case studies in the domain of firefighting (one of the domains included in this book) with the purpose of identifying common 'structural configurations'. These different purposes influenced the conceptual lenses used in each study, the selection of case material, and the ways in which it is 'made comparable'.

Our key point of reference is the perspective of sustainability and the 'sensitizing concepts' that help elaborate this perspective. Blumer (1954) suggested the term 'sensitizing' to account for concepts that are useful precisely because they provide 'a general sense of reference and guidance in approaching empirical instances' (p. 7). This, he adds, is not due to some kind of conceptual immaturity but reflects 'the nature of the empirical world which we are seeking to study and analyze' (p. 7). He continues:

> We do not leave aside what gives each instance its peculiar character and restrict ourselves to what it has in common with the other instances in the class covered by the concept. To the contrary, we seem forced to reach what is common by accepting and using what is distinctive to the given empirical instance. In other words, what is common (i.e. what the concept refers to) is expressed in a distinctive manner in each empirical instance and can be got at only by accepting and working through the distinctive expressions.
>
> (p. 8)

Working through material from different empirical studies allows one to progressively refine the sensitizing concepts, showing how they may help capture the aspects of an observed phenomenon that 'matter for design'. Comparing and contrasting helps highlight the existence of common practices, as Akrich and Rabeharisoa (2016) describe it, while also helping us to better understand the unique and specific ways the different projects deal with the issues at stake when trying to ensure the sustainability of design outcomes beyond the end of the project.

The research initiatives we compare from the point of view of sustainability are of a very different nature. Most of them follow a practice-based approach that combines fieldwork studies with IT development (in most cases using participatory techniques) and some form of testing and evaluation in a (close to) real-work context. While some of these examples are single projects, others are part of a research line developed over many years. Only a few of these projects reached the stage of full appropriation by a user organization or community. Other cases included in this book are mainly observational studies that were carried out from a practice-based perspective, following, for example, the development and deployment of an infrastructure over years or the adoption of off-the-shelf technologies by a user organization.

While the majority of projects are university-based, several of them have been developed within an industrial research context. Although the researchers in these projects have a strong academic background and publish internationally, the conditions for doing research differ from the typical externally funded research in academia. The two university spin-offs we had the chance to follow as examples of a particular strategy to keep an idea and/or technology sustainable in the longer term were managed differently again.

Our approach to comparing these numerous cases, which are diverse on so many levels, is partially inspired by Robinson's work on doing comparative studies in urbanism. Robinson (2016) argues: 'The approach I signpost here takes inspiration from comparative urbanism's openness to conceptual revision, and offers methodological and philosophical grounds for a new repertoire of comparative methods open to "thinking with elsewheres"' (p. 188). She suggests basing comparative work 'on comparative practice, rather than formal methodological requirements', advocating 'thinking with variation and repetition, rather than trying to "control for difference"' (p. 188). In this line, the sensitizing concepts are a starting point for capturing variation (and possibly repetition), with the aim of achieving some degree of conceptual revision.

SECTION II

CASE STUDIES

The case studies included in this section cover the different fields of activity and projects/cases from the perspective of the research teams as presented in the interviews and project publications. Table II.1 provides an overview of this variety of domains and projects, in some cases research lines, their duration, and the supporting funding schemes.

Table II.1. Overview of domains and projects

Domain	Project	Nation	Duration	Funding Scheme
Manufacturing in SMEs	EKPLO	Europe & Germany	2016–2018	EU & Regional
	CyberRüsten 4.0	Europe	2016–2019	EU & EFRE.NRW (Regional)
	Kompetenzzentrum Mittelstand 4.0	Germany	2017–2020	BMWE (National)
Firefighters	WearIT	Europe	2004–2009	EU (IP Project)
	Landmarke	Germany	2008–2011	BMBF (National)
	Koordinator	Germany	2012–2014	BMBF (National)
Emergency Management	Störfallkommunikation	Germany	2006–2008	RWE Rhein-Ruhr Netzservice (Regional)
	Infostrom	Germany	2010–2013	National
	EmerGent	Europe	2014–2017	EU
	KOKOS	Germany	2015–2018	(BMBF) National
Healthcare	WOAD (Web Of Active Documents)	Italy	2009–2015	Local University
	PICADo	France	2012–2015	Fonds Unique Interministériel (National)
	CALIPSO	France		Regional
	HADex	France	2016–2018	Innovaction Grand Est (Regional)
	Scanning	Norway		Local Hospital
	Videoconferencing	Norway	1993–2016	Sunnaas Rehabilitation Hospital

Continued

Table II.1. *Continued*

Domain	Project	Nation	Duration	Funding Scheme
	Telemedicine Toolkit	France	2012–2014	Regional Healthcare Agency
	Action-ADE	Canada	Since 2012 ongoing	CIHR (National), and various provincial funding agencies
	DocuLive	Norway	1992–2004	National
	B-EPR	Denmark	1996–2006	National
	SEP	Denmark	2000	National
	WelFare Technologies	Norway	2015–2018	National
Developing Countries	WiFi Mesh Network Mankosi, South Africa	South Africa	2009–2012	National Research Foundation (NRF) of South Africa Council for Scientific and Industrial Research (CSIR), EPSRC from the UK
	Zenzeleni Networks	South Africa	Since 2012, ongoing	NRF, DST, local telcos, EU H2020
	Ethnographic study in Namibia	USA	2010	Local Funding
	Ethnographic study in Bangladesh	USA	2013	Intel Science and Technology Center for Social Computing
IT Service Providers	Print Awareness Tool	France	2012–2015	XEROX—Grenoble
	TurkBench	France	2013–2015	XEROX—Grenoble
	Agent Performance Indicator	France	2013–2016	XEROX—Grenoble
	Request for Service Management	USA	2017–2019	IBM-Almaden
	Cloud Service Analytics	USA	2017–2018	IBM-Almaden
	Intelligent IT Configuration	USA	2017–2018	IBM-Almaden
Intercultural Computer Clubs	ComeIN	Germany	2005–2008	BMBF (National)
	come_IN@Palestine	Palestine	2010–2012	Deutscher Akademischer Austauschdienst
		Morocco	2015–now	
Crossing Domains	Living Lab Energy and Environment	Germany	2014–2017	MKULNV (Regional)
	Smartlife	Germany	2014–2017	BMWi (National)

3

Bringing Industry 4.0 to small and medium enterprises

Industry 4.0 is the name of the so-called fourth industrial revolution. The first three industrial revolutions, which spanned almost 200 years, were concerned with developing sources of power; shaping work organizations according to Tayloristic principles; and programming automation systems that helped reduce the physical work needed to manage the semi-finished products, perform basic operations, and assemble them to create a final product. The self-declared 'fourth industrial revolution' aims at the vertical and horizontal integration of the production system by controlling and coordinating the internal and external supply chains through 'smart', if not 'intelligent', technologies. Since both supply chains can have a global reach, Industry 4.0 needs to address the organizational and technological issues related to the globalization of the economy and its effects on the production systems.

Although there is no unique definition of Industry 4.0, all of them share some basic features (see Thoben et al., 2017 and Brettel et al., 2014 for an overview from a scientific perspective and Gilchrist, 2016 for a more commercial perspective). Industry 4.0 aims to increase the automation and integration of all the production activities—making pervasive use of recent IT concepts such as the (Integrated) Internet of Things (IoT) to enhance the Internet of Services, 'big data' collected through these services, and data analytics to support optimization of the production—and progressively substitute the workforce when decisions have to be taken and production flows have to be accommodated during unexpected situations.

Recently, the convergence of these concepts has been made explicit in the term 'Cognitive Internet of Things', which aims to 'empower IoT with high level intelligence' in order to keep human intervention to a minimum (Wu et al., 2014). Irrespective of the term that is used, the envisaged main advantages include an increase of product quality, a reduction of waste from ecological

Future-proofing. Wulf et al., Oxford University Press.
© Carla Simone, Ina Wagner, Claudia Müller, Anne Weibert, and Volker Wulf (2022).
DOI: 10.1093/oso/9780198862505.003.0003

and economic perspectives (Stock and Seliger, 2016), and improved customer relationship management as products and services become more personalized and their designs involve the customers themselves. Moreover, workers can concentrate on more 'creative' activities under the condition that they update their skills and competences according to the new paradigm.

In the literature, the successful cases illustrating the feasibility and positive effects of Industry 4.0 mainly concern big enterprises that, in general, have well-defined organizational structures and production processes that are already supported by enterprise resource planning (ERP) technologies and often also by knowledge management (KM) technologies. This is the case in the United States, where the phenomenon is more pragmatically referred to as 'industrial internet' or 'integrated industry' (e.g. Gilchrist, 2016; Gökalp, Şener, and Eren, 2017), whereas much of European research contributes to a literature focusing on SMEs, where the scenario can be quite different. An extensive survey of the German industry (Sommer, 2015) shows that the size of the industry significantly influences the awareness of, interest in, and readiness for Industry 4.0 principles. It also demonstrates that the actual inclination of SMEs to invest in the related technological innovation is limited to aspects that do not dramatically change the organization of the production processes. Another survey of European industries and Industry 4.0 experts (Gabriel and Pessl, 2016) suggests that the innovation that is needed to face the changes induced by the globalized economy can be characterized more as an evolution from the current situation than a true revolution. In this trajectory, the future of work is taken as an important factor of the innovation, in addition to ecological concerns. The leading idea is to maintain the workforce as a central component of the decision processes and to provide training that enables workers to take advantage of the new opportunities. Moreover, concerns are voiced about the impact of the envisaged innovation on the quality of the working life, in particular with respect to the increasing levels of stress that workers may have to face. Industry 4.0 is funded by many research programmes all around the world.

In European projects, researchers are called to support companies, especially SMEs, in their path towards innovation. The projects that have been included in this case study have all been carried out with the University of Siegen as one of the main research partners. Interviews with Thomas Ludwig (quoted as TL), Christoph Kotthaus (quoted as CK), and Aparecido Fabiano Pinatti de Carvalho (quoted as FC), together with numerous project publications, have provided the material for discussing the sustainability aspects of IT projects in manufacturing, with a focus on SMEs.

3.1 Overview of research line

The line of research in industrial settings at the University of Siegen encompasses a number of projects: *Living Lab Energy and Environment* was about flexible energy management systems in manufacturing settings (described in Chapter 10); *CyberRüsten 4.0* was about supporting the work of machine set up with augmented reality (AR) and sensor technologies; *EKPLO* was about supporting production planning (PP) in SMEs.

EKPLO (Real-time Collaborative Planning and Scheduling; 2016–19) aimed to explore the potential of advanced planning and scheduling (APS) systems for SMEs. Funded by the European Union (EU) and the State of North Rhine-Westphalia, it cooperated with several manufacturing companies in the Siegen area. With support from one of those companies in particular, a prototype was developed to get process data from the shop floor in real time and improve the overall data/information quality. A gamification approach was used to motivate data input:

> So, if all workers told how many parts they produced and in which quality at the end of the shift […] the project focuses more or less on real time data and a quite clever way between how often do you trigger workers to enter data and what would be a good interval. The gamification approach was to trigger this intrinsic motivation for the workers.
>
> (CK Int, 22/11/2018)

The prototype was developed in collaboration with the workers. The team decided to use *OpenDash* (see Chapter 10) as a dashboard tool that has real-time features. This choice suggested itself, as *OpenDash*, which had been developed by colleagues in Siegen, offered an easily customizable dashboard for production planners to create the visualizations they actually needed for their specific roles on mobile devices that allowed them to 'run around in the company all the time and still do scheduling'. The prototype has been presented at a number of fairs and in the context of the Competence Center *Mittelstand 4.0* (CC), where it has provoked some interest from other active production planners.

The project *Cyberrüsten 4.0* (2016–19), funded by the EU and EFRE NRW (a special funding programme financed by the European Fund for regional development), deals with rotary draw bending in manufacturing and the usefulness of cyber physical production systems (CPPS) in supporting machine set-up (Abele et al., 2016). Ethnographic data collection in a subsidiary of a German company in the Czech Republic uncovered numerous problems, including: the storage of tools and parts; the difficulties of workers in identifying the appropriate parts for the set-up, as some parts are very alike; and the complex process of parameter adjustments, which requires an experienced installer. The findings of this pre-study suggested AR technology should be used for two tasks in particular: to capture complex set-up instructions using AR animations and short video sequences and to capture small tolerances by inputting sensory data (De Carvalho et al., 2018; Hoffmann et al., 2019). When the prototype was ready, the researchers ran several usability tests with students, but alas, the Czech company did not agree to install the whole set-up. Fortunately, one of the project partners provided a lab with a similar machine, which allowed the industrial environment to be replicated and the prototype to be tested with workers from several partner companies. After completion of the project, the manager of the Czech company that had hosted the pre-study invited the research team back to engage in another iteration to refine the system for another process. The goal was to initiate knowledge transfer between international sites of the company. Moreover, the CC provided the opportunity to present the tested prototype to other companies, several of which voiced their interest.

The *CyberRüsten* prototype was used in three implementation projects in total. The idea underlying one of those projects was to develop generic software that supports the production and playback of instructions. Within the second project, another software prototype was developed that used abstract (i.e. arrows and boxes) instead of concrete hologram representations (on the basis of CAD models of the machine). Both types of representation were compared in a user study. Finally, as both prototypes only support static set-up processes, the research team investigated the possibilities of using AR for dynamic adaptations of machine parameters, finding that these also work with 'very old machines' (Sven Hoffmann, additional information). A project that started recently (in 2020) uses the experiences of *CyberRüsten* to identify parameters that influence learning, information-sharing, and acting in semi-virtual workspaces.

Another building block for projects in manufacturing is the work of Ludwig et al. (2014, 2017a) on 3D printing, which investigated a range of possibilities for a technology to be able to recognize and remember how people used it, thereby supporting the appropriation process:

> We try to integrate a second level approach into the technology for discussing and articulating use practices around the technology with other people who use it, adding communication and cooperation layers. We call that 'sociable

technologies'. We started with this asking if it would be possible to integrate *Facebook* into the technology that was our idea, as a kind of appropriation support, moving from an Internet of Things to an Internet of Practice.

(TL Int, 22/11/2018)

This research helped identify a series of design challenges to make 3D print-ers more 'sociable'. A prototype was built and evaluated (Ludwig et al., 2014, 2017a). Although no funding was available, the research was continued with the CC. For example, projection mapping was implemented with a beamer mounted to the ceiling that projected how to operate a 3D printer onto the printer itself. The plan is to transfer the concept and design approach that was developed for 3D printers to production machines in manufacturing settings, putting functionalities for knowledge-sharing directly in the tech-nologies themselves. This seems a timely idea, as new complex and automated manufacturing systems are not easy to handle and control for the machine operator:

The capability of the production machines to report internal and external critical situations systematically and to present the production process to the machine operators is often limited; thus machine operators are often hin-dered in appropriating the complex production process. In other words: If an error in the machine—which is usually automated—occurs, the machine op-erator does not always know why it fails nor how to fix it, because the state of the machine depends on too many parameters both inside, but also outside the machine itself.

(Ludwig et al., 2016: 2)

3.2 The key role of the Competence Center *Mittelstand 4.0*

In my opinion, the CC as an institution is for sustainability. The main mission is to transfer knowledge and research from the university into practice.

(CK Int, 22/11/2018)

The Competence Center *Mittelstand 4.0* was established in 2017 in coopera-tion with other universities (Fachhochschule Südwestfalen, Ruhr-Universität Bochum) and the Fraunhofer Institute (FIT). It has a staff of ten people—four of whom are affiliated with the University of Siegen—with, in addition, a full position for public and media relations. The activities of the CC focus on the transfer of design ideas and approaches that have been developed at the university to SMEs. All funding by the Ministry of Economics goes to the participating universities. Companies that cooperate with the CC do not act as typical consortia partners in research projects, as they cannot receive funding through it.

The four team members at the University of Siegen mostly engage in IT consulting. They do this in the context of small projects that last from one week to four to six months. These projects require input, such as programming or hardware integration, and give rise to systematic reflection. In 2018, the CC served 250 companies with lectures, a workshop series, and twenty-five to thirty small projects.

> There is a huge amount of companies that are interested in working with us, because, things we do, we are not allowed to get money from them, because we are funded and this is one of the interesting things for companies—they get something for free.
>
> (TL Int, 22/11/2018)

Organizing a successful proposal for the CC was only possible because the research team was already in contact with companies from previous research. The CC now allows the extension and strengthening of this network through the different activities it engages in; some of the workshops the CC team organized, for example, stretched over the course of half a year. This enabled the research team to establish good connections:

> You meet them again and again, and after one workshop we went out to have dinner together and continued talking and some other projects resulted from this. And what we also sometimes do, we know the companies, we know the contact persons and know pretty much what they are doing, we consider them also for further research projects—in a manner of sustainability of these connections. We then find an interesting problem we were tackling first and maybe we can look at this a little deeper and then try to get funding to continue this research.
>
> (CK Int, 22/11/2018)

Organizing events is a large part of the CC team's work. *Digital scout*, for example, is a series of workshops that introduce concepts of digitization to companies. The series was initiated by the chamber of industry and commerce and the district administration, and went on to seek the knowledge and assistance of the University of Siegen to provide the local businesses with some advice with regard to digitization. They got in contact with us because they wanted to do something, but needed concrete ideas about the contents that would make sense.

(TL Int, 22/11/2018)

The series was started together with local partners such as the IHK (Industrie— und Handelskammer Siegen) and Kreis Siegen. The first workshop was about 'detecting process for modelling processes and how to derive improvements from their processes'; the second was about 'change management and how to detect people who are somehow affected by the introduction of digitization'. The third workshop was about innovation and new products, 'where we just provide new methods for getting or for deriving ideas of new projects and designing', and there was also a fourth regarding visualizing sensor data.

We started the first series, and we were hoping to maybe have around 15 people attending—and then we received more than 30 applications, and we admitted 30. And that was the starting point where we noticed: there is a definite demand for this. The second round of workshops was already scheduled and was fully booked in an instance. And so, the CC took on the arrangement of contents, and now is also advancing the initiative to other districts and cities.

(TL Int, 22/11/2018)

Moreover, the CC team developed an AR class for machine setters, instructing them on how to configure the machines, 'since using the technology is not that easy' (CK). Companies that are interested in this topic get in touch with the developers to discuss the application area.

We have done an exploratory study because 3D printing is a new technology that is not used so often in companies but the CC allows us to present the whole infrastructure and the way to visualize this to other companies and those who are interested in this, we have discussions about how these things can be transferred into production machines in a serious production context. We haven't done a project yet about this but as you know it depends on funding and we don't have staff to do this for two years right now.

(TL Int, 22/11/2018)

The CC presents a unique opportunity for the research team to present their work to a larger audience in the form of prototypes, with the aim of eliciting the interest and cooperation of companies to make further developments and adaptations to different manufacturing settings. Small cooperative projects also allow evaluation of prototypes that have been developed as part of a larger research project in more detail.

> Usually, it is hard even to reach the appropriation phase of a technology because appropriation is not just throwing the technology into some practice context but it is rather to see how the practice evolves: are there any changes in practice, what organizational changes and so on. [...] Really, with a three-year project after two years you have a functional prototype that works properly, probably and there's just one year left to evaluate the prototype in a practice context and usually appropriation is hard to reach.
>
> (TL Int, 22/11/2018)

The general strategy is to take design approaches and their prototypical realizations and put them into new contexts, so they can be developed further and may eventually be integrated into a real work setting.

> To get people to get involved with our prototypes, it takes a lot of work and care and know-how to get it right. It's simply very, very intensive: getting to know the application area properly, understanding the requirements correctly, and implementing them.
>
> (CK Int, 22/11/2018)

This is a strategy that Iversen and Dindler (2014) have described as *evolving*—that is, what has been developed serves 'as a springboard' for further development and even new ideas—'it will be a different tool in the end, a totally different tool but from the design approach it will be similar' (CK).

Examples of small projects on which the CC's researchers have collaborated with people from different companies are as follows:

> Companies do not have an ERP system, they are just interested in whether the offers they get from other companies are valid, and if they are worth the money.
>
> Other projects are—they are interested in getting data from a machine and visualize that data and we have here the concept and the technology where we are able to put these technologies in their context, set up the machines and after maybe 2, 3 or 4–5 weeks they have a kind of dashboard where they can visualize data.

Or we have plenty of topics, for example, a company came to us and wanted to have a workshop about future trends, the global market and how to qualify employees for this.

(TL Int, 22/11/2018)

One of these small project examples was run by a company that produces cranes to use inside production halls. This company has an issue with machine maintenance: its maintenance workers, who are only around in the morning shift, actually have many other jobs to do apart from maintaining and repairing machines, from odd jobs like building a fence to building prototypes for new products. Currently, they use a whiteboard for discussing issues, but prioritization is an unresolved problem—'nobody actually wants to take the decision on what has to be repaired'. When a worker personally asked for support for a minor issue, it was difficult to refuse. Hence, maintenance wanted to 'get more transparency' into that. The team from the CC used an open-source ticket system based on the idea of multilevel prioritizing to support the specific situation in this company and, combined with a new user interface borrowing from KANBAN in software engineering (Anderson, 2010),

> we put a standalone system here first because also they know that this will be up and running a lot quicker. Because they want to have that tool up and running and the connection towards the ERP system, which could be or they expected to be very problematic and expensive and time consuming. They don't want to have this now. They want to have this prototype first. Well it's not a prototype I think it will work in the end.
>
> (CK Int, 2/5/2019)

In this project the team did a small pre-study followed by participatory workshops, to foster the transfer of not only technologies but methods.

What suits a research context well and helps PhD students produce interesting papers for particular conferences may not be the best approach in a real work setting. In the *EKPLO* project, for instance, although the companies the research team contacted liked the approach, it became clear that it would be necessary to tackle the issues of data quality and timeliness in a slightly different way from in the previous company:

> So it could still be some kind of persuasive systems design but most likely nothing related to gamification but still a lot will be the same or the idea what can be a clever way to get process data from the shop floor, from the machines

in a manual manner, not in an automatic manner, not sent by the machine but tackle the issue of data that has to be manually collected from the shop floor.

(CK Int, 22/11/2018)

At the same time, it was important to have some of the key insights that had been gained in a research study confirmed; when, for example, a machine breaks down, it can be beneficial even in a small company to get machine data to all responsible people quickly and in a useable and non-disturbing way, to get production up and running again.

What the companies are interested in is a problem definition they can recognize and a design approach that solves the problem. For example, the work on 3D printing is used by the CC as 'a blueprint for operating complex machines'. In addition, in *CyberRüsten* further refinements and developments of the original prototype are needed to fit new processes or slightly different machines:

It is very domain specific, it depends on the machine that you have, so when you map, you map the machine, right, it depends on the parts the machine has, how the parts can be set up in the machine and what kind of software is involved in controlling the machine.

(FP Int, 11/6/2019)

3.3 Impediments to achieving sustainability

The research group at the University of Siegen follows a practice-based research approach, has built a large network of manufacturing companies, and engages in numerous dissemination and training activities. Still, the Industry 4.0 solutions developed in the context of research projects do not necessarily 'fit' the conditions of SMEs, and there is significant progress to be made before a prototype may eventually be implemented and evaluated in a real-use context.

We are aiming at somehow researching appropriation and therefore you need a very good high-fidelity prototype, not regarding IT security in their product level but the functional end and working level for the use case, for the scenario should be very good. And this is, where we are struggling most of the time to get these demonstrators fully into production, so into these companies for a longer period to actually get the basis for appropriation, because implementing actual products is not allowed by the funding agencies.

(TL Int, 22/11/2018)

The research team has undertaken a series of initiatives introducing design solutions into real working contexts in sustainable ways.

3.3.1 How to carry conviction for a design solution

Production planning in a small company is, to some extent, an integral part of work on a day-to-day basis. Those responsible for PP are usually good at it. Hence, a first problem is to have the conviction that a prototype needs to be implemented and probed.

> Running here a process invention you always feel like a disturbing factor although companies get funded within the project, doesn't change the attitude much in my opinion. [...] They know they have maybe some flaws in efficient long-term planning but well, they keep their people and machines busy every day—long-term effects, they don't know, they believe they are not so bad but if they are bad, they actually cannot even tell because they don't have real controlling. When you then come and say: hey, we have a user-centred planning tool for your actual work environment, they are interested. But when it comes to the actual work and you raise all the issues, that it is necessary to provide this data-demanding technology which also requires stable processes to acquire these data, then you are really changing the organization, even for such small companies and then they get nervous also.
>
> (CK Int, 22/11/2018)

The managers in an SME may see the long-term benefits of a particular innovation but still fear its potentially disruptive effects and their costs. This is different from the situation in large manufacturing companies that have the resources for creating artificial—that is, 'safe'—environments, as in the example of 'virtual' testing in the car industry. However, while large companies may employ highly specialized personnel for planning, one of the basic problems—how to provide these people with proactive planning data—is the same. Production planning algorithms depend on a lot of real-time data. Collecting these data is difficult, and this is why, first of all, the research team in the *EKPLO* project developed tools in support of data acquisition.

One of the insights from a small study was the reaction of the head of production to the idea of augmenting all the machines with AR technology—'I don't need that in the production hall because, if I'm in there it takes me less than a minute to walk through' (CK). Here the head of production refers to the fact that, given his expertise, he can get an overview by just looking at the machines, the boxes, and what the workers are doing; however, as CK states, 'what he needs is to get an overview, when he's not around'. This is an example of the well-known struggle between what would be technically achievable, and the needs of the users (Piirainen et al., 2010). It is about problem definition—finding the 'right' problem. To refer to Rittel and Webber's notion of 'wicked problems', 'Problem understanding and problem resolution are concomitant to each other. [... The] process of solving the problem is identical with the process of understanding its nature' (Rittel and Webber, 1973: 162).

Another insight from engaging with the company was that data acquisition is now 'way too complicated and unreliable' and automating the process is not an option for most SMEs—they don't have 'the most modern machines' and 'rely on manual tasks a lot', findings that are also reflected in Sommer (2015). But even in the case of more recent machines, paying for the licences would be too expensive: 'They would never do so. If they would pay for these licenses they easily could afford one or two other machines and they would definitely do that over paying for some data' (CK Int, 2/5/2019).

But there may also be a host of practical problems relating to the sometimes heterogeneous interests of the collaborating partners, the legacy systems in place, or a lack of experience with IT systems. This complexity

> makes it even harder to keep something like this alive. And that's also something you should think about right from the start: how to build such an architecture. It reliably works only if the communication and cooperation between the partners is sustainable. If this is no longer the case, then the house of cards will collapse to some extent. And that—for us—is then also the danger of losing the field of application. If a key component no longer functions properly, or cannot be further developed or adapted—then everything collapses.
>
> (CK Int, 27/5/2019)

A new partner in the *EKPLO* project was also a vendor for ERP systems. The idea was to implement this tool in the other partner company so as to have a common database for the tools. Also attached to the ERP system was a machine data acquisition function. While the new partner insisted on its own ERP system for data acquisition, the other company later refused to implement the system, because a parallel implementation of another ERP system was in progress in this company's headquarters and other subsidiaries:

> So, that was even here, from my perspective, ERP system even for such companies makes total sense, but they are really not liking the idea [...] because

it doesn't really support what they need. And, if they need to make changes they have to pay for changes for change requests to the company. In Excel they more or less can do it by themselves easily [...] The way the ERP systems work and how they are working doesn't fit. And this is like we've been working on that for more than half of a year and I don't see a real end to that.

(CK Int, 27/5/2019)

Apart from the data acquisition problem, for many SMEs an ERP system is just too 'big' and expensive: there is a tension between what might be useful and the high costs of investing in the future.

3.3.2 Evaluating a solution with real data/in real use

To be able to observe the appropriation of a design in use, a high-fidelity prototype is needed. Before such tools and the corresponding practices are in place, it is difficult to evaluate the system:

OK, we could program a demonstrator on fake data but this is of no use to these companies. If you want to have a real evaluation and if your aim is to get even close to appropriation you need to embed these systems into their business software as good as you can. The business software here is Excel. So, this was the main target and this is why we develop tools for workers to enter these data in a digital way, maybe in a more straightforward way than gamification.

(CK Int, 22/11/2018)

Here a key problem is also cost—evaluating a technology in a manufacturing context with real data may be expensive for a company:

It is not just the lack of [...] software running up, it is usually, we need to get access to the machines, we have some actual manufacturing processes where some material and resources got wasted and stuff like that. [...] We had a workshop at the last ECSCW [European Conference on Computer-Supported Cooperative Work] where we discussed it—evaluating technology in manufacturing settings is one of the most serious issues and there are right now no good facilities from a methodological point of view—how to evaluate this kind of technology. [...] Companies expect products and not prototypes. And if a prototype within actual manufacturing processes can cost a company up to 5000 Euro just because there is no current process running or a machine breaks or stands still. Or maybe even you have the wrong data and there may be the very harmful message that the system believes that the production orders are already done and they are not. Then you may be delayed for 15 or 20 customer orders, this is pretty critical [...]

(TL Int, 22/11/2018)

These risks—waste of material, breakdowns of production, and their consequences—are the reason why in the *EKPLO* projects last year the team did not manage to go beyond the stage

where in a workshop environment you can present a prototype with more or less realistic data. But it is not the current data and getting this into the actual processes is pretty difficult, especially for the small companies with so many roles per person and you cannot actually focus on something but on the actual manufacturing process itself to maintain it and keep it running and not play around with researchers.

(TL Int, 22/11/2018)

Another impediment to implementing a solution that in principle would be of interest to management and workers is the lack of technological know-how needed for maintenance and repair. Many SMEs have experienced the difficult situation when a new technical device breaks down and there is not the expertise on hand to manage the situation:

One of the managing directors told me, we know him now for quite a while, but he hates IT. He hates it. Every new consultancy and every new dependency on the technology he hates, because it adds up and he starts hating it more and more, when it's not working and he can't repair it. He loses time in repairing it, asking others who don't know.

(CK Int, 2/5/2019)

The fear is that inevitable breakdowns will delay the primary processes—and companies hesitate to take this risk. Even the partner company in *EKPLO* that is a vendor for advanced planning scheduling systems has problems because of technology issues. The tool depends on correct and complete data. An incomplete database will result in errors and inconsistencies and be perceived as non-functional and 'useless' by the users. So whenever there is an issue with data analysis due to bad data quality and users 'see an error', they put the tool aside because they don't have the time to identify the problem.

> They don't know where the problem could be and even trying to repair this through trial and error [...] they are afraid to break something else to cause an effect that someone else will be affected by. So, they just don't do it. They put it aside, close it and get back to Excel or sheets of papers and so [...] this is a constant struggle.
>
> (CK Int, 2/5/2019)

This reluctance to use a tool without having the competence to understand and effectively handle breakdowns is understandable, as small companies often have a very narrow profit margin. So, 'everything has to work smoothly for them to earn money'. An economically critical situation can make remaining committed to the project near impossible, as was the case with one partner company:

> And this is also I think one of the main reasons they are struggling with the ERP system so much, because it takes a lot of effort and a trial and error until this process innovation in a sense can become productive. They didn't have the resources to actually focus on that. They rather stuck with their old processes, which they knew and somehow knew that they work.
>
> (CK Int, 2/5/2019)

Hence, to be able to install a tool in a real production context, a lot of favourable circumstances have to come together: a reliably working 'high-fidelity' prototype, the ability of the company to resolve at least small problems with the software internally, and a stable economic situation that allows the team to deal with early problems in the expectation of future benefits. The *EKPLO* team mentioned the case of one of their students who actually managed to implement a PP tool in an associated partner company. This was only possible because 'he was a working student, very talented, and the CEO has an informatics background' (CK). He was allowed to connect the PP system, which had been designed to help see whether a production order was in danger or not, to the other systems in the company. One of the implemented features looked at who was using the system, when, and for what purpose. He collected usage data from fifty to sixty people.

> For example, some other department heard about the PP system: e.g. sales used it to inform customers about the status of a production order; the overhaul department used it to find better time slots for overhaul work so as not to interrupt ongoing work. One effect of the PP was also that the morning meetings became shorter. New requirements were defined.
>
> (TL Int, 22/11/2018)

3.3.3 Limitations of university-based research

Research and IT development with manufacturing companies as partners requires technically competent and self-confident young researchers. Hence,
master's and PhD students that enter this context need the knowledge and assistance of their supervisors to be able to succeed. Manufacturing processes
are complex and understanding them requires an extended period of immer-
sion in the environment to fully grasp their needs. At times, this requirement
collides with short-term recruitment policies, along with master's and PhD
students being involved in the project work.

> If certain people leave, then the structures that they have built up would be
> ruined. And that is actually bad with regard to long-term research.
>
> (TL Int, 2/5/2019)

> It is also bad from the perspective of the users, who are relying on those struc-
> tures. They have nothing then. They will survive that situation. But it's not
> nice. [...] Especially for smaller companies that don't have their own IT de-
> partment, I think that's out of the question (that they would otherwise get
> involved). They need external help. And then, I think you as a researcher need
> to have a set of arguments. Otherwise it will be difficult.
>
> (CK Int, 2/5/2019)

The other problem is connected to the requirements for doing good research,
which are not necessarily compliant with the kind of work that developing and
implementing a working prototype in a manufacturing company requires. This
holds especially for PhD students, who are under pressure to produce papers
for highly demanding publication venues, eventually also apply for funding,
and get some teaching experience.

> The more you develop just useful tools for industry, the less you are a re-
> searcher. You are then more of an IT consultant or service provider. That's
> extremely difficult to reconcile. If you look at the really successful tools in
> companies, they frequently are badly published from a research perspective.
> And then extremely well published tools are often not fully usable for in-
> dustrial companies. This is a field of tension in which our PhD students are
> actually constantly moving. If you want to build tools that far, then there is
> little time for all the other stuff. So, you collect data all the time and keep
> implementing [...] but then they come with new requirements, with new
> questions, then you have to keep them happy, all these social factors too,

which all play a role. It is always a lot of work, so that sometimes you slip a bit into the role of a consultant or service provider. This is a field of tension in which you move all the time—this holds especially true, when you look at it from a sustainability perspective: is sustainability what I produced on paper afterwards, or is sustainability that the company can then work sensibly with a sustainable piece of software? Of course, at best, both. But it puts lots of pressure on our PhD students.

(TL Int, 2/5/2019)

Furthermore, the structure of funding plays a role. It is a common understanding among funding agencies that they advance research but do not necessarily engage in all the groundwork that is needed to embed a technical solution in a real work environment. For example, 'If you spend four or eight weeks just implementing some IT security mechanisms that doesn't push people forward' (CK). Moreover, the more you reach the product phase, the less interesting it gets for publications. For these you need fancy new technologies. But companies look for various pieces of software that improve and slightly modify existing processes (CK). Also, the stakes are high. And when managers in a company realize that the results don't meet their expectations, 'they get rid of you as soon as they have the chance' (CK Int 22/11/2018).

3.4 Types of innovation

In large companies, projects are often about technological innovation and process inventions, with a focus on very specific processes of one single machine or one single production line. From a technology point of view, this is easier to model than a system that seeks to support the planning processes within the complex organizational and technological work environment of people with different roles. When it comes to PP, it does not make much sense to focus on a few machines and/or one or two products. Efficient scheduling takes all production orders into consideration. Moreover, in small companies employing twenty to forty people,

the processes just grow depending on the people that work there and they only focus on product inventions. [...] doing work on improving work planning processes in such small companies is different from improving from a machine engineering perspective. This is really two pairs of shoes.

(TL Int, 22/11/2018)

A second factor that shapes what kind of innovation IT projects in SMEs may aim at is to do with the distinction between prototype development and product development. IT research projects are geared towards developing prototypes as proofs of concepts and getting research questions answered. Companies look for actual products that come with service level agreements concerning maintenance, security, and so on, and this is very difficult to provide, especially for PhD students. This is why companies prefer to cooperate with other companies or spin-offs,

> because they have a legal framing, they have clear conditions about how to deal with each other, they are able to set up some contracts and so on [...] and it is hard for universities to provide the same kind of sustainability for SMEs or even large companies without getting paid. [...]. Companies, they want, for example a reaction of about 4 hours—these are parts of an agreement we cannot meet. We go out from the CC, do our project for about six months and to fit our schedule as well, and they expect us to come at very short notice and even have that in a contract. We cannot provide such a service level, and this is why it is more interesting to collaborate with companies that have another mission than we at the university.
>
> (TL Int, 22/11/2018)

Hence, dealing with the exigencies and constraints of an SME defines what kind of innovation is possible. A company may not need and/or be able to afford and handle the most advanced technical solutions. However,

> [i]t depends. Advanced means also to meet all the requirements from an interface perspective, because you have to implement all the interfaces that are currently available in companies usually. [...] all the technical interfaces. And usually other projects in completely different domains usually start from the scratch, developing some new fancy prototypes. But in smaller companies the technologies are more advanced from a technological level, but they are not that advanced from an innovative state of the art perspective.
>
> (TL Int, 2/5/2019)

Hence, engaging in collaboration with SMEs in real manufacturing settings brings numerous issues of integration—that is, making a technical system work with the base already installed—into the foreground.

3.5 Summary

In the manufacturing industry, projects have little chance of achieving the sustainability of design solutions unless they develop more long-term relationships with companies. For the set of projects discussed in this section, establishing the CC was a crucial step towards such a long-term perspective. It allowed the researchers to present prototypes to a larger audience and find new partners that invited them to further develop a prototype for a specific context and purpose, get it ready to be implemented, and eventually evaluate it in real use. Hence, the ambition is to transfer design solutions to new contexts by adapting/modifying them and evolving their potential for new and/or additional tasks.

Apart from network-building, the CC also serves as a training centre that helps prepare companies in the region for automating their production. A key strategy here is not just to present technical solutions but to adopt a practice-based approach to designing them.

The stories of these projects help us to understand some of the impediments to installing design solutions in manufacturing. Some of these impediments are to do with the particular situations of SMEs. First of all, it is not easy to carry conviction for a system that may be useful in the long term but has no immediate priority, as many of these companies are quite successful at handling their 'installed base' of machines and surrounding technologies on a daily basis. This applies, for example, to PP, which is usually done as an integral part of the work. Considering the probing of a new system with real data in a real production context, the stakes are high. There is the risk of a temporary breakdown with all the associated costs. Moreover, a new system increases the company's dependence on IT expertise in effectively handling repair, maintenance, and necessary further adaptations of software.

A particular problem that is not unique to SMEs in manufacturing is data acquisition. Automation is often not an option, as it may be expensive, and asking workers to do manual data work adds to their workload without necessarily making their work easier or more effective.

A final point concerns the problems university-based researchers have in providing the services that a commercial provider would offer, in terms of availability for maintenance, troubleshooting, solving mundane IT security issues, and so forth. All these are activities that do not help to produce papers. Moreover, manufacturing processes are complex and young researchers at a PhD level may not have the courage to enter the field and spend the time needed to get to know the application area properly.

4

Emergency and crisis management

Emergency management (EM), also called crisis management, is a domain that crosses several fields, including economics, ambient ecology, and healthcare. It receives increasing attention, since critical situations can occur in all these areas, and in recent years many of these situations—including floods, terrorist attacks, or incidents in nuclear plants—have had a significant impact both locally and globally (Graham, 2010). Emergency management takes on distinct connotations in each specific domain but shares common features and challenges in all of them.

The literature describes four phases of EM (Haddow et al., 2017): disaster *mitigation* is oriented to prevention; disaster *preparedness* is oriented to planning the management activities and training the involved people; disaster *response* is oriented to handling the immediate reaction to the specific critical situation; and, finally, disaster *recovery* is oriented to restoring the previous state of affairs. The four phases raise different challenges and can be supported by different IT-based solutions. Mitigation and preparedness are the outcomes of long-lasting processes that mainly involve data analysis and the definition of organizational strategies in view of a possible disaster. In contrast, the response phase has to be performed within a very short time, in disrupted settings, often involving situations in which people may panic. The acquisition of the information necessary to rescue people and goods is difficult. Immediately after the occurrence of an adversity, when intervention is highly critical, the quality of the information may be very low and real-time decisions have to be taken with a high degree of uncertainty. The recovery phase has less demanding time constraints. However, the expectation of having the damaged setting restored as soon as possible requires timely interventions to solve the most urgent problems.

Many actors are involved in EM: the citizens, communities, or organizations that live and/or work in the damaged area; rescuers with different responsibilities, depending on the gravity and nature of the disaster: police officers,

Future-proofing. Wulf et al., Oxford University Press.
© Carla Simone, Ina Wagner, Claudia Müller, Anne Weibert, and Volker Wulf (2022).
DOI: 10.1093/oso/9780198862505.003.0004

medical emergency teams, expert technicians for the functioning and recovery of a damaged setting. Increasingly, volunteering citizens and communities play an important role in EM. They may assume the role of 'sensors' in the damaged area, providing detailed information and receiving directives to support the activities performed by the professional rescuers (Palen et al., 2010). The presence of several actors can generate tensions and contradictions that make the reconstruction of the situation difficult (Mishra et al., 2011). Finally, there is the need to integrate physical activities performed on site and to monitor and guide citizens' behaviours through technology (typically social media) so that they avoid putting themselves in critical situations (Ludwig et al., 2015).

The nature of the IT-based solutions that can be used in support of the various phases is quite different. The research reported in the literature on EM pays specific attention to the response and recovery phases in reaction to some of the recent disasters, their increased occurrence, and their media impact all around the world. Experience gained in the context of disasters allows researchers to better understand the highly distributed and time-critical nature of EM, helping to tailor technological support to fit the communication, information-sharing, and coordination needs of different actors. To fully apprehend the practices that characterize EM and identify appropriate collaborative technologies, a multidisciplinary approach is necessary (e.g. Pipek et al., 2014).

In addition to that, researchers need to pay attention to the mitigation and preparedness phases of an emergency. One of the essential tasks of, for example, firefighting organizations is to define and effectively communicate the general norms and procedures that the situated and dynamic behaviour of the rescue teams in each specific critical setting is expected to comply with. These norms are subject to an official and often lengthy certification process that is to guarantee the effectiveness of future actions. They have a strong institutional value.

As in many work situations, there is a potential conflict between predefined norms and procedures and the situated unfolding of an event, such as a fire or flooding, in unpredictable ways. This conflict, which is well known in the design of coordination technologies (Cabitza and Simone, 2013), may be aggravated by an IT system (e.g. a workflow system) that does not allow action to be flexibly adapted to the contingencies of an evolving situation. Another source of uncertainty and potential misunderstandings may arise from the differences in education, professionalism, and experience of the various actors that are involved in and contribute to the management of an emergency (Zettl et al., 2017). These differences may generate terminology problems in communication (Reuter et al., 2017), differing interpretations of the current conditions with the consequent misalignment of behaviours, and limited trust in the reliability of actors, and volunteering helpers in particular (Reuter et al., 2012). The nature of the incidents the rescue teams handle requires high levels of reliability and safety. To this purpose, the services these teams provide are regulated by institutions that set precise rules and standards, and any new procedure, device, or technology has to respond to established certification procedures. This results in a 'gated market' which research teams struggle to enter with their IT-based solutions, irrespective of the potential benefits these would offer.

In general, communication among the involved actors is a crucial aspect of EM in all phases (Ley et al., 2014). In particular, the highly risky nature of the rescue processes in the response phase raises the issue of how to ensure the safety of the (professional) team members, with well-established ad hoc procedures guaranteeing their mutual protection. For example, in the case of firefighters, the teams are normally divided into two groups: one group operates in the burning area and a second group operates outside it, monitoring their safe state through a set of conventional communication patterns that convey the location of the firefighters, their well-being, and the important details for rescuing them in critical situations. During the recovery phase, communication plays a crucial role in keeping the damaged people aware of the evolution of the restoring activities and the expected time necessary to bring the electrical power distribution, transportation networks, damaged houses, and so on back to an (at least minimally) operational state. Finding the appropriate technologies and means of communication for such a variety of different and often critical contexts, whose needs may be hard to identify, poses considerable challenges.

This section describes research lines developed by researchers from the University of Siegen that address the specific practices and needs of rescue teams in two different contexts. The first set of projects focuses on the response activities of firefighters when they have to move within closed spaces to rescue endangered and possibly injured people. The second series of projects aimed at providing computer support to professional rescue teams and volunteers in emergency situations, taking the breakdown of an energy supply and the need to prepare for potential incidents during large-scale events as examples. The section is based on publications from these projects as well as on interviews with Matthias Betz (quoted as MB), Volker Wulf (quoted as VW), and Volkmar Pipek (quoted as VP).

4.1 Projects with firefighters

4.1.1 Overview of the research line

Research on firefighters started with the large ('Integrated') EU project *WearIT* in 2003 upon the invitation of a group of artificial intelligence (AI) researchers from the University of Bremen. After 9/11, several funding schemes sought to address security issues. The project was about finding application domains for ubiquitous computing. One of the fields of activity included in the proposal was firefighting, with a focus on wayfinding in an unknown building. The partners were firefighters in Paris. At the beginning of the project, there was a 'positivist view' of the problem, with the idea that firefighters may benefit from a routing system that navigates them. Researchers at this point were simply not aware of the fact that firefighters are excellent at navigating unknown terrain under difficult conditions. The idea was to develop automatic map generation based on small robots and sensors in support of navigation: 'The key person [...] had the idea of system sensors being spit out of the boots of the firefighters' (VW). Prototypes in virtual reality (VR)—for example, an ego shooter game—were developed, with the first sketches of a solution embedded in the game. The game was then played with the firefighters: 'I have the strong impression that these guys were laughing at us' (MB).

At some point in the project, an alternative vision gained ground—one that involved not just automation but also supporting the social navigation capabilities of the firefighters. The 'opposition group' wrote the *Landmarke* proposal, which received German government funding for three years. In this way, a technology-driven EU project environment helped develop a new agenda. *Landmarke* (2008–11) was based on a collaboration with firefighters in Cologne (Germany). This collaboration turned out to be extremely useful, and good personal relationships developed. The research team worked with the firefighters in workshops, where they had the possibility of playing with design ideas. One of the application partners, the Institute of Firefighters of North Rhine-Westphalia (with its seat in Münster), has the second-largest training facility in Europe, with an eight-floor building that you can enter with fire engines and ladders. Hence, the research was performed in a controlled environment. Participating in and also devising training sessions provided the team with a good understanding of the practice of firefighting.

The firefighters appropriated the *Landmarke* solution, demonstrating that 'it worked'. At that point, an additional design idea resulted in a new research proposal. The idea was to use chosen 'landmarks' as network nodes for the

communication between the firefighters in the building and the comman-
der outside. The *Koordinator* project (2012–14), which also received national
funding, had nearly the same partners but changed the focus of the landmarks
from navigation support to communication infrastructure. Some *Landmarke*
firefighters, in addition to a group of volunteer firefighters, became members
of the *Koordinator* project.

> This is a nice example of sustainability, empirically spoken: getting continu-
> ity in a research line, with three independently funded projects: of how the
> thinking/the vision developed, broken by conflict. The continuity is with the
> people. The strategy is to play with money so that people can get their PhD
> done and the group can follow up on a research line. [...] When MB left, the
> whole group disintegrated, there is nobody left to continue, and another pub-
> lic funding is not available. We lost the research line! The question is how to
> share this knowledge of the project team members in a 'transgenerational'
> way: across research generations. We don't even have any landmarks left!
>
> (VW Int, 19/12/2017)

4.1.2 Design strategy

Using the controlled environment of a training site was a necessity, as
observing real firefighting events would not have been feasible. Also, there
would have been major insurance problems for the participating researchers.
However, only being able to be part of and observe training sessions was a clear
limitation of the project. The research team entered the site seeking to gain an
understanding of wayfinding in practice, looking into how firefighters navi-
gate. They were committed to providing safer conditions. Their role was clearly
defined: 'We were the clever guys with technologies from university—"they
will give those to us"' (MB).

Collaboration took place in a series of two-day workshops, one session every
three months, with a group of fifteen participating firefighters who performed
their practices. For example, a standard scenario would be one of rescuing a
person from a flat. Such a reconnaissance mission may have been reiterated
up to five times ('they were really tolerant because this was boring for them'—
MB). While the researchers aimed to get a profound understanding of the
practice of firefighting, the firefighters learnt to reflect on their practices, as
the researchers' observations led to intense discussions: 'We were able to observe this slow process of raising awareness: maybe these practices can fail in
certain situations?' (MB).

Once the design idea took shape—with three iterations of the system constructed in total (*Throwies*, *UFOs*, and *Wedges*)—the research team used the evolving prototype in 'breaching experiments': 'The initial prototypes of the system were designed intentionally without a clearly defined form of use and the semantics of the artifacts emerged and were progressively defined throughout the design process by means of user involvement' (Ramirez et al., 2012: 1029).

4.1.3 Finding a 'real problem'

The research team focused on observations and the metaphor of an (artificial) landmark. This metaphor reflects a feature of the practice of firefighters, which includes using landmarks—such as eye-catching objects, stairways, things they can easily remember—for wayfinding. The design idea was to augment the environment, enabling firefighters to place additional landmarks wherever this seemed relevant to them while moving. The question then was: what is a landmark? Is it interactive, optical, acoustical?

An unusual scenario is that of a comrade having an accident. This topic came onto the table halfway through the project—should we practise such a scenario?

> Accidents are really rare, as practices in Germany are rather defensive, hence pretty safe. The firefighters from Köln were professionals and they had an accident on their mind, a really bad accident. One comrade had died because he did not find his way out, his breathing apparatus went empty and he got entangled in his rope. Accidents are not part of the training of firefighters and their leaders felt we should not talk too much about accidents.
>
> (MB Int, 22/3/2018)

Although it was deemed problematic to bring up the topic of accidents, it became the object of an intense discussion in one of the workshops with a representative from the firefighting institute who supported the idea of practising a critical incident. He consented to prepare a situation where the participating firefighters would fail. The fears of the leadership were countered with the argument that the Cologne firefighters were well equipped, professionally and mentally, to enact a critical incident and reflect on it.

> This gave a really intense drive to the project: we closed doors, locked them and brought them into this crisis situation. It was the first time, where they

actually failed in wayfinding. This was the main question: it was about failing. And the leadership's fear was pointless. It was a great experience, a magical moment: we can change our educational approach. After that we let them fail like hell in each workshop, providing lots of stuff for reflecting.

(MB Int 22/3/2018)

This experience confirmed the usefulness of landmarks in critical situations. It also exposed ongoing problems with radio communication which routinely fails, such as when firefighters enter a basement or a large parking garage where in summertime a huge area may fill with smoke really fast, with the electricity shutting down:

By simulating breakdowns on common navigation tools, such as fire hoses cut in half or entangled in the pillars of the parking lot, the instructors were able to produce scenarios that created situations of partial or complete loss of orientation.

(Ramirez et al., 2012: 1037)

One of the design ideas was to use the landmark for communication by changing its colour, for example, or letting it beep through remote control. This is relevant with respect to a basic rule saying that a group leader who has had no communication with his team for more than two minutes since they entered a space has to assume that there was an accident. At this moment everything changes, as others are called in and the target is to rescue their comrades. In this scenario, a firefighter may change the colour of the first node in the landscape of landmarks (next to the entrance) to red and change the colour back to blue when he feels safe; each change is broadcast to the network. In fact, the researchers observed the firefighters

appropriating the beacon's colour codes to deal with the problem of unstable connectivity on their voice-over-radio communication between indoor working teams and their commanders outside the building. We observed how they used the feature to remotely set the colour of each beacon to articulate simple questions such as 'Everything ok?' and their responses, like 'Yes' or 'No'.

(Betz and Wulf, 2018: 468)

These instances of firefighters appropriating the platform for navigation support led to the disclosure of other, probably even more immediate, problems in indoor firefighting.

The researchers used the *Koordinator* project to develop a grounded understanding of many details of reconnaissance missions and the problems with radio communication in particular. The firefighters, who follow a two-in, two-out policy in these situations, share one channel, which means that only one person can talk at a time and all others can hear it. This requires strict discipline, as the channel quickly gets overcrowded. There is also not always a stable connection. Fumes and heat aggravate the situation. Regulations mandate firefighters working in a danger zone to wear a self-contained breathing apparatus (SCBA) and special protective clothes. The SCBA provides a limited amount of breathing time and its use is very exhausting.

A fact that caught the researchers' attention was that firefighters use a number of routines for reporting—for example, calling the leader outside upon entering the first room. When firefighters communicate (which is very difficult in a burning building), they do this in a very standardized way, using a kind of 'command language'. The researchers decided to extract all the routine communication (the part that is never changing) from what is special, and enhance the device that they always carry with them with text-based features. Much work was spent on structuring this catalogue so as to support the smooth flow of action:

> Some messages come always in the beginning, some at the end. They regularly have to report the status of the breathing apparatus and adapting your breathing to speaking whilst you are active is really difficult, you have to talk through a mask, there is the noise of the engines of the pumps, so the quality is really bad. So, we added the protocols of calling someone to the landmark control device, in both directions, text-based, following the question-answer way, embedding a list of possible answers. This was a design challenge, how to create message packages, and it worked out really well.
>
> (MB Int, 22/3/2018)

The speech act model worked very well in this setting. The *EmergencyMessenger* turned out to be particularly helpful for the firefighter volunteers, who may see no more than two fires in a year. They have to fulfil the same regulatory requirements as professional firefighters 'and have so much stress that they just forget to do the radio communication properly; they sometime forget to report the breathing level' (MB). They appreciated the catalogue on their device, which provided a guideline for the firefighters working indoors, helping them to avoid missing out on the next relevant report in the ongoing tactical proceedings.

The project also involved new partners, with a view to turning the prototype into a product. One of the new partners, Dresdner Elektronik, was interested in developing the solution, 'helping to move from Tupperware prototypes to a product'. In addition, a specialist in sensor-based activity recognition from the University of Karlsruhe supported the team in developing an algorithm for motion/acceleration sensors that recognizes when someone is climbing a staircase, crawling, kneeling—based on a classification of firefighting activities.

4.1.4 Relationship-building

A key aspect of both projects was the amount of time and effort that was spent on relationship-building, work that often remains invisible in reports and publications but may be critical to achieving a solution that promises to provide support to users in practice. For example, the team spent lots of time optimizing the ergonomics of the device. Introducing a 3D printer helped prototype the casing. As a consequence, they were able to show up 'with three new casings' every three months. Having a 3D printer available also helped build relationships when firefighters brought a USB stick to the workshop with a design to print out: 'A kind of professional friendship developed. We started to open up a bit, they invited us to their "Feuerwehrfest" in their local community, with a barbecue and beer, and we stayed some hours longer' (MB). An important element of collaboration was stability:

> We never skipped one single appointment, even if we had nothing new to show. You know that these guys discuss their experiences in their weekly reunions, they always create their own results, their findings. So, let it settle down, let them have their discussions, their fights when they discuss their practices—they have become researchers of their own practice. The most exciting part was to observe how they have become researchers, how they changed their way of how they see themselves. Also you learn so much; you know how to disassemble a water pipe, you start to help them (after a training session), they start to trust you, the two cultures merge.
>
> (MB Int, 22/3/2018)

For the firefighters, the most valuable outcome was the possibility of jointly discussing and reflecting on their navigation practices.

One of the firefighters who had already participated in *Landmarke* continued in *Koordinator* as a paid consultant or observer. He acted as an important bridge between the two projects and wrote parts of the *Koordinator* proposal. He had a strong commitment to the project and spent half a year bringing the new firefighters to the level of knowledge of the previous project: 'He was a backbone when he explained the design decisions in *Landmarke*, he was much more efficient with these guys who listened to him, a real professional firefighter, a hero!' (MB).

4.1.5 Impediments to sustainability

The research team had been extremely lucky in its choice of project partners. The institute not only provided the site for collaborative training sessions; it also runs a school for firefighters and is the main department for developing firefighting practices and rules/regulations: 'This strategic role was not clear to the research team at the beginning: "we were lucky". When *they* say, well, this technology helps change our practices, then this is accepted. It also has to fit into the legal regulations' (MB).

In spite of the impressive research and development work done in *Landmarke* and *Koordinator*, it did not result in a product. While a lot of interesting research results were created, the firefighters, who had put an enormous amount of work and commitment into the project, offering their free time, did not see a design result that they would have been able to integrate into their practice. Although they appreciated the learning and had had the opportunity to reflect on and think about ways to improve their practice, this was a disappointment.

What were the reasons for this failure to produce a sustainable design and, ultimately, a product? *Landmarke* had the Draeger company as a partner, a large provider of firefighting equipment. They participated out of interest, without requiring funding, and were good to cooperate with, but in the end they decided not to commercialize the project. Their main question was about the added value of a device which firefighters only need in a crisis, when something fails: 'we need something for all incidents to be able to sell it' (MB). The city of Köln also did not want to invest in the landmarks. Their argument was that spending resources on a device that offers support primarily in critical situations that are extremely rare did not make sense to them. Moreover, for the firefighters, the use of the landmarks as a communication device (the part developed in the *Koordinator* project) had turned out to be more valuable than the landmarks themselves. This would have required a business partner with a different profile:

In *Koordinator* we had two small partners that were technically very good. One of them, Vomatech, built large-scale visualizations of emergency situations but they were not in the business of building communication devices. They had a strong network that also included firefighting and wanted to make a step forward to include the first liners, the firefighters on the ground. It is not clear if they are still working on this idea.

(MB Int, 22/3/2018)

At some point the researchers themselves thought about creating a spin-off and selling the knowledge around the devices, also hoping that big actors like Draeger would see the results and decide to invest. However, the fact that the market for firefighting equipment is 'gated', with only two main suppliers and public administration customers, deterred them. Moreover, the lifecycles of existing solutions are long—roughly twenty to thirty years.

The people were really gifted. One problem was that we never achieved a level in the security domain to build something for real world practice, only for training situations. There are high security layers, lots of certification steps needed, the hurdles are so high! This is one of the reasons why firefighters are so conservative as regards new toys and tools.

(VW, 19/12/2017)

4.2 Supporting professionals and volunteers in emergency situations

4.2.1 The research line

The work of Volkmar Pipek's group on emergency/crisis management developed over a period of almost ten years. It started with a small project (*Störkommunikation: proaktives Kommunikationsmanagement für den Störfall*, 2006–8) in close cooperation with the biggest German electricity provider (RWE) following an accident that had occurred in 2007 when several power lines broke down in parts of North Rhine-Westphalia. The company funded the project to study how media technologies could support communication in emergency situations (Reuter et al., 2009).

The follow-up project—*InfoStrom* (2010–13)—continued this collaboration while broadening its focus and also including several research centres (University of Siegen, SAP Research, Fraunhofer FIT, PSI Transcom). This was a much more complicated set-up that involved two partner regions (the counties of

Rhein-Erft and Siegen-Wittgenstein) which have different topographies and network structures, making it necessary to deal with rather different structures in EM. Siegen-Wittgenstein is a densely wooded, hilly county in the middle of Germany. The main industries are tourism and a number of SMEs in mechanical and electrical engineering. Rhein-Erft, the area around the city of Cologne, has Germany's most important transportation infrastructures, like highways, airports, railroads, and the river Rhine, which carry specific risks. There are also several large chemical plants and many companies have specialized emergency plans.

From the very start, the idea was not just to develop specific applications but to build a more generic communication infrastructure called *Security Arena*, which would support informal procedures in contrast to the highly regulated official ones. The basic component of the *Security Arena* concept is a web-based inter-organizational social network called *SiRena*, together with a map that allows the assessment of situations on the basis of geo-located, aggregated information (Pipek et al., 2013, Ley et al., 2014). From the very beginning, the participating workers—firefighters, police—asked:

> 'What's in it for me? Why should we participate in your project?'. [...] But at some point, they really understood: Okay, this is a research project. This will end. And at that point we really—that was about 4–5 months into the project—came under some pressure to clarify that after 3 years after the research project is gone, that not everything would fall apart. Then there was also a demand from the users to have something more sustainable, even though the users were unpaid to some extent to be users. But anyway, they wanted to have some return investment, as they wanted to have sustainability.
> (VP Int, 31/3/2018)

The researchers guaranteed to provide the platform by the end of the project and also promised to keep a dedicated server 'as is' after the project end—that is, without any improvements or updates. The promise was kept. Hence, there was a commitment to sustainability from the very beginning.

The follow-up project *EmerGent* (2014–17), an EU project, grew out of the *InfoStrom* project when, in a workshop towards the end of the project, the emergency services complained about some serious issues with social media regarding the coordination of volunteers. This project focused on the issue of how to coordinate the efforts of 'spontaneously emergent' volunteers during an emergency or crisis. *XHelp* was one of the prototypes that grew out of this project. It supported coordinating contact within specific Facebook groups, for example groups that offer some help or ones where people can request help or resources such as water and food. For example, *XHelp* supported matching these (Reuter et al., 2015). It was evaluated during the European flooding crisis in 2013. *KOKOS* (2015–18) was an additional nationally funded project on the same topic. It collaborated with several organizations and associations (the Protestant Church, a large sailing club) which have been described as 'intermediate organizations' (Zettl et al., 2017). When organizing large-scale events, these entities need to, to some extent, set up their own emergency response organization in collaboration with local police and local firefighters, as well as volunteers.

When starting work in the *KOKOS* project, the research team realized that the voluntary workers with whom they collaborated

> have a much lower level of liability of their activities and so they are much more open to actually use whatever public information exchange platforms are available. [...] it turned out that many of these organizations were already using some kind of platform and this monolithic approach of the *Security Arena* just was not feasible for this kind of crowd.
>
> (VP Int, 31/3/2018)

Hence, the *KOKOS* project focused on developing applications to support crowdsourcing during disasters, such as the public display *City-Share*, which can be used for communication and assigning of tasks even when there is no internet connection. Researchers made use of Raspberry Pi, which provides a local Wi-Fi network and a mobile web app (accessible via a QR code), making it possible for content to be shared on people's smartphones (Ludwig et al., 2017b). Another application, *CrowdMonitor*, seeks to passively collect and display social media information (publicly available from ordinary people) alongside volunteered information in response to public requests (i.e. from knowledgeable volunteers). This allows emergency services to create requests for particular information or targeted alerts, which can then be pushed to the users' mobile app (within a particular location) (Ludwig et al., 2016).

Although this research line was thematically strongly connected, the platform that had been developed in the *InfoStrom* project was abandoned because it had become obsolete for reasons that will be explained in the following section.

4.2.2 Limited malleability: Technology choices

With respect to long-term sustainability, a key decision in the *InfoStrom* project was the choice of technology, which, in turn, was based on an empirically grounded understanding of the nature of EM. Although emergency workers use formal procedures, they also strongly rely on improvisation (Ley et al., 2012):

> Improvisation becomes necessary when beforehand planned decision-making does not work for any reason. [...] The necessities to judge highly novel problems and to act quickly reduce the chances of extensive planning: 'Decision makers in emergencies must be prepared to improvise' [...] Without improvisation, emergency management loses flexibility, without preparedness, emergency management loses efficiency.
>
> (p. 1528)

Recognizing that many activities during an emergency situation are informal, the research team decided to build a platform ('similar to Facebook') that would support emergency workers to exchange and update information as the events were unfolding. The system 'should focus more on people and not so much on data' (VP).

Looking for a robust and well-maintained platform, the researchers first considered a commercial CSCW platform (called *Social Engine*), but this would not allow any modification of the code. This is why they decided to adopt ELGG, an open-source platform that has a thriving community of developers, is JavaScript-based, and has functionalities similar to Facebook. Since EM has a demographic dimension and organizing the work in terms of having a map and moving things on the map is natural to emergency workers, a map tool with web-based and mobile versions was added to the platform.

The decision to use ELGG had some far-reaching consequences, not all of them positive. The research team soon realized that modules that had been promised were not really functioning and well documented. There were also some 'ugly surprises'—some of the modules that the open-source community had reported as being fully functional and fully usable were not, so work on debugging the software was required. More dramatic was that the platform did not support hierarchical directories. At some point, the team decided to change the kernel and open a separate branch in order to be free to implement modifications without having to comply with the rather bureaucratic requirements of the community. The application process requires a lot of documentation, for which the team did not have the resources:

> So, we basically, by that decision we established our own branch of the platform software and disconnected ourselves from the development and the community. This meant that we actually later ran into many problems. […] At some point, we were not able to do the updates anymore. That was one problem, the other problem was that the platform did not offer a very clear way to add new functionality as a module.
>
> (VP Int, 31/3/2018)

On top of this, it turned out that using updated modules offered by the open-source community was as cumbersome as offering a new module, and there were difficulties with the user interface, as the map required the full screen. Offering something like a map-based tool is also quite a dramatic change when it comes to interface design.

A more fundamental problem had to do with privacy and access rights, a key user requirement. With the new set of data items connected with the map functionality, it was no longer possible to use the access rights system offered by the platform. This created problems in real use. For example, firefighters may find it interesting to see where all the fire engines are. However, they do not want to share this information with the general public and, more surprisingly, they do not want the neighbouring firefighting stations to see where their own fire engines are. Although firefighters are committed to helping each other, they also feared that everything being visible could invite questions regarding why, for example, a particular fire engine had not been dispatched. Although it was possible to change the access rights strategy, this turned out to be too expensive to share with the open-source community.

> We decided for an open source platform; it was difficult to connect to the access right system, so we decided to implement a map module that by its functionality was very much valued by the users, but we couldn't go through with it because then again, we would have to have to change the access right management system of the platform. Although we would have had the option to do it, the work of doing it and connecting the changes of feeding back the changes to the community, that was way too much work.
>
> (VP Int, 31/3/2018)

In the end, the privacy and connected liability issues that matter to professional emergency workers remained unresolved. On the other hand, the experience in *KOKOS* showed that people that are engaged in civic society are inclined to use what is ready to hand, like WhatsApp and YouTube, as they don't have the same liability issues to take care of.

These experiences have influenced the technical choices for the new research stream (*INF*: Infrastructural Concepts for Research on Cooperative Media; since 2016), which is about building infrastructures for managing research activities and exchanging data. ELGG was no longer so interesting at this point. Its technology was also perceived as outdated by the PhD students in Siegen, and it is no longer active. There was a stronger interest in new technologies, in moving towards a new ecology of tools. In the context of *INF*, the decision was made to move to *eXo*, a new open-source platform that was selected since it is Java-based and has a programming interface and an operating system with a suitable open-source database. Following an approach similar to that of the IBM Eclipse (which has a basic version for the general public and a commercial one for companies and internal use), it has a commercial branch that manages the community with commercial interests but is still open source. This environment is more suitable for sustainability and more reliable. The research team is not dependent on a community, as there is a commercial company behind this. But the platform is still open source; hence, the research team can reprogram what they need more reliably for reuse. The group has also invested in adopting the Raspberry Pi platform for IoT and has bought Lexor for speech-based assistance. These decisions have been taken knowing that the technology is evolving.

4.2.3 Practical impediments to appropriation

Although much effort was dedicated to rolling out the technologies and encouraging the practitioners to make use of them and observe, evaluate, and redesign them, participants did not appropriate them as was intended and hoped, for a variety of reasons. With respect to project *InfoStrom*, Ley et al. (2014) mention that some participating organizations did not have the necessary IT infrastructure to run the system in place. The outdated web browsers in the control centres did not support JavaScript or WebSocket, which were necessary to run the application. Although the participants had access to a stand-alone computer where a suitable web browser was installed, this made integration of the system into the work context impossible. This limited the usefulness of the system in the eyes of the users, who felt that this would require that it is 'used by everybody and if it is accessible to everybody. It must

not be used in a voluntary manner but has to be an inherent part of our work'
(Ley et al., 2014: 376).

Another issue Ley et al. mentioned was that the system's map service information compared unfavourably with users' experiences of the geographical
information available in existing systems: 'Basically we have everything in our
GIS. When I am in an operation and have my GIS on the screen, why should
I open another GIS?' (p. 375).

The main problem with *InfoStrom*, however, was that the technology that
had been conceived for emergency situations was not usable during an emergency due to liability issues.

> In the professional arena of crisis management, you learn which is your role
> and the related liability. You are growing up, you're being schooled also in
> what it means to have this responsibility. [...] And that means, that you're
> also very clear about your liability issues, that come with your role. [...] With
> this background, it is difficult to organize the activities through Facebook:
> somebody may read your data, exchange of sensible material 'on some server'
> and you may be held liable. [...] So, the people that we worked with in the
> triangle of *Infostrom*, they really wanted to have something separated. [...]
> The voluntary workers that were working on *KOKOS*, people who work in
> churches, who work in sports clubs, and so on, they have a much lower level
> of liability of their activities and so they are much more open to actually use
> whatever public information exchange platforms are available.
>
> (VP Int, 31/3/2018)

In their empirical study of 'improvisation practices during coping and recovery work at emergency response agencies', the research team had already
identified reliability of information as one of the key conditions for a system
and/or person to be trusted: 'Trustworthiness is directly connected to reliability and plays a significant role in sharing or retrieving information, especially
for those kinds of information which have high impact on complex and lifesav-
ing decisions' (Ley et al., 2012: 1534). As the system was not capable of solving
information uncertainties reliably, the platform turned out to be mainly considered for supporting strategy planning and maintaining the communication
and relationships between emergencies. For a short while, the platform was
also successfully used for training purposes (Reuter et al., 2009).

There are some indications that the web-based part of the platform (not
the map-based functionality) was used by local people from the Siegen-
Wittgenstein area. There are about 1,000–1,100 registered users. 'And what is

really surprising is that even in the last two years the platform got between 200–300 new users. I can't tell you why, because there was no moderated activity from our side in any way' (VP).

4.2.4 The arena of emergency management: Politics and heterogeneous interests

Emergency management is a complex, heterogeneous, and highly regulated field that makes establishing results from an external research and development project extremely difficult. *InfoStrom* addressed issues concerning the collaboration of diverse players—such as the police, fire department, and citizens—in major emergencies, with RWE, a big electricity provider, as the main project partner.

One of the problems was that insisting on an open-source solution, which made perfect sense from a research point of view, made building a business case difficult and problematic, as the researchers did not own the technology. At the same time, there was no institution available to pay for the system, host it, and maintain it.

> If you look at the *Infostrom* scenario, then, basically, it would have been the counties that have to pay for such a platform if they want to have such a platform. And the counties are not aware of this additional value of digital tools that they could bring. They only see the cost. And the costs, they fear, are too high. And it's making them dependent on a technology and they don't know what this dependency would mean for their work. [...] Because the emergency management field is completely dedicated to the problem of infrastructures breaking down. Those people have a very clear awareness of what it means to connect your practice to a new infrastructure. This is something they really are very concerned about.
>
> (VP Int, 31/3/2018)

In addition to a scepticism towards new developments in the EM field, there are so many different approaches and ideas without a single coherent plan for which direction to take. One insight from these experiences is: 'We were not fast enough with respect to both our capability to build a company and the technology evolution although our users can use our ideas: no sustainability from this perspective' (VP Int 31/3/2018).

The problems of gathering support for a particular solution are exacerbated by the complexities of decision-making in a politicized field with competing authorities:

> In the *Infostrom* project we had two different counties to work with. The county is the level at which the first operational decisions are being taken. So below the county level on emergency management it's basically that every fire brigade responds to whatever emergencies are being reported but when it comes to strategic decisions the county level at which the first strategic de-cisions are being taken. [...] Because the professional fire brigade they also have their own network and their own strategic development lines you could say and these are independent of counties.
>
> (VP Int, 31/3/2018)

Initially, the BBK, the public authority for EM in Germany, had shown some interest in the system, but after the main contact for the project left for an-other job, further attempts at connecting failed, mainly 'for political reasons'. Moreover, the BBK released an alternative app to report on EM that became mandatory by regulation. Hence, maintaining the link with the BBK just did not work out.

While Siegen-Wittgenstein relies on voluntary firefighters, the county of Rhein-Erft has professional, fully paid fire and rescue services. The researchers had underestimated the impact of the differences between these two cultures of firefighters who act out their (identical) roles in a different way. While the voluntary services rely a lot on informal communication and do not neces-sarily record content in between emergencies, professional firefighters follow well-ordered routines and report much more formally.

> Because if you are in the professional fire brigades you can actually tell the people what to do and they have to do it. As the voluntarily firefighters in times of emergency of course you can also tell the people what to do and they normally would do it but when there is not an emergency, it's much more difficult to get hands on the people. So, the voluntary organization in Siegen Wittgenstein are much more appreciative of the additional value such a platform can bring.
>
> (VP Int, 31/3/2018)

On top of these differences that shaped users' perceptions of the additional informal communication tools offered by the project, a group of firefight-ers in Rhein-Erft, not being sufficiently informed about the research and development work done as part of the *InfoStrom* project, created their own platform to exchange news.

Although the research team had carried out an in-depth study of practices which helped shed light on the intricacies of what they understood and analysed as improvisation work during emergencies in both sites (e.g. Ley et al., 2012), there was a 'political' side to the project that was not sufficiently transparent for the team to be able to react.

4.3 Summary

The two types of emergency/crisis management represented by these projects address different aspects of how to make IT solutions sustainable in and for future use.

The work with a team of firefighters started with a focus on how to support navigation in a building on fire, with the aim of contributing to providing safer conditions. Although the resulting design solution—*Landmarke*—worked, it did not respond to a 'real problem', given the firefighters' competent and efficient practices of wayfinding. Such a potentially 'real problem'—a critical incident—had to be found in collaboration with the team of firefighters and well understood. This collaboration brought their problems with maintaining radio communication while in a building to the fore as another challenge. This gave the project a new and fruitful direction. Finding a design problem that matters in practice was only possible because of the time and effort the design team put into working with the team of firefighters. This allowed design ideas to evolve in numerous discussions and experiences to be shared, resulting in a series of design solutions. This relationship that grew over time also secured the continuity of the research line. It is an example of the invisible work a research team may need to engage in to achieve a potentially sustainable design result.

Another insight from the project is that, as experimenting in the context of a real firefighting event would not have been feasible, the project was restricted to the controlled environment of a training site. Consequently, the firefighters' possibilities of actually using the emerging designs were limited to simulated events—appropriation did not happen in real use but as part of the process of codesign.

Also, the next step—from a working prototype to a product—did not happen, because of the nature of incidents such as fires. Due to the criticality of such events, solutions have rather long lifecycles, as they have to go through numerous certification steps. As a consequence, the market is 'gated', with only a few suppliers, and there is no economic incentive to invest in a solution that mainly offers support in the rare event of a critical situation.

The projects with firefighters also highlighted the importance and value of learning. Firefighters benefitted from the various project activities that invited them to reflect on their navigation practices. Although they appreciated this opportunity, not being able to actually use the design outcome in the future was a disappointment.

The projects on emergency/crisis management started with a power-line breakdown, changing the focus of subsequent research activities on crowd-sourcing during disasters and supporting the coordination of volunteers as a new type of user. One main lesson from this research line is to do with the consequences of technology choices. *InfoStrom* sought to support the infor-mal, improvised procedures of firefighters and police during an event such as a power outage. The users expected a sustainable solution in the form of a guaranteed platform from the beginning of their engagement with the project. The choice of platform turned out to be unfortunate due to a number of short-comings, in particular the failure to resolve the privacy and connected liability issues that matter to professional emergency workers. Another practical im-pediment to appropriation was that not all participating organizations had the necessary IT infrastructure in place. This experience motivated a move towards a new ecology of tools that provide a more reliable basis for reuse and which would ultimately also resolve the information uncertainty in an emergency situation in a dependable way.

Another insight gained by this project is that in a specific context—emergencies—a solution that fits professional workers is not necessarily portable to new types of users such as volunteers, who tend to use technologies that are ready to hand and may not have the same liability issues. The research line also demonstrates the difficulties a research team can have in adequately responding to the heterogeneous and potentially conflicting interests of stake-holders in a complex, highly politicized field where the stakes may not always be transparent.

5

Healthcare at the hospital and at home

The healthcare domain as an object of study touches almost all research
disciplines, for some obvious reasons. The delivery of good healthcare services
is one of the main commitments of any government and one of the biggest
sources of public expense; governments, through national and international
funding agencies, invest significant resources in improving the effectiveness
of the care processes. This is not a straightforward task, as care delivery and
the management of the involved structures are complex processes. They generate a multiplicity of worksites (Strauss et al., 1985) that differ in terms of the
involved professions, medical devices, and technologies, as well as patients'
illnesses and the care activities performed.

Different theoretical approaches and methods are needed to study them.
This complexity raises challenging research questions. While the progress of
the medical field is a primary aim, other main focal points are technological
innovation in all phases of the care process, from diagnosis to rehabilitation
and prevention, and organizational models of care and hospital management.
Healthcare research also requires attention to be paid to psychological and
ethical issues concerning the relationships between patients and care professionals. Finally, there is the need to study if and how progress made in different
sections of the healthcare system concerning diagnosis and treatment can be
harmonized so as to achieve an overall improvement in the care delivery, considering its fragmentation in terms of both specialized care and the multiplicity
of institutions that deliver care.

Healthcare work includes both the activities that are targeted towards the
improvement of patient health and the creation and management of the
documents that trace these activities. Documentation practices serve the ac-
cumulation of information regarding a patient's diagnosis and treatment and
coordination between the activities themselves (Berg, 1999). They also support
accountability, the monitoring of the care processes, and, finally, the recording of data that are useful for clinical research. These documents amount

Future-proofing. Wulf et al., Oxford University Press.
© Carla Simone, Ina Wagner, Claudia Müller, Anne Weibert, and Volker Wulf (2022).
DOI: 10.1093/oso/9780198862505.003.0005

to a huge number (e.g. many thousands for the patients of just one hospital unit), differ according to the care activity they document, and are often interrelated, as they share the same data or method of elaboration; this generates what has been called positive redundancy (Cabitza et al., 2019). They are created by care professionals in support of their activities, often combining formal documentation with informal annotations; and they are produced in the different places that patients visit as part of their illness trajectory (Fitzpatrick, 2004).

IT-based solutions have been sought to manage this complexity, with the aim of facilitating the work of care professionals (and also informal carers) and improving the quality of the care and of the documents themselves. Electronic patient record (EPR), electronic health record (EHR), and electronic medical record (EMR) are typical technologies conceived with this aim in mind, although with limited adoption (Jha, 2008) and questionable success (Heeks, 2008: 127). The literature is rich in research contributions that demonstrate how the introduction of EPR systems in hospitals becomes problematic when the research does not take local practices and needs into account (Fitzpatrick and Ellingsen, 2013: 619–25). The conception of a hospital information system (HIS) has to face the conflicting relationship between the direct care of the patients at the bedside, which is typically supported by an EPR application, and many other purposes, including the improvement of the hospital's performance in terms of cost reduction and the successful treatment of patients; the precise classification of diseases and treatments in discharge letters for the purpose of reimbursement by insurances; and the high quality of the data delivered for clinical research. These purposes are also supported by applications serving more administrative purposes. In any case, an IT project entering this complex field has to account for the 'installed base' (Hanseth, 1996), with an already existing HIS as its main component which brings its own corresponding functionalities, affordances, and constraints. Often, projects in the healthcare domain seek to test a solution in a limited set of units and then scale it to other units, if not the whole hospital. This aim adds complexity to a potential solution, as the transferability of the technology and work practices between units becomes a fundamental requirement.

In recent years, the twofold aim of creating a better care environment and reducing the costs of care has motivated a move towards a model of care that is delivered at home, where the patient can enjoy a more comfortable and familiar environment. Telemedicine is an umbrella term for different types of services that may be remotely provided: from telediagnosis to monitoring chronic patients to the remote management of acute diseases (Grisot et al., 2019). As in all distributed settings, a technology cannot fully support awareness about the remote situation. Consequently, it becomes more difficult to reconstruct the patient's state of health during the evolution of an illness. In this situation, caregivers (whether formal or informal) may need additional documentation, some of which patients themselves may be able to contribute, to trace specific phenomena and uncover critical trends. This is critical to being able to personalize the ongoing remote monitoring of patients. The emergence of private agencies to which some activities (e.g. data collection and maintenance) are outsourced makes identifying the in-frastructure to support this highly distributed setting even more complex (Kempton et al., 2020).

In this challenging arena, each project has to carve out its specific context to be able to focus on a manageable set of problems and try to offer appropriate solutions. This chapter presents five projects that are grouped according to the approach they have chosen: either developing novel socio-technical solutions that fit the needs of the target setting or adopting off-the-shelf solutions that can be immediately experimented with in real contexts. In the first case, the sustainability of the solution depends on both the study of the target setting and the conception and implementation of the prospective technology; in the second case, the sustainability of the solution depends on how the adoption is planned in view of the appropriation by the target users. The projects in each group are concerned with both situations: care activities within the hospital and home care supported by telemedicine.

Two of the projects included in this chapter belong to the first group: the *Web of Active Documents* (*WOAD*) project proposes a different conception of the EPR inside a hospital to make it more flexible; the *PICADo* project and its follow-ups seek to support the work of agencies that mediate between patients in a home care situation and the hospital in charge of them. Three projects are about the adoption of off-the-shelf solutions: the *Scanning* project describes the process of introducing scanners in a hospital and developing work prac-tices around them; the *Videoconferencing* and *Telemedicine toolkit* projects aim at supporting the interactions between patients at home and their caregivers, the first one in the rehabilitation phase and the second one in the handling of emergencies. The descriptions of these projects are based on interviews with Carla Simone (quoted as CS), Myriam Lewkowicz (quoted as ML), and Mar-gunn Aanestad (quoted as MA), as well as on numerous project publications co-authored by them.

5.1 Designing in support of existing healthcare practices

In the healthcare domain, the construction of new technological artifacts tends to follow two different scenarios: either users of an existing healthcare solution are uncomfortable with the provided technology, which they perceive as constraining their current work practices, or the project is set up to respond to a 'gap' which can be filled to support the complex caring process. Projects that follow a practice-based approach start with a study of the existing situation in close interaction with the prospective users, involving them as codesigners of the solution and helping them to appropriate the design in 'real use'. The two following projects exemplify this approach.

5.1.1 Towards a more flexible EPR: The *WOAD* project

The *WOAD* project began by identifying two problematic issues: (1) the rigidity imposed by an EPR on the structuring of the information supporting the caring processes at a ward level; (2) the need to preserve forms of redundancy of information that are useful in practice but which digitalization projects usually disregard and seek to reduce.

The sources of the problem
The WOAD project started in 2005 in the ambit of the Advanced Research and Education Programs of the University of Milano-Bicocca and lasted until 2014. This financial support allowed the recruitment of master's and PhD students working on the project themes. The project was rooted in an interest in the role of artifacts in cooperation (Schmidt and Simone, 1996) and, more specifically, in their role in the healthcare domain, a specific interest of a member of the research team (Cabitza, 2011), who had developed personal relationships with some doctors working in hospitals located in the Lombardy region. In the course of the project, the research team had several encounters with these doctors and nurses and decided to collaborate with them. Their shared aim was to understand why the prospective or early-stage introduction of an EPR in the hospital was problematic and generated discontent and strong resistance among the clinical staff. Doctors complained that their involvement in the design of the technology was rather limited; the involvement of nurses was even more marginal. In Italy, healthcare technologies, and EPRs in particular, were—and still are in some cases—in the hands of strong providers whose marketing strategy was to propose, if not impose, predefined solutions

that could be customized at most. These one-for-all solutions conflicted with the clinicians' local practices, which are tailored to the different departments in each hospital.

These issues are pervasive in the healthcare literature, as reported, for example, in Fitzpatrick and Ellingsen (2013). The *WOAD* project confirmed this common experience. Particularly frustrating experiences included the time required to satisfy requests for small modifications to the interface or to the order of the actions enforced by the technology. Doctors were used to define local documents to support a new clinical procedure or changes to an existing one, or to improve the coordination of the clinical activities under their responsibility. With paper, these changes were easily implemented and put to work almost in real time. Hence, the rigidity of the EPR system was the main issue from the very beginning and shaped how the project evolved. This issue 'naturally' captured the interest of the research team in the design of malleable technologies.

The design strategy

From the beginning, the project took a constructive approach to answering the key questions: is an alternative solution possible? What would it look like? One of the doctors claimed that the only way to influence the ongoing digitalization process was to demonstrate to the main decision-makers, namely the management and the IT department, an alternative approach that would take the clinicians' work practices into account. This claim triggered a mutual learning process about what in the current paper documents it would be important to preserve and improve, and what might be digitalized using an alternative design approach that focused on the emerging requirements. The aim was also to contrast the 'residual scepticism' regarding any sort of technological intervention in the healthcare domain.

The process begins by identifying and confirming the key requirements. First and foremost, it should be easy to define and modify the structure of a document in order to preserve what in a paper world is easy to convey through the mutual position of pieces of information and their possible multiple occurrences. Moreover, it should be possible to define and modify classes of documents with different levels of precomputed information to reduce the burden of replication, as happens with paper documents. It should also be possible to annotate the documents, as is done with paper documents. Annotations can be contingent to drive the reader's attention to a specific piece of information, or they can be predefined to enrich the meaning of the content (Cabitza and Simone, 2017). In the first case, annotations serve the purpose of making the reader of the document aware of a specific situation; in the second case, annotations can reify conventions that express the strength of a specific feature—for example, the extent to which it is relevant to execute some actions in a specific order and the severity of the consequences of breaking the order.

This was typical of emergency departments, where care protocols have to be executed under time-critical conditions. Under less severe constraints, annotations can also serve the purpose of reporting the existence of workarounds to deal with situations that are not foreseen but that occur with increasing frequency. This additional information, besides conveying a real-time awareness of an unusual situation among the collaborating clinicians, is useful for those in charge of defining the structure of the information or planning the related changes.

Finally, it should be possible to express different kinds of relationships among pieces of information within and across documents, typically concerning the same patients in a specific care trajectory. This feature is present in the proposed healthcare standards (e.g. HL7) but, again, it is too rigidly defined and therefore difficult to apply. Doctors expressed the need to flexibly define the relationships they deemed useful and understandable in their work contexts, and a requirement for support in ways that are contextual to the documents in use. They also suggested the meanings of these be made explicit when needed, and, finally, that the abovementioned relationships should be able to be visualized upon request (Cabitza et al., 2019).

Impediments to sustainability

In an iterative process, the research team constructed several mock-ups and some prototypes in response to these requirements, proposing different ways of expressing and visualizing the various kinds of annotations (Cabitza and Simone, 2017). The mock-ups were discussed and validated with the doctors and nurses to assess the implications of their potential adoption in a workable solution. Since the general opinion was positive, a step was taken to identify situations where it might make sense to 'automate' annotations. An already existing visual rule editor was adapted to the specific case in order to check if it was possible to define a few relevant rules. The preliminary evaluation was positive, but the limited resources of the project did not allow the team to experiment with integrating this component in the other prototypes.

The doctor interested in conducting a feasibility study of this alternative solution contacted the management of the hospital in order to discuss the possible outcomes of the project. He aimed to establish a more formal and comprehensive collaboration with the research team. His proposal was to construct a prototype that was sufficiently robust as well as interoperable with the hospital's EPR and to evaluate it in the field. The management's response was negative: they perceived investing in the project as a waste of the (limited) available resources, but, more importantly, as an action that conflicted with the policy of standardization governing the technological investments of the hospital. This negative response concluded the first part of the *WOAD* project. The experience in the healthcare domain had been very productive in terms of ideas and partial solutions that the prospective users considered valuable and, in a way, sustainable. But the researchers found the healthcare domain too difficult for experimenting with solutions that conflicted with the mainstream policies of both the technology providers and the public institutions.

Moving from healthcare to other domains: Struggling for resources
The difficulties they had experienced in the healthcare domain led the research team to look to other domains where the mature functionalities could be challenged (Cabitza and Simone, 2017). In a project in the agricultural sector, prototype annotations were tailored to collect the opinions of a class of experts about the usage and dosage of fertilizers and pesticides that were part of a document defining the norms and standards for the main cultures in Lombardy. However, the project and its resources were mainly devoted to the automatic collection of data to extrapolate statistical information on these cultures and did not allow for a more comprehensive implementation of the prototype. In the elderly domain, a simplified version of the *WOAD* prototype was experimented with to share memories between elderly people and younger members of their families in view of promoting intergenerational relationships. These experiences led the researchers to develop a highly malleable conceptual architecture where documents could be locally defined and annotated to improve collaboration and to critically reflect on the role of the designers (Cabitza and Simone, 2015). An additional feature was to enable the selection of parts of the information and convert them to a different format so as to ensure interoperability with an information system in support of the managerial strategies as well as supervision (Simone, 2018).

Along with this conceptual work, the researchers tried to find resources to implement the *WOAD* prototype, moving in two complementary directions. On the one hand, they tried to involve colleagues with a strong experience in distributed architectures. This goal was impossible to achieve because these colleagues would have had to change their view of the role of the users in design:

Our colleagues could not appreciate the basic principles on which the conceptual architecture was grounded [...] user oriented malleability raised new issues in respect to the design-oriented malleability and in addition were demanding to implement [...] then they were not keen to start this challenging and upsetting (for them) adventure [...], 'So what? the game is not worth the candle' they said.

(CS Int, 22/03/2018)

The second direction was to move towards commercial partners. Contact was made with a small software company that was fascinated by the challenge but at the same time worried, since the project would require a long-term investment in development and marketing with uncertain revenues in the short term: a risk that it could not take. Contacts were also made with a publisher of online books that had the idea of augmenting them with the possibility of a rich interaction among the authors and their readers. The publisher appreciated the functionalities that were proposed in *WOAD* and found them inspiring, but in the end, he considered them too demanding in terms of implementation and fell back on a simpler solution.

The last act of this troubling story seemed to lead to a happy conclusion. In 2014, the Italian branch of an international company contacted some universities in the Lombardy region, among them the University of Milano-Bicocca, to redesign their technology in use according to what they called 'the last outcomes of the research efforts in the field of information systems'. To this end, some young IT professionals had been hired. The research team involved in the *WOAD* project met the executive officer to explain the approach and define the scope of a possible collaboration. His reaction was very positive: he appreciated a strategy that started from work practices rather than the commonly presented top-down approaches, since his worry was that the current organization might be upset by the introduction of a new technology. He believed that this was not the case because the functionalities of the WOAD prototype were aligned with the work habits in the company.

The local situation was very favorable: the branch was quite autonomous in organizing its local procedures. The central information system managed by the headquarters was very old: basically, it was a sort of database where some information relevant for their centralized control had to be stored according to their logic.

(CS Int, 22/03/2018)

This was a cumbersome procedure, worthy of being digitalized without dramatically changing the local practices. After some meetings with the managers of the various departments, the mutual commitment was very clear: the researchers had to perform the analysis, define the high-level design of the system in collaboration with the various stakeholders, and supervise its implementation that was in charge of the local IT department. The latter welcomed the idea, since its young IT professionals were interested in experimenting with new technological approaches. An adverse event abruptly interrupted this story: the headquarters blocked the funds for this unscheduled investment in favour of the introduction of a new information system that would provide more integrated and standardized procedures across the various international branches. In 2017, the research team dissolved for personal reasons or changed research interests.

5.1.2 'Domomédicine': A French initiative offering research opportunities

With the expansion of telemedicine, interactions between hospitals and patients living at home are increasingly mediated by agencies whose aim is to improve the quality of the services provided. In France, this goal was named 'Domomédecine', a concept that was defined by the French Academy of Technology and experimented with in the 'Grand Est' region. It

> describes a health system that keeps the patient at home while allowing it to benefit from a set of medical and care acts comparable in number, and in quality, to those that could be done at the hospital. [...] These medical and care acts can be complex, in that they exploit the most modern technologies available. Therefore, the best part of certain acts can be at home or during the socio-professional activities of the patient and the hospital becomes a contributor in this health system.
>
> (Lévi and Saguez, 2008)

The research team at the University of Technology in Troyes got involved with this approach to telemedicine in a small project (*Modèle de l'Internet pour le Soutien Sociale* (*MISS*); 2008–11) that was funded by the university's strategic programme. They worked on this project with informal caregivers (mostly family members) of patients suffering from memory loss, involving them in the design of a social support solution (Tixier and Lewkowicz, 2011). The project was an important step towards 'an active social support community of family caregivers' (p. 8). Moreover,

> in this project, we built a strong relationship with the local health care network, in particular with one psychologist. We were able to participate in support group meetings for spouses who acted as caregivers and they started a social network on their own (RéGéMA).
>
> (ML Int, 21/03/2018)

The follow-up project was *TOPIC* (2013–16), which was funded by the European Commission in the frame of the Ambient Assisted Living (AAL) programme. In *TOPIC*, the consortium developed a solution that could not actually be deployed and experimented with in the participating countries, for a number of reasons. One was the difficulty the participating software company had in adequately responding to the requirements that were articulated by the researchers in view of the complexity and variability of the local situations:

> the system had to align to the needs of three countries, it was not *their* system that had been made with them. You want to do basic features but for the company they were too basic. We had lots of fights about—we wanted light weight features, about interface issues.
>
> (ML Int, 12/03/2018)

PICADo (2012–15) was funded by the French Inter-Ministerial Agency, which supports innovative projects led by industry. Its aim was to design, develop, test, and evaluate the first operational system that complies with the new approach to care delivery, with a focus on patients with cancer, neurodegenerative diseases, and diabetes. The research team had the opportunity to conduct an observational study of the work of *E-Maison Médicale*, an association that incorporates 'different private health workers and professional caregivers, mainly located in several cities of the Troyes agglomeration (N-E of France)' (Abou Amsha and Lewkowicz, 2014). Their aim was to improve the quality of home care by creating interprofessional informal care teams in response to the care needs of patients living at home. This association was deemed interesting because it operates in a region that has a growing ageing population and because it 'is one of the few successful examples of collaboration among different private health professionals for home care in France, where solo-based practices are more common between health workers' (Abou Amsha and Lewkowicz, 2014: 5).

The association is an interesting case of a dynamic work organization.

Unlike many organizational settings [...] inter-professional home care teams are dynamic and each team member may participate in multiple home care teams. Team members are changed depending on the evolution of the patient's health and social situation, and on the patient's perception of their quality of life. Every change in the configuration of the team is negotiated collectively, together with the patient and their family caregivers.

(Abou Amsha and Lewkowicz, 2014: 8–9)

A successful initiative

Observations of the activities performed by the home care teams and interviews with individual caregivers helped deepen the understanding of their work practices and of some of the coordination mechanisms (Schmidt and Simone, 1996) which support the collaborative delivery of home care. One of these coordination mechanisms was based on a coordinative artifact called 'liaison notebook'—a simple notebook in which the different actors jot down their observations, report on telephone conversations to address emergencies, and record meetings to discuss complex issues. A liaison notebook may be more or less structured, depending on the patient's condition, and may also just contain freestyle messages.

While the observational study had yielded many valuable insights, the complex solution that the consortium of *PICADo* proposed was not well accepted by the members of *E-Maison Médicale*. This is why the research team in Troyes decided to build a small system called *CARE* (Abou Amsha and Lewkowicz, 2015; Abou Amsha and Lewkowicz, 2017), which was a real success. It offered a simple solution that accounted for the fact that caregivers often deal with issues beyond the medical scope in order to ensure a good quality of life for patients. Organized in dynamic teams that are open to newcomers, caregivers collectively address emerging medical, unexpected social, or logistical problems (such as how to assist a patient in the case of a family breakdown). The 'liaison notebook' plays a key role in coordinating these actions. Although they were satisfied with their current practices, they agreed to consider how IT could help them make their open and flexible collaboration smoother.

The research team organized design workshops to discuss typical scenarios, for which dedicated technological mock-ups were constructed (a detailed description of the mock-ups can be found in Abou Amsha and Lewkowicz, 2015). The positive reactions of the members of *E-Maison Médicale* led to a full implementation of the *CARE* application according to three main principles: first, [...] tracing the challenging issues in patients' trajectory, to facilitate the integration of new care actors by giving them the necessary information about the patient. Second, enabling a discussion-based documentation to provide a flexible way of documenting patients' information and by then to be aligned with the current way of solving problems and adjusting practices. Third, offering an open indexation of documented information to facilitate highlighting the most important information for each care actors.

(p. 7456)

The association members raised two additional issues. One was how to guarantee open access to the application for one-time users that are not part of the association. The other had to do with privacy and security issues concerning the notebook, which members considered a 'shared secret', knowing that practices of sharing sensitive information did not conform with the privacy rules of the healthcare system. A deeper analysis of these issues was left to the deployment and validation of the *CARE* application in the real work context. Apart from that, the *CARE* prototype was a starting point for new projects.

The follow-up

The knowledge acquired in the *PICADo* project offered important input for the follow-up project, *CALIPSO*. This new project opened up the possibility of studying the coordination practices of hospital-based caregivers that perform home visits and comparing them with how self-employed caregivers organize coordination among themselves. *CALIPSO*, which was funded by the region of Troyes, involved a hospital in the city, the local association of medical doctors, nurses from the city, the university, and a local software company which had already collaborated with the hospital for several years. The idea was

> to add the small, self-built system to the HIS as a 'new brick'. It supports coordination, the sharing of information with the family, practitioners in the hospital and in the city. As this is a sensitive setting, we also look into the role of anonymity in on-line platforms. It is a simple solution.
>
> (ML Int, 21/03/2018)

Hence, the *CARE* prototype was transferred to a new project, helping to develop a simple solution that could be easily appropriated.

A first step in the *CALIPSO* project that targets the two kinds of caregivers was to identify the types of data they needed. While collaboration with the members of *E-Maison Médicale* was easy due to the long cooperation with them in the frame of previous projects, it was more difficult to motivate hospital professionals, who are not used to a practice-based, participatory approach. Hence, the first important achievement was to establish mutual trust and a collaborative atmosphere. This was essential, not least because of the necessity, in this new context, of facing the problem of how to regulate the exchange of sensitive data.

One of the findings of the previous project had been that there were several versions of the 'liaison notebook', even for a single patient. Hence, the new notebook was presented as a medical, social, and familial *carnet de liaison* testifying to a clear commitment to positioning the health of a patient in a larger system of actors than just the perimeter of medical professionals (Berthou, In Press). The notebook, which runs on a tablet, was tested by five users in their own homes for about two months. Berthou (In Press) concludes towards the end of the project that at that moment it was still 'not possible to know to which extent the tablet would play a supporting role in the coordination or as a data bridge between the town and the hospital'.

A change of strategy towards sustainability

Myriam Lewkowicz describes some of the strategic choices she took as part of her role as senior researcher and leader of a research group in Troyes. Having participated in several European research projects, she had experienced the positive and problematic aspects of those projects. Being sensitive to the issue of achieving sustainable outcomes, she decided to flank her traditional research activities with efforts directed towards establishing relationships 'with the society' in the French context, aiming to create occasions for smaller-sized projects with fewer bureaucratic constraints on the one hand, and have a greater impact on the French healthcare context on the other. In line with this strategy, she organized and/or took part in seminars 'with the society', including, for example, the 'week of caregivers' to share her research experiences with professional and informal carers in the domains of healthcare and elderly care. At a more strategic level, she decided to target the insurance companies as potential project partners, since these play a relevant role in the healthcare supply chain. More recent political changes have led her to change strategies in order to be able to further develop her research approach and ideas (see her contribution to the Epilogue).

She currently acts as vice president of *MADoPA* (http://www.madopa.fr/madopa-missions/), an association created by Jacques Duchene, one of her colleagues and an expert in sensor technologies and their use in applications that aim to alleviate the lives of fragile old people. The association is run by four people that participate in national French and EU projects and promotes studies in the field of healthcare for ageing people. The current president is head of a regional branch of a social insurance cooperative:

> A goal is to make changes in the ways social insurances deal with technology. In France, this is a question of trust. People don't spend money on technical devices unless they have an official label. [My goal] is to change the long-term vision in a political way, to change how some stakeholders see the things [...] to have an association that could own the design result and keep it alive, supported by the university. End user organizations are normally overwhelmed. This was not achievable in the TOPIC project because of the rules of the Ambient Assisted Living (AAL) program funding it.
>
> (ML Int, 12/03/2018)

These goals have been pursued in the *HADex* (*hôpital à domicile*) project, a precursor of *CALIPSO*:

> the idea is [that] you are treated at home like in a hospital, for instance you ring a bell and the nurse comes, but it is less expensive of course. This is for example important for children with cancer who will be treated at home.
>
> (ML Int, 12/03/2018)

HADex (2017–18) was part of a regional call for social innovation where the prerequisite for the project coordinator to come from 'civil society' was one of the unavoidable constraints. In the case of *HADex*, this was 'Mutualité Française', an institution managing the national health services. The role of *MADoPA* in this project 'was to envisage a new organizational way to manage the patients at home to make the solution sustainable' (ML Int, 12/03/2018). The research team in Troyes developed a mock-up that was validated and appreciated by both the head of the organization and the care professionals, and it was discussed with a local software company that had a good working relationship with the local hospital, to see if they could offer this solution in their portfolio. The project ended before this could actually happen. A political change at the regional level made this objective more difficult to reach, since the new strategy of the regional agency is to push more standardized solutions for the interactions between hospitals and patients at home. In this situation the research team had to work out a change of strategy. They decided to collaborate with this new agency, which has become a big player in the region:

> We decided not to go against the agency/political strategies; we did not want to be the little village fighting against the big players. Instead, we decided to go to the agency and bring practice-based design in.
>
> (ML, additional notes)

The pursuit of both issues—home care (as in *CALIPSO*) *and* the 'hospital at home' solution (as in *HADex*)—has been on hold due to the COVID-19 problems. However, there has already been some success with the new strategy, as the regional agency decided to develop a proprietary application based on WhatsApp that is similar to the *CALIPSO* solution. Another successful move was to reinforce the research team with younger researchers educated in different disciplines and to put them in contact with the local hospital to deal with a variety of problems:

> And now the hospital has realised that people from our group are really helpful. They want to work with us. [...] they have realized that our group is really helpful for them—before they were into algorithms and so on.
>
> (ML, additional notes)

This is congruent with the insight that advocating the principle of practice-based computing with decision-makers is more important than promoting specific research tools.

5.2 Adopting off-the-shelf technologies

Sometimes a project needs specific devices or general-purpose applications that can be bought off the shelf; hence, it makes no sense to redesign them. Sometimes using off-the-shelf technologies is a specific choice. This is the case when a technical solution for a problem (that is often well defined) has already been developed and can, at least in principle, be reused in the situation at hand. However, this choice can be problematic and may require a specific effort despite the simplicity of the solution and its apparent limited impact on the flow of activities. In any case, introducing a new tool has implications for work practices, the organization of work, and the existing ecology of technologies that need to be accounted for.

5.2.1 Supporting clinical documentation management: The *Scanning* project

Clinical practices generate a huge amount of data and documents that have to be managed in an effective way to support the care processes and administrative activities in the hospital. Digitalization is one of the main strategies to limit the burdens of managing paper-based documentation. However, digitalization has to follow its own trajectory, and this is sometimes conflicting with the pressing needs of an effective and efficient hospital. The *Scanning* project had to face exactly these challenges.

The sources of the problem
The Norwegian *Scanning* project was promoted by a hospital in which an EHR had been introduced, with the goal of drastically reducing the presence of paper documents (Aanestad and Jensen, 2016). This goal was difficult to achieve for many reasons, among them being repeated design changes to the EHR and the need to archive the paper versions of documents that have a legal value. The hospital had to face the management and archiving of an increasing amount of paper documents while the EHR was not yet ready, so its management team decided to purchase scanners to compensate for these delays. This was conceived as a temporary solution while a more definitive one was awaited. Four departments started to pilot test the scanners, without having additional human or financial resources. One of the four departments, the Women's Clinic, was considered the most interesting one and key to understanding how the scanners impacted the clinical work processes.

Design strategy
Meetings with the clinic's staff as well as observations of the scanning activities that were carried out by clinical secretaries revealed that nobody had a clear view of these impacts. The IT department suggested starting from the referral documents and incoming mail and then scanning more complex bunches of documents produced during the care process of a patient, up to the complete record files of patients that were due to be admitted to hospital. In addition, the archive department issued guidelines and a document categorization scheme that followed the prospective structure of the EHR.

It immediately became evident that each department had specific documents that required ad hoc scanning procedures. In order to account for this observation, the design of the overall scanning process was organized according to a 'Level 1 Procedure' for documents valid at the hospital level and a 'Level 2 Procedure' for those local to each department. Alas, it turned out not to be easy to identify and define the second type of documents, and the idea of changing existing procedures created some reluctance. Hence, the project management team organized a series of workshops where clinical staff together with IT department representatives questioned the current procedures and discussed how they should be adapted to the use of the new technology. After that, each department acted autonomously to reach a finer level of detail.

> In general, the redesign process was complicated by the need of detecting such typical constraints that would shape the available redesign space. This discussion was pursued through collective negotiation about the various possible procedure changes, with the collective aim of detecting and preventing adverse consequences of proposed changes.
>
> (Aanestad and Jensen, 2016: 20)

Several factors influenced the negotiation process: above all, the constraints posed by the evolution of the EHR and its limitations regarding privacy standards; the concomitant upgrade of the local area network that created some incompatibility with the purchased scanners and the need to access dedicated workstations to use them; and the technical impossibility of linking together documents that had been scanned at different moments of the care process. A workaround was to use the same scanning date, but this solution had to be accepted in the overall hospital before being applied.

Achieving sustainability

The management took positive action to stimulate departments to define their local scanning procedures.

> The project management sought to manage and coordinate these local redesign processes across the hospital, since several personnel groups and departments were linked in multiple and complex ways within the hospital's work system. Local changes in the work processes thus had to be negotiated and coordinated with other processes.
>
> (Aanestad and Jensen, 2016: 22–3)

When all four departments had defined their procedures, the next step was to harmonize and optimize them: some Level 2 procedures were moved to Level 1, since they were deemed crucial for the overall hospital (e.g. the mail-handling procedures). Moreover, the approach was based on considering the suggestions coming from all stakeholders (doctors, nurses, and secretaries) in order to avoid the changes disrupting their work practices.

> The redesigning of work routines continued as the pilot departments gradually expanded their scanning activities to encompass other documents. Eventually, the scanning took off, but the paper documents were still in use for a long time. A year beyond the intended deadline, the amount of paper sent to the archive was finally starting to decrease, and the work processes utilized primarily digital information.
>
> (Aanestad and Jensen, 2016: 22–3)

5.2.2 Supporting remote rehabilitation:
The *Videoconferencing* project

The rehabilitation process is a good candidate for partial outsourcing, as some of the related activities can be performed at the patient's home. However, this requires good communication to be established between the hospital and the patients at home. The Norwegian *Videoconferencing* project sought to achieve this goal by adopting a videoconferencing (VC) technology that had the double advantage of being a standard commercial product and being familiar to the hospital workers, as it was already used as meeting support for care professionals in the hospital.

The sources of the problem
The project was initiated by the Sunnaas Rehabilitation Hospital, which provides specialized rehabilitation services for patients with spinal cord injury, serious burns, neurological diseases, traumatic brain injury, stroke, and multitrauma conditions (Aanestad et al., 2017a). The project lasted from 1993 to 2016. Its aim was to use the VC technology to allow patients to stay at home during rehabilitation and receive the necessary care and services there. It was motivated by the knowledge that for these patients, mobility can be a challenge, so even reaching the hospital could be problematic for them; meanwhile, the hospital has to manage a huge number of patients but is only capable of hosting a limited number (a total of 159 beds for over 3,000 hospitalizations).

Design strategy and measures towards sustainability

The project traversed three phases: experimentation (1993–2007); routinization (2007–10); services extension (2010–16). The first phase leveraged the
experience gained in the 1990s about the use of VC technology for purposes
other than rehabilitation. In the years before the start of the project, the hospital had already experimented with this technology in some limited application
to evaluate the costs and benefits of its adoption in rehabilitation, with positive
outcomes.

> In 2007 the hospital management decided to introduce a full-time position
> with responsibility for telemedicine, establish a working group for the de-
> sign and placement of videoconferencing rooms headed by the Chief Medical
> Officer, and equip two new videoconferencing rooms located closer to the
> clinics.
>
> (Aanestad et al., 2017a: 50)

In the second phase,

> the project funded a project manager (external) and a part-time internal
> coordinator. The other participants in the project received no economic com-
> pensation and had to find time for the project in their daily work schedule.
> There were participants from all clinical departments; most of them were
> team coordinators.
>
> (Aanestad et al., 2017a: 51)

The presence of team coordinators was important, as they had direct knowledge of the rehabilitation needs and procedures, which vary considerably
across the hospital's departments. One of the first actions was to revise the
discharge procedure in order to incorporate the voluntary acceptance of the
telemedicine treatments by the patient. A 'telemedicine team' was formed,
consisting of a physiotherapist and two technicians, whose task it was to
maintain the service and solve potential technical problems. As an additional
measure,

> [a]n extensive training program was conducted across the organization. [...]
> The training aimed to reach all staff and was offered to one department at a
> time, and also as regular 'refresher' sessions where individuals could drop in.
> Standardized user guides and similar interfaces were created for the video-
> conferencing rooms. The sharing of individual success stories was important
> in mobilizing new participants [...] the videoconferencing facilities were also

used for patient consultations [during which] the patient and therapist could talk directly to the responsible person at the Norwegian Labor and Welfare Administration (NAV) and discuss the preparations before returning home.

(Aanestad et al., 2017a: 51)

In this way, the bureaucratic procedures were simplified. Another type of video-supported meeting, for example, involved a member of the hospital staff and several people from the Norwegian Labor and Welfare Administration (NAV) communicating with the healthcare staff located at the patient's home. The laptop was moved around in the house and gave everyone an immediate, visual sense of the barriers (doors, steps, etc.) that had to be removed before the patient could return home. The joint discussions during the virtual meeting enabled a speedier decision-making process than was usual (Aanestad et al., 2017a). The VC facilities were also used for project meetings dedicated to negotiating and planning the adoption of the technology by the different departments. In addition, the facilities were expanded and regularly upgraded as a standard organizational process. The last achievement was an agreement between the project leader and the NAV to give all health workers free access to the NAV's VC rooms and related services. It included assistance in establishing the related connections. This outsourcing facilitated the expansion of the services nationwide and relieved the hospital of the burden of management of the technical infrastructure.

In the third phase, the role of the team coordinators was crucial to sustaining the expansion of the services. These professionals formed a network that regularly discussed the telemedicine needs and requests of the various departments. One request was regarding allowing direct communication between the patients and the care staff. This required the adoption of a specific technology in response to legal constraints concerning privacy. It kickstarted dedicated action that, starting from a pilot test, culminated in a service that is now in regular operation. Another request came from the departments caring for patients that were supposed to stay in isolation for a long time. These patients wanted to be able to participate in the teaching activities regarding their rehabilitation and to stay in touch with other patients. This was achieved by distributing tablets to those patients and giving them access to the appropriate rooms in the VC system.

All these measures show that the hospital's management was conscious of the fact that the main problems concerned not the technology but the surrounding (work) organization. Its choice to listen to the local requests made the adoption and appropriation of the VC technology sustainable, as testified by the fact that the technology is still in use.

5.2.3 Handling emergencies: The *Telemedicine toolkit* project

Emergency situations in nursing homes need efficient communication between different stakeholders to promptly react to the call for assistance and
share the relevant information. As in the previous projects, the approach was
to adopt an off-the-shelf solution, but this was problematic and led to unexpected outcomes. The evolution of the project was observed by a French
research team; the study is reported in (Gaglio et al., 2016).

The sources of the problem
The *Telemedicine toolkit* project followed the introduction of a telemedicine
toolkit that aimed to improve the relationship between caregivers in nursing
homes and the French regional Emergency Medical Dispatch Centre (EMDC)
that is tasked with responding to urgent medical problems that are communicated by telephone. Responses could include simple indications on how to
manage the problem, up to the assignment of an ambulance or the delivery of
complex medical equipment to the nursing home that contacted the EMDC.
  The telemedicine toolkit had been designed to help caregivers offer timely
responses and avoid undue hospital admissions of patients that could be
assisted in their nursing homes. The project involved ten nursing homes operating in the city of Troyes and the local university, which conducted an
observational study focused on the 'domestication' of the toolkit in these
different settings. The telemedicine toolkit

> is a suitcase that includes devices with which the nursing home staff can
> perform an electrocardiograph, measure blood pressure and determine how
> much oxygen people have in their blood; it uses a Tablet PC with an inte-
> grated webcam to transmit the data gathered using these instruments to the
> emergency medical dispatch center so that the nursing home staff can discuss
> the situation with the medical regulators.
>
> (Gaglio et al., 2016: 223–4)

The university's research team observed the 'deployment processes, to look at
them from a user's perspective, and to determine how these users are able, or
not, to appropriate the systems' (p. 224).

The adoption strategy and the appropriation problems
Ten nursing homes installed the toolkit mainly due to the availability of the
support of a regional healthcare agency that allowed its acquisition free of
charge. In the words of the research team, the suitcases were 'parachuted [...]
where nobody was particularly looking forward to getting them' (p. 226).

The adoption encountered some technical problems related to the internet connection and issues of data privacy that were somehow solved during the experiment. More serious impediments concerned the integration of the suitcase in the work practices of the different nursing homes. In contrast to trained nurses, the orderlies working in the nursing homes had never had any formal electrocardiogram training. Consequently, they feared being given

> responsibility for acts that had not been specified in the regulations describing their duties, despite this being a professional milieu where tasks were often undertaken by parties other than the ones for whom they had originally been conceived. For instance, orderlies were not authorized to take people's blood pressure but often did this with permission from nurses.
>
> (Gaglio et al., 2016: 227)

The consequence was that orderlies refused to actively engage in domesticating the suitcase. But nurses also had difficulties in deciding whether the situation of an elderly person required the suitcase to be used, since the definition of 'emergency' was too vague and contrasted with the usual way of interpreting it. One reason they reduced the usage of the suitcase was to avoid possible criticisms by the management of the nursing home. Another was that in the face of a 'true' emergency the activation of the suitcase would have required too much time, impeding the timely treatment of the emergency and reducing the possibility of staying close to the elderly people in the most critical moments.

An unexpected sustainable outcome

Since the management promoted the use of the suitcase, the nurses had to find acceptable ways of doing this. There were two main advantages in support of its adoption. First of all, the suitcase proved helpful in monitoring the health conditions of the elderly patients and in identifying those that may require a consultation with the EMDC professionals. Its use also helped create a baseline from which to compare the evolution of conditions and evaluate the criticalities that arose. This more relaxed way of communicating with the EMDC staff (in comparison with an emergency situation) improved their mutual interactions.

In this more favourable climate, another problem was solved. The EMDC complained that the orderlies were unable to properly describe the problematic state of the elderly because 'they don't speak their language' (Gaglio et al., 2016: 227). This problem was resolved by a doctor working in one of the nursing homes in cooperation with a doctor working in the local hospital's geriatric department. Together they defined a form guiding the interaction between the orderlies and the EMDC professionals. This form played the role of a sort of 'Esperanto', since it categorized symptoms and listed typical questions to facilitate the mutual understanding of the two groups. The questionnaire was appreciated by the project management, became an integral part of the suitcase offered by the technology provider, and was considered as the most successful part of the overall project.

5.3 Summary

The projects presented in this chapter adopt different strategies depending on the type of technology and whether the aim is to design a new piece of technology or adopt an off-the-shelf solution. The projects that chose the first strategy had two quite different outcomes, although in both cases researchers put much effort into the pre-study of the target situation. The *WOAD* project was not able to reach a version of the prototype that could act as the starting point of true experimentation in the field; the *PICADo* project failed in its main goal but produced a good understanding of the users' needs, and the *CARE* component was successfully transferred to a subsequent project (and possible follow-ups). The different outcomes of these projects are due to several factors, one of which had an influence beyond the projects themselves. The *WOAD* project aimed at changing the way an EPR is conceived in order to make it flexible enough to support the varied work practices. As such, it should have had a direct impact on the HIS of which the EPR is a fundamental component. This situation resulted in a technological component that was quite complex to construct and which the hospital management was opposed to testing in real use. The complexity of the prototype made transferring it to other domains difficult. The *CARE* component that had been developed in *PICADo* was much simpler and only marginally interfered with the existing technologies, as it basically flanked them 'from the outside'. Its validity was positively evaluated by the direct users, as in the *WOAD* project (although with a different level of technological maturity), without interventions from external stakeholders.

The projects that adopted the second strategy had different outcomes. In the *Scanning* and *Videoconferencing* projects, management was aware that the introduction of these technologies had to be carefully considered. Hence, they devised and implemented organizational procedures and learning processes designed to make it a success: in the first case, they took this opportunity to negotiate the distinction between global and local processes and reorganize them with the involved stakeholders; in the second case, they leveraged the existing experience with the technology and built a suitable infrastructure in terms of training, technological support, maintenance, and updating and generating stable practices. In the *Telemedicine toolkit* project, the technology was 'parachuted' into the nursing homes without any further support. The appropriation of the technology as such was difficult because the toolkit was perceived as a 'foreign body' that disrupted the informal relationships between the nurses and orderlies and had a negative impact on the communication between them and the EMDC staff. The adoption of the technology evolved towards an 'unanticipated use' (Robinson, 1993)—that is, for purposes other than those planned. The definition of a shared terminology (the 'Esperanto') made the project somehow successful and the technology sustainable, although not in the way the management team expected.

6

Integration of healthcare services and technologies

The healthcare domain suffers from a fragmentation of the management of care. The outcome of poorly coordinated initiatives (Mykkänen et al., 2016), it has encouraged the development of different local solutions in a trend that makes the delivery of care increasingly complex. The result is a rich space of IT systems that reflect, and at the same time contribute to, this fragmentation. This situation is commonly considered undesirable by the healthcare institutions, since it causes different kinds of problems and potential inefficiencies, including difficulties in cooperation and information-sharing among the different agencies that deliver care; a lack of uniformity in the quality of the services they provide; and, finally, the challenge of controlling the economic resources that are mobilized by this important public sector.

Each country has its own hierarchy of care structures that define the strategies for reducing these problems and taking the relevant operative decisions. This elaborate process involves several authorities, as well as politicians and technology experts. Each decision process can last several years and generate conflicting opinions, since the interests may diverge. They require a mediation that is not simple to reach.

In recent decades, integration and interoperability were the keywords commonly used to refer to possible strategies to limit the effects of these issues. They followed a rationalization approach that could take different, although often interconnected, forms. As part of this approach, the definition of standards absorbed significant resources at the international level, with dedicated committees aiming to create a reference set of concepts in relation to disease classifications, care data/documents, and processes (Benson, 2010; Begoyan, 2007). At a more local level, the integration of data conceptual models or local ontologies helped to rationalize the existing incompatible data representations by proposing unique representations that could make data and information exchange possible (Stumme and Maedche, 2001). This approach indirectly

Future-proofing. Wulf et al., Oxford University Press.
© Carla Simone, Ina Wagner, Claudia Müller, Anne Weibert, and Volker Wulf (2022).
DOI: 10.1093/oso/9780198862505.003.0006

regularizes the processes using and producing healthcare data through the implementation of prescribed data flows within healthcare applications.

This effort was flanked by the generation of guidelines and clinical pathways (Wakamya and Yamauchi, 2009), which were issued and sometimes mandated by the health authorities responsible for any level of the care hierarchy. The aim was to disseminate 'good practices' in order to improve the quality of care, monitor its efficiency and costs, and collect data for clinical research. The multiplicity of these purposes blended the conflicting needs of three different ambits—care, its management, and clinical research—leading to applications that were not (fully) satisfactory for the related stakeholders, as the advantages are not homogeneous and often lead to collected data of poor quality (Greenhalgh et al., 2009). This scenario was made more complex by the evolution of the organization of care; the latter is increasingly distributed among new and sometimes autonomous agencies that support specific services designed to increase the safety and well-being of patients (e.g. elderly care, telemedicine, or risk prevention during care delivery).

Consequently, integration still encounters barriers that are related to both the hierarchical structure of care (often called 'vertical' integration) and the distributed nature of care delivery (often called 'horizontal' integration) and their obvious mutual influences. For example, Auschra (2018) describes barriers on six levels that influence each other: administrative/regulative, funding, inter-organizational, organizational, service delivery, clinical. The sustainability of the outcomes of the integration initiatives depends on the ability to reduce the impacts of these barriers.

As aptly discussed by Fitzpatrick and Elligsen (2013), the role of researchers in projects aiming at integration is limited by the complexity of the target contexts. Researchers are rarely called to directly participate in the integration process. Their task is more to report post hoc on how a project developed, critically evaluating its outcomes, or to compare the strategies towards integration adopted in different contexts. The research literature takes different perspectives on how to evaluate the success of an integration initiative, and these fall between two extremes: (1) a managerial perspective based on performance indicators with respect to the optimization of time and costs (Angst et al., 2011); (2) (less frequent) the perspective of the CSCW and PD literature, which values the impact of the proposed solution on the existing work practices and on its appropriation by front-end employees. The initiatives considered in this chapter mainly adopt the second perspective and illustrate the involvement of both CSCW and PD researchers.

The *ActionADE* project was developed in Canada to respond to the need to improve the collection of data regarding adverse drugs events (ADE) and make them available on a province-wide level. The research team started the project and was directly involved in all steps, having to face the increasing complexity of the context.

The other projects covered in this chapter are observational studies of initiatives in Norway and Denmark, in different contexts. The *DocuLive* project was started by a Norwegian consortium of primary hospitals with the aim of establishing an EPR solution that could be applied at the national level; the Danish *B-EPR* and *Standardized Extraction of Patient Data* (*SEP*) projects pursued a similar goal in response to specific policies promoted by public healthcare institutions; the *WelFare Technology* project is an example of the integration of public and private technologies in remote care.

6.1 Integration across different agencies/institutions

Modern medicine increasingly requires the availability of information about various aspects of healthcare delivery in order to improve it and, in particular, avoid undesired events. For effective communication between the agencies collecting the data and those storing the data to make them accessible for authorized usage, (part of) the HIS that is local to each hospital should be integrated with the technological structure of the receiving institution, which operates at the wider regional/national level. This integration is not a simple technological problem; it also involves strategic and organizational issues that may have to be defined 'on the fly', especially in cases of 'novel initiative'. In this process, rather different conceptions of the technology and its development may come to the fore.

This is the case in the *ActionADE* project that has been developed in Canada with Ellen Balka (quoted as EB; Simon Fraser University) and Corinne Hohl, an emergency room doctor with an MA in epidemiology, as project leaders. The aim of the project is to design a system that supports reporting of ADEs on a province-wide basis to help ensure patient safety. The integration of such a design solution with a provincial pharmacy system (*PharmaNet*) posed a number of challenges, as it required interaction with different hospitals, the regional health authorities, and additional stakeholders, each with their own views and procedures to follow. This still ongoing project tells a complex integration story.

6.1.1 Background

The *ActionADE* project was formulated in response to a Canadian law—Bill C-17 (Vanessa's Law)—that was passed on 6 November 2014 in an attempt to bolster drug safety by strengthening post-market surveillance and research in Canada. More specifically, its aim was to reduce the risk of ADEs,

> unintended and harmful events associated with medication use, and represent a leading cause of ambulatory and emergency department visits and unplanned hospital admissions. Poor documentation and lack of communication of ADE information between care providers, and across health care settings, are likely to contribute to frequent re-prescribing and re-dispensing of culprit drugs.
>
> (Peddie et al., 2016: 2)

In Canada, electronic ADE documentation currently occurs within online reporting systems hosted by organizations external to care delivery (e.g. the United States Food and Drug Administration). From the point of view of managing ADEs, the problem is that:

> [...] although this documentation is structured and somewhat standardized across systems, it is cumbersome and time-consuming to enter such information into existing systems. [...] ADE reporting within these websites is disconnected from the needs of clinical care providers, and clinicians rarely report such events, as immediate patient care-related activities supersede the data request of external agencies.
>
> (EB Int, 13/12/2018)

In other words, these systems have been conceived from the perspective of these agencies and are disconnected from the care practices of the people that should provide the ADE documentation.

The leading idea of the *ActionADE* project was to anchor the collection of ADE data in the care processes so that this effort would not be considered an additional burden. On the contrary, it should develop into an additional source of support for the care processes themselves:

> Our main goal is therefore to design a patient-oriented and provider-centered ADE reporting system that is fully integrated into an EMR. Ideally, this system will be used by clinicians to facilitate ADE documentation and information flow between care providers and across health sectors (e.g. between

ambulatory care settings, hospitals, and community pharmacies) to prevent unintentional re-exposures to harmful drugs.

(EB Int, 13/12/2018)

6.1.2 The design strategy

The *ActionADE* project started as a participatory design project that involved all stakeholders: emergency departments in the province of British Columbia, clinical pharmacists, the Ministry of Health (MoH), and the provincial health authority (HA). A first step was to systematically survey the existing ADE reporting systems in order 'to distill a compendium of data fields from individual reporting systems into a list of *core fields* which are currently used to communicate ADE content in existing reporting systems' (Peddie et al., 2016: 4).

The survey showed highly variable reporting systems which used different definitions and terminology:

Within the systems reviewed, we frequently encountered the use of composite data elements. In contrast to single data elements targeting one concept (e.g., 'dose'), the use of composite elements contained multiple elements (e.g., 'dose, frequency and route used'), making it difficult for reporters to prioritize constructs, and possibly more likely to omit critical information.

(Balley et al., 2016: 26)

The variability of reporting systems has a direct impact on the quality of the collected data in terms of completeness and interpretability. On the one hand,

[t]he lack of standardization between systems is likely to limit the comparability of the data being generated using different systems, and may undermine efforts to pool and analyze data across cohorts for improved signal detection of rare and emerging signals.

(EB Int, 13/12/2018)

On the other hand, the analysis of all the fields present in the forms and systems used to gather information about ADEs showed that the data they captured tended to support regulatory needs more than clinical care needs. Attempts to capture data required for regulatory purposes (e.g. the lot number of a drug) often served as deterrents to clinicians (EB Int, 13/12/2018).

Therefore, standardization and integration with care practices were the two main concepts leading the next steps of the project, which deeply involved three main kinds of care professionals: doctors, nurses, and clinical pharmacists. Focus groups with participants from study hospitals, primary care offices, and community pharmacies in British Columbia convened 'to iteratively refine a set of data fields that would be relevant to clinical work' out of the core fields that were extracted from the aforementioned survey 'and discuss the practicalities of diagnosing, documenting, and reporting adverse drug events' (Hohl et al., 2018: 3).

In parallel, a qualitative study investigated the practices put to work to manage ADEs through observational field studies shadowing clinical pharmacists and physicians in emergency departments. The main focus was

> on pharmacists because identifying, documenting, and reporting adverse drug events are central to their role [and] on emergency department settings because our prior work showed that patients with clinically significant events commonly present to emergency departments, where the diagnosis is often first suspected.
>
> (Hohl et al., 2018: 2)

Observations and focus groups highlighted the complexity characterizing the management of ADEs. First, it is controversial how to categorize ADEs and to decide which ones of them have to be deemed clinically significant. Secondly, the diagnosis of ADEs is performed under stressing conditions, such as high numbers of patients in the emergency department with limited information about their medication and medical history. For this reason, decisions are often temporary and need to be confirmed at a later time by considering the actions of other caregivers and the evolution of the patient's conditions and by informally contacting (external) care professionals that might have had responsibility of the patient.

> Despite these difficulties, the clinicians are interested in documenting ADEs and would welcome reporting mechanisms that meet clinical needs while allowing them to observe the direct impact of reporting on clinical care. [...] Electronic reporting systems could facilitate communication by automating the electronic communication of standardized adverse drug event reports between clinicians or creating patient-level alerts [...] [that was considered] as highly relevant and would motivate the use of a reporting system.
>
> (EB Int, 13/12/2018)

The project proceeded in three funding cycles under three different funding schemes, a fact that in itself created some challenges.

The initial PD project resulted in the electronic version of the ADE paper prototype being implemented on iPads in a teaching hospital. At the end of the second cycle, a fully functional stand-alone solution was running and used in the hospital, and a significant amount of provincial-level work for integration with the province-wide pharmacy system had been achieved. Planning the provincial roll-out of an integrated system happened in the third funding cycle, at the end of which the MoH had taken over the project.

6.1.3 The first prototype: Getting ready for appropriation in real use

The qualitative studies allowed the construction of a paper-based form for ADEs that was mature enough to be validated in a pilot testing (Chruscicki et al., 2016), with the aim of reaching 'a more mature design, and introduc[ing] revisions at lower cost, than if revisions were required after all programming costs have been incurred' (EB Int, 12/10/2019).

The clinical pharmacists perceived the paper-based ADE form as an efficient, user-friendly, and intuitive way to record ADEs. Users preferred the form on a single page and checkboxes over drop-down menus and free text and felt that some data entry fields could be omitted while others needed further clarification or simplification. Altogether, the fieldwork helped end users and researchers anticipate how the ADE form's functionality could be improved to assist clinicians in communicating relevant ADE information between care providers on different wards and across healthcare sectors, and to act as handover tools. This enabled the research team to anticipate the need for electronic linkages between different components of the EMR being implemented, ideally including a bi-directional link with drug plan data.

As the overarching objective of the project was to develop a documentation tool that supported communication between care providers (rather than communicating events to external agencies), the name of the form was changed to 'Adverse Drug Event Communication and Documentation Form' to highlight its intended purpose. Most importantly, the pilot system was to allow for updates or modifications after a report was generated, which none of the reporting mechanisms available at that time supported.

We hope that our findings highlight the need for a culture shift around ADE communication, from an approach that serves to generate health data for external agencies, implied by 'reporting', to a patient-safety oriented approach that focuses on communication and documentation for prevention of repeat events.

(EB Int, 12/10/2019)

At the end of 2018, the project team had programmed the pilot-tested set of data fields into an electronic application called *ActionADE*, which was prototypically implemented on iPads and is now in use in a teaching hospital in Vancouver, British Columbia. An agreement with the MoH let the collected ADE information be temporarily stored in a secure server provided by the main technology partner. This concluded the first part of the project and opened the second phase, which aimed to integrate the *ActionADE* application with the provincial drug information system so that standardized ADE data could be communicated between providers and across health settings.

The project is now running in the Health Agency as a stand-alone project and a significant amount of the provincial work for integration has occurred. We are starting to do the build of the integrated solution. The stand-alone solution is running in our hospital. To integrate it *PharmaNet* needs to make changes.

(EB Int, 13/12/2018)

6.1.4 Towards integration with a provincial pharmacy system

To reach the goal of becoming a scalable solution at the provincial level, the *ActionADE* application had to reach full integration with *PharmaNet*, a centralized, real-time database of most outpatient prescription medications dispensed in British Columbia (BC) (Smolina et al., 2016: E253).

It was established in 1995 as a claims database to link community pharmacies with government to support billing for medications [...], and community pharmacists are legally required to enter prescription details of dispensed medications for all patients. [...]. *PharmaNet* is the definitive information source for medication dispensing histories for the province.

(Balka et al. 2018: 2)

From the very beginning, the integration process 'faced significant delays due to a range of unanticipated policy and governance issues related to its system-wide integration' (EB Int, 13/12/2018). These delays were to do with a number of unforeseen and challenging hurdles, including:

- The problems the province-wide initiative in the frame of the Canada Social Transfer programme had in bringing one new information system to most of the hospitals in the province, a project that stalled and had to be completely rebooted;
- A data privacy breach at the MoH, unrelated to the project, which for many months made it difficult to build up collaboration;
- The huge amount of invisible work that was necessary to increase conviction in the project, comply with the requirements and procedures of different funding schemes and institutions, carve out agreements, etc.

These 'unanticipated policy and governance issues' created a situation which Ellen Balka likens to a set of balls, all of them in constant motion:

Over the course of 2 and ½ years, we interacted with 38 organizations in an effort to [...] build support for our project, and motivate the provincial Ministry of Health to plan for and fund *ActionADE*'s integration with *PharmaNet*. We often initiated stakeholder engagement with customized briefing notes that provided an overview of the project, its status, and challenges we were facing, which served as a basis for soliciting support. We presented the project to numerous stakeholder groups in our effort to locate the locus of decision-making power related to *PharmaNet*.

(EB Int, 13/12/2018)

6.1.5 The challenges

An unanticipated major hurdle appeared when the second funding envelope, the Electronic Health Information Partnership Program, required a commercial company to be brought on board to implement the pilot version of *ActionADE*. The software company that was hired was not part of the MoH's list of approved vendors, a fact that created an enormous amount of work. Carving out a service agreement and drafting a privacy and risk assessment with this industrial partner, both of which were not ready, turned out to be time-consuming tasks. A particular problem associated with this was a conflict between the university hosting the research project and the industrial partner that owned the server where the data were memorized, as the latter wanted to hold the full property of this server. To ensure data privacy and protect against any incorrect use of the data themselves and thus comply with ethical principles to be guaranteed by the university, this latter required technical information about the server that the industrial partner deemed to be part of its own intellectual property.

> So a bunch of issues came up in relation to that, like if there is a data breach, is the company even allowed to enter the data farm to fix it and who is responsible for maintaining the servers located in the university, who is liable to keep the work going, all that, and who you know, what kinds of service agreements are in place. It is sort of amazing to me how this company and other companies as well had servers in another institution's server farm and there had not been a privacy and risk assessment which is required by law. There were no agreements in place about who had access under which circumstances, who owned the server, who is required to fix it, and so on. So that was about a year of negotiation with the university and the company.
>
> (EB Int, 13/12/2018)

Another conflict that arose concerned the different statuses of the ADE data collected in the project, which was based on the leading principle of anchoring ADE information collection in the caring practices of the hospital:

> In order for the project to qualify for review by the *PharmaNet* data stewardship committee and constitute 'research data', all data would have to be de-identified. Yet, this would render our ADE data meaningless for clinical care, where clinicians need to know which patient had suffered an ADE to ensure they would not re-expose the patient to the culprit drug. From an operational perspective, the new ADE data does not yet exist and will be created through a PD research process, and therefore, could not simply be considered 'clinical' data. Thus, *ActionADE* fell into ambiguous territory, subject to both research and clinical care guidelines—neither of which accounted for the possibility of a health IT project attempting to create new data and evaluate the impact of sharing data on clinical decision-making.
>
> (Balka et al., 2018: 3)

Moreover, although the project received letters of support from the MoH and *PharmaNet*, 'the greatest challenge we faced was determining who within the Ministry could set in motion the collaboration required for *ActionADE*'s integration with *PharmaNet*' (EB Int, 13/12/2018). Several attempts were made for about two years to find the right people—but even in the best cases, the answers reflected a generic appreciation of the project without any practical effect. Then, suddenly, things started moving, since a fully hidden obstacle was removed: the industrial partner that was tacitly opposed by the MoH left the project due to the slow timelines.

In addition, the MoH activated an initiative to remove barriers that were preventing innovative projects from moving forward 'in the form of a 'Transformation Office (TO) … ActionADE is in the first cohort of projects supported through that office' (EB Int, 13/12/2018). Becoming part of this initiative, however, required the research team to comply with the processes of this new agency. This, again, meant engaging in time-consuming activities:

> You have to go to their weekly meetings and you have to enroll your project in their management system, set key performance indicators for phases I, II, III, and all of the sudden we go to meetings every Monday, entering information into their project management system, which has nothing to do with research, but true to their word, if we have a problem they help us solve it.
>
> (EB Int, 13/12/2018)

One of the problems the TO helped to solve was connected to the decision to run the pilot *ActionADE* on a tablet, a device for which the HA had no policy. This decision involved finding a tablet that would be compatible with the HA's security requirements. Ordering this tablet through the HA meant following their internal procedure,

> but we don't have a budget line number to order hardware which means we can't go through their vendor. We spent a few weeks until somebody gives us a number and we place the order for the hardware and then somebody tells us that we have a security problem […]
>
> (EB Int, 13/12/2018)

Creating a sustainable solution that is scalable, hence useful and used in all healthcare settings and pharmacies in the province, required the research team to interact with several institutional actors and to comply with their specific rules and procedures, developing new kinds of relationships. As many of the activities that were necessary for development and integration had not been done before—'everything we did we were literally the first people to do it' (EB Int, 13/12/2018)—the team had to initiate new procedures. For example, *ActionADE* was one of the first projects that went before the province-wide project approval process. Hence, 'in meetings with 15–20 people from different divisions at the Ministry', action had to be taken

> to get integrated into a process that normally does not involve entities outside unless the Ministry has initiated those relationships. Then we had to go through the corresponding budgeting process and at the same time we were doing similar processes at the HA (Health Authority) with the TO (Transformation Office), a brand-new process; at the same time, we are working with HA's IT department which is being reorganized and they have new processes.
>
> (EB Int, 13/12/2018)

The research team's position was that of an outside group trying to influence the *PharmaNet* development process. This was a venture that required a significant budget and a brand-new process.

From the perspective of the research team, the downside of all this work that helped push the project forward was the feeling of having to do many things 'nobody ever uses':

> So, anything anybody ever asked us to do we did. People wanted briefing notes, presentations, detailed specs, we did them. Half the time people were asking us to do things that they never used. My personal favorite was a year before we got any traction with the Ministry of Health they asked us to fill out a project charter and a business case development for them. We don't know if anybody ever read it [...] they tried to exhaust you.
>
> (EB Int, 13/12/2018)

In sum, the engagement of the research team in non-research activities that are largely invisible in the academic world was key to the project's progress. In discussing these challenges, they conclude:

> Our ability to pilot-test and progress with *PharmaNet* integration reflects perseverance, our willingness to participate in multi-sector politics, the eventual alignment of diverse stakeholders, and arguably, timing and luck [...] we often received feedback from stakeholders suggesting that if anyone could influence change, it would be our senior team members, supported by an excellent team.
>
> (EB Int, 12/10/2019)

6.1.6 A continuous effort towards sustainable integration

From the very beginning, the *ActionADE* project aimed at scaling up the ADE reporting application from the local hospital to the hospitals of the region. With this in mind, the research team undertook various types of action. So the survey of the existing systems was not only instrumental to the construction of the prototype; it also demonstrated the solidity of the research effort and its usefulness to the institutions that could support the development of the application and its adoption in other hospitals. Given that these institutions might wish to consider other systems, it was profitable to show deep knowledge of the existing alternatives, as it allowed the researchers to compare these alternatives and make a convincing argument for the proposed reporting system.

Moreover, at quite an early stage in the project, the researchers presented the general principles underlying the *ActionADE* solution in influential publication venues. This was also done in anticipation of other potential proposals by the research community in response to Bill C-17 (Vanessa's Law). In Hohl et al. (2015) the authors support the argument that the shift from 'reporting' to 'documenting' requested by this law is not suitably supported reinforced by the existing reporting systems. They also provide a description of their project agenda, focusing on the care-centred approach that would inform the proposed solution and the pilot testing (illustrated in Chruscicki et al., 2016). This added to the credibility of their approach. In addition to that, the researchers presented five main guidelines based on the qualitative studies (Peddie et al., 2016).

6.1.7 Achieving integration changes the contextual conditions

At the end of the second funding cycle, the research team was ready to start planning the provincial roll-out process to community pharmacies. However, irrespective of the effort to create the condition for a sustainable integration, the successful transition to this stage of the project was (and still is) open.

The research team successfully competed for a new grant. The requirements of the funding agency, though, obliged them to engage in a process called 'outcome-based contracting':

> Since May, we've been in meetings of 10 hours a week with the Ministry. We had to go through the Ministry's change management process, the requirements specification process, the Ministry of Health contracts out the

development of *PharmaNet* to a private company, so then they were at the table, and then we had bi-weekly project management meetings with the Ministry's PM team and our PM team [...] So, we have been in this very intensive planning process which is culminating now.

(EB Int, 13/12/2018)

Although the outcome of this process was successful, as the relevance of the *ActionADE* solution was confirmed, the new contract changed the relationship between the research team and the other stakeholders. The requirement to explicitly involve the institutional agencies and the 'outsourcing' of the development of *PharmaNet* to a private company resulted in the research team having much more limited control over the integration process. From the very beginning of the planning phase, problems and tensions came to the fore. The private IT company did not have a detailed knowledge of how the solution to be integrated had been constructed. Moreover, their language was completely different from that of one of the institutional actors and the co-leader of the project, who was a medical expert not so familiar with technical issues. One of the consequences of this misalignment was that, for example,

the classification schemes by which the *ActionADE* solution had been constructed were questioned, thus underestimating the effort and approach that we had taken in its development. It is a continuous game and the question is: who wins? and on the basis of which motivations? There are several interests around the table.

(EB Int, 12/10/2019)

As a result, the number of meetings increased dramatically and the decision process became more complex and frustrating for the involved researchers. The time to be dedicated to the meetings increasingly conflicted with the other duties they had to fulfil as academics. These stressful conditions, together with the limited impact of the project leaders on the integration process, challenged the harmony within the team: 'We were confident that the data generated by *ActionADE* were properly delivered [to *PharmaNet*], but how they would be displayed to the users and integrated with the applications they normally use remained completely obscure' (EB Int, 12/10/2019).

With the new constellation of actors, the relevance of the role of clinical pharmacists as users underlying the construction of the *ActionADE* software was completed underestimated:

Our software had been conceived with the focus on clinic pharmacists: extending it to other kind of users would require additional research effort to fit their needs. In particular, in many hospital departments the role of the nurses in collecting ADE data is crucial: they are not used to do that [...] we have to understand how this could be possible.

(EB Int, 12/10/2019)

In other words, the integration project no longer followed the principles the research team had adopted in the previous phase: 'The pace of the process is defined by other kinds of goals [...] We were used to tiring but fruitful discussions with the government representatives to solve problems but this is no more the case' (EB Int, 12/10/2019). These were all indications that the change of ownership could threaten the original project vision.

The feelings of the research team in this situation—at the point where the provincial roll-out was about to start—were characterized by ambivalence. On the one hand, there were many sources of frustration for the research team. In fact, the MoH had taken over—'from their standpoint now that we have proven through a proof of concept, they don't actually need us' (EB Int, 13/12/2018). On the other hand, the pleasure of seeing the results of their previous efforts being exploited in the new richer regional context motivated the search for solutions that could help meet the challenges of this new stage: 'The project still progresses [...] we feel overextended and exhausted. If we succeed to have the system going beyond the pilot [...] this would be the most successful project of my life!' (EB Int, 13/12/2018).

In a sort of résumé, the project leader provided a condensed description of the challenges she and her team met, as well as the difficulties of reconciling this type of long-term engagement with academic work:

The story about sustainment is that when you interact with a large system you are interacting with moving parts, it is never stable. You are interacting with a constant change in who your team is, and so on. And there were really no structures in place to support this kind of work. We had to push the various institutions that we interacted with to create structures. [...] So, if I really give you a one-liner about sustainability [...] It is not a short-term undertaking. It requires new structures and new processes. And all of this is invisible in academic work. So, you don't want to do this as an assistant professor.

(EB Int, 13/12/2018)

6.2 Technology integration and standardization

Research on information infrastructures (IIs) in healthcare started in the mid-1990s with a set of seminal papers (e.g. Hanseth et al., 1996; Monteiro and Hanseth, 1996; Bowker et al., 1996). Researchers began studying the making of large-scale national e-health solutions, looking into how the technical issues of standardization and integration with an 'installed base' were approached and more often reporting failure than success. Most of these studies were carried out from an ethnographer's perspective. This was also the case for Margunn Aanestad (quoted as MA; University of Oslo), who suggested a series of projects she had been involved in to the authors of this book. A key problem in all these projects was that they started out with a top-down view, seeking to impose standard ways of doing. She points to several characteristics of IIs. One is the fact that

> IIS is large, shared by many actors [which] implies the need to negotiate the standards, there is this collective dimension that shapes the local-global connections [...] so it's the collective quality of the solution that has been the challenge to make them sustainable, not the appropriation by the users but the negotiations between the actors—do we support this?'
>
> (MA Int, 20/11/2018)

Another characteristic of national e-health initiatives is their long-term nature: 'The temporal [...] observing IIS in development and use requires a longitudinal perspective, you need to follow them for a long time' (MA Int, 20/11/2018). She refers to her observations of more than thirteen years of efforts to establish a digital solution for prescriptions in Norway throughout the healthcare system. This was a project that also shed light on the difficulties of bringing all relevant stakeholders around the table, as well as the special challenges of having to have vendors on board:

> Due to the comprehensive functionality specified, the project required extensive work from the vendors´ side. The vendors had to develop new and quite complex software components, modify their existing solutions, and integrate them to the national e-prescription solution. This resulted in a situation where the overall project became dependent not only to the activities of the vendors directly involved in the e-prescription project, but also to the overall situation within the vendor organizations.
>
> (Vassilakopoulou et al., 2017: 3)

When you cooperate with vendors, 'you have to deal with long backlogs, jobs may get delayed for years' and you have to 'fit into their strategic plans' (MA Int, 20/11/2018).

The projects presented in this section partially encountered the same challenges as the *ActionADE* project. What makes them different is that while *ActionADE* started from local practices and tried to integrate a locally successful application with a province-wide system, the projects studied by Margunn Aanestad and others took the opposite path. In all cases they, at some point, had to meet work practices at the local level, assuming different strategies.

6.2.1 Disruptive conflicts: The *DocuLive* project

Hanseth et al. (2007) had the opportunity of conducting a longitudinal study that made it possible to reconstruct the story of the development of an EPR system in Norway through its implementation and adoption in the Riskhospitalet, a large, specialized teaching hospital in Oslo. We name this initiative 'the *DocuLive* project' from the name of the involved EPR. The project aimed to construct a standard EPR system for adoption in all Norwegian hospitals. It started with five of the most relevant hospitals in the country. The goal was ambitious since its deployment would require strong integration of the work practices and information structures supporting them. Indeed, the envisaged EPR was supposed to be 'complete'—that is, it should be an integrated record of all patient information.

The design strategy and its problems
The project activities started with the firm intention to take a bottom-up approach by involving representatives of the various hospitals and focusing on the work practices characterizing them. Unfortunately, this process soon became unmanageable. Participation decreased and 'the need to continuously find a common agreement turned the intended bottom-up approach in a top-down one' (Hanseth et al., 2007: 123).

The project consortium included a big software company that had commercial interests in several European countries, and when it became a US company during the project its commercial interests in *DocuLive* took on a worldwide dimension. The consortium in Norway decided to live with this trend in order to guarantee the continuity of the project and anchor the sustainability of the EPR system through the involvement of such a strong company. This choice suddenly became counterproductive. The possibility of the Norwegian consortium governing the design choices was constantly diminishing, as their requirements had to be harmonized with an increasing number of requirements coming from completely different settings.

The involved hospitals took different paths to reach the initial goal. One hospital incorporated the *DocuLive* technology in its solution. Interestingly, the efforts to make this feasible in a sustainable way led to its progressive downsizing: first as a component of the overall architecture managing the documents produced by a subset of stand-alone applications supporting the patient care trajectory; and then as a simple element of a constellation of stand-alone applications whose documents were accessed through a web portal. Obviously, this solution was made possible by the evolution of the available technology infrastructures towards web-based architectures. However, it is interesting to note that the trajectory from an all-encompassing centralized solution, as foreseen at the beginning of the project, towards its fully distributed version in one of the hospitals depended not only on technological considerations but, more importantly, on the problems that the centralized solution generated during the project. In the word of the authors, 'an important factor behind the failure [was] complexity' (Hanseth et al., 2007: 123).

Indeed, any attempts to reduce complexity by imposing a new order on the activities and the documents they generated according to the 'one patient-one record' principle resulted in an additional level of complexity that made the design increasingly intricate, and finally unfeasible and not sustainable. Respecting the autonomy of the agencies involved in the patients' care trajectories emerged as the unique sustainable approach that the evolved technology was happily able to support.

6.2.2 Two contrasting experiences in Denmark

Aanestad and Jensen (2011) report on a qualitative study of two Danish healthcare initiatives that sought to address the problems of non-integrated EPRs in the country. The aim was to compare the strategies adopted to construct the prospective solution in the two initiatives and investigate the reasons why the first one failed while the second one was successful.

A failure story: The B-EPR initiative
The *Basic Structure for EPR* (*B-EPR*) initiative was promoted by the Danish MoH and started in 1996. Its aim soon evolved from the definition of a less ambitious communication standard to exchange data across EPR systems towards

a national standard for representing the content and structure of patient data; a standard that software vendors were expected to comply with in the construction of any EPR system in Denmark. The story of the project followed the steps typical of the definition of a standard. Between the start and the end of the project, the National Board of Health in charge of the standard definition released several versions that were shaped by the ambition to not only govern how EPR systems had to be conceived but also

> to replace the patient national register that since 1977 had collected data on patients diagnoses. Such a register would require more structured data in the EPR systems, including the standardization of clinical terminology and datasets, as well as a coupling of the information to the ongoing clinical process.
>
> (Aanestad and Jensen, 2011: 166)

In 2004 two companies had developed two prototypes that were too immature to be tested in the field. It was only possible at that point to assess the readiness of the hospitals to adopt the system and to collect the opinions of a number of clinicians before and after a limited trial in one hospital. Clinicians appreciated the process-oriented nature of the support offered by the system but found it too complex. They also thought that 'this way of working was not easily transferable to clinical practice' (Aanestad and Jensen, 2011: 167) and wondered why such a problematic standard would be further developed. Irrespective of the generalized scepticism, the standard was further refined until 2005, when its development was meant to be frozen to allow vendors to implement the last version and the hospitals to test the related prototypes. But this never happened. In 2006 a national public observatory reported that the objectives of the project had not been met and the report of a private consultancy agency (Deloitte) 'questioned whether the B-EPR model was realizable at all. […] As a consequence, the Minister of Health decided to put the B-EPR development on hold' (Aanestad and Jensen, 2011: 168); the focus of the initiative has since been oriented towards other issues.

Learning from failure: The SEP project
The *SEP* project started in 2000 and evolved in response to the progressive failures of the previous *B-EPR* project.

> The idea behind the project was sketched by a consultant physician and former employee in the Danish National Board of Health. The purpose was to make electronically registered patient data available between hospitals within

counties and across county boundaries in Denmark. The philosophy behind SEP was that, as hospital owners, it should be possible to make patient data registered in EPR systems, Patient Administrative Systems (PAS), and other hospital systems on currently and previously admitted patients available to other hospitals in the county.

(Aanestad and Jensen, 2011: 168)

The strategy was driven by rather pragmatic considerations, as the architect of the model explained:

The counties had spent a lot of money to be in a leading position in the EPR area, and so had the three IT vendors. They were not interested in scrapping all existing systems that did not cohere with the B-EPR standard [...] They were interested in relying on what existed and then gradually working towards something in common.

(quoted in Aanestad and Jensen, 2011: 167)

In practice, a *SEP* standard was based on an analysis of existing health information systems. Then predefined elements of patient data were extracted from existing PAS and EPR systems, structured in a *SEP* database according to the standard, shared between the cooperating hospitals, and accessed through secure internet access via an internet browser.

Unlike the *B-EPR* case, the pilot testing of the standard in two hospitals was possible because the vendors were involved in developing its definition. The outcomes were positive, as testified by the evaluation reports. The users who were involved in the pilots emphasized that *SEP* was significant because it

makes it immediately possible to have an operational access to viewing and comparing data across the various information systems, including EPR systems, and thus it largely contributes to solving one of the most significant healthcare information problems [in terms of information sharing and data access].

(Aanestad and Jensen, 2011: 169)

Few technical issues were mentioned in the assessment of the solution, and the evaluation group stated that 'the data structure appears simple, logical and in accordance with common clinical practice' (Aanestad and Jensen, 2011: 169). The conclusion by the member of the EPR Observatory was: 'SEP is a practical, improvised solution in a situation where you have different systems that cannot communicate. It is not an ideal solution but it is a practical solution if the alternative is that you are not able to see the data' (Aanestad and Jensen, 2011: 169).

The winning strategy of the project has been described by the researchers as follows:

> The SEP system was an addition to the existing procedures and tools, and as such, the project could approach stakeholder mobilization differently from the B-EPR initiative. First, it did not require the same number of actors involved, as it initially included only the immediately concerned user departments, involved vendors and the consultant. Secondly, the approach did not require that the stakeholders took large risks. Since the SEP solution required that vendors developed only a small, add-on functionality to extract data from existing EPR systems, their development costs were small. Also for the hospitals, this was a low-risk investment, as the hospitals did not need to replace any of their existing systems, or change the users' clinical practices and documentation practices. The prototype tests provided proof that the SEP solution actually worked and offered immediate use value, which strengthened stakeholders' commitment. SEP structured the way the extracted data was stored in the database, but it did not impose any novel structure onto the pre-existing EPR systems, or the documentation practices, since it was based on the existing data structure. [...]. Thus, all EPR vendors were able to adapt to and utilize SEP with minor investments.
>
> (Aanestad and Jensen, 2011: 172)

The positive outcomes of the pilot tests convinced other counties to use the same solution. Currently, the solution covers almost all of Denmark.

6.2.3 Recognizing different value paths: The *WelFare Technologies* project

Telemedicine involves the integration of technologies and devices that offer specific services. This type of integration raises interesting issues, especially when the solution has to reconcile the needs and strategies of several stakeholders. The Norwegian *WelFare Technologies* (WFT) project is about these issues. It was the object of a study by a research team whose outcomes are reported in Kempton et al. (2020).

The *WFT* project— which was conceived within the frameworks of two programmes: the Norwegian National WelfTech programme initiated by the

Norwegian Directorate for eHealth and the Norwegian Association of Local and Regional Authorities (KS) programme—started in 2014 with the aim

> [of coordinating] a wide set of autonomous or semi-autonomous organizations with separate agendas and separate resources, like governmental agencies, municipalities, health technology spin-offs and established software vendors. The program is centred around a politically set policy problem, described as an increasing demand for health care services at the same time [...] The program targets two subcategories of WelfTech: safety technologies (alarm-based systems like safety alarms and fall sensors) and remote care technologies (data-based health systems like digital medical devices linked to a communication software).
>
> (Kempton et al., 2020: 5)

The project had the resources to start the implementation of a *WFT* architecture supposed to overcome the fragmentation and limited flexibility of the existing commercial solutions, with the goal of mobilizing the interests of technology providers and other hospitals.

Over the course of the project, the overall integration strategy changed due to a series of problems. In the first phase, the team proposed an architecture that was based on an open standard to allow the recombination of *WFT* at the patient's home, where a hub would be linked to a core module that collected data which could be used by health service applications. The recombination would promote the innovation of *WFT*, which could easily be plugged in while the core module remained stable. But this solution contrasted with the commercial strategies of the main technology partner of the project (HealthTech): 'As the CTO of HealthTech explained that [...] his company needed to control the chain of data from device to platform, to be able to detect and fix errors, and thus ensure robustness' (Kempton et al., 2020: 8). A few other technology companies also followed this strategy, offering closed solutions that, once forced to become open, could make the market difficult for *WFT* providers to innovate in.

For these reasons the vision for the second phase was changed:

> In May 2016 the government released a new digitalization [...] [that] emphasized that sector-spanning digitalization projects should develop common modules and infrastructures that could serve needs across the domain of the public sector. [and] led to the definition of a new architecture [...] centred on a digital platform offering shared resources. The devices and systems [...]

should use platform resources to support their own functionality and for data integration.

(Kempton et al., 2020: 9)

Since coordination at a national level turned out to be difficult, a similar initiative by the City of Oslo which was already ongoing was taken as a starting point for a national infrastructure, in the hope that its potential impact at the national level would attract technology vendors. However, the response was negative, as the vendors considered the effort required was too great for a product perceived to have limited commercial value. Moreover, the institutional complexity related to technology procurement at the national level, as well as the need to work out the related regulations, made the implementation of the architecture appear problematic.

In the third phase the strategy changed again, moving towards a more decentralized architecture based on a core integration module:

[…] the hub is now an integration module, receiving data from welfare technology systems, transforming it into a data structure the EPR systems can handle, and then transferring this data to EPR systems connected through the secure health network. The modularity of the systems, outside of the core, is not specified.

(Kempton et al., 2020: 10)

To solve the many problems that were raised by the various stakeholders, a public infrastructure was provided via a public enterprise—the Norwegian Healthnet (NHN)—which already operates national network infrastructures for public health organizations via a cloud service. This solution solved the problems:

Developing the core hub of the platform internally and incrementally allowed accommodating institutional resistances. The problem of procurement was accommodated by utilizing NHN as an already established service provider for the municipalities. The resistance posed by legal issues regarding the handling of health data was accommodated by affording a close collaboration between developers and the legal expertise at the directorate.

(Kempton et al., 2020: 11)

Understanding that the choice of a centralized and rigid solution was unsustainable led to the conception of a more articulated ecology where the different value paths of the involved stakeholders were accommodated and, ultimately, to a successful solution.

> With the caveat that the platform is still being developed and expanded, and will be evaluated during 2020, the new architecture seems to successfully have accommodated initial needs and requirements of the involved actors.
>
> (Kempton et al., 2020: 12)

6.3 Summary

The integration initiatives described in this chapter were promoted in relation to regional or national public policies aiming to reduce the fragmentation of local solutions or to standardize the management of delivering new services. As such, they enjoy a favourable situation, since the public decision-makers are directly committed to reaching positive outcomes. At the same time, however, the many and various complexities of the public sector and the diversity of the involved stakeholders create impediments and conflicts that make this goal hard to achieve.

In the case of the *ActionADE* project, the problems arose when the local solution to collecting data about adverse drug events in a specific hospital had to scale to the regional level and then became a more widely applicable solution. In this transition process, the research team that had developed the local solution in collaboration with clinical pharmacists—and created the conditions for its sustainability—progressively lost its role in the new and broader decisional space for various reasons. A lot of effort had to be invested in making the project progress. This involved: understanding what caused it to slow down; clarifying procedures or defining new processes; and finding ways to interact with different stakeholder organizations and comply with their rules. One of the most difficult parts was to sensitize the new owners of the process on the regional level to the necessity of additional investigations in the field in order to make the partial solution operable in a wider context while keeping the characteristics that made it locally sustainable. The new strategy taken by the decision-makers did not fully consider this complexity: they were more inclined to adopt a top-down, more standardized approach. Despite experiences that were disappointing and frustrating at times, the researchers continue to seek ways of influencing 'what our data will look like in varied community pharmacy systems in use in our province' (Balka, in this book).

Illusions about the feasibility of a strong standardization process were the main source of problems in the different e-health projects. The numerous obstacles and conflicts the projects encountered required them to change perspective. In all cases, the solution was to implement the minimum standardization necessary for the exchange of information across the existing systems, while leaving a maximum degree of self-organization to the local agencies and respecting local strategies and work practices. The projects offer examples of conflicting situations. In the *DocuLive* project, the conflict concerned the main technology partner's need for taking a worldwide perspective and the Norwegian consortium's need for a solution tailored to their work processes. In the *B-EPR* project, the standard under definition generated a solution that was too complex and did not fit the local practices. The problem was solved in the *SEP* project, which from its start decided to create a highly distributed solution. Finally, the *WFT* project met two main conflicts, since the initial solution was centralized although technically highly modular. The first conflict was between the devices/applications, which sought natural and autonomous evolution, and the main technology agency, which required a high level of robustness in its integration and Researchers can observe and document deeper control of the data flow process. The second conflict arose from the difficulty to coordinate the construction of a shared infrastructure to support integration at a national level, while a solution developed for a single hospital conflicted with the commercial interest of its provider. The sustainable solution was based on a minimal infrastructure guaranteeing a controlled data flow without imposing any constraints on single integrated devices/applications.

Altogether, these projects show that when huge integration initiatives have to be put in place, the development of technology is just one of the problems. Indeed, its development is strictly interlaced with external factors that follow a different dynamic. Researchers can observe and document these processes in longitudinal studies to increase awareness of this complexity. When they are involved in the process itself, they have to learn how to cope with them, irrespective of the required effort, in order to be able to play a role in making the solutions sustainable.

7

Learning across cultures and communities

Some phenomena that have an impact on many places in the world may invite and sometimes also oblige a research team to consider the issue of learning across cultures and communities. Migration from countries where poverty impedes the population from reaching an acceptable level of quality of life is such a phenomenon. Poverty may have different causes: authoritarian governments and/or corruption; climate change making the soil unproductive; small-scale wars (in most cases civil wars) that force people to escape from their homes and become refugees in hosting countries. These refugees seek places with higher levels of security because it is impossible for them to live in towns and cities where bombing and military attacks challenge their lives every day and destroy their minimal means of support. Also, and from a more positive perspective, students move from developing to more wealthy countries to receive a better education and improve their job opportunities when they return to their native places. This kind of student movement brings a new sensitivity and new research topics to the hosting universities. When looking for research funding opportunities that target the improvement of living conditions in developing countries, these universities can take advantage of the presence of these students in their research teams. These diverse phenomena generate contexts in which different cultures come into contact and pose diverse challenges.

Migrants and refugees, who have recently come to Western countries in large numbers, are confronted by the need to settle down and find a home in completely new surroundings. This includes the need to learn about and integrate into a new culture and community. Integration is increasingly interpreted not as a prescriptive set of norms to adapt to, but more as the inclusion of newcomers in a multicultural society where differences and mutual learning become a source of richness. The structural aspects of integration are concerned with equal access to all parts of everyday life, such as education, work, justice, institutions, and healthcare, whereas the social and cultural aspects of it focus on the negotiation of a common basis for living, rooted in shared

Future-proofing. Wulf et al., Oxford University Press.
© Carla Simone, Ina Wagner, Claudia Müller, Anne Weibert, and Volker Wulf (2022).
DOI: 10.1093/oso/9780198862505.003.0007

values and mutual respect. Both forms of integration can be reached through activities that facilitate the understanding and appropriation of the resources the new social ambit makes available. Literacy in the language of the hosting country is one of the first steps. This includes digital literacy, which is key to being able to fully participate in the hosting society.

Around the 1990s, the concept of 'computer clubhouses' was put forward in the United States to describe a place that fosters the IT literacy of specific groups of young people. A computer clubhouse is a setting where people can acquire IT competences through a situated and collaborative learning process that is based on a constructionist approach. Since then, computer clubhouses have spread around the world and their success is well documented in the literature (Resnick et al., 1998; Kafai et al., 2009; or, with an example of a computer clubhouse targeted at senior citizens in Australia, Boulton-Lewis et al., 2007). Learning in these places is often combined with initiatives aiming at network creation and community-building among club members. In Europe, the same idea was given the name 'computer club' and this has found different applications, especially as a place to teach young people IT skills through activities they find valuable, enjoyable, and worthwhile (e.g. Mumtaz, 2001).

7.1 Learning in intercultural computer clubs

In the same tradition but with a wider goal, in Germany the computer clubs evolved into 'intercultural computer clubs' (ICCs) when people took the US computer clubhouse concept and further developed it in response to the problems of migrant communities seeking to improve their living conditions in new, and often hostile, social environments. The ICC research line has been developed within the *come_IN* project by a group of researchers at the University of Siegen (Weibert and Wulf, 2010; Schubert et al., 2011; Weibert et al., 2017).

In Germany, political decisions had created a favourable climate for this research line: in 2004 previously separate discourses about different migration movements—of Germans as well as people of German ancestry from the East, guest workers from other European countries, and refugees—'merged into *one* public discourse on migration and its societal consequences' (Weibert and Wulf, 2010: 94). This development culminated in the German Bundestag and Bundesrat agreeing on new immigration laws, 'acknowledging on the highest political level that Germany is an immigration country and sees itself as such' (p. 94).

This discourse and the ensuing new law influenced the approach to creating ICCs. The research team set up different instances of ICCs in various German cities that had a high presence of migrant families. It also carried the idea to the completely different contexts of two Palestinian refugee camps and the Imazighen community in the High Atlas, Morocco. Hence, the concept of ICC was transferred within a single cultural framework as well as across cultures.

7.1.1 The ICCs in Germany

In Germany, transferability was based on the idea that ICCs had to become spaces where the integration of migrants and the hosting society could be promoted in a sustainable way. A first choice was to locate them at social institutions—typically, schools were chosen, as they were a common ground in the neighbourhood, at least for everyone who had children. Moreover, schools were able to offer human and material resources for the ICCs themselves. Over the years, a network of ICCs in various cities in Germany has grown, each having their own local characteristics but all sharing the same basic principles. A key decision was to be decidedly not like a school and not follow a fixed lesson plan, but instead to cover questions and topics that the young and adult participants brought in from the neighbourhood. Another choice was to encourage the active participation of children and adults in designing the programme, hoping that learning that had started in the ICC would be continued in the home and neighbourhood contexts (Schubert et al., 2011). Open-access policies are a characteristic central and common to all ICCs. Their members can join or leave without restrictions.

Forging close topical as well as institutional links with the neighbourhood is of major relevance to the ICCs. In the case of an ICC that had been set up in a quarter of one of the mid-sized cities in the Ruhr area characterized by a combination of high levels of migration and unemployment, the participating school was concerned with increasing the children's IT literacy and creating a welcoming atmosphere for the parents. It saw the ICC as a means of reaching this goal as well as promoting the adult level of education and integration.

One teacher runs the CC (also providing a link to the school), parents became involved. Pretty soon there was a waiting list because kids took the CC experience outside in the form of created artefacts—thus, it advertised itself. The school has a big entrance hall which is like a market place; with an atmosphere that makes the parents see the school as a place where they can go. The

> CC is part of that. Kids start in 2nd grade and leave in 4th grade. Every once in a while, older kids may return when they have a free day [...] Adapting the CC concept 'came naturally' when talking to people locally. Central to the idea is that it is all about that specific place.
>
> (AW Int, 20/03/2018)

Still in the same neighbourhood, another ICC, this one located in a community centre, directed its activities mainly towards women and their children. Here, computer literacy was seen as an important prerequisite for having access to various parts of public life, and the proposed computer club was expected to provide good help in this regard.

> All women are migrants, some of them Rom: the ICC focuses on their problems. The women are in fact family managers: they take care of the official letters, of bills, the kids, their problems in school, and so forth. They have many kids, they have a hard time finding a job because of their background. So part of the ICC is: they bring a letter, or ask to 'help me find a flat'. But we also do projects together. In one of them the women interview each other about their lives, producing audio files that they then combine with photographs in interactive digital stories.
>
> (AW Int, 20/03/2018)

Moreover, the women's original culture, which is based on male predominance within the family, limited their ability to take decisions by themselves. These boundaries were difficult for them to overcome. The club was perceived as a place where their independence was acknowledged (Aal et al., 2015).

> 'The elements you carry to a new CC are: it is open, free of charge, we want learning to be continued in the home without us; and we take the available tools with us' (AW Int, 20/03/2018). This openness reflects the fact that the research team has understood at an early stage the necessity to 'be in a process of constant negotiation with the neighborhood participants in order to best meet their needs. It lies in the nature of the concept that it does not imply guaranteed success' (Weibert and Wulf, 2010: 101). It expects its young and adult participants to be willing to be active and attentive at all times; 'to ensure that all voices and opinions equally be heard'; and to be prepared 'to step back from the expectation to "be entertained" or to "be educated"'.
>
> (p. 101)

In all ICCs, the activities were organized in weekly meetings and dedicated to joint work projects that involved all the participants in their specific role.

The children and their parents/relatives defined the topic of the project together, to motivate participation and ensure that the experience was perceived as useful. Negotiating a topic strengthened both intergenerational and intercultural integration, as it stimulated a mutual learning process among the participants, speaking to their experiences and valuing their skills.

Although all projects aimed at capacity-building in IT through the construction of IT artifacts, IT was not the starting point or the main focus. It was considered as an enabler of a cooperation process that helped participants to arrive at solutions that fitted their expectations. Indeed, the ICCs explored infrastructural choices consisting of interconnected laptops and software environments (such as *Scratch*), which were easy to appropriate and enabled a constructive attitude irrespective of the initial familiarity with IT. This choice was not only motivated by access to limited human, financial, and technological resources, but also responded to the basic idea of letting the projects emerge from the participants' creativity and expectations, without the influence of any (maybe) more powerful, but also distracting, technology (Weibert and Wulf, 2010; Weibert and Schubert, 2010). Common to the digital as well as the more tangible activities in the ICCs is a double learning process concerned with the appropriation of a given piece of hard- or software, as well as the negotiation of an agreement on its appropriate handling (Barricelli et al., 2011; Schubert et al., 2011).

With this structure, the ICCs have grown into a network that by now has outlived research funding structures and have formed an association to continue their work.

7.1.2 The ICCs in Palestine

The collective reflection on transferability was challenged when the research team, after some contact with Birzeit University in Palestine, decided to extend the *come_IN* project to a completely different environment: the Palestinian refugee camps.

The Palestine project started with Volker's colleague Ibrahim from the computer learning center at Birzeit University. The idea was to create a CC for refugees, who are often perceived as dangerous, and normal Palestinians and a proposal was made to the German Ministry of Foreign Affairs in 2011. Ibrahim found an NGO partner in the Jalazone refugee camp—which was funded for the purpose to collaborate with us. They received money from us to buy computers, set up a server (that was expensive), and provide a room. George (from Birzeit University) took over the responsibility but he didn't understand the concept at first. So he came to Germany to work on how to transfer the computer club idea to the Palestinian context.

(KA Int, 21/03/2018)

The very notion of integration that was at the basis of this initiative had to be contextualized:

The existence of the refugee camps more than 60 years after their establishment is politically a highly sensitive issue, since they symbolize the need and desire of the Palestinian people to return to their land which was lost to Israel in 1948. The positioning of the refugee camps' population within the Palestinian society is a complex one. While their continued existence is seen to be a political necessity ("right to return"), the in-camp population is looked upon in a demeaning manner and they are often regarded as second-class citizens. They are generally considered to be poorly dressed, behave aggressively, and use street language. People expect negative interaction with them due to perceived differences in morals, values, and attitudes. In general, members of the Palestinian middle class would typically prefer not to enter any of the refugee camps and very rarely do so. There are also severe economic and social obstacles to be overcome by refugee camp inhabitants who want to move out. So there is little social esteem and exchange with regard to the inhabitants of a refugee camp.

(Aal et al., 2014: 113)

Moreover, the administrative context of these camps influenced the decision regarding where to locate the ICC. All refugee camps, and in particular their schools, are managed by the United Nations Relief and Work Agency (UN-RWA). The limited resources and bureaucratic nature of UNRWA made it difficult to have relations with the local schools. So, other solutions had to be found.

The first ICC was located in the Jalazone camp (Aal et al., 2014), which is situated in the West Bank between the northern neighbourhood of Ramallah—the city where the Palestinian National Authority is located—and the location of Birzeit University. The refugee camp is also close to an Israeli settlement and a military outpost. This proximity generated an extremely tense atmosphere due to the frequent clashes between young people in the camp and Israeli settlers and soldiers. Moreover, the soldiers sometimes used the camp for military training purposes in full combat gear. These exercises involved the camp's residents and generated clashes and panic among them. This influenced the regular activities of the club and also resulted in the children not attending regularly. To make the ICC possible, the mediation of a local politician was instrumental to

> get in touch with the head of *Dima*—Association of Creativity. This newly formed organization was quickly registered as an NGO, just in time to host and run the computer club […] While the installation of the technical infrastructure and the introduction of weekly activities of the computer club were relatively quickly established, other issues appeared. The building is also used for other activities, e.g. as a gym, and was therefore very often crowded and busy, which often disturbed club sessions.
>
> (Aal et al., 2015: 115)

The selection of the tutors was facilitated by the fact that at Birzeit University students have to mandatorily perform 120 hours of community service. Most of the students choosing to support the ICC as tutors lived in the Jalazone camp. They perceived their tutoring activities as a means to gain visibility in the camp, although the work in the club was seen as more demanding than other community service options such as planting trees or working in a youth centre.

Another unexpected difficulty had its origin in the traditional structure of Palestinian schools, which are mono-educational—that is, classes are boys or girls only. The initial attempt to break this habit clashed with a 'spontaneous segregation': classes naturally divided into two homogeneous groups. The high number of children attending the school and this natural attitude led to the organization of separate sessions. However, this was not an optimal solution, since children of the first session liked to remain for the second one, thus recreating the same problems. Moreover, the tense atmosphere of the camp was reflected in the conduct of some children, who showed a lack of responsibility, aggressiveness, and unwillingness to cooperate in their work. As a consequence, more tutors than were present in the German clubs were necessary to organize and maintain some order in the children's activities.

The projects the children engaged in were similar to the ones in the German clubs. Storytelling implemented with *Scratch* was about 'the history of the camp and the hardships of living there'. The equipment available was also similar to that available in the German clubs. However, 'the lack of both professional maintenance and IT skills has led to virus issues, configuration issues, system slowdowns and similar sys-admin problems' (Aal et al., 2014: 117). In Jalazone, Facebook was used as a communication and data-storing infrastructure. Students and teachers of Birzeit University use it frequently and the children adopted it quickly to communicate with their tutors.

To enhance the experience of ICCs in the Palestinian environment, a second ICC (Yerousis et al., 2015) was set up in the Al-Amari camp that is located in the south-west quarter of Ramallah. The location of the camp is not directly influenced by the presence of the Israeli army but still suffers from the political tensions that are going on in the West Bank. In the camp, the post-school initiatives are managed by the Palestinian Child Center (PCC), 'a community outreach non-governmental organization that caters to school-age youngsters up to grade twelve. This center is seen as the only safe and productive place for in-camp school kids to participate in meaningful extra-curricular after-school activities' (KA Int, 21/03/2018).

For this reason, it was natural to locate the ICC in a free room that the PCC made available after completing some renovations. The PCC also provided available personnel to facilitate the ICC sessions. It was motivated by the practical failure of most of its educational initiatives and attracted by the reputation derived from collaborating with Birzeit University. The positive experience of the Jalazone camp suggested that the same technological configuration could be replicated. Additional laptops were provided by the university in the ambit of its summer camp programme for school-age children. This created some logistic problems but helped provide the necessary number of computers. Internet access was provided, after a PCC request, for one year by one resident who worked in a technology-providing company. The tutors were again recruited among the university students through a selection process that carefully checked their commitment and competences. In general, these students lived in Ramallah: unlike in the case of Jalazone, the public transportation was efficient and the trip safer. Most of them had been involved in community services (e.g. assisting disabled people) away from the camp but found the new possibility more attractive and formative. Since the recruiting was done in several rounds, the newcomers were involved in a well-established handover workshop, where they acquired sufficient information about the approach and activities of the club. To sustain their level of engagement, they received a laptop that they had to give back to the next cohort of incoming tutors. Specific attention was given to maintaining the continuity of work. This was done by involving the tutors in bi-monthly workshops that were designed to bring up, discuss, and mitigate important issues related to the work of the volunteers. A substantial amount of time in the workshops is spent on reflection regarding past work and future planning of activities in the computer club, while capitalizing on and re-using past practical experience and knowledge. Personal safety issues in the camps were a frequent subject of discussion.

(Yerousis et al., 2015: 3753)

The attendance of the children was still irregular since the camp was not immune from tensions and political conflicts related to isolated events (like the killing of a young Palestinian man resident in the camp, who had been partaking in protests in a nearby settlement), but less than in Jalazone.

The projects were influenced by the children's experiences in the camp. One of them was inspired by the dramatic experience of a tutor during an episode of the Intifada that caused her family to abandon their house and live through a period of violence. The memory of this experience combined with her university education in architecture inspired the idea of using the 3D printing facility made available by the University of Siegen to imagine and construct a model of an ideal house in which the children would like to live. Other projects concerned the construction of simple artifacts based on an electronic learning kit that was provided by Birzeit University.

The two ICCs in Palestine systematically increased the mutual learning between people living in the camps and people living outside (in this case, students), who before working in the ICCs had had limited knowledge of what it means to live in these camps, despite living nearby (Yerousis et al., 2015).

7.1.3 The ICC in Morocco

The experience acquired in the ICCs in Germany and Palestine was transferred to a quite different setting, where the goal was not to reach integration, but rather to explore the influence of IT on education in communities of transition. The target population was an Imazighen community which is not of Arabic origin (although most of its people are Muslims). The community lives in a valley in a region of the High Atlas in Morocco. This region underwent a radical change, including better access to the valley through newly built roads, internet access, increasing tourism, but also the broader political participation of Imazighen in Morocco. The research team spent several weeks in the field. One of them, an anthropologist, then lived in the community for nearly a year to observe how the local population made sense of the ICC and used the provided tools (Rüller et al., 2019).

The research team's strategy was to invest a considerable number of resources to acquire a deep understanding of the local conditions and to work with a local NGO that was very active in the valley:

> Right from the start it proved indispensable to work closely with a local NGO, which was focused on improving infrastructures in the valley, hosting cultural activities, empowering women and supporting children in their school career. This NGO had been working in the valley for the past 13 years and enjoyed the trust of community. This was reinforced by the fact that the founder and members all originated from the same valley. Being an integral part of the community, itself meant they had access to crucial knowledge about local social relations, local ways of proceeding and local concerns. This collaboration enabled us to gradually develop for ourselves a better understanding of the specific situation and setting.
>
> (KA Int, 21/03/2018)

This collaboration took place in the course of the project from 2015 to 2018. The first two years of the project were dedicated to building relationships with the local stakeholders in order to prevent possible resistance and conflicts. The local NGO played a relevant role, since it enjoyed an outstanding reputation. The research team benefitted from this reputation, as it helped them establish trust and build a good basis for communication with all the involved actors. The NGO was also able to solve difficult situations. Its members played the role of interpreters with the local people whose main language was Tamazight: only the men speak Arabic to different degrees, and children learn Arabic and French in schools. The members of the NGO speak English since they are involved in tourism initiatives; many of them also hold a bachelor's degree. The NGO was also in charge of finding the human resources for the organizational and tutoring tasks at the ICC and was useful in the solution of the legal problems related to the definition of the formal contract with the German university.

Unlike the German experience, the NGO wanted to have a voice in the construction of the ICC. It found it more appropriate to tailor the offer specifically to school children and to implement it as part of their educational programme. This was the outcome of a negotiation in which the two parties recognized their specific competences—knowledge of the technology versus knowledge of the local conditions.

The NGO already had a tutoring program in place, aimed at improving school children's education. This provided an excellent interface to combine existing practices with new media technology and the idea of the Computer club. The implementation took the form of enabling the tutors to expand their teaching to include ICT and playfully enrich it with project examples especially designed for children.

(KA Int, 21/03/2018)

In cooperation with the local partner, the decision was made to build a new house next to the school which would be accessible outside school hours.

In the second year of the project, the ICC started with a kick-off workshop which was open to both the children and the adults. This first hands-on experience made their generally low IT literacy evident. People in the community typically use smartphones to chat by means of Facebook and WhatsApp and to watch videos on YouTube. Some legal issues prevented the acquisition of technologies locally. Also, they were of a low quality. This is why all the equipment had to be brought from Germany and would have to be returned at the end of the project.

The experience in Morocco had many similarities to the ones in Germany and Palestine; however, some stark differences made this experience unique. Apart from the problems connected to local regulations, the main difference concerned the role of the local NGO, which shaped the activities in the ICC in line with its educational initiatives. It guided the children's choices and definitions of projects to work on. But it fully appropriated the ICC concept as an open, informal learning space and conveyed this idea to the teachers that were used to more traditional methods. In the words of one team member, the collaboration with the NGO was fruitful and also methodologically inspiring: in future attempts to build an ICC, the team should more systematically explore and leverage the local in place (KA Int, 21/03/2018).

7.1.4 Special challenges and measures taken towards sustainability

A key factor in ensuring the transferability of the ICC experience from one setting to another was that the research team, in close collaboration with the local stakeholders involved in the ICCs, regularly reflected on the experiences and consequent adjustments of problematic aspects. For example, through the experience of the first ICC in Germany, the need emerged for plenary opening and closing sessions to be held at each meeting to collectively plan activities and document their outcomes in order to create a shared awareness of the achievements and open issues. This became part of the usual way of conducting the subsequent ICCs. At times, the fragmented pace of the meetings left projects partially completed and the related material not well organized. This was problematic for the participating children and the authors themselves, as well as the newcomers or other people interested in similar projects, who had difficulties in reusing this documentation. Moreover, activities became difficult to plan.

To alleviate these problems, the research team dedicated special effort to identifying the needs of all the involved stakeholders. It resulted in a set of requirements, including that: the artifacts and the data produced by ongoing and past projects be shared, and their retrieval made simple and effective; the privacy of the collected information be protected through increasing levels of visibility; mechanisms be implemented for sharing expertise regarding technical solutions and how the children's groups are organized. These requirements also concerned the time in between the weekly meetings, making the interactions easy and extending access to the materials beyond these meetings. As the commercial solutions were inadequate, particularly in terms of usability and flexibility, the research team decided to construct a key ICC tool themselves: the community platform *come_NET* enables digital artifacts to be stored as well as shared, and allows networking across ICCs in different places. A gamification element supported the children in their first digital steps in this shared space, which was secured and only accessible from within the ICCs (Aal et al., 2018).

Overcoming some of the effects a different background/culture may have on integration is one of the main challenges in all ICCs. Above all, the wide spectrum of goals that ICCs aim to achieve in comparison to the more traditional CCs—which are mainly focused on acquiring technical competencies for their members— have to be confronted with the surrounding socio-political situation; these might create obstacles, if not explicitly oppose, these initiatives. Reaching these goals can be difficult when the surrounding political and social climate is less favourable—or becomes less so—as is the case in Palestine, which is characterized by experiences of conflict, hostility, and, at times, violence. Giving space to expressing these experiences in the ICC, as well as fostering a mutual learning process between the children living in the camps and people from outside, helped sustain the work of the ICCs in these difficult situations.

7.2 Summary

The goal pursued in the conception and set-up of the German ICCs was to promote the integration of migrant children and their families, with a focus on equal accessibility of the participants and, possibly, their neighbourhoods (structural integration). An important step in this process was to identify the needs of the participants and the support the ICCs were able to provide. A key concern was to promote mutual learning and understanding (cultural integration). The sustainability of these initiatives was rooted in both kinds of integration and, importantly, in a participatory action research approach designed to facilitate early and continuous 'ownership' of the different ICCs by the local people involved. The trust that was established not only laid the grounds for the continuation of the ICCs beyond the research project but also resulted in follow-up activities concerning key topics. This was the case in two cities, where the Siegen research team built a digital platform to help refugees and migrants upon arrival in a new place. Here, the previous experience with the ICCs provided the basis for actively involving refugees and migrants, as well as their volunteer and professional helpers. So, at the end of the PD process, a platform with a number of digital features was built (Weibert et al., 2019), which—again—outlived research project structures and was continued and kept by local volunteer associations.

Cultural differences generate challenging contexts when the technological interventions are located in non-Western countries that are involved in local conflicts and wars. These contexts add further complexity to the previous issues, since the researchers have to face a climate of insecurity and aggression and often also have to manage interactions with international institutions that operate in these problem areas. This was the case for the two ICCs located in Palestine. The two Palestinian contexts raised similar challenges, irrespective of their slight differences. In this country, the teaching system excludes the possibility of girls and boys staying in the same class; this has an impact on the teaching organization and its effectiveness. Also, the geo-political situation exacerbates the difficulty of searching and managing the resources necessary for the clubs' survival and creates strong emotional behaviours in the children and tutors, creating positive and negative effects that both need to be managed. Finally, the camps, although somehow connected in a network of mutual help, are perceived by the rest of the country as a separate world, a world with different values, expectations, and living experiences; as such, the very meaning of integrating the people living in a camp with the 'outside world' to reduce their isolation and increase their wealth is challenged by serious and conflicting political issues.

The ICC in Morocco encountered a different situation, which required a change of strategy. Setting up the ICC would not have been possible without the support of the NGO which acted as a mediator between the research team and the local community. Due to its mission and strong presence in the community, the NGO, which was fully committed to the vision of the ICC, was in a position to align its activities with the ICC's educational programme. A next step is 'planned to build and integrate a mobile MediaSpace to reach the far-off villages in the valley and the nomads living on top of the hills who hardly would visit the MediaSpace in the centre' (Aal et al., 2018: 17).

8

Projects in developing countries

8.1 Background: Issues in ICT for Development research

ICT for Development (ICT4D) research, which dates back to the early 1980s, is
used as an umbrella term for projects that make use of information and communications technology (ICT) to improve the living conditions of people in
so-called developing countries. For researchers that have been trained in Western countries, engaging in ICT research means entering a new and, in many
respects, different socio-cultural context. Emphasis is often placed on the relatively poor members of those societies, who may live in rural areas. In many
cases, being able to work in this context means having to engage with NGOs
and government institutions. A key insight from ICT4D research is that experiences made in other contexts and technology-based solutions that have
proven useful there cannot simply be transferred to a development environment. The kinds of technologies that are needed might be very different due to
the different levels of maturity of the technological infrastructures that are in
place. Moreover, understanding the everyday living conditions of people and
their practices may take time, requiring researchers to immerse themselves in
a local context that may be unfamiliar and not easily accessible.

Some key questions are: what is meant by development, innovation, and
democracy and how might developing countries benefit from ICTs (Kleine
and Unwin, 2009)? These questions received different answers in the course
of the evolution of ICT4D, from initial efforts aiming at innovative solutions
conceived 'on behalf of' the target communities (e.g. telecentres), to innovative solutions developed 'alongside' these communities to let them participate
in the design of innovation, and, finally, to innovative solutions developed
'within and by' the communities themselves (Heeks, 2008). These different approaches can coexist and may be useful, as long as it is clear that they serve
different purposes: defining general policies (e.g. pricing of technology); increasing the knowledge of the technology and its affordances and limitations;

Future-proofing. Wulf et al., Oxford University Press.
© Carla Simone, Ina Wagner, Claudia Müller, Anne Weibert, and Volker Wulf (2022).
DOI: 10.1093/oso/9780198862505.003.0008

or leveraging local capabilities to identify products and business models that are appropriate for a particular place. A crucial condition for achieving sustainable outcomes in the context of ICT4D research is a participatory approach that deeply involves users, allowing them to develop an understanding of their practices and needs, as well as multidisciplinary interactions with policy-makers and (local) experts to develop solutions for the different issues that are at stake.

A provocative and inspiring proposal to overcome unjustified and/or simplifying distinctions between 'there' (the developing countries) and 'here' (Western countries), and between the West and the 'Rest', has been made by Philip et al. (2012) in a call for 'postcolonial computing':

> Our goal is not simply to bemoan the problems that arise when methods fail to move easily and stably from one setting to another but to understand design efforts as always already processes of hybridization. While many translational design problems arise primarily in 'obvious' postcolonial contexts—in ICT4D projects, for example—our arguments are broader in scope. [...] we notice methodological innovations everywhere, suggesting commonalities across the West and the 'Rest'. On the other hand, incommensurability appears to mark relations not only across cultures but within them. As similarities and differences cross cultural boundaries, the boundaries themselves are called into question. Postcolonial Computing advocates a focus not simply on the negative critique of [a priori] constructions of cultural difference, but on the productive possibilities of 'difference' itself. The seams among differences are not simply a source of undesirable unevenness and aberration, but also sites of creativity and possibility.
>
> (Philip et al., 2012: 7)

As always, attention to diversity and the particularities of a specific context are necessary to avoid streamlining these into a narrowly defined set of presumed 'typical' difficulties and needs.

ICT4D projects take place in different national and cultural settings and they target rather different domains, hence they have to tackle different challenges. Rural ICT, for example, seeking to enhance existing rural development activities, may see reaching out to particularly poor segments of the farming population, training and capacity-building, fostering entrepreneurship, and encouraging ownership as major steps towards sustainability (e.g. Pade-Khene et al., 2011). Projects introducing ICT in healthcare institutions may have to focus on capacity-building for generating and documenting patient data

(Kimaro, 2006) but are also confronted with issues of scaling, as 'to make effective decisions on resource allocation for a district, the manager needs health data from all the clinics in the district and not just from an isolated and limited set of clinics from a preselected pilot area' (Sahay and Walsham, 2006: 186). Common issues of projects in developing countries are economic (or financial) sustainability, given the scarcity of resources and the often resultant dependence on donor institutions (Ali and Bailur, 2007), and, related to that, technological sustainability, which means that technologies have to be not only affordable but also easy to maintain and repair locally.

Walsham (2017) proposes several issues to consider in ICT4D research. While 'what is meant by development and how ICTs can contribute to it' (p. 25) is still open to debate, women and ICTs is a rather neglected topic, in spite of the key role of women in education, healthcare, agriculture, and entrepreneurship in many developing countries. Another area is that of 'new ICT enabled models', with initiatives to 'connect the excluded', text translations into local languages, and 'new social enterprise models', as well as uses of ICT as instruments of information-sharing and coordination in the context of disasters, conflicts, and emergencies as examples.

How to ensure the transformative potential of ICTs is at the heart of the projects we present and discuss in this chapter. The first example, which Nicola Bidwell (quoted as NB) has provided together with personal comments and visions, concerns work with a rural community in South Africa in two steps: the set-up of a shared audio repository and solar charging stations for mobile phones (Bidwell and Siya, 2013; Bidwell et al., 2013b; Bidwell, 2016), then the rolling out of a wireless mesh network (Rey-Moreno et al., 2012, 2013). It also touches upon worldwide initiatives for building community networks (Rey-Moreno et al., 2015b; Global Information Society Watch, 2018). The second example concerns issues connected with the repair and maintenance work ICTs require, based on fieldwork by Steven Jackson (quoted as SJ) and collaborators in Namibia and Bangladesh (Ahmed et al., 2015; Jackson et al., 2012, 2014).

8.2 Different paths to achieving sustainable outcomes

The projects in rural South Africa have been developed over time in the Mankosi community by a team that included several inhabitant researchers and were carried out in close cooperation with the tribal authority (TA). The community consists of almost 600 households belonging to twelve villages of different sizes, 'geographically scattered across about 30km^2 of very hilly and grassy land, scored by rivers and smaller water pathways, and dotted by the remaining clusters of indigenous forest and a generous sprinkling of grazing cattle' (Rey-Moreno et al., 2013: 3). There was mobile internet available at that time, but it was inaccessible due to affordability. Hence, people were not able to charge a phone or tablet. Some of the problems local people have in communicating within and across villages had become obvious in previous projects, where researchers had built a solar-powered Wi-Fi network between a rural clinic and hospital in order to trial health information prototypes (Tucker et al., 2007) and designed a digital storytelling application (Bidwell et al., 2010; Reitmaier et al., 2010, 2012). The team installed solar charging stations in Mankosi to power an audio repository for sharing voice recordings and communicating synchronously (Bidwell and Siya, 2013; Bidwell et al., 2014).

The design of the charging stations was strongly connected with ethnographic explorations of walking as a basic shared practice of people in rural Africa:

> [...] we elaborate on how walking is involved in knowing, perceiving, feeling, wanting, and using resources to orient thinking about links between walking and sustaining social and environmental infrastructures in rural Africa. We seek to show that designing to address electricity constraints cannot merely interpret walking and electricity use in Western concepts, such as about convenience [...], but must situate walking in local social relations and local meanings in rural Africa.
>
> (Bidwell et al., 2013b: 3)

Inhabitants decided where to install the charging stations. Bidwell et al. (2013b) described several routines they developed walking to (and from) the stations, when, for example, recording voltage and connecting phones, fixing stations, charging phones, receiving, returning, and organizing phones, and so on. They maintain that attention to these practices that evolved around the charging stations is key to understanding their acceptance and continuous use by the community:

> Inhabitants' practices in using the Stations interconnect with the many ways that their walking creates, expresses and 'reads' relationships in their social and physical environment. By walking, their bodies acquire literacies in the traces and rhythms that walking produces and reproduces. Thus, we posit

that walking was involved in the literacies that grounded various people's perspectives on sustaining the Stations.

(Bidwell et al., 2013b: 31)

As a next step, the researchers discussed the potential of a wireless mesh network with the TA and started creating an intranet on the basis of which the inhabitants installed solar-powered public phones in the villages (Rey-Moreno et al., 2012). This made free calls between public phones possible. Next, a not-for-profit locally owned cooperative, *Zenzeleni Networks*, was established in the community with the aim of reducing the cost of communication of the community members. Two surveys that were carried out in 2012–13 and 2013–14 showed: mobile phone ownership in the community had considerably increased; people still used the solar charging stations (at a low cost), although some of them had also installed their own solar energy solutions to charge phones; and a high proportion of people's disposable income was spent on a rather constrained set of mobile phone services. This made having *Zenzeleni Networks*, which is a CN, as a lower cost alternative particularly important (Rey-Moreno et al., 2016).

The sustainability of all these development efforts is always at stake in a poor rural community, and an enormous effort has been made to support appropriation and continuing use.

8.2.1 Robust technology

In a longitudinal multiple case study in rural Tanzania of telecentres and the (government) services they provide, Furholt and Sæbø (2018) contend:

> [...] we note that radio, an old and widespread technology, still is the most important information disseminator in rural Africa and that integrated solutions, based on the interaction between Internet and ICT, mobile phones, and radio are becoming increasingly important for bridging the digital divide. Simple systems based on robust technology that work in harsh conditions succeed.

(p. 11)

The projects in Mankosi also followed this insight, aiming to 'afford flexibly siting, moving, using, protecting, repairing and customizing the Stations' (Bidwell et al., 2013b: 33). The stations have been built using the cheapest components that could be locally bought—'it cannot be anything that is going to crash or you need an upgrade on or it's got to be like the car battery, the car charging thing, the plastic box that you get from a supermarket, so, component based' (NB Int, 3/6/2019). To facilitate maintenance, the installation had been constructed in a modular way, 'allowing each piece of the system to be disconnected for repair independently, e.g. a panel with a user console on top and the wiring beneath, and a separate breathable area to house the batteries' (NB Int, 3/6/2019).

When setting up technologies in poor countries, keeping them affordable and easy to maintain and repair are prime considerations. This also implies ensuring that spare parts do not have to be shipped from far away and can be assembled on site. Moreover, when building the wireless mesh network, practical questions concerning the physical constraints given by the terrain as well as security had to be considered, which required intimate knowledge of the community. For example, the households for the mesh nodes were selected according to a prediscussed set of constraints:

> Meet the physical constraints required by the wireless mesh nodes, e.g. electromagnetic line of sight among nodes considering the Fresnel zone; link budget calculations to check that the received power over a certain distance is above the receiver sensitivity, with a maximum distance of 1 kilometer, a constraint given the radio characteristics of the mesh router chosen; and the concept of a mesh node, with each node having to 'see' at least three others. [...] Provide security for the installation, to prevent theft of devices, specifically by having some kind of fence around the house or at least many people living in and around the homestead.
>
> (Rey-Moreno et al., 2013: 4)

The need to provide robust and reliable technologies may resonate well with donor agencies that have experience with ICT4D. However, it may be in conflict with ideas to bring technically innovative solutions to a potentially large emerging market. It also requires a sense of practicability and sensitivity on the side of developers that have been trained in a more affluent context. Electronic devices may not last long:

> Sometimes it is due to heat affecting the routers used in the case of Namibia, the dust in the computers, as is common in the rural areas of Zambia or Zimbabwe, or the fake Ethernet cables detected in Nigeria. The high cost and lack of local availability of rugged equipment prevents low-income communities from making use of them. Other materials required to set up a community

network, such as electrical and solar equipment, poles, etc., are not available in a common hardware store in Africa and [are] expensive to import.

(Rey-Moreno, 2017: 12)

As the initiative has matured, they have been able to install industry-standard transmission equipment for internet backhauls.

8.2.2 Capability-building

For it to be sustainable it needs to work across that, those things, it needs to be embedded in the community. It needs to empower and capacitate individuals in that community.

(NB Int, 3/6/2019)

A number of ICT4D researchers have taken up the notion of 'capabilities' that has been suggested by economist Amartya Sen. It is to do with what people are actually able to do and acknowledging the importance of agency (and not just 'utility') in the development process. Martha Nussbaum proposed an open-ended list of such capabilities which she sees as helpful in constructing a normative concept of social justice and as providing 'an attractive way of understanding the normative content of the idea of development' (Nussbaum, 2003: 34). In the context of ICT4D, the notion of capability—what people can do—relates to agency (the ability to use, maintain, repair, adapt, and further develop a particular technology) as well as to learning (being able to use the skills acquired in one project to set up new projects, ICT-related or not).

The ICT projects in Mankosi have been successfully taking care of all these aspects. First of all, both the original audio repository and wireless mesh network project not only employed a local champion but a network of local research assistants that took over a variety of roles. The approach was to provide training to appointed members of the community, including transportation and food:

In the initial training sessions, we covered the theory and then moved on to hands-on practical exercises, e.g. working with wood to construct custom boxes to hold the batteries, installing and dimensioning solar and storage systems, building the connection panel for the electrical installation, configuring and installing the routers, and aligning their antennae. However, once a first 'sample' was constructed by a trainer, e.g. a solar battery storage box or Mesh

Potato pole mount, the trainees implemented additional units by themselves under the watchful eye of a trainer.

(Rey-Moreno et al., 2013: 5)

In this way, the project built a competent local maintenance team, and end-user training was also carried out by locals. As the initiative has matured and expanded, members of the cooperative have needed to gain increasingly sophisticated business and legal expertise, and part of the work of *Zenzeleni Networks* is to ensure local people have access to support and mentorship in this.

Capability-building activities had even more far-reaching results. One of the PhD students involved in the team set up a CN (*Zenzeleni Networks*) in South Africa:

And that's what commenced it. So he set up this community network, facilitated them to set up a community network which is now, that started in 2013. I think in 2017 it connected to the internet. It's the first not for profit internet service provider in South Africa. By becoming a cooperative it has changed South African law to make it legal to have for non-profits to have spectrum licenses […]. And it has absolutely galvanized the whole movement in Africa.

(NB Int, 3/6/2019)

Among the other success stories from the projects are: one of the local researchers from the village, who was mentored in the project, wrote about work done in the projects from her own perspective (Kaschula and Dlutu, 2015) and then went on to do a PhD. Another local researcher established the operations of a social welfare NGO in Mankosi (https://www.onetoonechildrensfund.org/enable)

which is called 'Mentor Mothers'. Basically, she works with mothers to help them in preventative healthcare scenarios. Because there is a lot of people that die quite young there. That sort of issues. Poverty-related healthcare issues. So, there was this process aspect that I felt good about because this had a different level of sustaining.

(NB Int, 3/6/2019)

At first, the connection of the people in Mankosi, through an intranet between the twelve villages, helped with planning meetings and joint decision-making. The second stage, full internet access at an affordable price, was used 'as we all like it, socializing, entertainment' (NB Int, 3/6/2019). But it also had more last-ing effects, as Bidwell and Jensen (2019) found out in their follow-up impact research in 2018:

> […] students who were on work placements were really very adamant and they said you know, our English has improved. Now we have better English, we can work in the hospitality area. Why has your English improved? Because I can stay on YouTube, look up an English word […]. I don't feel panicked […] So, what was beneficial for them was not frantically worrying that airtime was going to run out or maybe they needed to save some airtime for something else […]. And they had time to learn. They had time to look after their kids, do that, come back do a bit of learning […] and getting employment. […] Then there were other stories about people finding long lost relatives, very, very pointing stories. In that time which I suppose it probably was seeded when I started there but then gained momentum over the years. The number of youngsters going to university in that area has gone from one in five years to last year it was about twenty.
>
> (NB Int, 3/6/2019)

An article in Saab News from 29 February 2020, 'Mankosi in Eastern Cape develops SA's first community-owned internet service provider', quotes two students:

> Student Phatheka Siya says the network helped her apply for university on-line. 'The network helped me to apply online in university with other group of students. We were from high school then and it still helping us because we are able now to look for internships online while we are here. It helps us also to look for business opportunities to start our own business and it's much affordable than the other networks.'

> Job seeker Bongiwe Dlutu says the network assists her as she doesn't have to go to town to apply for jobs. 'The network is assisting me as a freelancer because I don't have to go to town to apply for jobs. I search for jobs online and do freelance online. I use the network before freelancing to apply for job opportunities for people in the community to apply for tertiary institutions,' Dlutu explains.

These long-lasting benefits for people in the community reflect the list of ca-pabilities that Martha Nussbaum proposed as fundamental entitlements that need to be endorsed to achieve social justice in a society.

8.2.3 Financial sustainability

In a study of digital inclusion projects in developing countries, Madon et al. (2009) found that 'most projects are started with funding from local or central government, aid agencies, or NGOs. However, long-term financial sustainability implies the need to develop indigenous funding sources and sustainable revenue streams' (p. 96). In a literature review of ICT4D projects, Chipidza and Leidner (2017) argue that 'power asymmetry among stakeholders might increase the resource dependency of beneficiary communities on donors, and might lead to the former resisting further ICT interventions' (p. 1). In their view, resource independence is key to reducing the power asymmetry between stakeholders and local communities (see also Chipidza and Leidner, 2019).

In Mankosi, the TA proposed to charge a low rate for intra-community calls as a way to make the mesh network financially sustainable, 'so that a local support team can make a living from maintaining, and even expanding, the network' (Rey-Moreno et al., 2013: 3).

> So, then they said, ok we are going to charge three rands per charging and this is going to go into a kitty for when things need to replaced. This was still forty percent cheaper than the alternative charging, so it was still cheaper for people to do it.
>
> (NB Int, 3/6/2019)

As the research team worked directly with the community members and not with NGOs or government institutions, there was more freedom to develop a business model that fitted the needs and expectations of the community (Rey-Moreno et al., 2012). In fact, rates were fixed by the community and the billing system was codesigned with them (Rey-Moreno et al., 2015b). Another step for generating additional and, as it turned out, indispensable income was to look for businesses in the area that would use the internet and pay for it:

> The way that they do it is they provide higher quality, faster internet to two or three medium sized businesses in the area. At a price which slightly undercuts competitors, but it only slightly undercuts competitors. And they buy bulk internet at the fastest speed [...] And then the money they make as a profit from that then goes back into the system to enable them to charge a ridiculously small amount to the communities. The community contribution really doesn't, it only, it doesn't really sustain it's the, this mixed model of getting medium sized enterprises to offset it.
>
> (NB Int, 3/6/2019)

8.3 Community networks

Community networks pre-date the commercial internet:

> They have their roots in the early email and electronic bulletin board systems (BBSes) that emerged in the mid-1980s. These systems grew into networks, which were adopted by enthusiasts as technologies that could be easily built with dial-up modems and the newly emerging, low-cost personal computers. These networks were also adopted by social activists who immediately saw their potential for improved organising, knowledge sharing, and awareness raising.
>
> (Song et al., 2018: 7)

Today, with smartphones delivering powerful generic services as well as more specific apps, community networks offer an essential infrastructure for people's lives, in particular in developing countries. *Zenzeleni Networks*, one of the main outcomes of several projects in the Mankosi community, resulted from the decision of the community members to organize themselves as a cooperative. This was necessary in order to benefit from formal licence exemptions and be able to provide services legally.

> There are all these community networks popping up all over the places. Now the reason they need it because in rural areas, it's not like in Europe where you have often regulation of spectrum, is closely tight to anti-monopoly rules and in Africa we haven't got quite such good anti-monopoly issues and what this means is if an area isn't profitable for a mobile provider to provide to, it will provide very poor service and it is relatively, incredibly expensive for people. Phenomenally expensive. Some of the most expensive internet access in the world. So this is the reason it's needed.
>
> (NB Int, 3/6/2019)

Making the CN legal, financially sustainable, and affordable has already made a difference in people's lives, providing access to resources that would otherwise not be available and new income streams:

> Their sustainability in a way is well beyond the product. It's changed law, it's developed people's careers, it's enabled them to start to build little apps, wind cells for their own purposes, all at the point to humble level at the moment.
>
> (NB Int, 3/6/2019)

The indigenous community networks in Mexico are another outstanding example. Talea de Castro—'The Mexican village that got itself talking' (BBC, 15/10/2013)—is one of them. The Talea Cellular Network was created using technology from a US-based company and expertise from a non-profit organization called Rhizomatica when villagers understood that the main network provider in Mexico would not be installing a mobile phone antenna for them (see also the report by Bidwell and Jensen, 2019).

> They have their own local GSM mobile service where they confirm other members of the community, send texts to other members of the community and then for an extra charge phone out of the community to elsewhere in Mexico which they couldn't do none of that before.
>
> (NB Int, 3/6/2019)

Moreover, 'This equipment belongs to the whole community. Now we can be autonomous, self-sufficient and self-reliant without having to ask to be breastfed by anyone!' ('The Mexican village that got itself talking'—BBC, 15/10/2013). Before that,

> they had to go to a satellite phone in the center of the little nearby town and then they had to book an appointment for call [...] So they told me stories about how by being able to have their mobile phone services they were able to pick up a man who had a heart attack in the field and bring him back and get him to the clinic in time. Because they could now call for a taxi to come and pick up the man rather than anything else. People told me about managing to go and see loved ones before they passed away they said, I mean, a large number of save your life situations by this connectivity. And then more privacy they said was very valuable and the also huge impacts to the local businesses because now rather than walking all the way from your village to the nearest shop which was two or three hours walk.
>
> (NB Int, 3/6/2019)

For this to happen, a certain legal provision concerning spectrum regulation was important (Global Information Society Watch 2018: 179):

> Rights to spectrum, like you have a right to land and it's the only country in the world and it's all based on these indigenous groups doing this [...] So, there's, you know, profound sustainability over an idea because what it now

does, when you start moving regulators and policy makers in those directions then other sustainable things that we can't even imagine will come out.

(NB Int, 3/6/2019)

Another remarkable example is the Ugandan CN. Battery Operated Systems for Community Outreach operates in Northern Uganda—'the worst place in the world to be a child: remote, war-affected, culturally scoured, and deeply isolated over more than two decades of brutal insurgency' (Global Information Society Watch 2018: 239). It puts emphasis on fostering economic develop-ment and reaching out to adolescent refugees, offering them opportunities to connect and find material and spaces for learning (Bidwell and Jensen, 2019).

They had a lot of local innovations. And empowering people to sell their agri-cultural products at fair prices rather than being ripped off, so they would consult market information and then tell people in that villages 'oh look, you know the price of sorghum is this. The price of rice is this. Don't let the guys coming to trade with you and undercut you.'

(NB Int, 3/6/2019)

A lot of the discussion about community networks focuses on sustainable ac-cess, which refers 'to the ability of any user to connect to the internet and then stay connected over time' (Oghia, 2017: 26), with the pressing and not easy to resolve problem of how to power it and keep it operational, which Oghia (2017) defines as among the main barriers to scalability and lowering costs. *Zenzeleni Networks* provides one example of how to possibly achieve long-term sustainability of access.

8.4 Designing with repair and maintenance in mind

An interview study with ICT4D practitioners and end users about the technology-related challenges they face found: 'These practitioners consistently suggest that electricity is the most important hardware-related concern, followed closely by cost, robustness/ruggedness, and ease of mainte-nance/repair' (Hosman and Armey, 2017: 648). Houston and Jackson (2017) point at 'a growing body of ICTD work that affirms the value and complexity of repair work in Southern contexts, and the deep skill and ingenuity associ-ated with repair under what are in some ways technologically marginalized and resource-constrained environments' (p. 209).

'Maintenance and repair are in fact essential to sustaining and keeping infrastructures going [...] and that work needs to be accounted for and compensated and attended to' (SJ Int 19/4/2019). Steven Jackson thinks of maintenance and repair as important aspects of innovation, also arguing that 'big players' in the computer industry spend much time not on developing new types of software but on repairing—fixing—code. Moreover, most of the technologies we use are old or ageing, broken, and in need of maintenance and repair. In developing countries, the additional problem is to do with the fact that just 'throwing away' a piece of malfunctioning technology may not be an option, and there is an urgent need for spare parts. There is a growing body of literature on e-waste and its toxicity, but also the possibilities of reusing materials and parts (e.g. Davis et al., 2019).

8.4.1 The projects

Coming from an ethnographic background, Steven Jackson and his colleagues engaged in two projects investigating practices of repair and maintenance in rural Namibia and in Dhaka, Bangladesh. The first project focused on the national Tech/NA! programme, a nationwide computerization initiative that supported the set-up of labs and training centres at the Rundu College of Education, two teacher resource centres, and several senior secondary schools. Another associated initiative was 'Computers for Kwando', which was started by US Peace Corps volunteers. Computers were shipped in and set up in smaller regional schools. Fieldwork on computing practices in the area, most of it carried out by former Peace Corps volunteers, brought 'the maintenance and repair angle' to the attention of the researchers 'because it was the clear central point of failing in the formal development project' (SJ Int, 19/4/2019). Nobody had thought of repair of broken computers as a key issue:

> The irony in that case is that when things broke the only recourse they had was to send all the computers back to the capital, to Windhoek [...] but at the same time there actually was a local repair sector that the former dimensions of the development program, the contracts basically, excluded. So, when they set up this program, this is the tragedy of that story and many of these stories, that the skills and the expertise are sometimes there in the local environment but they are excluded by the formal institutional setup [...] the only thing you can do is send it back to the capital. Well, it's two months to get things back to the capital and they often get further broken on route or lost or they disappear. So,

effectively nobody sends anything back to the capital and if they do it rarely comes back.

(SJ Int, 19/4/2019)

The researchers looked into the practices of a great number of mostly small private repair shops, including an informal repair market in Rundu and the Rundu Institute of Computing, documenting the activities and skills people had built through years of learning, mostly through apprenticeships, which enabled them to handle computer problems on top of repairing broken cell phones, which was their main business. This included reusing and recycling parts.

The main researcher in the project in Dhaka, Bangladesh, started his work by participating in a training programme at a local mobile phone repair training centre, followed by a three-week apprenticeship at another repair workshop:

So he spent a lot of time actually learning the techniques that various kind of repair techniques and cleaning techniques and short-cut techniques and so what we were centered on there was really the forms of skill and innovation, as we would call it innovation, that we saw happening in that environment [...] what we found is that there is actually enormous skill, there is enormous skill, people skill, that is not accounted for in that understanding of technology in the world. And it lived in this environment and we were really interested in that, that was really what we wanted to see. And so that was the center of that work. It was really trying to understand and document what are the practices that are going on an affirming this is skilled technological work.

(SJ Int, 19/4/2019)

Like in rural Namibia, most local IT users were connected to small repair shops, some of them operating individually, others cooperating, some of them part of the Gulistan Underground Market.

8.4.2 Making skills visible, learning

The wide range of skills that repairers acquired in both places—rural Namibia and Dhaka—mostly through apprenticeship relations, not only allowed them to build up highly specialized expertise but also paved the way to innovation. Jackson et al. (2014) provide three perspectives on repair work—repair as craftwork, repair as collaboration, and repair as creative repurposing—describing a variety of practices undertaken by repairers. Like Houston (2019), who has done similar work in Kampala, Uganda, they stress the importance of collaboration and learning for building repair knowledge. Repurposing is a particularly noteworthy practice, as it points to a potential for innovation:

> By sorting and redirecting the flows of broken and partially functioning devices (some on to recyclers, some back to other fixers) bhangaris play a crucial role in the material flows and networks by which repair activity in Dhaka is accomplished. This work too requires talent, skill, and creativity—to select and buy the right devices at the right price, to cultivate an appropriate network of buyers and sellers, and to see such objects through to their final destination, whether by recirculating them into other repair activities or on to Chinese recyclers for disposal.
>
> (Ahmed et al., 2015: 4)

This has also been observed by Wyche et al. (2015), who, through drawing exercises with repairers of mobile phones in rural Kenya, tapped this potential for innovation. Repairers in this study pointed out a mismatch between mobile phone design and the context of use, mentioning dirt or sand getting inside the phone and damaging the parts that receive and emit sound, broken screens, and so forth. Wyche et al. (2015) argue for 'incorporating local innovators' expert knowledge into the technology design process' as well as 'supporting the local design and manufacture of mobile phones in rural Kenya' (p. 471). Jackson et al. (2012) point to the importance of acknowledging what they call 'broken-world thinking' as a viable way to sustain technologies in developing countries. They cite the owner of a phone and computing repair shop in Madagascar as an illustration of this thinking:

> Here's how Rakoto describes his introduction to his current line of work: 'When cellphones first came to Madagascar, I was curious to see how they functioned, and how they might break. So I bought one, threw it into the river here and then took it apart to see how the water and soil damaged it, and how it might be fixed'.
>
> (Jackson et al., 2012: 115)

Engineering education in developing countries emulates the focus of Western universities on theoretical engineering knowledge, instead of helping students to develop and heed more practical skills:

It neglects many of the things that might be specific to a Bangladeshi context some of that tactile engagement and some of the appreciation and understanding, not only for the production of the new innovation or the next or new form of code. But also, that maintenance work was part of the process, that kind of physical and material anchoring both important and very valuable. So it's a way of sort of balancing how we approach different kinds of learners as well so that computing [...] is not only for the people who think about the world in this abstracted only numbers, only code kind of way but also has room for kind of a greater dimension of craft and technical engagement.

(SJ Int, 19/4/2019)

8.4.3 Legal and policy issues

While for the survival of community networks it was crucial to get formal licence exemptions and be able to provide services legally, the need for repair and maintenance requires taking additional conditions for sustainability into account. Jackson et al. (2012) point out 'the stubborn tendency to over-privilege artifacts or systems to the neglect of the supporting contexts in which their coherence and efficacy is sustained. This too is a basic lesson of social worlds scholarship' (p. 115).

One of the key legal and policy issues is to do with what has been called 'planned obsolescence'—that is, intentionally shortening the lifespan of a product to force customers to replace it. Another issue is to do with the need for fair repair legislation, which started in the car industry:

There's a number of principles that run behind it one of them is things like free and non-discriminatory access to schematics, right? Like if a company has a schematic of a phone that shouldn't be locked behind commercial walls or proprietary walls. Companies often want to do that because they often want to find ways of extracting additional value in the practices of repair

[...] people who have brought lawsuits against people who wanted their repair manuals online using copyright. They'll say, 'This is copyrighted, you shared it online, you didn't have permission, we are going to sue you'. So, there is a variety of, what I would call closure mechanisms. They are trying to shut down and manage and control this world'.

(SJ Int, 19/4/2019)

8.5 Conditions for sustainability in research

There are a number of issues that concern both sets of projects we are discussing here: a tension between the requirements of academia and funding
institutions in the long-term sustainability of ICT-based solutions; the challenges connected with operating as an outsider in another social world; the
need for and ability to access transnational information as a critical issue; and,
finally, the (lack of) inclusion of women.

8.5.1 Academia versus the requirements of researching in another social world

Growing an academic presence in Western countries is one of the significant
tensions for researchers to cope with when working in developing countries.
While a standing in academia requires lots of publications in top journals and
conferences, working in a project in places such as rural Namibia requires
engaging deeply with the people to gain their trust, getting involved with
myriad practical issues and, above all, having ample time. There may not be
academically valued results to report on after the first project year, and many
practicalities may not necessarily add up to making a novel argument.

As concerns the work on managing maintenance and repair, this is not a
highly ranked topic for funding institutions:

> [...] the work we do as academics, we get funded to say we are going to do
> new stuff, right? [...] but if I want to get a grant from our national science
> foundation I can't say 'Look there's this long running program of work that
> I want to keep going because the value here is the long running program',
> right? The value is that we have, I mean, god we even had ten years' studies,
> we would do wildly far ahead and I feel, but that's not the story you can tell
> to institutions because institutions, grant institutions want to hear a story of
> the new.
>
> (SJ Int, 19/4/2019)

Often, the only possibility is to look for small spin-off grants 'that is going to get
us started on that and we are going to see if we can build from that to something
a little bit larger once we have some better results' (SJ Int, 19/4/2019).

Another issue is connected with the role of an outsider:

So even though I live in Namibia, or my colleagues live in Namibia, we're still outsiders. So I have a village or I have a community network ten minutes away and I know a lot of people in that village. But I still, I'm not part of that village. I don't sleep here, walk here, be part of it. I mean I can go there every day but I'm still not, I still don't know what it feels like to wake up at five o'clock in the morning to go and get water like I did in that walking, whenever I decided that I wanted to live that life to try to feel that life. So most of us don't do that.

(NB Int, 3/6/2019)

This means that it is essential to co-opt local researchers into the team and support the kind of capacity-building that Nicola Bidwell describes. Also, Steven Jackson stresses regarding his research:

in every instance [...] it has relied on local partners and work and collaborators, sometimes students with deep knowledge of the area and connections in the area. And there's never, I have never done a study where, that wasn't available. So, I have never just kind of showed up at a place without a collaborator who had those connections [...] yeah I'll see you for the next two or three years and then the grant will be done and I'll never hear from you again. I think people get that, I mean, I think that really challenges our ability to have responsible relationships with communities and partners and actors out in the world.

(SJ Int, 19/4/2019)

Apart from the fact that local experts are crucial for having access to people and their way of living and thinking—e.g. the 'broken-world thinking'—building relationships is also to do with the social responsibility of researchers who engage in often deeply participatory endeavours with practitioners in other social worlds (Robertson and Wagner, 2012).

8.5.2 Access to transnational information as a critical issue

Respect for local knowledge and ways of thinking does not preclude the fact that local researchers and local practitioners may need access to a wider community of practice:

To what extend does a rural person who is fixing things, what level of sophistication of devices must you connect into a wider community of practice to share information to fix things. [...] As soon as you get to software or devices or electronic components [...] that are more complicated and with the constant addition of new components. How do people connect into the wider knowledge systems and sharing knowledge about things?

(NB Int, 3/6/2019)

On the one hand, local experts build their own networks, as in the case of Uganda, where repairers have developed their own ways of sharing information that allow them to do their work:

There is sensitive information system across WhatsApp. So every time they opened up a phone or opened up an amplifier and found a new component. They take a picture of it and build up a prepositive of questions where nearly a thousand different repair guys in Uganda look at their WhatsApp 'oh I, now that component. Ok what you got to do'.

(NB Int, 3/6/2019)

In her study of mobile phone repair work, Houston (2019) mentions two important sources of information: online libraries of firmware files and the virtual community of technicians known as the 'GSM Forum', which contains 'stories' about solutions found in particular situations.

The GSM hosting forum is a huge online user chat forum, which specialises in how to fix and repair problems in mobile phone handsets. It covers virtually all mobile phone models, and users post detailed descriptions—often literally pictures—of problems or malfunctions, as well as similarly detailed instructions on how to fix mechanical or software problems. The forum embodies an enormous, global, crowd-sourced and user-driven knowledge base, which provides valuable and practical knowledge to people interested in repairing mobile phones.

(Toivanen et al., 2012: 29)

However, the circulation of knowledge from the 'official' centres is restricted to particular accredited locations of repair. This makes it difficult for small, independent repair shops to get access to knowledge

about the design of mobile devices, strategies for repair, firmware files and tools to intervene into embedded software systems [...] because information is routinely withheld by manufacturers who choose to share this information with particular repair businesses through relationships of 'authorisation'.

(Houston, 2019: 131)

8.5.3 (Lack of) inclusion of women

A widespread experience is that women in developing countries, although responsible for health, education, agriculture, commerce—areas where ICTs have been introduced—and often also for family finances, participate much less in technology-related activities. For example, they use the CN and hotspots less than men and usually do not engage in repair work that may provide them with an important independent income. Nicola Bidwell argues that the inclusion of women as active participants in these and other activities may be a condition for long-term sustainability.

> My particular position which is part informed by data and part informed by feminist influences is that unless you have an inclusive platform you may run the risk of not being sustainable. So, evidence from data about that is an intervention in India where women can't use their local Wi-Fi services whichever those are they might be connected to the internet or they might because of very extreme social constraints that don't give them safe access to places, private access or cultural issues don't let them go to those places. Those women, in particular the younger women, start to use the mobile operators because they have no choice.
>
> (NB Int, 3/6/2019)

For example, Rosner and Ames (2014), who have studied practices of repair in Paraguay and California, observed gendered ways of addressing the work of repair:

> [...] by articulating differences between material practices of craft and technology tinkering, participants distinguished male and female competencies and reaffirmed divisions between gendered metaphors for technology design, e.g., low-tech and high-tech, soft and hard, gentle and rough, shy and fearless, and so on.
>
> (p. 329)

These gendered views and practices are not restricted to developing countries, as shown, for example, in a study by Dunbar-Hester (2008), who studied a group that tinkered with and built radio hardware: 'They are also concerned with combating the gendered nature of hardware skills, yet in spite of their efforts men tend to have more skill and familiarity with radio hardware than women' (p. 201).

Looking into the participation of women in the *Zenzeleni Networks* in Mankosi, South Africa, Hussen et al. (2016) stress that, on the one hand, women are excluded from meetings and decision-making. However, 'when it comes to working on a daily basis to materialize the goals, the task is easily delegated to the women as part of their domestic role' (p. 19). Changing these culturally ingrained gender inequalities is not something that can be done in one project. With respect to community-based telecoms, Bidwell et al. (2019) state:

> Men dominate global discourse in telecoms techs, policy and lobbies and advocacy about regulation […], which influences perspectives on what makes telecoms viable and sustainable, and what labor is valued […]. Women are often underrepresented in CNs' decision-making […] and undertake labor that is invisible or not as highly valued as software and network engineering.
>
> (p. 3)

8.6 Summary

The projects discussed in this chapter represent only a small part of the work done under the umbrella of ICT4D research, and they may not even be typical. However, some sustainability issues that are of more general significance stand out.

The contexts that these projects share are the lives of poor people, some of them in remote villages, in cultures that place a strong value on community. As ready-made technologies often do not 'fit' these contexts and resources are scarce, there is a need and also talent for improvisation and 'making do' with what is at hand.

In such an environment, a participatory design approach is essential, as it allows design solutions to be anchored in the life world of the participating community, as well as enabling local capability-building, both of which help pave the way towards achieving sustainability. Key to participatory design in a community, such as Mankosi, South Africa, is that all decision-making is in the hands of the community and/or its elders. Capability-building concerns the involvement of local researchers that may be able to take a project further, supporting appropriation and planning follow-up activities. It also means developing the skill base for people that are capable of maintaining and repairing the technologies in place and/or providing training.

A participatory design approach in connection with capability-building enables the community to take ownership of a technical solution. One of the unresolved problems in this context is the inclusion of women that, although responsible for most aspects of daily life, participate much less in technology-related activities.

Another major issue is financial sustainability and, associated with this, the need to become independent of donor organizations. The technologies that have been installed in Mankosi, for example, are made from components that are available in a supermarket and hence cheap, and the technical solutions are robust as well as relatively easy to maintain and repair locally. Another cornerstone of the project's sustainability was the decision to create a business model together with a billing system, both of which have been worked out with members of the community and are supported by them. This, together with efforts to create additional incomes, allowed the community to exercise its ownership independent of donor organizations or government aid, which may have interfered with its ideas of how to maintain and use *Zenzeleni Networks*.

In this context, fighting for legal provisions and taking the required organizational measures may be necessary, with a view to being able to provide services legally and keep them affordable to those who most need them.

A key insight derives from research revealing the ecology of repair shops found in many developing countries that has developed independent of particular ICT4D projects, contributing to the sustainability of IT-based solutions. This repair culture is based on learning through apprenticeship, collaborations, and techniques of 'creative repurposing'. It expresses the 'broken-world thinking' without which sustainability would hardly be achievable. It rests on the availability of huge amounts of e-waste and the willingness of many to access and sort this waste, disregarding its potential toxicity, as a strategy for survival under harsh circumstances.

9

Research projects in IT service companies

Industrial innovation requires a constant research effort that companies organize in various ways according to their dimension, strategies, organizational structure, and available resources. Boutellier et al. (2013) offer a survey of the research structures and strategies of 'best-in-class companies' in various sectors such as the pharmaceutical, food, chemical, automotive, electronic, and software sectors. The survey is interesting, although not fully up to date, as these companies are in constant transformation.

Usually, research activities are conducted within the business units of the company, as their role is to have an immediate impact on the production of the goods or services that characterize the company's mission. In addition to this, big distributed, often multinational, companies typically have their own research laboratories or centres, with a well-defined organizational structure. These labs are specifically funded, and their members are rewarded according to criteria that are distinct from the usual productivity parameters applied in the business units of a company.

In general, research centres conduct their activities in the scientific domains characterizing the products or services of the hosting company. In addition, they may support the related production processes in order to make them more effective. This is typical of companies working in the IT sector, whose products are intrinsically linked with the business processes of their clients. The experience acquired while improving the internal business processes to manage IT products or services can then be leveraged to make their commercial offer more complete and more appealing to clients.

In order to be able to innovate their products or services and the related processes, industrial research centres need to align their activities with the leading-edge research conducted within academia and public research institutions. One of the criteria widely adopted for rewarding researchers in this context is the number of publications in top-level scientific conferences and journals that constitute the main occasions where academic/public and

Future-proofing. Wulf et al., Oxford University Press.
© Carla Simone, Ina Wagner, Claudia Müller, Anne Weibert, and Volker Wulf (2022).
DOI: 10.1093/oso/9780198862505.003.0009

industrial research meet and mutually influence each other (Cohen et al., 2002). In highly technological ambits, the acquisition of patents defines an additional measure of research performance (Arundel, 2001). The consultancy of public researchers in industrial projects and the participation of industrial research centres in publicly funded research projects are other ways of letting the two worlds cooperate on shared research topics. This requires specific research programmes as well as regulations concerning intellectual property rights that make the collaboration more complex and sometimes more problematic to achieve.

It is not uncommon that additional research activities take place in the various distributed business units of a big company with a dedicated research centre. This raises the problem of the relationships between these two research ambits, which often have different goals and approaches: to put it simply, the former are more oriented to the future and to innovative solutions, while the latter are more oriented to the present and dealing with its contingent issues, aiming at directly applicable solutions. Strategies are needed to solve this problem, since the collaboration between the two ambits is vital for a productive transfer of knowledge and experiences between them, and ultimately also to justify the existence of the research centre itself. As we shall see in the projects presented in this chapter, the different paces of the two research ambits have an impact on joint projects and the sustainability of research results.

This chapter presents six projects that have been part of the research efforts of two research centres: three projects at the former Xerox Research Centre Europe in Grenoble (France) and three at the IBM Research—Almaden (California). They all concern the development of solutions in response to issues raised by either the hosting company or some specific business units. The projects cover different business activities and offer a solid basis for discussing how industrial research is conducted to achieve this goal in various contexts.

The *Print Awareness Tool* project at Xerox dealt with the idea of aligning the company with the current ecological trend by promoting the reduction of paper usage in its business processes; the *Turk-Bench* project investigated a crowdsourcing business model for delivering data services in the healthcare domain. The *Agent Performance Indicator* project was set up in response to a high degree of turnover in a call centre operated by one partner company. The projects conducted at the IBM Research Center were all oriented to find solutions for specific commercial activities of the company: the *Dashboard* project dealt with monitoring the client's *Requests For Services* status with a view to improving their effective management; the *Cloud Analytics* project sought to let the sales force preview the client's fidelity to the newly offered cloud services; and, finally, the *Intelligent IT Configuration* project dealt with the provision of intelligent tools to ensure the more effective compliance of an IT solution with the complex requirements defined in the client's *Requests For Proposal* documentation. Information about these projects was sourced from numerous project publications, together with interviews with Antonietta Grasso (AG), Tommaso Colombino (TC), and, remotely, with Jeanette Blomberg (JB), who is located in Almaden.

9.1 Projects at the former Xerox Research Center in France

The Xerox company has a research history that dates back to the early 1960s. The initial centralized structure of research activities at Xerox has evolved into a number of research centres that are centrally promoted and funded but have specialized research interests and are managed autonomously. The famous and influential Palo Alto Research Center was later flanked by two research units in Europe, one located in Cambridge (UK) and one in Grenoble (France). These shared an interest in studies of work organization and collaboration at work, with a specific focus on how such studies might be used in the production of innovative workplace technologies. This shared view was reinforced when Graham Button left the directorship of the centre in Cambridge and became the director of Xerox Research Centre Europe in Grenoble. In 2017 the French centre was acquired by Naver Labs, a South Korean company that operates in the domain of innovative internet services and which wanted to establish a stronger scientific link with Europe. This acquisition oriented the research interests of the team performing ethnographic studies (led by AG from 2005 to date) to the domain of ambient intelligence, still keeping the user-centred approach to inform design.

Just before the change of the centre's ownership, AG and TC were involved in three projects that they deemed to be interesting and connected to the theme of sustainability because they reached different levels of maturity in the development of the technology (AG Int 31/05/2019). The change of ownership had an impact on their outcomes, but AG emphasized that other reasons had been relevant with respect to the sustainability issue. In her words: 'For us sustainability [still] means doing research in a way that it is not only contributing to the production of knowledge but also producing assets that can survive the research itself' (AG Int 31/05/2019).

9.1.1 The *Print Awareness Tool* and *Turk-Bench* projects

The *Print Awareness Tool* project was conceived in response to a call for project proposals issued by the Xerox CEO with the aim of promoting the development of more environmentally friendly services and products for its customers. The research team was involved in a project that aspired to monitor the usage of printers by making them 'intelligent' using machine learning techniques. In this framework the team proposed a tool that would help employees to reflect on their use of office resources, including the paper used to print their documents.

Building on a study at Xerox Palo Alto Research Center about the usage of printed documents, which had identified several document categories, the project focused on two of these: 'ephemeral' documents (those that are printed and soon disposed of) and documents that are seldom used, despite having been printed. The team constructed a monitoring system that tracked the printers used by the employees, providing feedback about their printing volumes and proposing reference thresholds to reduce the amount of printing. The system was conceived 'in a systemic view à la CSCW' that considers not only the individuals but the organization as a whole and the local departments that stand in between the end user and the whole company (AG Int 31/05/2019).

The system incorporated a portal accessible to the whole organization that showed both individual and aggregated efforts to meet the envisaged printing reduction according to the thresholds expressing the target of the company. Moreover, the portal described in which specific measures to reduce energy consumption the saved money was invested. It turned out that this was important information, as the employees felt more motivated if they knew what the savings were used for. It also explained some of the company's environmental actions, which were funded with the achieved savings. The system also provided an intermediate interface dedicated to the team the employee belonged to. Each team leader was in charge of fine-tuning the machine learning algorithm and planning and monitoring the measures oriented to a reduction of printing. Since different teams have different document needs and ways of reaching their objectives, the option of employees adapting these measures to the local context was helpful. Previous attempts based on the definition of general imposed and fixed thresholds had led to workarounds and complaints about the overall initiative.

The system was the object of internal experimentation to tune its functionality and was then adopted by an external early adopter, a big French retail company. Since the system was well accepted by the employees of this company, Xerox decided to turn it into a full product. The outcome of the project was positive. However, it raised some critical issues. Although the system was relatively simple, its development took many years. The software engineers in charge of the development did not fully appreciate the value of the system's different interfaces:

> [...] since there is the division between research and engineering it was difficult to transfer the idea to the engineers and something was lost in this translation. In the end only one of the three parts of the service went into production: the part for the individual. That was the main loss. Especially the intermediate interface was not perceived of any value and did not convince them.
>
> (AG Int 31/05/2019)

While the researchers focused on the aims and needs of the clients and the related innovation, the engineers mainly saw the challenges involved in developing and implementing the system. Their reluctance resulted in the limited implementation of the system's functionalities in relation to the initial requirements—that is, the additional interface for the managers was never taken into consideration. The project devoted its main efforts to managing the deployment of the system at the early adopter site. The problems to address were not only technical but also about

> [...] the many issues you encounter when you deploy a product in a real productive organization: since it was not yet a product it was necessary to find champions, to have the right connection to people that can promote and take care of the adoption; you need campaigns and find people willing to try; some people complained not to be involved in the campaign others complained about the way it was done.
>
> (AG Int 31/05/202019)

Another issue was how to motivate users:

> Xerox is living off the paper; the system was saying that the world is changing and it was difficult to convince people that even a sheet of paper is a resource.

> The world is going to the digital and the old business model based on paper
> and printing was no more sustainable.
>
> (AG Int 31/05/2019)

In addition to the saving of paper, a key message motivating the client companies was Xerox's awareness of the need to reduce the consumption of resources.
The system contributed to fostering the company's trustworthiness in its role as
a 'companion' in the digital world. While the client companies understood the
reason, part of the management at Xerox was perplexed. The people deploying
the system at the company site also often asked why Xerox would propose such
a system 'against its interests'.

The *Turk-Bench* project was conceived in response to a request by the management of Xerox to evaluate the possibility of exploring the crowdsourcing
business model for internal data-entry services concerning the healthcare
domain. The management was not sure of the potential advantages of the
model:

> Although the action is simple it requires competences to interpret and input
> the correct data, especially in the case of medical forms. There was a dis-
> cussion about the possibility to outsource that operation and maintain the
> desired parameters of quality.
>
> (AG Int 31/05/2019)

The project started with an investigation of the crowdsourcing phenomenon in
order to understand the Turkers' work practices and the kinds of relationships
that link the Turkers and the service requesters. One of the main issues was
to identify the problems affecting the acquisition and completion of service
requests. Some members of the research team participated in a forum (called
Turker Nation) where US Turkers shared their concerns, strategies, and technical solutions to mitigate their problems (Martin et al., 2014). In addition
to that, a 'technology probe' was used to find out about the characteristics of
the crowdsourcing market (Hanrahan et al., 2019). The combination of these
two methods helped identify the problematic aspects of this special kind of
labour market: its speed; the difficulties Turkers experience in accessing the
information they need to acquire rewarding requests by potential clients; their
inadequate infrastructural support—a result of a poor understanding of how
the Turkers generate knowledge about the flow of work they are engaged in and
about the service requesters with which they need to interact; and, finally, the

poor level of investment in the platform (that is, Amazon Mechanical Turk), which disregards the true nature of the labour market it supports. The study

> raised a lot of issues about the fact that the platform in use conceives people as machines disregarding the effort to generate knowledge about the work providers. [...] While the mundane view of crowdsourcing was about getting pocket money or fun, in that setting it was real work to survive. The idea was to build a platform that could improve the employer-employee relationships.
>
> (AG Int 31/05/2019)

The conceived platform was supposed to go beyond the idea that each single job is new and should promote learning:

> In principle, it should have guaranteed the dispatch of the requests and created some memory of the tasks a person has performed with which requester; expose some rating of the employer; create connections between workers engaged in similar kinds of data entry.
>
> (AG Int 31/05/2019)

But because of the identified problems, the project did not reach the development phase and the platform was never implemented since the company abandoned the adoption of the crowdsourcing business model.

9.1.2 The *Agent Performance Indicator* project: Crossing corporate boundaries

The context

Customer contact centres, or call centres, are a widely spread component of the customer relationships management (CRM) organization of companies in a wide number of sectors (Deery and Kinnie, 2004). Outsourcing these activities is considered a way of reducing costs and simplifying the organizational structure, as these activities are perceived as routine, hence easy to delegate to dedicated structures. A number of studies (e.g. Wegge et al., 2006; Procter et al., 2016) contradict this view, showing that call centre agents have to mobilize professional knowledge to accomplish their work. That makes call centres 'knowledge work environments' that are, however, 'built around a fairly strict productivity model and division of labour' (Colombino et al., 2014). In general, call centres are endowed with complex data and information management systems that crystallize this strictly ruled work organization. There is an evident conflict between the efforts management invests in achieving efficiency through standardization and the agents' need for flexibility, given the variability of the situations they face when interacting with multiple clients. This conflict makes call centres a problematic work environment, rich in feelings of frustration and tensions (Houlihan, 2004). For these reasons, call centres 'provide an interesting but challenging context for technological innovation' (Colombino et al., 2014) as testified by several attempts to understand how to improve their performance, especially from the management perspective (Ibrahim et al., 2016; Mehrota and Fama, 2003). Other studies have examined how to bring innovation to call centres that have been conceived from the agents' perspective (Martin et al., 2007), as well as from a more comprehensive CRM perspective (Saeed et al., 2011).

The setting investigated in the *Agent Performance Indicator* project (Hanrahan et al., 2019) was the service provider partner *Alfa*. It manages call centres that offer services to the clients of a number of telecommunications companies. The aim of the project was

> to look at the work of the call centre agents and their management, with an eye towards those parts of the job, such as compensation mechanisms and performance management practices, that were likely to be drivers of the high level of attrition they were experiencing. [...] attrition was higher than it could or should have been.
>
> (Colombino, et al., 2020: 55)

In the tradition of the Xerox Research Center, the project

> was a technology development project driven by the findings of an ethnographic study; it was a collaboration between the research and business arms of a large corporation; it was organized according to standard and recognizable principles of project management, with a plan, tasks, deliverables, etc.
>
> (Colombino, et al., 2020: 55)

The project had three distinct phases: the ethnographic study that sought to identify the sources of attrition within *Alfa* and generate ideas on how to design a system that would help improve the agents' situation; the construction of an IT prototype to support the work of agents and their supervisors; and the deployment of the prototype in the socio-technical infrastructure of *Alfa*.

The ethnographic pre-study

The business model of *Alfa* was based on two main principles: labour arbitrage 'defining and standardizing those organizational processes and policies which are directly connected to workforce management, such as compensation, performance, management, human resources, etc.' (Colombino, et al., 2020: 57), and optimization of overhead costs. Its activities are shaped by the interactions between four main actors: the management of *Alfa*, the agents, their supervisors, the customer outsourcing the service, and the clients that benefit from it. *Alfa*'s management aims to create the most profitable relationship with each customer according to a specific service level agreement (SLA) that governs the service delivery and the performance that has to be guaranteed and reported to the customer. Supervisors have responsibility for a small group of ten to fifteen agents. They monitor the group's performance and promote its service provision quality through specific actions, as and when needed. The agents interact with clients to provide the requested service according to the related SLA and the additional rules imposed by the supervisors to increase their performance.

The resulting structure is strongly hierarchical and the flow of information among the various roles is shaped accordingly. Central to this information flow are the data necessary to compute the key performance indicators (KPIs), which are used to assess the performance of the organization at various levels and are linked to the compensation the agents receive: 'The KPIs are derived from the call centre telephone switch and from assessments performed by quality analysts who listen to recorded phone calls and "score" the agents' performance on a set of pre-defined categories' (Colombino et al., 2020: 57). Moreover, the data are collected from different sources. *Alfa* has

> a centralized [technological infrastructure similar to an] Enterprise Data Warehouse. This warehouse collects all of the phone switch and qualitative data from various [call] centres. The source of this data is a point that varies as well. For some functions within the call centre the data is pulled directly from the phone switch, and for others it is pulled from the data infrastructure of the client organization.
>
> (Colombino et al., 2014: 280)

The observations showed that the data are used for three different activities: (near) real-time monitoring of the agents' activities during a call; managing the agents' performance and providing them with feedback; and upstream reporting. The way the data were aggregated reflects the priorities of the organizational hierarchy and privileges standardization, as well as control over the operational autonomy of the agents and supervisors.

However, management, supervisors, and agents have different needs with respect to the granularity of the data. Management needs data at a coarse level of aggregation for its overall control and reporting to the customer. A finer aggregation and more frequent updates would generate undue overhead costs that management would be unwilling to afford. This attitude and strategy shaped the overall construction of the technological infrastructure supporting the management of the performance data. Supervisors need more timely and finely aggregated data than this technological infrastructure is able to provide, especially in their interactions with the agents under their responsibility. They compensate for this shortcoming by local elaborations, typically with the help of ad hoc spreadsheets that they can flexibly organize according to their needs. The agents are in the worst position: they would need real-time data to modify their behaviour in order to reach the level of performance of the KPI and influence their compensation, as well as comply with the overall performance goals of *Alfa*. Unfortunately, the data that the agents receive are almost useless for this aim and presented in a rather simplistic visualization. They have no workarounds to compensate for this fact, since they have limited access to their overall performance data. However, management

'rightly or wrongly, [does] not want to provide agents with easy access to data that may either distract them from their core activity [...] or indirectly encourage them to work to the numbers'—i.e. leverage their understanding of the performance assessment and compensation mechanisms in order to hit the highest compensation rates without necessarily providing the best value to their organization—if not outright game the system.

(Colombino et al., 2014: 283)

From the agents' perspective, the business model that shapes the organization targets performance criteria that seek to fulfil the SLA and reduce costs. Their core activity of providing the clients with the best answers to their requests is measured only in terms of time optimization and not in terms of the quality of the information they provide.

The construction of the prototype

The research team proposed a solution that takes heed of the needs of agents and their supervisors, starting from the view that agents perform knowledge work:

Customer care work is rarely routine—product launches, system updates, changes in the organization can always affect the volume and complexity of the calls coming into the call centre. We therefore believed there would be a benefit to providing decision making tools to layers of the organization that are normally not involved in defining performance management strategies and expectations, but are nevertheless responsible for putting them into practice. The challenge for us was therefore to help agents and supervisors identify and respond to unfolding situations more rapidly and effectively than the call centre as a whole was able to do.

(Colombino et al., 2020: 62)

Based on these insights, the researchers took a series of design decisions. They took special care in designing the interface for the agents, using a nuanced characterization of their skill set to avoid the reduction of performance assessment to a subset of performance metrics. The proposed visualization was rejected by the project stakeholders, but not because of its readability or technical quality:

What was being questioned was the ability and willingness of a low-skilled knowledge worker to interpret and make constructive and legitimate use of data which, from an organizational point of view, was not immediately related to ongoing call-taking activity.

(Colombino et al., 2020: 62)

The interface was simplified to make the 'in situ' deployment of the prototype possible.

The problematic deployment
The concluding phase of the project was dedicated to the deployment of the prototype in the hosting context. In this process, an increasing mismatch between the vision that had inspired the construction of the prototype and the expectations of *Alfa*'s management came to the fore, starting with the request to change the interface. The researchers' understanding of a 'good' agent was in conflict with the organization's performance management and compensation practice. Another issue concerned the integration of the prototype with the existing legacy technologies in use.

We had a significant amount of interaction with both the IT staff of various call centres as well as the development teams of [Alfa] [...] to understand how to support our initial round of experiments, how our tool would fit into their overall infrastructure, and what capabilities would need to be developed by whom. Fitting our tool within the existing infrastructure and obtaining data with the required accuracy and timeliness that we required for our applications, turned out to be next to impossible. [...] In the cases where our tool was eventually, successfully deployed, the amount of effort required by the IT and development organization was in the order of six to eight months.

(Colombino et al., 2020: 64)

This clearly contrasted the management's goal of reducing costs.

Moreover, the researchers, in accordance with their socio-technical approach, had envisaged an iterative deployment leading from the prototype to a true product. The organization's management did not agree with this approach, asking for an immediately fully operative application and refusing the idea to cover any additional cost that the iterations could generate. The initial aim of reducing attrition was thwarted by very concrete and practical issues or, better yet, by *Alfa*'s culture. At some point, the researchers lost the ownership of the technology. Although the prototype became a product in use, they found themselves excluded from following how it was adapted to the new organizational requirements. The project was considered complete, and at that time Xerox Grenoble was acquired by Naver Labs.

Different views on sustainability
From the management perspective, the project was a partial success, since the prototype was the starting point of a product whose full development was achieved outside the project. From the perspective of the researchers, the project generated a diffused sense of frustration that can be described in terms of different kinds of misalignments. One of these misalignments concerns the adopted business model and the role of the technology that had been foreseen by the call centre's management:

So if you have on the one hand our [research] management that tells us that the goal of research is not to deliver short-term gain but envision a long-term benefit through innovation so in this case might mean rethinking the business model, thinking about technology as a way to become sort of value-added instead of a cost-cutting exercise whereas the management of the call center had a very different perspective. So there was already right there a problem of misalignment.

(TC Int, 11/06/2019)

As a consequence, the researchers found themselves in a difficult position that raised a basic ethical issue: to what extent should they 'push' their critical perspective and mission, and to what extent do they have to compromise on the existing situation?

> [A] consequence of the confrontation between the researchers and the business group was ethical. The potential for tension between the researchers and the business group was always there, in the form of the question of whether research is done purely in service of the organization's goals, or if it does in fact also have a remit or the authority to redefine what those goals are.
>
> (Colombino et al., 2020: 56)

Related to this, the researchers point to the different levels of accountability in relation to the outcomes of the project:

> The confrontation between researchers and the business group 'in the wild' therefore brought to the fore very different experiences of organizational accountability, where the managers of a business group had to shoulder a heavier burden of accountability (to a bottom line and to a rigidly hierarchical reporting structure) than the researchers whose bottom line (so to speak) was less likely to be affected by the relative success or failure of a single project.
>
> (Colombino et al., 2020: 56)

The decision to apply an iterative model, although in a simplified version, resulted in a misalignment between the pace of activities envisaged by the researchers and the timeline set by the business unit. This points to a problem that is common to many projects: the time needed to investigate a setting—in particular if this is a new one that might open a new business perspective—and arrive at the first prototype to be experimented on 'in the wild' is in conflict with the financial scheme that has shorter and fixed reporting cycles:

> If you do observational studies you start, maybe you open a new domain, so you have to do foundational studies to understand the domain, you have to understand what the interesting issues are, then maybe you start thinking about the technology, then you start building, then you do ideation, then you do a sort of mock-up or prototype, you start iterating [...] it can take more than a year before you even get to some kind of functional prototype [...] so the 12 months cycle, it was something that had to be worked around.
>
> (TC Int, 11/06/2019)

This misalignment also affects the business units involved in the projects:

> In an organization there should be a consistency between the vision for what research is, inventing the future [...] all corporations have their own way of describing long-term research and how important it is but then there is an operational reality and it is bureaucratic and it is built around layers of management and middle management who work and report on cycles, financial reports in cycles.
>
> (TC Int, 11/06/2019)

These multiple sources of misalignment would suggest that a more radical rethink is needed for the ways the company manages its research projects:

> because there is no middle management, no research director that is going to challenge that kind of organizational structure, [...] it would need a clear decision by someone who is placed on a very high level to subvert or revolutionize the organizational bureaucracy to change the incentive mechanisms [...] I don't see it happening.
>
> (TC Int, 11/06/2019)

The research condition in the new company (Naver Labs) shows that a different organization of industry-based research is possible:

> It's not impossible, *Naver* is different. They have more resources to invest. So they are less worried about accounting with that kind of granularity. They are happier with a system which says, here is the budget, do what you want, and come back and talk to us when you have something interesting to show. That allows you to plan your research activities over 2–3 years [...] my experience (and also that of other people) is when they have money, they let research do their own things, if they don't then they start tying research down to that cyclical and more short-term accounting mechanism, which also allows them to measure or believe they are measuring return on investment in research projects.
>
> (TC Int, 11/06/2019)

Another aspect of the new situation is the possibility of working with IT specialists that are hired by the research teams: this reduces the tensions experienced with these professionals when they belong to the client organization:

Moreover, in the new situation it was possible to hire engineers that are re-sponsible to guarantee the continuity of the research from the field study that highlights the requirements up to the implementation of systems that can be deployed in the real world according to the spirit of the new company.

(AG Int, 31/05/2019)

9.2 Projects at IBM Research—Almaden in San Jose

IBM has a long research history that was initiated in 1945 and had a con-siderable impact on the evolution of IT systems and services. Nowadays, the research is organized across twelve research laboratories that are lo-cated in all continents. These laboratories specialize in different research areas and constitute a network of more than 3,000 researchers collaborating to generate breakthroughs in basic research and its applications and pro-vide solutions that respond to worldwide needs, paying attention to regional conditions.

IBM Research—Almaden is located at San Jose, California in Silicon Val-ley. It hosts scientists, computer engineers, and designers that are focused on leading-edge technologies including artificial intelligence, healthcare and life sciences, quantum computing, blockchain, storage, Internet of Things, and ac-cessibility. This work builds on a rich history of breakthroughs, especially in the management of huge amounts of data. The three following projects fit this research tradition perfectly.

9.2.1 The *Request for Service Dashboard* project

The *Request for Service Dashboard* (*RFS-D*) project was initiated by IBM ex-ecutives who were concerned that the processes for managing these requests were not efficient. An important motivation for the project was the company's strategy to increase the use of available operational and transactional data to run its internal business operations. The project started as a technology-driven intervention and evolved into a more socio-technical design approach.

Their solution was to develop a workflow tool to track the progress of the request for service (RFS) business. However, early experience with the work-flow tool was problematic in that the data generated by the tool could not be trusted and this created an inaccurate picture of the RFS business.

(Blomberg, 2016: 1)

The executives responded to the unreliability of the RFS data by requiring that the RFS managers produce reports based on the inaccurate workflow data. This request created frustration on the side of the RFS managers 'because the reports did not give an accurate picture of state of affairs and yet they were being assessed as if the information was correct' (Blomberg, 2016: 1). For this reason, the research team was asked to help understand the problem with the workflow data and find a solution. The first phase of the project was dedicated to studying the work practices of RFS managers, for whom interacting with clients and creating custom reports about the status of the client's RFS was a key part of their work. The research focused on understanding how the new workflow tool might fit into and align with existing practices.

On the basis of their findings, the research team developed an application based on a dashboard

> that provided the ability to easily customize reports for particular client situations and collaborate with clients over the progression of individual RFSs. Our dashboard made the work of the RFS managers easier and more efficient, with the additional benefit of increasing client satisfaction.
>
> (Blomberg, 2016: 1)

This simple solution motivated the managers to use the workflow application and, consequently, the data it generated gave a more accurate picture of the real status of the RFSs. They also 'could update this status (and the reasons for delays) in collaboration with their client counterparts' (Blomberg, 2016: 2).

The dashboard was successful and was used together with the workflow tool. Its sustainability was achieved by taking a socio-technical approach that looked into the reasons for the poor adoption of the workflow tool and focused on how to support its appropriation: 'The dashboard sustains itself because it responds to real needs. We have been acknowledged for its success. It is still in use, and we guess it will be as long as the workflow is in use' (JB Int 15/10/2019).

9.2.2 The *Cloud Services Analytics* project

The project targeted an internal group of sellers and their managers working in the global cloud IT infrastructure-as-a-service (IaaS) business (Blomberg et al., 2018). The aim was to provide them with analytics that would help them improve their selling performances. The managers' motivations were twofold: one related to monitoring the sales of new cloud services that are typically consumed 'on demand', which is different from the more traditional long-term contracts. The second motivation was to show that 'the business unit was on the cutting-edge in using tools that leverage innovative AI technologies that are part of the current IBM strategies' (JB Int 15/10/2019).

Therefore, the Research Center was involved in the project that was thought of as the initial phase of a long-term project initiative. In the next step, it had the ambitious goal of targeting a larger set of managers and sellers and incorporating a wider set of data sources in order 'to enable the cloud sales organization to become a leader in enterprise cloud solutions by providing them with the analytic tools to grow the cloud business, including basic reporting and advanced analytics' (Blomberg et al., 2018: 284).

The initial focus of the project was

> on sales leaders responsible for specific geographic territories (geo leaders), sales managers, and sellers as our users. We developed a starter set of analytics that included risk of defection (e.g. customers likely to terminate their contract) and growth or shrinkage of client and offering revenue. Our initial data sources were ledger data and client registration data. In the longer term, we envisioned enabling others in the company to use our 'platform' to add new data sources, analytics, and users.
>
> (Blomberg et al., 2018: 284)

The project strategy and the necessary actions

In order to achieve the goal of the project, the research team had to assemble different kinds of expertise. They included a machine learning mathematician and an operations researcher, both with prior experience in the field, as well as an anthropologist.

Several actions had to be taken before starting the technical work of developing the sales analytics. First, it was necessary to get access to the relevant source data: 'This involved obtaining many approvals where we had to argue for the importance of our project and also demonstrate how we were going to protect the security of this highly confidential data' (Blomberg et al., 2018: 285). Secondly, some programming was needed to guarantee that the ledger data were updated according to the project needs. Moreover, the data had to be aggregated in order to reduce the complexity of the prospective algorithms to extract the required analytics. The decision was to aggregate the data 'by a three-month moving average enabling us to update our predications monthly' (Blomberg et al., 2018: 285).

Another problem to solve concerned the source data. This implied finding the people that understood the database structure and resolving the problems resulting from the fact that there was 'no a priori "right" way to aggregate and name entities'. This was not a trivial task, and the researchers felt 'pressure to get our results to the sellers for their feedback on the usefulness of the predictions' (Blomberg et al., 2018: 286). Also, the development of the algorithms required defining a strategy and a choice of where to start in developing the analytics: 'Our algorithms deployed supervised machine learning approaches, where we [initially] focused on developing models (or patterns in the ledger data) to identify which client accounts were at risk of defection' (Blomberg et al., 2018: 286).

The solution was implemented using a simple but sufficiently predictive formula: 'Through machine learning experimentation we discovered that a single analytic feature […] was a good predictor of accounts that were likely to defect in the following six-month period' (Blomberg et al., 2018: 286).

The next step was to refine the analytical capabilities, which entailed additional decisions on how to tune the model so that the predictions were adequate and in particular on how to present them to the users:

> The percentage of growth or shrinkage could be set to between 0% (defection) and 100% (double revenue). For our initial reports we set the percentage to 50% growth or shrinkage. The results were sorted by geography and country and ranked by a relative score between 0% and 100%.
>
> (Blomberg et al., 2018: 288)

Additional information was provided to help the user interpret these percentages.

The interactions between the sellers and their managers were useful to find additional bugs but were also problematic: 'While we always applauded the sellers when they pointed out anomalous results, we also knew this was a double-edged sword, as too many such errors could ultimately undermine their confidence in our analysis' (Blomberg et al., 2018: 291). Nevertheless, the sellers provided valuable suggestions to make the analytics more useful to them, such as aligning the frequency of the reports on the analytics with their 'temporal rhythms' (moving from the initial four-month intervals to monthly updates) and finding the related technical solution.

Difficulties in the sustainability of project outcomes

Although the design strategy was based on observations of the sellers' work practices and on interacting with them and their managers, the initial version of the tool providing the analytic results encountered some problems in terms of its appropriation. In this context, appropriation can be interpreted as the ability of the sellers to 'make sense' of the provided output in relation to their current work practices and to have the knowledge to work with the results.

The researchers' observations revealed that, with respect to the likelihood of a client to defect, the analytics were not difficult to interpret and, consequently, could be trusted. On the other hand, in the case of the model predicting growth/shrinkage, the output was not as interpretable—for example, in relation to the '50% chance of defecting':

> What proved to be challenging for some sellers was to understand what was meant by the statement that accounts on the list had a 50% chance of defecting in the next six months. At first glance for some it seemed like a coin toss to say 50% of the accounts on the list would defect and 50% would not.
>
> (Blomberg et al., 2018: 292)

Indeed, the more sophisticated machine learning techniques used to make the predictions made it difficult to 'intuitively' make sense of their outcomes:

> The growth and shrinkage model took into account multiple features, producing highly accurate and precise predictions. However, the results of these models were difficult to reason about as some of the features were abstract and not easily mapped on to the sellers' everyday experiences [...] it was difficult to see the direct link between the revenue data and the predictions, and impossible to explain in everyday language exactly how the model arrived at the predictions. [...] The analytics found patterns in the data that humans could not 'see' requiring a level of 'blind' trust on the part of the sellers.
>
> (Blomberg et al., 2018: 292).

One possible way of coping with these problems was to let some feature of the model be parametric. This approach, which had been successful in other cases, resulted in the sellers getting easily confused because of the complex and obscure contexts in which the parameter values had to be set.

The second problem related to the sellers' expectation of being supported in defining the action they had to take in response to the various risky situations highlighted by the analytic outcomes. The main reason was that the model did not, and could not, account for factors that could potentially lead to a risky situation:

> Had there been a reorganization at the client company? Had the client started to use a competitor's services? Was there a recent major service outage? In addition, knowing what courses of action would best address the client situation were not informed by the model. [...] In addition, sellers did not always understand why an account was no longer on the list for risk of defection. What actions had been taken, if any, to turn the account around?
>
> (Blomberg et al., 2018: 293)

In an attempt to solve these problems, the system interface was augmented by adding direct questions to generate the required information:

> Not only did this sales executive want to understand what might have caused a change in a client's risk profile, we too wanted to know what actions sellers might have taken and the impact of their actions had on changes in revenue.
>
> (Blomberg et al., 2018: 293)

However, these questions remained almost unanswered, because recording such information was not part of the sellers' work practices. On a more general level, it clearly emerged that what needs to be borne in mind is 'how the users are engaged with the results and not only on developing better models' (JB Int 15/12/2019).

Moreover, at the organizational level the question of what information about clients should be available, beyond disclosure agreements with the clients, became an issue that received more scrutiny within the company, as access to this information could have unexpected impacts 'on career opportunities, how marketing dollars were spent, prompt additional oversight on sellers' activities, and so on' (JB Int 15/12/2019).

While the project was progressing, the company's executives decided to change which services were to be sold by which divisions within the company, thereby also changing the allocation of responsibility for their sales, with consequences for the data that were being fed to the models and, in turn, the predictions. The research team found it difficult to keep up with these changes:

> While we tried our best, realistically we could not keep up with all the organizational changes that were occurring and likely would occur in the future.

Instead we had to 'assume' that these changes were not significant enough to undermine our analyses, taking some comfort in the continuing precision and accuracy of our analytics. However, this suggests that data scientists will have to stay connected to their analytics so they can make adjustments to data cleansing strategies, entity resolution schemes, and algorithmic choices that are responsive to organizational change.

(JB Int, 15/12/2019)

After two years the project ended, for a number of reasons. The first was the reaction of the prospective users, who continued to make sales decisions based on information beyond what the system knew: 'Actually, we observed that they continued to take their decision outside the system as they didn't see enough advantage in using it' (JB Int 15/12/2019). An additional reason was the changes at the executive level of the company: 'Organizational changes meant that we had to (re)socialize our work and its value and convince our new stakeholders that it was feasible for our analytics to keep up with future organizational changes that inevitably would come' (Blomberg et al., 2018: 296). Moreover, to make the outcomes of the project sustainable, the hosting organization would have had to include people able to carry it on once the research team moved on to other projects: 'There were no IT people in the business units [...] who will take over? [...] Research labs generate ideas and models and the business units ultimately have to take responsibility to maintain the systems' (JB Int 15/12/2019). Irrespective of the initial ambition and long-term goal, as well as the efforts, the project was concluded: 'In the end, the calculation was made that these potential challenges outweighed the immediate and short-term benefits of the analytics' (Blomberg et al., 2018: 296).

Nevertheless, the research team acquired valuable experience in what it takes to deliver 'actionable analytics' for the enterprise. One key insight was: 'The problem is not [only] the technology but the complex dynamics surrounding its development. [...] The technology has its momentum and it is difficult to reorient its development' (JB Int 15/12/2019). This means:

We must temper hype with organizational realities. As in our case, even for a company that develops and sells analytic systems and services, there are challenges to adopting them internally. Realizing the full potential of data analytics requires awareness of the technical and organizational complexity of acting on analytics in the enterprise.

(Blomberg et al., 2018: 297)

9.2.3 The *Intelligent IT Configuration* project

This project started with the aim of supporting IT service designers (called 'architects') within IBM as they prepare architectural solutions and create bids in response to Requests for Proposals (RFPs) from clients. RFPs include several unstructured documents: 'most of the data within the RFP is unstructured text, which architects must transform into more structured formats (e.g., copying a text string from a document into a spreadsheet cell)' (Wolf and Blomberg, 2019a: 143:5). This is the first step of a workflow that is followed by three main additional steps:

> This structural transformation enables various kinds of downstream analysis, as the text requirements are mapped to their numerical baseline values (e.g., how many units of a given item, as well as if/how those quantities are expected to change over the life of the contract). These requirements and baselines are then further mapped to higher-level IT services frameworks, […] and then ultimately matched to different sets of IT offerings (bundles of services that meet various service requirements).
>
> (Wolf and Blomberg, 2020: 194)

A concluding phase optimizes the coverage of the client's requirements and accounts for additional features such as costs, pricing, prior business with the client, and the like.

The conceived support was an intelligent tool to alleviate the effort of extracting requirements from RFPs and propose an architecture suited to respond to them. The two main technologies at play were: natural language processing (NLP) tools to provide the requirements extraction and an optimization model to find the best-fitting solution.

The tool development project adopted the Agile software method that is based on the 'continuous delivery' principle: each delivery allows for validation and tuning of the next plan and functionality for preparing the new release. According to this method, the project went through several phases: from the initial interviews to an 'early adopter' programme where architects provided early feedbacks via a 'think aloud' method while completing a series of tasks. The next phase was a 'general availability programme' where all the architects had access to the tool in multiple sessions. The last phase was devoted to asking some architects to experiment with the tool as part of live deals with their clients and collecting their opinions.

The research team charged with providing user feedback and assessing the fit of the tool with the practices of the IT architects became involved in the project after its inception. Their task was to investigate the project's progression and what was achieved as well as any problematic aspects, and to possibly change its trajectory (JB Int 15/12/2019). The results of the study, which lasted nearly two years, are based on the analysis of data gathered through interviews and usability sessions where the participants interacted with incremental versions of the tool. Additional data were gathered through focus group sessions with members of the broader 'early adopter' cohort and solicited feedback via email surveys and an online chat forum (Wolf and Blomberg, 2019b).

The ambivalent attitude towards the tool in progress

Although the architects that were involved in the project approached it with a positive attitude, they also expressed concerns regarding the tool and its development. From a sustainability perspective, this mixture was not disruptive. The research team's approach kept the architects always actively involved in the development of the tool, as well as in the executive meetings showing the progress of the project outcomes. They were asked to 'honestly' report about their experiences and point out achievements and problems that were still unresolved. This strategy helped convince the executives that it was worthwhile to further fund the project. Also, the tool responded to a genuine need: the need to diminish the effort required by a time-consuming activity (requirements extraction) in combination with the complex process of finding the best solution for the client. Hence, despite some serious concerns, the architects wanted the project to be successful and maintained highly active participation.

If the distance between the project today and its imagined tomorrow undermined healthy progression, why did it persist? Conceptual distance between the two—and in particular, reinforcing the allure of the system's imagined potential—was necessary (even advantageous) for a number of reasons. Demonstrating one's 'buy in' of the strategic vision of the 'cognitive enterprise' (which the project symbolized) showed one's relevancy and eager engagement with the changing nature of contemporary work. No old-fashioned, out-of-touch or resistant workers here! Instead, pride was taken in being on the cutting edge, not only open to the 'future of work' but actively participating in shaping that future.

(Wolf and Blomberg, 2020: 199)

In other words, the many serious problems that were encountered and that could have resulted in resistance—and, in the end, failure—were counter-balanced by the architects' constructive attitude. They were committed to proposing ideas about how to overcome the problems and thinking about how to incorporate the tool in their current practices.

The problems were of different kinds. For example, architects involved in different parts of the same solution for a client usually interact to align their choices, make colleagues aware of critical decisions, and so on. The tool does not adequately support this collaboration; nor is it able to take care of routine checks such as 'if this requirement and the associated technological component is present, then that requirement and the associated technological component is obviously present too'. A suggestion was to augment the tool with the possibility of adding annotations to the produced documents and to promote awareness information concerning the deal under their concern (Wolf and Blomberg, 2020).

Another problem was how to classify the different portions of an RFP text. Architects use a list of IT service categories to identify the requirements of the prospective solution. These categories are then 'carried forward in the tool' to support 'optimization modeling that aids the architect in designing a technical solution to cover the requested services' (Wolf and Blomberg, 2019a: 3). The level of reliability of this process was difficult to interpret, in particular as some portions (called 'white spaces') were not classified. Architects requested that the tool should make clear whether this lack was a 'choice' by the algorithm (that is, it classified the text as 'irrelevant') or a 'bug' that they should correct with a manual classification so that the system could be 're-trained' to avoid the same mistake in the future. In this respect, they were unsure that this problem could be effectively solved:

> This part of the new process introduced confusion over the meaning of the white space—and what it was communicating to the user. Does white space mean the NLP dos not think it is important? [...] During the usability test, solution designers wondered if all the white space in a document would need to be manually labelled.
>
> (Wolf and Blomberg, 2019a: 4)

This problem led to two complementary solutions. The first was to allow architects to skip the classification and add the data from another artifact in use (called 'Market Sheet') to the optimization model. However, this 'workaround' required the extra effort of transferring the information in the 'Market Sheet' to a format that was understandable by the optimization module. Moreover, the possibility of skipping the first 'intelligent' support provided by the tool was perceived as a partial failure of the overall expected advantages of an 'intelligent tool'. In the final phase of the project, what was conceived as a temporary workaround became the most widely adopted solution. This, however, was not satisfactory:

> Solutioners expressed disappointment over the system's current inability to deliver on its grand time-saving vision, and frustration over the extra effort it required over BAU [Business As Usual]. In some sense, the system was indeed transforming their everyday work practices, but in ways that confounded rather than enhanced those practices.
>
> (Wolf and Blomberg, 2020: 198)

The second solution was to let the interface provide the level of reliability of each extracted requirement, but, again, interpreting this level of reliability was difficult.

These are only a few examples of the problematic issues that came up in the project. They show not only how the design of 'intelligent tools' concerns their algorithmic capabilities and levels of reliability, but also how the outcomes of a hidden algorithm can be interpreted, given that the current work practices follow a different 'logic'.

> What makes a smart system 'explainable' for a given context? What are the key enablers (and inhibitors) to end users contextual understanding of such system? [...] Scholarly attention is needed to chart the interacting aspects of ML interpretability and how sense making and coherence dynamically emerge through interactions between users, smart systems and their deployments.
>
> (Wolf and Blomberg, 2019a: 1)

In the end, it is the huge effort required from all the involved stakeholders to make the tool usable in practice that prevented the actual deployment of the project's results: 'The problem was in the initial conception [...] if there is no reconceptualization of what you are building [the project] likely will not be successful' (JB Int 15/12/2019).

9.3 Summary

Each of the research projects presented in this chapter started with the company hosting the research lab (Xerox Grenoble and IBM Research—Almaden) requesting help finding a solution in response to a specific need that had been identified within the company or a client organization. As such, on the one hand, each project has a predefined set of target users and a natural ambit where the solution can be experimented with, and, on the other, it has a stable set of available resources within a broad timespan. According to the cultural tradition of the two research labs, all projects spent their initial phase studying the target setting and the needs of the prospective users, combining ethnographic studies (observations and interviews) with iterative methods to construct the envisaged solution in the event that the prototyping step was reached. Irrespective of these overall similarities, the projects had different outcomes that characterized their different levels of sustainability.

The *Dashboard* project ended up with a well-established technology that the users found easy to appropriate and that could sustain itself; it adequately responded to their needs, as they had been identified during the pre-study.

In the *Print Awareness Tool* project, the prototype reached the stage of becoming a product, although with a reduced functionality in comparison with the richer one identified during the pre-study. Here the full sustainability of the initial idea clashed with the limited readiness of the IT professionals implementing the product to accept and understand the value of the interface, which they decided to drop.

On the other hand, the *Turk-Bench* and the *Cloud Service Analytics* projects both failed, as they were deemed unsustainable, although for different reasons. In the first case, the management was unprepared to recognize the knowledge work of the Turkers; it then decided not to invest in a technology that supported this business model. In the second case, the lack of sustainability was mainly related to the kind of technology (AI innovative tools) that was at the core of the solution: the problems experienced by the users in making sense of the analytic outcomes and integrating them into their daily work practices were challenging. In addition, the effort to maintain the operability of the solution in the presence of new and changing sources of data along with organizational fluctuations in leadership turned out to be too much to sustain the project. This was also the case in the *Intelligent IT Configuration* project, which had a longer life before it ended, irrespective of the difficulties it encountered, including the cut of the NLP-based component. The project was continued for a longer period because the users, the IT architects, wanted to make it successful and convince the management (and to some extent themselves) that this was possible. This shows how the positive attitude of the users can play a role in making the development of the solution more sustainable, until some other factors make this impossible.

The initial prototype developed in the *Agent Performance Indicator* project reached the experimentation phase in the target organization. Its development continued outside the influence of the research team, who lost track and control of its evolution and had no guarantee that the initial vision of increasing the power of the call centre agents was maintained.

The presented projects shed light on what can be considered innovative research in a corporation: innovation as improvement of the working conditions of the prospective users, as in the case of the Xerox Research Lab projects; or innovation as construction of solutions based on leading-edge technologies with commercial potentiality, but complex in design and appropriation, as in the case of the IBM Research Lab projects. In the first case, the projects show the limited understanding and appreciation of the articulated outcomes of the ethnographic investigation by both the management and the IT professionals involved in the projects. In the second case, simple (or simplified) solutions can be suitable for the users and are then likely to be sustainable, as in the case of the IBM's *Dashboard* project, if they answer the users' needs appropriately. On the other hand, the complex models that are incorporated in various ways in the intelligent technology can hardly account for the articulated and subtle, often invisible, means by which human agents make their decisions and are then unsustainable, as the agents perceive them as too far removed from their work practices.

10

Beyond individual projects:
University spin-offs

The forming of a new company by a researcher who left a university or research organization to start the company 'while still affiliated with the university, and/or a core technology (or idea) that is transferred from the parent organization' (Clarysse et al., 2011: 1421) can be considered a way of keeping an idea and/or research outcome alive in the near future. While the literature gives much prominence to the image of 'dynamic high-growth potential spin-offs', Harrison and Leitch (2010) suggest that 'most university spin-off companies start small and remain small, reflecting founder aspirations, capabilities, and resource endowments' (p. 1241). While academic entrepreneurship has become fairly common in the field of engineering, far fewer spin-offs grow out of practice-based research. This may have to do with the challenges of motivating companies to explore the potential of socio-technical solutions. As one of our interview partners summed up, 'The willingness of a company to go along with such a process—in my experience organizations are only ready for such a type of change if they are unusually far-sighted or in strong acute pain' (JG Int, 26/06/2020).

The two initiatives we have selected for this book represent different types of USOs, with contrasting aspects in several dimensions. The first one, *Ximes*, founded in 1997, grew out of research at Vienna University of Technology and a strong relationship with the Austrian trade union movement. It offers 'consulting, software and knowledge' to companies on three interrelated topics—working time, wage and salary, and workforce requirements—on the basis of a participatory approach. Starting with the dissertation project of its founder, Johannes Gärtner, who developed software in support of shift planning at STAHL-AG Linz, Austria's formerly state-owned steel plant, it evolved over the years to attend to the needs of different work domains, learning how to account for the complexity of situations and develop solutions in close

Future-proofing. Wulf et al., Oxford University Press.
© Carla Simone, Ina Wagner, Claudia Müller, Anne Weibert, and Volker Wulf (2022).
DOI: 10.1093/oso/9780198862505.003.0010

collaboration with all stakeholders in a company. *Ximes* was able to mature not only due to its growing practical expertise but also because of its continuing academic interests and activities.

The other initiative is *OpenDash*, a web-based visualization framework that was developed at the University of Siegen. It supports visualizing any digital data, such as energy or mobility data. *OpenDash* is special in that end users can easily create their own content for this dashboard, deciding for themselves which data they want to see and when they want to see them. The system offers a set of pre-defined visualizations but also supports free customization based on an end-user development (EUD) approach, as well as the ability to make one's own visualizations. The story of *OpenDash* shows some of the strategies that researchers may develop in order to ensure the continuity and transferability of a design outcome. The spin-off that resulted from several years of development effort in several projects is now in a position to guarantee continuous support to the practitioners and their organizations involved in the projects and let the solutions be replicated or evolve to serve other settings— that is, to enter the free market and respond to its rules. This section is based on interviews with Johannes Gärtner (JG, *Ximes*), Nico Castelli, Martin Stein (NC and MS, *OpenDash*), and Corinna Ogonowski, CO all from the University of Siegen, as well as numerous project publications.

10.1 The story of *Ximes*

The story of *Ximes* goes back to the early 1990s when Johannes Gärtner, at that time at GPA (the Austrian union for private-sector white-collar workers), decided to write a dissertation on how to support the collaborative planning of working time arrangements within a company. This was a topic that connected his interest in politics with computer science, legal issues, and ergonomics:

> It was easy to get started from my trade union background, as I knew the people and then I fell in love with the topic and arrived at some exciting insights that did not find favor with computer scientists, in particular the participatory aspect.
>
> (JG Int, 26/06/2020)

He completed his doctoral thesis at Vienna University of Technology in 1992; the first software in support of shift planning was ready in 1995; in 1997 the company *Ximes* was created; and in 2002 Johannes Gärtner left the university and became self-employed after having completed the 'Habilitation'.

One of the big stumbling blocks at the beginning was finding a company that would be willing to embark on a common shift-planning project. As soon as an arrangement with STAHL-AG Linz had been found, Sabine Wahl (still at *Ximes* as manager and head of software development) joined the project as part of her master thesis. After the successful completion of the project with *SHIFT-PLANASSISTANT V 1.0*,

> it was clear that the project would stop with Sabine leaving, so I offered her a deal that exceeded my monthly salary but I was confident to be able to win additional projects [...] and that worked out reasonably, but it was tight for a long time. Projects brought us money but what we earned went into development. However, the feeling that this is an important topic and the approach useful and that we can make a living from it, this feeling stabilized.
>
> (JG Int, 26/06/2020)

It also took time to develop an approach that would persist and eventually also grow. The focus on working time was extended to include issues of wage/salary and workforce requirements; at the same time, the approach, which is participative (inclusive of all stakeholders), interdisciplinary (depending on the issue), and scientifically grounded, was further elaborated. The Working Time Society (otherwise known as the Committee on Shiftwork and Working Time, International Commission on Occupational Health (ICOH)) had an important role in this respect, providing a forum for debate as well as access to international collaborations.

10.1.1 The approach

Ximes grew out of the initiative of one individual, who was able to impart his ideas and his political commitment to a small group of young colleagues. Central to the project was a deep political commitment to the humanization of working life and to workers' health, as well as an approach to system design that was participatory and interdisciplinary. Based on criticism of an understanding of scheduling developed in management science and operations research at that time, Gärtner and Wahl (1998) defined the scheduling task as one that gives the user the role of exploring design options of a schedule in their work context and also assessing a chosen option, including the organizational change issues that need to be addressed:

First, it does not deal with the vagueness and the ambiguity of real-world requirements as neglectable shortcomings of pure scheduling problems. On the contrary, these features often allow better solutions (e.g., by considering organizational changes). This led us to requirement handling by design and participatory planning. Second, we give the schedulers a much more active and responsible role.

(Gärtner and Wahl, 1998: 223)

Hence, organizational change as a consequence of a new practice of scheduling working time was considered from the beginning.

Based on these insights, two complementary tools were developed: one that assists designers in the pre-analysis of a scheduling problem and one that supports the actual design of the schedule. The shift-scheduling assistant offered several functionalities:

Support of flexible and refined planning; tools for manipulating shift models; tools to support the analysis/preservation of overview; support of various visualizations that help improve overview; support of the interactive development resp. evaluation of shift models in cooperation with managers resp. working groups.

(Gärtner, 1996: 13)

The consulting activities that the group at *Ximes* engaged with and further developed were inspired by PD. Participatory techniques were used in the design of new working-hour arrangements and new reward systems, both with encouraging results. First of all, design decisions became more transparent and the pressure to provide arguments for a particular solution increased for all participants. Gärtner and Wahl (1998) see these as the main benefits of their approach, which also convinced their clients to spend time and money on negotiating instead of mandating a shift schedule:

The relevant implications of individual planning decisions (distribution of burdensome shifts, income) become available immediately and with minimal effort (in many areas in less than ten seconds instead of hours of calculations). As a result, these moved closer to the discussion and attention.

(p. 16)

As it is difficult for people to talk about their use of time in abstract terms, they need to be supported to understand the different facets of a problem such as working time and develop alternative solutions that can be compared:

As people are not able to keep all facets of a complex problem continuously evident, what I have to achieve is that those implicated in a decision take account of the problem in its complexity, and I have to manage to get the answers from the software as fast as possible—does this comply with the laws, how about the weekends, how much will it cost [...] that I have a quick response to many of these questions and avoid that the discussion process is interrupted.

(JG Int, 26/06/2020)

10.1.2 Widening the perspective

The transition from having a stable position at the university to being responsible for a company which was growing fast was facilitated by favourable conditions. The most important condition was the possibility of Johannes Gärtner continuing at the university on a part-time basis for several years until the company was ready to take off. This provided plenty of time to build experience and brought 'lots of confidence', but also lots of anxieties that were not easy to handle.

One of the most striking experiences during this transition period was being forced to think about certain issues and keep an eye on them, such as finances, taxes, mid-term perspectives, and over time we developed a second company, since you can't be too vague, you need a focus. We like to experiment, invest heavily in R & D, want to have a good life but this is not the main idea, it is more about doing good, meaningful work.

(JG Int, 26/06/2020)

The second company, *calcuLex*, actually a spin-off from *Ximes*, offers software in support of 'calculating' work-related legal requirements.

A key insight was that it is important to generate a substantial income in good years to be able to survive in bad ones. A strategically important decision was to have a set of topics that will be relevant in the long term. While the ideas about working time, wage/salary systems, and personnel requirements may change over time, they will always be at the heart of companies and organizations, and it was to be expected that these might continue to be interested in getting support for developing solutions.

At the beginning, the group had a somewhat 'naive notion of the market'— 'the idea was what fits the STAHL-AG will fit half of the world' (JG Int,

26/06/2020). The question in steel production had been how to optimize the shift schedule for quite a homogeneous situation: the assumption that a certain number of people with relatively similar skills are needed to operate a workstation for twenty-four hours from Monday to Sunday. The task, then, is to develop a long-term shift plan based on standardized shift times, observing laws, costs, free time, and so on: 'Almost every word in this description has been modified over the years—shift times, homogeneity, regularity [...] it gets "softer" and we have learned to handle much more complexity' (JG Int, 26/06/2020).

This gradual softening of notions that had been taken for granted made progress possible, as it opened up new design spaces. One of the challenges for the group at *Ximes* was that these developments were not easy to anticipate and required investments to be made in research. One example is that shift work and flexible working hours had been considered as parts of totally separate worlds—shifts work for industry and flexitime for office work. 'Now all these blend and we introduce flextime in shift models'. Another example is personnel requirements that 'had been thought of in terms of 7.8 persons needed for a task—now personnel requirements is a social construct, dependent on the notion of quality, responsibility [...]' (JG Int, 26/06/2020). The first big contract after a series of smaller projects with steel companies was with a social work organization—a totally different world.

What allowed *Ximes*, that had started with a rather particular topic and approach, to continue and even grow with projects in different work domains and countries was the importance it placed on research as part of its long-term strategy. Recently, *Ximes* hired a young colleague with a strong academic profile. Apart from collaborating with international researchers from the working time community, *Ximes* is interested in getting funding for research projects from companies or advocacy groups and sometimes also funds its own research on 'exciting questions' if economically feasible. They also apply for research and development projects, some of them more commercially oriented and some using more basic research. In general, the strategy is to look for contracts with a research component.

The academic work is crucial for the survival of *Ximes* in several ways:

The key question is, do they [the companies] find us and do they trust us. And there is the question how do they come to us and here our academic or close-to-academic formats have proved successful, that means writing a book (e.g. the 'Handbook Shift-Plans'), writing an article for an academic journal, presenting at academic conferences and as a researcher at trade-union events, there it has been extremely successful that there were people that accepted us in this role and recommended us […] while the classic advertising strategies have hardly had any impact, it is this more indirect academic input that results in people contacting us.

(JG Int, 26/06/2020)

The group at *Ximes* discovered that academic status is valued by its clients and may be helpful for both the client and *Ximes* itself in the case of a conflict. Recently, *Ximes*, together with partners in Germany and Switzerland, founded the German-speaking sister organization of the *Working Time Society*.

One of the limitations of the approach is that it has grown out of a particular central European culture. Attempts at 'exporting' it to Japan or the United States have not been successful due to the different 'sociopolitical settings'. Factors such as different legal systems but also differing industrial traditions and cultures—'a rotating shift plan system means something totally different in the US than in the European context' (JG Int, 26/06/2020)—make its transferability difficult.

10.2 The story of *OpenDash*

10.2.1 Designing for eco-feedback in an industrial context

The research line around *OpenDash* started with *Living Lab Energy and Environment* (*LLEE*, 2013–17), a nationally funded project about developing an integrated energy management system for companies and households. The basic idea was to support awareness of energy consumption of individuals and organizations and to help them optimize their energy behaviour. The project, which focused on the industrial context, involved four companies as associated partners: a local savings bank; a large producer of fastening technology for the car industry; a producer of meat and bread; and a company producing metal products. In first contacts with these companies, the research team got to know their current practices to ensure energy efficiency, as well as their objectives for improving energy management. The team also helped the companies plan for the installation of sensors. It then conducted an interview-based empirical study with representatives from different departments—maintenance, purchasing, machine operations, IT, and management—to find out about their contact with energy data. The aim of this study was to understand how energy data could help employees in different jobs integrate eco-feedback into their daily practices. The result of this study was a first concept for a data management system, which identified the need for energy-related data for different roles in the companies and how to best visualize these data in support of ongoing operations as well as analysis and planning.

> We identified that there are different needs for different roles in the companies (both data and their visualization): we developed the concept of role-based energy management (see Castelli et al. 2015). Then we started developing this system. We called it *OpenDash*. It is a web-based visualization framework. You can use any digital data like temperature or mobility data and visualize for different people in a very flexible way.
>
> (NC Int, 22/3/2018)

The project ran into difficulties when it turned out that the IT partner responsible for transferring the sensor data into *OpenDash* did not manage to do so within project time. It seems that this partner did not spend enough effort on building a reliable, well-functioning system. Hence, it was not possible to test *OpenDash* in the companies:

> So we had maybe two weeks data sometimes that we can show to the companies to evaluate in a design workshop the system. But we were not able to test it really in the wild, in the everyday usage. [...] That was a bit the problem of this project that none of the four companies could use the system after. So they were a bit disappointed.
>
> (NC Int, 22/3/2018)

Luckily, the researchers were able to test the *OpenDash* in the context of the *Smartlife* project (2014–17) with twelve participating private households for about a year and a half. Hence, one step towards a sustainable solution was to transfer *OpenDash* into a different context, where it was appropriated by another group of users.

The other strategy was to maintain a working relationship with the participating companies, although funding had expired. As the companies are now legally required to have an energy audit done, they were interested in receiving a working system as fast as possible. Although the research team had intended to submit a proposal for a follow-up project, the pending elections for a new government in North Rhine-Westphalia created a gap in funding. This gap was filled by resources provided by the Competence Center *Mittelstand 4.0* (CC) Siegen (see Chapter 3), with which the university is a partner. It was started in 2017 and supports small and medium-sized enterprises in the area of South Westphalia in their digitalization projects. The research team was able to recruit a new partner:

> They already had the technology to fix these problems we had with the sensor data. We asked them if they could help us and they were interested but they don't get any money from us: they sell their technology to the companies themselves. They were able to collect data from at least three of those four companies. Now we are trying to connect their database to our *OpenDash* to show the companies any data. In the fourth company the old IT partner still tries to fix their problem but I don't know if they can get it.
>
> (NC Int, 22/3/2018)

In mid 2018, a new project—*ASUP* (*Anwenderorientierte Smarte Umweltinformationssysteme in der Praxis*)—started, which provides the opportunity to build on the technology that had been installed in the first project, help the software to run, and add a few new functionalities. This project focuses on data analytics from a machine learning perspective. This research involves almost the same partners and continues collaboration with the four companies. The new layer for artificial intelligence is intended to create energy forecasts based on a company's history of energy consumption, with different methods 'so that the companies can see how their energy develops in the next periods to make better decisions in terms of process planning or if they need any new contract or something like this' (NC Int, 2/5/2019). Another objective is to add blockchain as a backend that supports distributed energy data in a network of multiple companies for reporting their energy data. The idea is to review these data automatically and inform them regularly about their energy performance. Key advantages of such a distributed infrastructure are that it prevents manipulation of data and provides multiple backups.

10.2.2 Parallel development: *SmartLife*

SmartLife (2014–17) was embedded in the *Living Lab* at the University of Siegen and formed part of the design of new smart home concepts with the goal of improving the user experience:

> Existing systems are too complex. Users need to know: a) which kind of system is best for me; b) they usually have to set up the system on their own and the technical overload has to be reduced (e.g. they have to define 'rules' when

they install a device); c) users often don't know what their needs and what is possible: they should think in a more future-oriented way.

(CO Int, 20/3/2018)

As this project was about collecting smart data for different uses in the home, the decision was taken to use *OpenDash*.

This project also started with an empirical study that investigated people's daily routines, needs, interests, and ideas on how to possibly use an eco-feedback system in their homes (Castelli et al., 2017). Participants were then provided with a plug and play smart home platform system solution that was available on the market, using it as a technology probe for gaining additional insights. After three months of hands-on experience with this system, some selected participants were invited to a creative design workshop with the goal of involving them in developing a first set of requirements for how to use *OpenDash*. Participants created their own paper-based smart home interfaces, which then informed the design of a flexible and highly customizable prototype.

> The system is based on a dashboard concept, allowing us to realize our general idea of multiple visualizations for the participants' needs and use cases as single web components that could easily be exchanged or configured during runtime. [...] Widgets can be dynamically added, rearranged, changed in size or deleted. [...] To allow a very personal customization and a detailed exploration of smart home data on demand [...], we developed an EUD environment to create custom visualizations of smart home data. Our visualization creation process consists of five-steps [...], following the visualization pipeline by Card [13]: selecting data (Data Analysis), selecting time (Filtering), selecting chart, configuration (Mapping) and adaption (Rendering).
>
> (Castelli et al., 2017: 858–9)

This was installed in people's homes and used to gain insights about how they use smart home data with the system. Hence, a large part of project time was spent on anchoring prototype development in people's lives.

10.2.3 The design strategy: Synergies from multiple projects

It was clear from the beginning that *OpenDash* had the potential of being used in many projects. Its layered architecture offers the possibility of developing visualizations for different contexts. The system solves a basic problem—visualization of data—that is common to many projects that collect data from many devices. Hence the decision to develop a modular system that is open source, since

> anybody who needs such a visualization framework can use it in other projects. That's why we have a good open source documentation, we have flexible modules so that can be changed and we did not want to focus especially in the core of the system on energy, on any context especially. So we have this open source core which is a fully flexible dashboard system where anybody can build on top maybe visualizations for energy, for mobility, and so on.
>
> (NC Int, 22/3/2018)

OpenDash was first used for visualizing time-based data. For example, mobility data can be visualized on maps, and data line and bar charts can be used for energy and temperature. The different projects the main developers of *OpenDash* were involved in provided opportunities for developing additional visualization forms. Hence, their main strategy was to look for new projects and take their needs and requirements as an opportunity to systematically ensure the transferability of *OpenDash* to new contexts.

In the beginning, *OpenDash* was just front end, basically running on the computer of the user, and got its data from various sources. What was missing was a middleware which would provide a mechanism for data collection. This was a source of many problems which stalled the subsequent development of the visualization component. The *Cognitive Village* (2015–18) project provided the opportunity to develop a new version of *OpenDash* that enhanced the visualization layer with a middleware for data collection and processing.

> In the earlier projects, we always had this problem that we were so dependent on the companies to deliver a mechanism for data collection. And then, in *Cognitive Village*, A. and I wrote a middleware that collected data, in order to be able to visualize something at all. However, this was originally meant as a provisional software as long as we had to wait for another research partner to finish their work and provide the proper middleware. But as this software could not be finalized during the project time, we used ours, the 'provisorium', and developed it further. And this was then continually used in our other projects later on.
>
> (MS Int, 20/1/2020)

The process of developing and integrating a reliable and robust middleware as an integral part of the *OpenDash* platform was based on a tortuous path that had not been planned. The decision to follow this path was influenced by a mixture of personal interests and contextual conditions. An important opportunity presented itself in *Cognitive Village* with the collaboration between Martin Stein, who was at that time employed at Fraunhofer FIT and Alexander Boden (also Fraunhofer FIT), with whom he shared an office. In *Cognitive Village*, Fraunhofer FIT was responsible for the usability of the software to be developed.

> To fulfill his task, A. originally had planned to use an open visualization tool, which seemed to work, but also seemed to be quite complicated in its usage. Then I said, 'hey, why don't you want to try *OpenDash*?' At that time, I knew how it worked because I had seen it in the other projects, we had talked a lot about it, and I also knew how it had been built. And then we both wanted to try it out. But to do so, we also needed a middleware. So, we started with building this provisional thing, which we then planned to having it integrated when the proper tool was delivered from the other partner. And then this middleware was left over. At that time, it was still quite simple, it didn't do much, it really only took data, saved it and put it out again. But after the end of *Cognitive Village*, we saw that it was needed in other projects, too. In *LLEE* new requirements appeared and also in the follow-up project *ASUB*.
>
> (MS Int, 20/1/2020)

The decision was taken to invest time in improving the software and to further develop this provisional solution: 'we had to exchange some parts which were still a bit shirt-sleeved, and built it stable' (MS Int, 20/1/2020).

In addition to the integration of the middleware developed in *Cognitive Village*, a command-line interface (CLI) was created—a tool chain that helps developer-users in a new project build their own basic configuration:

> So some, there are some commands, give it a name and then it will create the basic structure of the system that you need, so you don't need to do anything from scratch but it provides you with most of the basic stuff and it goes so far that it asks you 'Do you want to include standard widgets, that already have been developed?', 'Do you want to include certain data sources that already have been integrated?', 'Do you want to integrate […] ?'
>
> (MS)

The main motivation driving this process was to find a way of making *Open-Dash* usable for companies beyond project time. This was also the beginning of a spin-off that the developers created in response to the need for companies to have continuous technological support.

10.2.4 Bringing *OpenDash* into new contexts

The main developers of *OpenDash* learn through different communication channels about potential new contexts for the software and the components that different individual projects may need. One such channel is the CC *Mittelstand 4.0*; this collects requirements and solutions developed for individual companies which are then put 'into the basis—the building box' (MS Int, 20/1/2020). Other circumstances that facilitate knowledge transfer between projects include offices being situated close to one another as well as joint lunch meetings. These help the developers get up-to-date information about the current status of the different projects so that they know which tools and which kinds of data are being used. Knowledge exchange also happens in the other direction: when developing new ideas for *OpenDash*, the developers may make suggestions to researchers involved in other projects: 'this could also be quite interesting for you, right?' (NC Int, 20/1/2020). However, due to the growth of the group, opportunities for informal chats over lunch have become more infrequent. This hampers the exchange of mutual knowledge that in the past has led to fruitful collaborations: projects that may benefit from using *Open-Dash*; use cases that might offer interesting opportunities that are not obvious at first sight; application fields that the main developers of *OpenDash* are not fully familiar with. One strategy to change this is to pool interdisciplinary expertise in the group. An example is a workshop with care providers in which a colleague with nursing expertise participated, later helping to identify possible use cases.

The developers of *OpenDash* are not directly involved in the projects using the software but act as consultants:

> Everybody knows about the visualization system and we help installing and integrating the system and when they have problems. And we have one former student for this *OpenDash*, who is employed by us now as technician: he is expert in the code and teaches other students about how to use and how to develop for this system. Having something running motivates them to improve it. We have good documentation.
>
> (NC Int, 22/3/2018)

One of the projects using *OpenDash* is *EKPLO*, which focuses on real-time production planning in companies (see Chapter 3). *OpenDash* is used here to visualize production plans and machine data:

> We decided to use *OpenDash* as a dashboard tool that has real time features which is interesting for us. Since we know each other here —pretty much all colleagues, we know what they do, so the idea came to us to not reprogram something or so but to use *OpenDash* […] NC once said that we are using it totally differently than they usually […] it is for information, representation and combination of time serious data most of all. Which sensor reported, which value and to put that together in maybe one diagram.
>
> (CK Int, 22/11/2018)

The software had to be extended and made more interactive. It now allows users to read and manipulate the results of production plans directly in the application.

A new project that uses *OpenDash* is *GaNEsHA* (2017–20), which has supporting greater awareness of daily transportation activities in cities as its aim. At its core is a mobile crowd-sensing tool to track mobility activities to be used by municipalities and service providers such as utility companies. As attempts to get, for example, telematics data from traffic lights failed, the Siegen team came up with the idea of collecting location-based chat data from people on the way to the city and using these data to predict how crowded certain roads in a city are or will be. *OpenDash* is also used here for visualizing these data.

10.2.5 The spin-off

Looking at other big German universities and their sustainability strategies for particularly successful technologies, the team at the University of Siegen decided in 2018 to create a spin-off which at the moment is run by two developers that are still employed by the university; the income that is created by the spin-off is being 'collected' until the company is profitable enough to pay for the developers' salaries. This is only possible because the developers are prepared to work for long hours and during weekends: 'we have a great work-work balance'. Their personal benefit is twofold: first of all, 'programming is fun, is fun for us. So, it's like a hobby which you can combine with the company'; and: 'I think so for me the biggest point was I didn't want to stay in research' (MS Int, 2/5/2019). The university benefits from this arrangement as well, as 'we typically give everything back to university. So, all the new stuff that we develop in the companies of our clients, we also put it into the research projects' (MS Int, 2/5/2019).

This constellation includes a relationship with the CC *Mittelstand 4.0. Open-Dash* is on the server of the CC, together with lots of other systems that are being used as demonstrators—'for proof of concept you use this server'. Another advantage is that the CC can propose to interested companies the spin-off as a partner that takes care of the maintenance of *OpenDash* in the future. The developers call this 'predicted maintenance'. It includes installing the necessary components on the company's server and configuring them. These relationships need to be constantly (re)negotiated.

One aspect of this complex relationship is deciding what should be open source and what is only available commercially. One key distinction is between aspects that are not necessary for a research prototype and those that are crucial for a company, such as the connection of the system to an active directory server, process integration, access rights, backup strategies, monitoring of the system status, security, and so forth. These parts are not open source.

> Typically [companies] don't pay for the development, we had some modules that we don't open source. So, because we pay for other licenses as well. So, there are some parts that we have to pay as soon as we use it commercially and these parts we can't even […] I don't know if it would be possible to open source that easily.
>
> (MS Int, 2/5/2019)

University, CC, and spin-off are also connected when it comes to finding companies as partners or clients. In general, the Siegen area, with its large number of SMEs, many of them in manufacturing, offers a lot of opportunities, since 'basically every company needs systems like we provide' (MS). One good starting point is the CC, where the developers can come in to show the open-source version of *OpenDash*. If a company is interested in a system which is open source, hence available,

> then the next question is 'Can you maintain it?' And then we can say 'No, the university can't do that.' 'Is there anyone who can maintain it?' 'Yes, every skilled programmer can maintain the project.' 'But can you do that as well?' And then we say 'Yes, we can do that as well.'
>
> (MS Int, 2/5/2019)

The boundaries between research, the construction of the publicly funded CC— which is not allowed to subsidize activities that benefit a company directly—and the spin-off have to be carefully managed. In some instances, the developers 'have to wait until people find out by themselves that we have a company as well' (MS).

The spin-off depends on continuous development. As part of this, the framework underlying *OpenDash* was changed, as well as the middleware—'this is not a static thing'. The impetus for change comes from both research projects and collaboration with commercial clients:

> Every project that wants to do any data collection or data visualization, data prediction, data analysis, I just say 'Yes, we can do that' and I integrate this and as soon as I run into an issue there or if Nico sees something that needs to, especially with the visualization or something like that, that should be better, we just develop a new one. And release it open source. And that's quite nice, because as soon as we released it open source from the university we can make use of it in the company.
>
> (MS Int, 2/5/2019)

Recently, the spin-off was joined by a hardware company which has been promised 15%—'so typically they sell their hardware and we can install our software system there, so every client they have is a potential client for us then' (MS).

10.3 Summary

University spin-offs may embrace very different realities (Pirnay et al., 2013) and we have described just two examples from among a potentially enormous variety. *Ximes* is a well-established company, having been founded in 1997, and has grown into two tightly interconnected firms with bases in Austria and Germany, respectively, and more than twenty employees. *OpenDash*, on the other hand, is young, and its two founders are still employed by the university. Common to both spin-offs is the time they have had to mature in a supportive environment before becoming independent and having to earn their own resources. Other shared features are the focus on users and work practices, which each of the spin-offs pursues in a different way, and a continuing academic interest. Differences are found in the business models they follow and the attitudes of their founders. While consulting based on participatory techniques (in combination with technological support) is at the heart of

Ximes, *OpenDash* is technology-oriented, although closely connected with the work practices each project seeks to support. Neither company aims at 'hi-tech hi-growth markets'.

At the core of the story of *Ximes* is a mission—the humanization of work and workers' health—and an approach that turned out to be sustainable, although it needed to be adapted to highly varied situations in different work domains. This was made possible through the company's emphasis on participation and learning. Consulting projects offer ample opportunities for learning. The exploration of new contexts and requirements and the collaboration with new types of stakeholders may result in new participatory techniques as well as new or modified software tools. The group's research activities consolidate and deepen the learning in and across projects and also help them to find new resources. In addition, *Ximes* offers a 'working time management' course to its clients as part of a connected sustainability strategy. This helps to strengthen their approach and broaden their client base.

At the core of *OpenDash* is an IT artifact—a visualization dashboard with many potential uses that has already been probed and further developed in different contexts. The transferability and evolvability of *OpenDash* has been planned since (almost) the start. This was possible because the researchers are embedded in a work environment with multiple projects in different domains, including the CC *Mittelstand 4.0*, which encouraged them to think about designing for tailorability. Using the synergies from these different projects, the researchers engaged in the step-by-step development of *OpenDash* software components—the middleware, support for a variety of visualization forms, and a CLI. The projects offered ample opportunities to probe the software in contexts as different as manufacturing, energy management in industry and private households, mobility of elderly people, and so forth.

The construction of the spin-off that was created out of these research activities has an arrangement typical of many of its kind, with the developers still being employed by the university but also starting to acquire commercial clients to develop their economic base.

SECTION III
ANALYSIS AND DISCUSSION

11

Looking across and connecting

The aim of this chapter is to focus an analytical lens on the collection of projects and cases in different fields of activity by revisiting them from the perspective of sustainability. Several objectives can be met by adopting a comparative lens. One such objective is to refine the sensitizing concepts presented in Chapter 2 in order to arrive at a more nuanced understanding of the conditions required to achieve a sustainable outcome and the strategies assumed by researchers. Another objective is to capture aspects that 'matter for design' in support of sustainable outcomes: more specifically, to learn how to set up a project or research line, how to create alliances in support of sustainability, and how to arrange for future-proofing activities well before a project ends.

While the comparative analysis that is presented in this chapter is not able to systematically account for the characteristics of the different fields of activity covered by the projects and cases, it is important to keep these characteristics in mind as a kind of 'background' that can help explain the particular contexts in which the research teams moved. Table 11.1 provides a short summary as a reminder of these different contexts and challenges.

11.1 A diversity of purposes: Clustering the projects/cases

While the case study chapters emphasize the specificity of each context, this next step looks across the different fields of activity and seeks to identify commonalities and differences. The analysis underlines the idea of sustainability as taking place in a multidimensional space (see Chapter 2) and discusses the complex issues researchers face in the diversity of contexts the projects represent. The key insights that such a comparative perspective provides will serve as a basis for the concluding chapter, which aims to spell out a future perspective.

Future-proofing the outcomes of practice-based projects concerns two interrelated dimensions (see Chapter 1): (1) the technical maintainability and

Future-proofing. Wulf et al., Oxford University Press.
© Carla Simone, Ina Wagner, Claudia Müller, Anne Weibert, and Volker Wulf (2022).
DOI: 10.1093/oso/9780198862505.003.0011

Table 11.1 Characteristics of the application domain with respect to sustainability.

Field of activity	Characteristics with respect to sustainability
Manufacturing 4.0 in SMEs	• Complex production process with solid distributed knowledge base • Ability to manage the collaborative overview of the state of affairs • Use of innovative devices within production processes in a competitive domain • Focus on product innovation rather than process innovation • Difficulty in ensuring steady flow of work while containing production costs • Lack of solid IT competences that are expensive to acquire in the labour market
Firefighters	• Highly risky and time-critical domain where safety is of paramount relevance • Well-established institutional policies and local practices to manage the risk for all the involved stakeholders • Any innovation requires complex certification by the reference institutions
Emergency management	• A complex domain requiring the handling of different phases (disaster mitigation, preparedness, response, recovery) with different requirements and time constraints • Conflicts between predefined procedures and real-time reaction to contingent situations • Action in the damaged settings requires different actors to be coordinated and kept safe • Critical collaboration among professionals and volunteers with different education, experience, and responsibility
Healthcare	• Many stakeholders involved at different levels of the care hierarchy • Action close to the patients is time- and safety-critical and has to be accountable • Many places where care is delivered with specific responsibilities and needs • A wide range of formal and informal forms for different and sometimes conflicting purposes to support and document care • Enormous need for coordination and information-sharing among all stakeholders • Bidirectional relationship with clinical research to provide data and be informed about care innovation • Considerable local variations of care practices to account for local settings and conditions • Problems with integration between new technologies and the IT installed base • Big investments in global initiatives and general lack of resources for local innovation

Continued

Table 11.1 *Continued*

Field of activity	Characteristics with respect to sustainability
Developing countries	• Extreme levels of poverty and poor infrastructure • Community as a fundamental social structure • Different ways of learning about and appropriating new technologies • Robustness of solutions counts more than their innovativeness • Difficulty in accessing global information to complement and complete local knowledge • A need for reaching autonomy from external interventions (donors, NGO, charity, etc.)
IT service providers	• Mostly international, companies that invest in research and innovation • Often based on hierarchical organization with complex decisional structures • The hosting company is often an early adopter of prospective commercial solutions/services—innovation as a part of the external image of the company
Intercultural Computer Clubs	• Mission to promote learning across cultures and communities • Meeting points of different cultural backgrounds—Western researchers confronted with migrants, refugees, and citizens of developing countries, all usually living under difficult conditions • Technological literacy as a means to improve the social situation of people in critical settings • Attention to intergenerational relationships and effects • Solutions depend on the social, political, and infrastructural characteristics of the local context in which they are anchored • Importance of stable alliances with local players to guarantee the continuity of the action and promote integration

flexibility of the IT artifact; (2) the stability of the social practices that develop through appropriation work and the ability to further develop these practices. The particular relationship between these two dimensions depends on the particular focus and purposes of a project. Hence, one important point to consider when comparing the projects and cases is to account for their differences in terms of the type of IT artifact they seek to develop, deploy, and make useful: whether they are designing a technologically innovative artifact that is tailored to a particular field of activity or a more generic technology that can be used in different contexts; whether the aim is to adapt off-the-shelf technologies to a particular context; or whether a project deals with large-scale systems in terms of standardization and/or integration (see Table 11.2).

Another set of distinctions refers to the different levels of sustainable outcomes (Scheirer, 2005): *individual-level* outcomes in terms of access to useful technologies and/or services and occasions for learning and new ways

Table 11.2 Foci and purposes of projects/cases.

Focus/Purpose	Project/Case
Technological innovation tailored to a particular field of activity	Project line with firefighters IBM *Cloud Service Analytics* IBM *Intelligent IT Configuration*
Develop a generic technology that can be used in different contexts	*OpenDash* (spin-off) *WOAD*
Reduce fragmentation of large-scale systems through standards/technical integration	*B-EPR* (*Basic Structure for EPR*) *STEP* (*Standardized Extraction of Patient Data*) *WFT* (*WelFare Technologies*) *DocuLive* (EPR system, Norway)
Community development	*Zenzeleni* community network *Come_IN* (ICC)
Development and learning (users, decision-makers)	*SmartLife* (Smart Home/Smart Energy) CC *Mittelstand 4.0*
Improve (work) practices/quality of services	*ActionADE* (adverse drug events) Xerox *Agent Performance Indicator* (call centres) *WOAD* *Telemedicine toolkit* *PICADo* (home care) *CALIPSO* (home care) *HADex* (hospital at home) *EKPLO* (real-time collaborative planning and scheduling) *Cyberrüsten 4.0* (Machine set-up with AR) Project line on emergency management
Improve organization of processes	Xerox *Print Awareness Tool* Xerox *Turk-Bench* project IBM *RFS-D* *Scanning* project *Videoconferencing* project *Ximes* (spin-off)

of doing things; the *community-level* capacity to make use of technology to sustain particular activities as well as to take further initiatives and innovate; and, finally, the *organization-level* implementation of IT artifacts to improve, for instance, (work) practices and organizational procedures or the quality of products or services.

These distinctions not only matter with respect to what future-proofing strategies a research team develops; they also define the kinds of challenges and constraints that have to be mastered and/or the limitations to confront and deal with.

In comparing and contrasting the projects and cases, we analyse the set of sensitizing concepts, probing their usefulness but also elaborating and extending them to capture new insights. We start by comparing the project outcomes and then describe the different future-proofing strategies as well as the impediments to sustainability.

11.2 Forms of sustainability: Comparing project outcomes

The different forms of sustainability that have been suggested by Iversen and Dindler (2014)—*maintaining, scaling, replicating,* and *evolving*—are a good starting point for comparing the project/case outcomes, as they help explain under which conditions sustainability can be a feasible goal and what the specific impediments to realizing a future perspective may be. The case studies suggest adding two more categories—the *discontinued* form and the *(still) open* form. Several projects stopped or were stopped before their possible outcomes could be implemented in a real setting, for a variety of reasons. In spite of this negative ending, these projects generated positive experiences, mostly in the form of learning, which helped the involved stakeholders carry some ideas forward. The *(still) open* form applies to a number of long-lasting projects with open and complex internal dynamics that make future moves possible and the sustainability of the outcomes uncertain. Table 11.3 presents short definitions of the forms of sustainability that will be further articulated in the next sections.

An overview of the projects according to their achieved form of sustainability is provided in Table 11.4. It is important to note that the distinctions between the forms are neither clear-cut nor mutually exclusive.

11.2.1 The *discontinued* form

This form of sustainability covers situations where projects had started to produce promising outcomes but for various reasons stopped before these could be deployed in a real setting. Another case of discontinuity is when the roll-out of a project was abandonded at the end of the project. In a way, this is a fairly common situation for research with a limited duration of funding. Strictly speaking, these projects, which are mostly single projects, could be considered 'unproductive' from the perspective of achieving a sustainable outcome—that is, in producing an IT artifact that is useful and will be used. However, they

Table 11.3 The different forms of sustainability.

Discontinued form	Projects started to produce results but for various reasons stopped before these could be deployed in a real setting, or a roll-out was discontinued at the end of the project; partial achievements can have effects that last beyond the end of the project.
Maintaining form	Projects reach this basic form of sustainability when the design solution is deployed in the target setting with users starting to appropriate it and remains in the place for which it has been developed after the projects end.
Scaling form	Projects extend the potential set of users adopting the solution under similar needs and conditions; scaling requires a limited adaptation of the solution to the new situation from both the technological and organizational standpoints.
Replicating form	Projects transfer their outcome to new settings with substantially different contextual conditions.
Evolving form	Projects expand the solution with new and possibly innovative aspects; evolving builds upon successful forms of *maintaining*, *scaling*, or *replicating*.
(Still) open form	Projects require a solution whose socio-technical achievements may remain open for some time; this makes it difficult to evaluate when and in which way the project will reach some sustainable outcomes.

are interesting to consider. On the one hand, they can offer examples of the conditions that may make sustainability an impossible goal to reach. On the other hand, they may yield partial achievements that last beyond the end of the project. They may offer the stakeholders involved the opportunity to: learn about a specific field of activity, its complexities and challenges; prototype solutions that can be further developed under more favourable conditions; or become aware of potential problems in complex organizational contexts that are difficult to anticipate.

There is an important difference between industrial/institutional projects and academic projects: while in the first case it is mostly management that decides to terminate an initiative as a consequence of the encountered problems, in the second case the project reaches a 'natural' end that is usually defined by the funding scheme adopted. The possibilities of being able to further develop some of the project outcomes then depend on whether a research team finds new opportunities.

Institutional projects: The case of health information infrastructures
An almost classic example of a discontinued project is the *B-EPR* project. This was promoted by a national healthcare institution with a view to constructing a new EPR to be nationally adopted in Denmark to facilitate data exchange between health institutions. The initial approach—to develop a centralized

Table 11.4 The level of sustainability reached by the different projects or research lines where only the more influential projects are mentioned.

DISCONTINUED FORM	Xerox *Turk-Bench*
• Industrial/institutional projects: Discontinued by management decisions	IBM *Cloud Service Analytics* IBM *Intelligent IT Configuration* *B-EPR*
• Academic projects: Discontinued due to specific characteristics of the field of application	Research line with firefighters: *WearIT, Landmarke, Koordinator* *WOAD* Telecare: *CALIPSO, HADex*
• Academic projects: Discontinued due to qualities of the produced solution	*PICADo* (telecare) *EKPLO* (SMEs in manufacturing) Research line on emergency management: *Infostrom, EmerGent, KOKOS*
MAINTAINING FORM	IBM *RFS-D*
• Industrial projects	Xerox *Print Awareness Tool*
• Off-the-shelf technologies in healthcare	*Videoconferencing* (healthcare) *Telemedicine toolkit*
• Health information infrastructures	*SEP* (Healthcare) *WFT* (*WelFare Technologies*) *DocuLive* (healthcare)
SCALING FORM	*Zenzeleni Networks* (South Africa) *Scanning* project (healthcare)
REPLICATING FORM	*Come_IN* (ICC) Xerox *Print Awareness Tool*
EVOLVING FORM	*Come_IN* (ICC)
• Accumulating evolution of services	*Zenzeleni Networks* (South Africa) *Ximes* (spin-off)
• Evolution of a technology	*OpenDash* (spin-off)
• Opening up to new stakeholders	*Cyberrüsten* (SMEs in manufacturing) Telecare: *CALIPSO, HADex*
(STILL) OPEN FORM	*ActionADE* (healthcare) Xerox *Agent Performance Indicator*

solution based on the definition of a national standard—turned out to be impracticable and was discontinued because of the resistance of the involved clinicians. They came to the conclusion that the standard was incompatible with their local conditions. As a consequence, the development of the standard was stopped. Having learned from this failure, the SEP project adopted a more distributed solution, which valorized the investments and practices developed around already existing EPRs. This strategy created less conflict and greater positive involvement of all stakeholders.

The story of these projects suggests that, had their public promoters taken a decentralized approach from the very beginning, leaving more space for local practices and interests, the projects would have avoided the waste of time and heavy drain on public resources that the initial misconception caused. Unfortunately, examples such as these, which are also recognized in the information systems (IS) literature (Cecez-Kecmanovic et al., 2014), have not yet convinced public institutions and the (top) management of public and private companies of the need to deeply investigate the implications of 'centralization versus decentralization' from both the technological and organizational standpoints and implement the best balance between them (Hugoson, 2007).

Industrial projects: Closure/discontinuation by management

The closure of a project may also be driven by the insight that the initial project goals are unsustainable. This was the case in the Xerox *Turk-Bench* project, which was driven by top management with the aim of exploring the opportunity of a new business model for a specific healthcare data entry activity. Management soon had to recognize the risk involved in delegating data entry—a critical activity that requires knowledgeable actors to guarantee the required data quality—to an outside structure that would be impossible to monitor. Here, the negative outcome was one of the expected results, although not a desired one. In spite of its closure, the project helped to create awareness that an apparently unproblematic business change involving a seemingly simple activity was too critical to be implemented.

Sometimes an overambitious goal becoming impracticable at some point can be a reason for discontinuing a project; perhaps the solution that is sought does not meet the initial expectations or is not sustainable in terms of user acceptance and/or organizational costs. This was the case for two promising internal projects at IBM that moved at the forefront of AI-based solutions. The initial goal of the IBM *Cloud Service Analytics* project was to provide sellers and their managers with analytics that would help them improve their selling performances. However, the project team had not expected the difficulties the users would have in making sense of the outputs of the application and integrating it into their everyday practices. Moreover, the top management had hoped to transfer the application to other divisions of the company, underestimating the need to keep up with ongoing organizational changes and the work involved in making the necessary adjustments.

The IBM *Intelligent IT Configuration* project, which aimed to introduce machine learning technologies to support the company's IT architects in the configuration of solutions fulfilling client requests, was stopped in the end. In this case, the management's ambition had been to demonstrate the company's expertise with this kind of innovation and promote the technology's commercial diffusion. In the initial phase, the project encountered the appropriation problems of a complex and unintelligible technology that seemed to repeat the failure of the *Cloud Service Analytics* project. However, the *Intelligent IT Configuration* project survived the opposing forces for a longer period due to the enthusiasm of the IT architects and developers and their determination to meet the professional challenge set by the local management. In both cases, it was the nature of the solution envisioned—using machine learning techniques in support of highly professional 'knowledge work'—that led to the closure of the project.

Academic projects: Impediments to reaching an implementable solution
Academic projects usually have to deal with fixed project timelines and strictly limited project durations. It may be impossible to arrive at a design solution that is ready for implementation within this short period, particularly when the field of activity and the setting are complex. The case studies present two rather different examples of this situation.

Large national projects and EU-wide projects often ask for solutions that are replicable in different regional or national settings. Even when the researchers succeed in developing a prototype solution that is viable for one specific setting, the short duration of the project may prevent its transformation into a prototype that is robust enough to be deployed in a field where reliability is mandatory. An example of this constellation is the national *PICADo* project, which was financed by the French 'Fonds Unique Interministériel' programme. Its aim was to develop a solution that would improve the quality of telecare. While an observational study had created many valuable insights, the project consortium pushed for a solution that was considered too complex by the participating user association, 'E-maison médicale'. As a consequence, it was not possible to reach the level of maturity that would have allowed the solution to be tested in real settings. Although none of the prototype solutions survived, the project left the legacy of a field study to the French partner. This inspired subsequent initiatives, as well as a highly successful prototype (*CARE*), which was developed independently by the French team.

The German *EKPLO* project, which sought to bring Industry 4.0 to SMEs in manufacturing, exemplifies another set of difficulties. Its aim had been to support production planning in SMEs. Despite having established a good collaborative basis in an industrial partner company, the research team encountered several stumbling blocks that were difficult to surmount: the difficulties of finding a satisfactory solution for the acquisition of real-time data; the risks (and costs) connected with evaluating a system with real data; and the need for internal IT competence that SMEs may find difficult to afford. Continuing the project with two companies after the *EKPLO* project ended was unsuccessful since one of these companies (a supplier for the automotive industry) went bankrupt. More generally, however, the technology developed within *EKPLO* turned out to be difficult to transfer because it had to be 'unfeasibly flexible' to meet the substantially different planning strategies adopted in each company:

> It will be difficult to revive these activities. Primarily because of the technical side. The demonstrator is technically quite ambitious and consists of modules from different partners. As the fine planning of production is strongly dependent on the context and we don't have a fully adaptable solution, it is not possible to simply transfer the demonstrator to another context with a different, quite individualized planning situation. We have been confronted with this issue already several times, unfortunately.
>
> (CK, additional comment, 4/8/2020)

The research line in the field of emergency and crisis management met other types of impediments that turned out to be difficult to address. It was built around the idea of developing a technology that supports the coordination of professionals and volunteers operating in critical settings. The technology changed from one project to the next (from the *Infostrom* project to *EmerGent*, up to *KOKOS*) in response to the needs of the two different types of users. What caused the end of the research line were the appropriation problems that the researchers encountered while validating the prototypes in different contexts. It turned out that the technology was not usable during an emergency, due to liability and privacy issues that, given the choice of an open-source platform, were difficult to resolve. Working with open-source software, which made perfect sense from a research point of view, made building a business case difficult and problematic, as the researchers did not own the technology. Moreover, there was no longer-term mechanism in place to support the corresponding open-source community to continue development in the direction of the projects. Further, a solution that fitted professional rescue workers was not necessarily transferable to new types of users such as volunteers, who tend to prefer ready-to-use technologies and may not have the same liability issues.

However, the experience gained in how to support the communication among different stakeholders and facilitate the sharing of multimedia data led the research team to move to another challenging domain—collaborative research work—where their experiences could be leveraged. This new project (the *INF* project) focuses on the collection of already existing specialized components in view of a modular architecture that could offer various functionalities and be easily appropriated and configured by the distributed research teams.

Academic projects: Impediments that characterize the application domain

Certain fields of activity are difficult to 'conquer' for academic researchers, for different reasons. One of the reasons may be the restricted possibilities for those outside the field to launch a new type of device or application; another may be the requirement that an innovative solution has to conform to consolidated work practices and organizational procedures before it can be experimented with in a real setting; and yet another might be the resistance of powerful decision-makers in a field such as healthcare against approaches that aim to support the diversity of local practices.

The research line in the firefighting domain had a difficult start with the *WearIt* project due to a misperception regarding what kind of support would be useful for firefighters to be able to take a different direction in the subsequent *Landmarke* and *Koordinator* projects. The projects established productive relationships with the participating firefighters and validated solutions and prototypes in collaboration with them. Nevertheless, the projects encountered a series of difficulties. A big provider of firefighting equipment decided not to commercialize the prospective solution because it was too focused on the, fortunately rare, situation of a critical incident and involved communication features that were outside the company's interests. Similar reasons led a potential adopter (a big German city) to refuse the required investment. Finally, the research team that had thought of establishing a spin-off to commercialize the solution had to give up because the market for firefighting equipment was 'gated', with just a few big players. After the different members of the research team left the university for different industries, the research line stopped. The legacy of this project line was the deep learning process that made the firefighters more explicitly aware of the complexity of their work practices and of the mechanisms promoting their safety.

A different example is the *Web of Active Documents* (*WOAD*) research line, which was able to produce a set of prototypes towards an innovative EPR solution enabling doctors and nurses in a hospital to express different kinds of relationships between pieces of information within and across documents. This flexible, adaptable solution was appreciated and partially validated by a group of users, but it failed to reach the deployment phase due to the negative reaction of the hospital's top management towards this kind of innovation. IT companies were also not keen to take the risk of developing an innovative application in a domain strongly dominated by big healthcare application providers.

The stories of these two research lines show some remarkable similarities, irrespective of the differences between the domains, the amount of funding, and the number of involved researchers. A conclusion is that the sustainability of a research line can be hampered by important contextual conditions that escape the control of the researchers involved. One of these contextual conditions is a change of strategy of important actors, which can affect the sustainability of the goals of a research line. This change can be caused by the dynamics of organizational change within the institution hosting the initiatives but also, and in a more substantial way, the dynamics of the political choices of institutional decision-makers acting in the target application domain. In the case of both the *CALIPSO* and *HADex* projects, regional policy decisions led to a situation in which the fruitful collaboration of the academic research team with a small software company came to a halt, which resulted in the research team having to change its strategy and look for new alliances (see also the 'evolving form'). The ability to be resilient to external and asynchronous events is one important quality of a research team if it is to move the research line on beyond the discontinued individual projects.

11.2.2 Maintaining

Maintaining is the most basic form of sustainability. It accounts for the situation where the design solution is deployed in the target setting, where users start to appropriate it, and remains in the place for which it has been developed. The solution can be based on off-the-shelf or well-established technologies or may have been developed for the specific target setting. The *maintaining* form depends on strong support for 'learning-in-practice' and appropriation. One of the basic conditions for a design solution to be maintained is that it is firmly anchored in the local context and the community and/or organization is willing to support the changes of (work) practices and organization that are necessary for users to be able to benefit from the new technical artifact.

Two of the industry-based projects are successful examples of technologies that have been developed to enable new types of activities. Both projects spotted a potential real need; the critical task was to develop a technical solution that would be easy to use. The IBM *Request for Service Dashboard* (RFS-D) project started from the interest of the local management of the company's selling division in improving the collection of data about the ongoing requests for services by their clients. The solution, based on an analysis of the local work practices, was designed in cooperation with the involved stakeholders. The application is based on a dashboard flanking an existing workflow, which made it easy to integrate data collection with the current work practices and motivated the stakeholders to expend effort on improving the data quality. The Xerox *Print Awareness Tool* project was started by the company's top management with the intention of increasing the internal saving of paper and improving the company's image in relation to the increasing ecological sensitivity. Again, the analysis of the sources of waste and an investigation of what might increase the motivation for behaving virtuously inside an early adopter company inspired the construction of an application that was quite successful despite the difficulty of deploying a product in a client organization. This motivated Xerox to transform the solution into a commercial product, and this choice opened the path towards its transferability to other organizations.

The projects using off-the-shelf technologies illustrate a different path towards maintainability. The *Videoconferencing* project is an example of successful adoption of off-the-shelf technologies in the healthcare domain. It built on the target hospital's past experiences with videoconferencing technology in support of administrative tasks, extending it to processes related to rehabilitation services. The hospital management recognized the local work practices and took care to avoid changes that the frontline workers would find difficult to make sense of. Moreover, involving staff at all levels, it set up a series of learning activities that boosted the appropriation of the technology.

The case of the *Telemedicine toolkit* project is not as straightforward, as the toolkit meant to support the evaluation and handling of emergencies generated resistance. One of the reasons for this was that the tool had been 'parachuted' into nursing homes, disrupting the relationships between nurses and orderlies. In one of the recipient nursing homes, a doctor had the idea of developing a form that categorized symptoms and listed typical questions based on a language that was shared by both groups of workers. The form became an integral part of the toolkit, facilitating the communication process during emergencies. However, the other nursing homes participating in the project refused to use the toolkit. Their resistance demonstrates that scaling the solution to different contexts was not as simple as had initially been thought. It would have required paying heed to the specific conditions in these different nursing homes.

The Norwegian *DocuLive* and *WelFare Technology (WFT)* projects, both dealing with healthcare infrastructures, also reached the *maintaining* form, although only after a change of the initial design strategy. In the first case, the initial strategy had been to take a bottom-up approach, assuming that it would be feasible to converge on a shared solution. It resulted in an unmanageable negotiation process, given the great variety of practices and requirements. These difficulties, together with the conflicting commercial interest of a multinational IT company, prompted a drastic downsizing of the initial objectives, with the result that each hospital tried to find its own way to adopt the solution. The *WFT* project also worked out in the end, due to the decision to leave space to different 'value paths'. This was done by developing the core hub of the platform internally and incrementally, which 'allowed accommodating institutional resistances' (Kempton et al., 2020: 11).

These examples illustrate different future-proofing strategies, depending on the complexity of the technology that is developed and what kinds of learning and organizational changes are needed to make the solution sustainable. They cover a wide range: novel but technically rather simple technologies that fit into existing practices; technologies that are simple but require a substantial amount of learning and change; large infrastructure projects that involve many different stakeholders and, after a challenging period, have to acknowledge the need to make major changes (e.g. downsize, acknowledge different 'value paths') to be able to produce a result that can be implemented and remains. The ability to maintain a design outcome in a particular context depends on whether the solution respects the local practices and offers a potential that is valued by its users. It is also contingent on an organization's (or community's) willingness to invest in learning as well as provide supportive organizational measures. And it presupposes a certain degree of technical flexibility that allows adaptations to changing conditions.

11.2.3 *Scaling* and *replicating*

Scaling and *replicating* are forms of sustainability that are based on transferring IT artifacts, practices, concepts, and ideas to other places. *Scaling* is about transferring a technology to a larger group of people and/or similar places, while replicating means venturing into new fields of activity. The motivations and strategies behind these two forms are different. Both forms presuppose that a design solution has sufficiently matured and has proven its usefulness in the context for which it was originally developed.

Scaling

Scaling presupposes a certain degree of similarity in the needs and conditions of different sites. It requires the solution to adapt to the new situation in a limited way from both the technological and organizational standpoints. This is easier to accomplish when the solution is based on general-purpose applications or devices, as their services are specific to a particular setting to a lesser extent. While software engineering offers a number of issues to consider for the (future) scaling of the technology that might require new investments to upgrade it in view of the impact of a larger number of users, scaling from the organizational perspective requires strategies to support the appropriation in new local contexts.

One motivation behind scaling a design solution is to have more users benefit from it. The *Zenzeleni Networks* project in rural South Africa is an example of a solution that initially involved a limited set of users and progressively reached the whole community. An important strategic move was developing a business model that included reaching out to users (small companies in the region) that would be able to pay for the services the network made available. Rey-Moreno (2017) identifies 'sustainability and scaling' as the main concerns of community networks, pointing to the barriers that

> range from the lack of awareness of both the potential benefits of accessing information, and the Internet more generally, and the possibility for communities to create their own network, to the lack of income of the people who would like to start one.
>
> (p. 3)

Hence, in the context of developing countries, *scaling* is of prime concern, since the aim is to reach a great number of people.

Certain kinds of applications—that is, applications that require a critical mass of users to make the solution work appropriately—require researchers to face the scaling issues during the construction of the solution. This was the case in the *City Quarter* project (Meurer et al. 2018), which aimed to develop a neighbourhood portal offering different kinds of services to residents, with a special focus on older adults. One important lesson learnt was that particular services that had been codeveloped with the residents, such as an 'organizing common activities' feature, needed a larger number of users to become attractive. However, it turned out to be difficult to activate a larger group of residents to participate in the explorative project. As these residents did not have the opportunity to experience the possible benefits of the portal, they were not motivated to contribute. This threatened the sustainability of the project outcomes. One of the lessons to be drawn from this example is that when aiming at the long-term participation of a variety of local stakeholder groups, it is important to understand how to stimulate their engagement (as also demonstrated by the *Come_IN* and *Zenzeleni Networks* projects). In community-based projects, *scaling* may require a whole region (e.g. researchers, local organizations, and civil society actors) to be involved in developing a common vision on which to build long-term cooperation in socio-technical initiatives.

Organizations experience a different kind of problem when seeking to scale a solution. *Scaling* a design solution that has been successfully appropriated in one unit to the whole organization requires careful attention to be paid to variations of practices, procedures, and work relationships across the organization. Moreover, it has to account for the fact that the prospective new users need support to appropriate a solution that they did not contribute to the development of. Additional organizational stakeholders may need to be involved to create suitable conditions for this to happen. In the *Scanning* project, off-the-shelf scanning devices were first adopted in a specific hospital department and then successfully extended to the whole hospital. This *scaling* initiative was facilitated by organizational strategies oriented towards promoting a sense of community. An important part of this was to reflect on current procedures and on how they would be affected by adding scanning procedures, and to jointly plan the desirable modifications. In this way, the members of the organization were able to cooperatively make sense of the technology and of the changes it could generate and contribute towards recognizing and solving the emerging problems.

This is an important point: *scaling* requires specific attention and accompanying measures, as large organizations are often fragmented or regionalized (Clement and Wagner, 1995). Hence, *scaling* may require people to be motivated to adopt a solution that has been developed in another organizational unit without their participation. Moreover, each new set of users needs support in adapting the solution to their local conditions, which may be slightly different from the ones where the pivotal solution had been successful. A big energy company in Italy introducing an enterprise social media system (ESM) exemplifies this situation (Simone et al., 2019). The pivotal phase involved the IT department, whose management had introduced the ESM to actively involve its IT professionals in a requalification process ahead of a deep change in technological infrastructure. The success of this adoption led the top management to scale it to the company level without carefully designed accompanying action. The adoption was very problematic, since this technology was considered as a useless support that negatively interfered with the technologies already in use.

Replicating

Unlike *scaling*, *replicating* means to transfer a project outcome to a new setting with substantially different contextual conditions, making it useful beyond the initial framing of the project. Usually, this implies an expansion of the project or the formulation of a new one. While *replicating* can build on the practical knowledge acquired in the context in which a solution was originally developed, a serious analysis of the new context of use is needed: which of the concepts, research methods, and ways of developing and introducing IT artifacts can be kept, and what has to be adapted and modified? The *Design Case Studies* approach (Wulf et al., 2015) suggests the formulation of cross-cutting themes for systematically transferring learning objects from one field, case, project, or initiative to another one.

This is why maintaining a strong connection among the different cases helps make replication more effective. This process is easier if the IT artifacts and practices are 'carried on' to another place by a stable group of people, typically the original research group. If this is not the case and/or the previous experiences are not well documented, each replication requires a significant additional effort. Hence, documenting how a particular project or case evolves and the choices, decisions, and activities that made it progress is key for *replicating* to be successful. For researchers, this is not a common practice; it is time-consuming and not easy to maintain over the course of a long project, as it absorbs current resources for a future advantage. When a project solution becomes a commercial product, it is potentially replicable under the control of the provider and the hosting organization (as in the case of the Xerox *Print Awareness Tool*). *Replicating* is a common practice in the business world that often suffers from a lack of effort to understand the diversity of practices, as well as an insufficient degree of technical flexibility.

A particularly successful example of the *replicating* form of sustainability is the *Come_IN* project (which also had evolving elements). It started with establishing intercultural computer clubs (ICCs) in two German cities and later expanded the approach, transferring it to other sites in Germany and two countries outside Europe (Palestine and Morocco), with each site representing different local conditions and the associated challenges. Replication meant that the research team had to finetune the '*Come_IN* concept' to the local social, technological, and political context, eventually enriching it and further developing it. This '*Come_IN* concept' rests on a common vision, ethical-political inspirations, and a shared set of practices and experiences. The replication of this concept was sustainable despite the different challenges posed by each setting, and the fact that at each site new additional stakeholders had to be convinced of the concept and motivated to contribute. An important supportive factor was the cohesion of the research team itself. Although with different responsibilities in each replicated instance, they maintained the basic idea of what *Come_IN* could be: an open space where mentors and learners were invited to freely express what they wanted to do and supported in fulfilling their expectations under a continuous but flexible control. Last but not least, the great effort the researchers spent on developing a stable infrastructure in support of all these initiatives created synergies among them. Another key to sustainability was the fact that the group of researchers succeeded in establishing solid agreements with the local authorities and with the local people managing each initiative. Some initiatives are active without the presence of academic researchers.

Another example of how to combine *replication* and *scaling* is the HIS programme that was set up to design sustainable health information systems in developing countries. Braa et al. (2004) claim that 'local interventions need to be part of a larger network to be robust' (p. 341). In this spirit, they promoted an alternative network that was marginal at the beginning. (The platform is now the primary tool for health data collection and analysis in nearly seventy countries.) Once the initial solution was ready, the research team started to scale it to new sets of stakeholders, replicating the solution in the different contexts. Braa et al. (2004) use the 'networks of action perspective', which

> underscores at a minimum (1) the importance of establishing networks of sites, rather than singular locations, to facilitate the necessary processes of learning, and (2) suggesting mechanisms for the vertical and horizontal flows of software, training, and sharing of experiences'.   (p. 359)

11.2.4 Evolving

The *evolving* form of sustainability adds to the *maintaining, scaling,* and *replicating* forms insofar as it expands them with new and possibly innovative aspects. This means taking a step towards a more complex and challenging way to achieve sustainability. This is achievable if those who contributed to the solution were able to soundly root it in the (possibly scaled or replicated) target setting and at the same time were sufficiently visionary to imagine a future space of possibility. This is a typical outcome of an expansive-learning process (Engeström, 2001) that ideally involves all the involved stakeholders: the users, the researchers, the institutions, the management, the IT professionals. The evolution may regard the technological solution itself and how it can be further developed and/or it may concern the organization or community that has to take care of its functioning, including the broader context that contributes to making long-term sustainability possible. Again, the projects or cases illustrate rather different approaches to evolving a solution.

The 'accumulative' evolution of services

The 'accumulative' way (Iversen and Dindler, 2014) of achieving sustainability is exemplified by the *Come_IN* project, which succeeded in replicating the basic 'ICC concept' at different sites within and outside of Europe, but also used each new site to further enrich the approach with new activities and tools. An important additional step was the establishment of a platform (*NettWerkzeug*), for which the research team obtained funding. The platform offers a number of tools to support the integration of refugees into a local city community. The tools can be customized by local stakeholders according to their respective needs. This follow-up project builds on many years of experience of working with refugees in the context of the computer clubs and takes a step forward from a physical place of activity to a digital place for information-sharing, making connections, and learning (Weibert et al., 2017; 2019).

The *Zenzeleni Networks* project, while *scaling* from a group of users to the whole community, also succeeded in further evolving and consolidating the community network from organizational and commercial standpoints. An important step was to form a not-for-profit cooperative that enabled the developers and owners of the network to solve legal issues and to define and implement a business model that makes the network independent from external constraints (e.g. those imposed by NGOs)—a flexible strategy that is adaptable to different local conditions (Rey-Moreno et al., 2015). The idea guiding these efforts was to create not just a network but 'local economic ecosystems that enhance the lives of those staying in the community' (Rey-Moreno, 2017: 24). Going a step further, the research team took action to facilitate interconnections between community networks in Africa and globally.

Both projects are similar in the way they provide for the future by replicating a fruitful approach, while at the same time taking steps to evolve it so that it can live on, possibly under changing circumstances and independent of continuous input of external resources.

The story of the spin-off *Ximes* is much longer, going back to the 1990s when, after successfully completing a large collaborative shift planning project with the biggest steel company in Austria, the university-based researchers estab-lished a spin-off. It took them several years and a series of commercial projects to develop a well-thought-out portfolio of services in different domains. This evolution took place on three levels. First of all, the *Ximes* team expanded its expertise to cover a broader set of issues related to the planning of work, from working time to wages/salaries and workforce requirements. Secondly, it opened up to other fields of activity with totally different requirements. Fol-lowing this path, *Ximes* engaged with and adapted to major conceptual changes in the field concerning the meaning of 'shift times, homogeneity, regularity', the keeping apart of shift time and flexi-time, and so forth. This openness to conceptual changes and the ability to integrate them into their services is par-tially due to the continuing academic research interests which *Ximes* kept with many of their commercial projects. At *Ximes* the 'future-proofing' strategy was also 'accumulative' but over a much longer time span than the other projects: it started by scaling the approach and the supporting software to different steel companies to replicate it by transferring it to other fields of activity, thereby evolving the set of services as well as the approach itself.

The evolution of a technology

The story of the *OpenDash* spin-off is different from *Ximes* in two ways: first of all, the researchers started at an early stage to take steps towards a sustainable solution that could be transferred to different fields of activity. When the first attempts at making the dashboard work in an industrial setting for the purpose of monitoring energy consumption turned out to be difficult because of tech-nical and organizational problems, the research team moved to a project that worked with people in their private homes (*SmartLife*), where the technology was more easily appropriated. *OpenDash* evolved from this initial experience in several steps: the frontend application was developed into a more complete one, offering a backend middleware that made data collection easier and more integrated with the current technological infrastructure. The next step was to secure the 'survival' of the solution beyond its initial deployment in a par-ticular context by adding a set of end-user development functionalities that allow users to adapt the application to their changing needs, typically arrang-ing new information sources and data visualizations. In parallel, *OpenDash* was made open source: this facilitated its transfer to other projects of the Siegen group, with its developers acting as consultants and helping their colleagues to further evolve the dashboard functionalities according to the specific needs of a project.

The establishment of a spin-off completed the picture: its initial activities were focused on the deployment of *OpenDash* on the client side, while the functional evolution of the technology was delegated to different research activities, offering new functionalities that can be made open source. The *OpenDash* team then brings them to a more engineered state and supports their instalment and integration with a client's infrastructure. Several factors have made the success of this story possible: mutual trust between the small team that runs the spin-off and the different research teams that have adopted the technology within their different projects and made this path viable; the strong technological and market-oriented attitude of the spin-off members; and, finally, it being the kind of application that was likely to have a target market due to increasing attention to visualization issues in many different contexts. It was also important that this target market was not 'gated' by a complex of norms and rules or the presence of strong players (like in the case of the healthcare and the firefighting domains).

Opening up to new stakeholders and decision-makers

Success stories such as *OpenDash* and *Ximes* are due to fortunate combinations of favourable conditions that are not easy to meet. When one (or more) of these conditions are missing, the researchers need to identify other strategies to make the project outcomes sustainable in the long run.

CyberRüsten, a research line that targets SMEs in manufacturing by supporting the work of machine set-up through augmented reality (AR) and sensor technologies, developed several versions of the technology and, as a long-term sustainability strategy, promoted it in the CC *Mittelstand 4.0* initiative to keep potential users interested in its capability. The evolution of the *CyberRüsten* technology beyond the initial project was made possible by the acquisition of one of the participating companies by an Asian company. Convinced by the outcome of *CyberRüsten*, this company planned to use an extension of the solution—

capturing complex set-up instructions using short video sequences and abstract hologram representations of the set-up steps—in its manufacturing processes. In addition, based on the *CyberRüsten*-Framework, an AR-assistance system for in-process support of the parameter settings of a rare and difficult to learn metal forming process was developed and evaluated in practice.

(Sven Hoffmann, personal communication)

This kind of evolution is a positive follow-up to the participation of an European Regional Development Fund project that has created fruitful intercultural relationships. Altogether, the research team worked on three implementation projects in different companies. They first developed a more generic AR software for capturing and sharing instructions for machine set-up, comparing the suitability of both prototypes. They also performed a pilot study that demonstrated the feasibility of dynamically adapting parameters using AR, even in the case of very old machinery. While a proposal for a spin-off company for further activities did not succeed in obtaining funding, a new project that started in 2020 provides the opportunity to explore learning, information-sharing, and acting in the workplace within a semi-virtual space.

The evolution of the research line on telecare in France grew out of the experience of developing a technical solution within the *PICADo* project that was unsatisfactory from the perspective of the user organization. This inspired the local development of a component supporting care professionals that act outside the hospital. It was well accepted by the user organization and could be further developed in other settings, as in *CALIPSO*, where the research team 'added the small, self-built system to the HIS as a "new brick"' (ML Int, 12/03/2018). The option of establishing a spin-off around the *CARE* prototype was explicitly discarded, as the team members wanted to keep their researcher status. Instead, the project team decided to seek powerful partners that might support their approach in the future. They started building alliances with stakeholders in the insurance sector, since these play a relevant role in the healthcare supply chain. Another adjustment of strategy became necessary given a recent change of the regional policy which added a new 'gatekeeper' to the field in the form of a regional e-health agency (see also Myriam Lewkowicz's contribution to Chapter 13). The team decided to accept the new policy as an unavoidable contextual condition and to pursue their research interests within the new framework, while at the same time trying to 'push' the principles of practice-based computing into the agenda of the new agency. What was at first an impediment turned out to help evolve the design ideas. The agency has now adopted a tool, 'WhatsApp for doctor and nurses', which resembles the one developed in *CALIPSO*. Moreover, having had the opportunity to systematically compare different home care arrangements constitutes a basis for a broader collaboration with the agency in future initiatives, according to its agenda. Hence, showing patience and keeping project ideas 'on hold' until a favourable opportunity arises—and then pursuing it—is paying off.

These cases illustrate different ways of evolving a project outcome. One way is to focus on the evolution of the IT artifact itself, as in *OpenDash*, where new contexts are used to extend its functionalities and increase its technical flexibility. The accumulative evolution of services is another strategy. This may be done by broadening the scope of a service to include a wider range of purposes, as in the case of the *Zenzeleni Networks*, or by adding activities and tools, as in *Come_IN*. In some cases, the evolution concerns not only the IT artifact itself but, more generally, an approach to solving a problem, which can be developed further by opening a dialogue with new stakeholders and decision-makers. In practice, these strategies may overlap.

11.2.5 The *(still) open* form

Looking at the sustainability of design engagements in practice, their outcomes can still be open at a certain point in time for different reasons. One is related to the complexity of an envisioned solution, with different components being constructed in different phases of a project. In such a situation, the project's outcomes may remain open for some time, as it is difficult to evaluate how the interdependencies of these components will actually affect the sustainability of the overall solution. The *ActionADE* prototype, an application devoted to collecting data on adverse drug events (ADE), is an example. It grew out of a PD project based on an ethnographic study of the work practices of clinical pharmacists and was successfully deployed in a major hospital. The project entered a phase of difficulties when the research team started to scale up the solution in a next step, as this required integrating it with a system managing ADE data operated by a provincial institution (*PharmaNet*). One of these difficulties had to do with the requirements of the funding programme for this phase, which involved outsourcing the changes to *PharmaNet* to a private software company. The provincial roll-out and integration also required an extensive degree of collaboration with the Ministry of Health, which assumed an important role in the project. Growth and involvement of new stakeholders made it difficult for the team to preserve control over how the system was planned. The main challenge was to convince the new set of actors that the information captured through *ActionADE* reflects how work is organized in one specific local and regional setting and that the ADE classification system will need to be adapted not only to local variations but also to the needs of different health professions involved in adverse drug reporting. While system integration has progressed, the outcome of this process is still open. In this case, it is the complexity of the context—a regional network of stakeholders, each with their own processes, expectations, and understandings—that introduces uncertainties and new challenges. While the project is on a path to resolve these, its final outcome is (still) open.

A different situation occurs when the solution that has been constructed by a team is to be deployed in the target setting by a different team that, consequently, becomes the owner of its development. This happened, for example, in the Xerox *Agent Performance Indicator* project, where the researchers had developed an initial prototype on the basis of a strong ethnographic study and a mission to support the call centre agents. At some point, management took over the prototype and deployed it in a way that is closer to the commercial needs of the company than to the researchers' intentions, to respond to the local needs of the users. The research team did not even have the opportunity to follow the deployment of the application and get feedback about its sustainability in the target setting. Hence, the learning that may have occurred in the call centre and any possible benefits are uncertain.

This situation may be more typical of an industrial context, where projects respond to institutional demands or to strategies expressed by the company's management, which may decide to increase its investment and dedicate more—and possibly different—human resources to it to reach its goals.

11.3 Contextualizing the research

One of the common features of projects that arrive at sustainable outcomes is the effort researchers expend on contextualizing their work in a specific local context. 'Contextualizing' stands for creating access to users, communities and/or organizations; getting to know how practitioners do what they do and what reasons they have for doing it that way; and, finally, embedding an emerging design in these local practices.

It is tempting to conclude from the projects we reviewed that contextualizing in the sense it has been defined is a 'sine qua non' of making IT-based solutions future-proof. While this is not a new insight, the projects provide details about the kind of work this requires and also the particular challenges researchers have to handle in different contexts.

11.3.1 The work of embedding a design in a (local) context

The work of 'embedding' reaches beyond getting to know a local context. It aims at deeply grounding an IT artifact in the practices of a worksite or community or home, using these as a starting point from which to develop design ideas. For the community-based projects *Zenzeleni Networks* and *Come_IN*, 'embedding' was one of the central activities. The series of projects in Mankosi was carried out in close cooperation with the tribal authorities with the participation of local researchers that offered the benefit of 'being from there'. Inhabitants acted as codesigners, took part in all design decisions, and the solutions grew out of their daily practices (e.g. the central role of 'walking'), taking local resources and living conditions into account. The ICC projects took an approach that had been originally developed in Germany to culturally vastly different sites (in Palestine and Morocco), adapting it to the specific local contexts and further evolving it. At the centre of this work was getting to know a place and neighbourhood, the particular people that may be motivated to participate in an ICC's activities, their perspectives and interests, and the available local resources in terms of sites, skills, and connections. This also required an understanding of local politics and the ability to manoeuvre complex relationships.

There are conditions that may push the work of embedding into the background, as in the *ActionADE* project, which started out in close collaboration with clinical pharmacists in a particular hospital as a specific group of users. The prototype was developed on the basis of a deep understanding of the work practices of this group and the complexity and variability of documenting and reporting ADEs. Another crucial step towards ensuring the implementation of the prototype in a hospital was to apprehend the institutional complexity of the healthcare system and the multiplicity of actors that needed to be informed, consulted, and, eventually, more actively involved. The step of scaling the prototype made taking care of variations of practices, both locally and between different user groups, difficult to maintain. The researchers were only recently in a position to add a nurse practitioner role to the software, and this still needs to be fully researched. Also, the software company in charge of integration was not open to the need to contextualize software development by accounting for different local practices.

The projects at IBM Research that use artificial intelligence (AI)-based modelling of complex practices demonstrate another type of challenge. Both projects—*Cloud Service Analytics* and *Intelligent IT Configuration*—aimed to support and ultimately improve the work of an internal group of sellers, respectively IT service vendors (called 'architects'), in collaboration with them. Although much effort was made to understand the work practices, embedding was made difficult by the choice of AI-based tools that failed to capture the complexities of the real practices and, hence, were not suited to support them effectively.

A conclusion from these project examples is that embedding design work in people's practices may be impeded by other choices. In the case of the *ActionADE* project, scaling the software temporarily diverted effort from investigating the practices of additional user groups. The case of AI-based tools and approaches poses more fundamental obstacles due to their limited ability to capture the decision-making of knowledgeable workers who have developed the skills required to (cooperatively) manage large amounts of data.

Creating the conditions for situating a project in real-life settings

Future-proofing presupposes the possibility of bringing a design outcome to a real-life setting. While this may not be so difficult when a community or organization initiates a project with the intention of working on a problem jointly with the researchers, when projects originate in the research community the researchers may find it hard to convince the stakeholders to open up for real-life interventions.

One example is bringing Industry 4.0 solutions to SMEs. In this case, the difficulties of implementing and evaluating a prototype on the basis of real data are to do with the constraints that SMEs in this sector face (Ludwig et al., 2016). As a consequence of the economic pressure these companies experience, which leaves few if any resources available for taking risks such as disruption of production, management needs 'immediate results' to be convinced of the value of exploring novel technical solutions. The researchers had to learn that investing in computer support that may offer potential for improving processes in the future is not necessarily a priority for these companies, as tasks such as production planning are usually carried out as an integral part of work and done rather well. The CC *Mittelstand 4.0* can be seen as an attempt to prepare the grounds for fruitfully collaborating with SMEs.

The *ActionADE* project draws attention to another set of conditions. It progressed in quite separate phases—local development, integration, and scaling—which raise different issues. In the first phase, the researchers had to expend an enormous amount of effort on creating the conditions for being able to finally implement a successfully tested prototype in the real-life setting of a hospital. This work included, among other things: finding the right people in the provincial Ministry of Health as well as the health authorities to collaborate with; clearing the way for hiring a software company that was not part of the Ministry's list of approved vendors; manoeuvring the different privacy and security requirements of the involved stakeholders; understanding the budget rules of a public institution; and so on. From the moment in which the project expanded from the first PD of the ADE reporting system and its implementation in a local hospital, new actors had to be convinced and their particular outlook on the project and operating conditions had to be identified and understood. This included the funding bodies for each cycle and their particular requirements. In this case, future-proofing required multiple challenges resulting from the institutional complexities of a sector such as healthcare to be tackled and surmounted.

A different set of conditions shapes the possibilities of intervening in emergency situations. The safety criticality of many of these operations does not allow new technical solutions to be experimented with in real-life events. In the projects with firefighters, the researchers managed to get access to a fully equipped training centre that allowed them to study firefighting practices as well as test design ideas and prototypes together with the participating professionals. In this case, the possibility of doing the research and developing solutions depended on the availability of a safe site. Others working in safety-critical areas have come up with methods such as 'Future Laboratories' (Büscher et al., 2008) to make up for the unfeasibility of having access to real sites of action by 'introduce(ing) functional prototypes into realistic enactments of work' (p. 7). Here simulation is used as a method of experimenting with technical solutions in areas where disruptions and delays may cause dangerous situations, as also demonstrated, for example, by the work of Bardram et al. (2002) about video prototyping in a hospital setting.

In their collaboration with a team of firefighters, the researchers were able to develop a potentially useful practical solution in support of the navigation practices of firefighters, due to their commitment to regularly and reliably communicating and collaborating with a team of professionals over several years. However, in the end, the sustainability of this joint research effort was thwarted by the fact that the critical nature of the work mandates long and costly certification procedures for any product aiming at this market. As this was not within the reach of university-based researchers, they would have needed the full support of a company established in the field to turn the prototype into a product.

These vastly different projects demonstrate that understanding the rules and procedures of institutions that may host a design solution and/or have an important role in this process is a critical task on the way to sustainability.

The 'invisible work' needed to keep a project going

Computer-supported cooperative work (CSCW) research has a long tradition of making visible work that remains invisible in official job descriptions and is often undervalued (Star and Strauss, 1999). While the invisibility of the skills needed in, for example, office work, nursing, or call centres (much of it women's work) is well researched (e.g. Balka and Wagner, 2021), less attention has been paid to academic work from this perspective. Practice-based research that aims at a sustainable outcome requires engagement in activities that are considered 'practical' but that are nonetheless an important element of academic work. However, funding schemes often do not cover types of work that may be critical to achieving sustainability, taking them for granted and/or underestimating the effort and time that they require.

Among the activities that often remain invisible in workplans and project budgets are relationship-building with users (which turned out to be one of *the* central activities in the firefighting projects and in all of the community-related projects); 'alignment work' with project partners, such as clarifying misunderstandings and negotiating what kind of work should be done by whom, including motivational work; time-consuming learning activities that are necessary for potential users of a technology to be able to participate as codesigners. This is an observation made by, for example, Meurer et al. (2018) about design work with older adults, who point out the time and effort that had to be 'spent on getting the elderly participants acquainted with mobile phones and build confidence as well as a "habit" of using them' (p. 509). They also stress that activities such as these 'may lack the necessary funds because their relevance is not perceived or cannot be fully anticipated' (p. 522). In the *SmartLife* project, which involved families in monitoring their own energy consumption (Ogonowski et al., 2018), a lot of effort went into keeping particip-ants motivated and providing continuous support, answering questions and helping to resolve problems with the software: 'To get all this going is a lot of extra work in a project which often remains invisible' (CO Int, 20/03/2018). A similar observation was made by Ellen Balka about the myriads of mundane tasks that needed to be accomplished to keep the *ActionADE* project going: 'So if I really give you a one-liner about sustainability [...] It is not a short-term undertaking. It requires new structures and new processes. And all of this is invisible in academic work' (EB Int, 03/12/2018). Much of this work resembles what Strauss et al. (1985) have termed 'articulation work'.

Bødker et al. (2017) refer to these (and other) types of invisible work as happening at the backstage of a (participatory) design project. They consider them 'messy' and 'less photogenic', arguing: 'The front stage is the pretty im-age of success, whereas the back stage is the often-hidden chaos of conflict and turmoil' (p. 250). We would not stress so much the 'messiness' of the back-stage but the relevance of practical, sometimes 'mundane' activities in keeping project work going, on different, interrelated levels, and their invisibility or low visibility in academic work as it is traditionally presented. While venues for publishing CSCW and PD research are open to accounts that describe the sometimes cumbersome processes of arriving at a design outcome, the special commitments, the skills, and the time involved in achieving such an outcome seem undervalued by other venues and, in particular, funding agencies. Future-proofing may require even more 'invisible work', as it requires researchers to deal with an even larger network of actors and with contexts outside their immediate reach and experience, compelling them to assume new roles such as facilitators and technical support persons. Making all these activities visible and accountable and properly honouring them are important steps towards more sustainable IT research and development.

11.4 Temporal dynamics

Temporal issues play a particular role with respect to achieving a sustainable design outcome. Georges Gurvitch (1964) was one of the first to describe different cultures and/or social groups with respect to their particular temporal practices and experiences of time. Time horizons and temporal patterns vary widely, both culturally and depending on the specific organizations and/or activities people engage with (Egger and Wagner, 1992; Wagner, 1994). In a practice-based project, the time horizons and rhythms of different stakeholders meet and have to be aligned to some extent. As regards the sustainability perspective, Saad-Sulonen et al. (2018) introduced a distinction between project-based and future-oriented temporality, arguing that stakeholders in a project may have different time frames and that these may clash and have to be reconciled (if possible). The projects we discuss in this book contribute to an understanding of the relevance of temporal issues for future-proofing, on several levels.

11.4.1 Funding institutions impose temporal structures

Funding institutions impose particular timelines on research teams in terms of deadlines, milestones, review meetings, and so forth. This imposed temporal structure may deeply influence the dynamics of a project, eventually also threatening a design outcome that corresponds with what users see as useful and potentially enriching their practices. An example can be seen in EU-funded projects:

The ways these projects are evaluated are also problematic. There is the mid-term review, everyone is stressed, starts building too early to have something to demonstrate. After this event, everyone is relaxed and it is impossible to have them do more work. People make design decisions because of the review. So, the project tends to be lost from the beginning. For example, something had been hard coded just for the demo but after the review it was not developed properly. Tests based on scenarios were done but there was no time to really use them during project time.

(ML Int, 12/3/2018)

Funding cycles are often short—between one and four years (at most)—and this makes planning for a sustainable result hard. Private companies have also established funding and reporting cycles, as in the case of Xerox, Grenoble, where

contracting took place yearly, it was a 12 months cycle. So basically, that meant every year you had to start over again. So, a project lasts a year, basically, which means that if you want to continue a research activity beyond a year, you have to transform the existing research activity into a new project which is a continuation of the old one.

(TC Int, 11/6/2019)

So, researchers had to 'work around' a twelve-month cycle.

There is a strong relationship between the business model, the technical infrastructure, and the performance management processes in place in hierarchical organizations. This relationship creates a temporal structure that is not easy to reconcile with the rhythm of research activities and may, ultimately, prevent future-proofing activities from unfolding and being maintained. The different academic research lines described in this book—for example, the projects in the areas of firefighting, emergency management, and healthcare—describe different strategies and workarounds to productively deal with given timelines and/or to 'stretch' activities further into the future.

(Vastly) different time horizons

The stakeholders that participate in a practice-based project may have (vastly) different time horizons, depending on their field of activity and their own temporal practices. Some of the key stakeholders in the *ActionADE* project were not attuned to working with a research team. Collaborating with an external team of researchers on what was considered an 'in-house' IT system (*PharmaNet*) was in many ways new to the regional Ministry of Health and the regional health authority. Hence, to make collaboration possible in the different phases of the project, the researchers were required to engage in lengthy negotiations (and attended frequent meetings) on a series of issues as they presented themselves; a process that took 'between one and two years' (EB, additional comment). Clearly, in this project the temporal patterns of research that proceed according to their own 'protocols' (Pedersen, 2007) contrast with those in bureaucratic organizations, where a certain degree of fragmentation of decision-making in combination with procedures of accountability may 'retard time' (Gurvitch, 1964).

A quite different type of temporal lens may be introduced by the user (or community) in a project. For example, decision-making processes in the Mankosi community, South Africa, not only involve the whole community, but are also slow-paced:

> Community owned initiatives can take considerable time to negotiate and resolve issues since issues that might seem small within other socio-technical systems can be much larger for people whose wellness and security depend on 'working together'.
>
> (Bidwell et al., 2013b)

> Meetings need to be called and people walk long distances to attend. Indeed, it often took days and repeated attempts to confirm research activities because the phones of people involved were off/uncharged.
>
> (Bidwell et al., 2013a: 102–3)

The researchers not only tried to understand and adapt to people's practices of timing, but also engaged with their temporal rhythms in interface and interaction design, expressing the intent to 'engage more deeply with "African Time"' (p. 104).

There may also be clashes between the time horizon of individuals and those of a project. Some of these differences are to do with the rhythms of the everyday lives of project participants, such as families with children, very old adults, or people doing shift work, which may make it difficult to fit in research activities. The solution that Joshi and Bratteteig (2016) developed in their work with very old and frail people was to subdivide the work into smaller projects so that participants could just contribute to those they felt fit for, and still feel involved.

In particular, the last two examples indicate that potential design solutions may have to be rooted in an understanding of the temporal practices and time horizons of a community or group of individuals. Protocols of research may also need to be adapted to the special rhythms of the target community in order to arrive at a design result that will be appropriated and prove useful in the future.

Different goals and purposes imply different temporal structures

There are projects and cases that by their very nature imply a long-term view. In general, integration projects point from the past (which may have the form of an 'installed base') to the future, as 'infrastructure development is a visionary and political process with a moving target. It deals with an extended time span, as infrastructures are designed today to address future and unknown needs of users' (Aanestad et al., 2017a: 27). Another reason for the extended time span required by the building of infrastructures is the dependence on multiple stakeholders that need to be invited and kept on board: 'For example, to get patient data out of the EPR or into it requires years of negotiations. [...] When you cooperate with vendor companies, you have to deal with long backlogs—jobs may get delayed for years' (MA Int, 21/11/2018).

An additional source of conflict in infrastructure projects may be the different time horizons of developers that participate over limited time spans and are trying to deliver a design on time and those who look at how to manage an infrastructure over time. This was the case in a project described by Karasti et al. (2010) who identified a mismatch between 'developers' project time and information managers' infrastructure time' (p. 401): 'The users' temporal orientation of infrastructure time led to different prioritizations than the designers who had a temporal orientation of project time' (Aanestad et al., 2017a: 47).

Finally, there are projects and cases that assume a long-term view because their aim is to scale and/or replicate a solution within a large organization or in similar places. Aanestad et al. (2017b) describe the *Videoconferencing* project as a case of 'participatory continuing design' that 'has unfolded for two decades in relation to a single technology' (p. 46). They argue that the users in this case had the opportunity to 'live with the system', understand how to use it in their daily work, and reflect on the possibilities it offered in a process of evolving use.

With respect to sustainability, these examples point to the need to account for the different temporalities that are at stake during project time but also beyond it. In some cases, achieving sustainability may necessitate continuous action over an expanded period of negotiations, learning, and, as in the last example, 'living with the system'.

11.5 Creating alliances

A large part of the work of embedding a project in practice is about building the kinds of relationships that may help sustain it in the longer term. The projects we investigated shed light on a variety of strategies and ambitions.

11.5.1 A variety of strategies

One main purpose behind the 'tying of knots' (Bødker et al., 2017) in a project is to find the right partners and contact persons in the field that are in a position, as well as willing, to provide support. Creating alliances may already be critical for writing a successful project proposal. Many projects do not just arise 'out of the blue' but can build on previous work in a particular field.

Having experienced the problems of making project work in healthcare sustainable, the research team at the University of Troyes started to seek out the main players in the field, the social insurance associations, as allies for doing project work in the future, arguing: 'In France, this is a question of trust. People don't spend money on technical devices unless they have an official label' (ML Int, 12/03/2018). The team leader, Myriam Lewkowicz, is also 'active with the society', participating in events such as 'the week of caregivers', which allow her to communicate her approach towards issues such as telecare and at the same time get to know potential partners and allies. When the new strategy at the regional level changed the contextual conditions, she established an alliance with the regional agency that was in charge of the new strategy implementation to promote the practice-based design of the new solutions. This is the strategy of an individual researcher who realized that she needs to reach beyond academia for her projects to have an impact in the French healthcare system. In a similar way, the 'Inclusive Ageing Group' at the University of Siegen puts a considerable amount of effort into forging alliances with the main stakeholders in the field; this includes acting as speakers in important events and sitting on committees that shape the future federal research agenda.

In some cases, it may not be clear from the beginning who the important allies will be. *ActionADE* proceeded from a successfully implemented prototype to scaling and integration, taking on the challenge of identifying potential funding programmes. In each phase, steps had to be undertaken to find the right people to talk to in the different healthcare institutions that needed to be involved (which took time), getting to know their expectations, ways of working, and constraints. Creating alliances can also require a certain kind of versatility in how the project is presented—the ability 'to make your case' again and again, without compromising on its mission. The researchers in *ActionADE* used the network they had built—which included emergency departments, physicians, pharmacists, the Ministry of Health, and the health authority—to strengthen the conviction in their approach with a view to long-term sustainability:

> The other thing we have done is to try to agenda set quite a bit—get our work on the radar of national organizations in hopes that the standards we have created will be adopted more widely than our project.
>
> (EB Int, 03/12/2018)

For projects in the manufacturing sector, building a network and extending it were critical for future-proofing the design ideas and prototypes that had been generated, such as *EKPLO* and *CyberRüsten*. With the CC *Mittelstand 4.0*, the researchers succeeded in creating a large network of manufacturing SMEs interested in versions of Industry 4.0 applications that are oriented towards skilled workers, and they acquired resources for workshops and small projects with industrial partners. This offered the opportunity to present design outcomes with future potential to a large audience of company representatives. Here the strategy was to create alliances that allowed a solution to be developed to a level of maturity that could be tried out in real manufacturing setting.

For *Ximes*, the university spin-off that offers services to companies in the areas of working time, wages, and workforce requirements, creating alliances is a matter of survival. What is special about *Ximes* is that it grew out of strong relationships with the Austrian trade unions. It has maintained these relationships while also building a network of business partners, taking care of them in different ways—for example, by contributing to events or offering a portfolio of educational resources in addition to consulting services.

In all these examples, creating alliances is critical not just to be able to enter a field of activity but also for extending practice-based research beyond the end of a funded project and finding ways to further future-proof design results and eventually have them implemented and appropriated in a real-world context. As seen from the perspective of regional development, creating alliances within a region is also a way to achieve social change in the long term, through partnering with different stakeholders in interrelated project activities.

Understanding the politics of a place

Building alliances often requires political work. This is clearly the case in the ICC projects in Palestine, where the German researchers connected with Palestinian refugee camps. The researcher experienced the impossibility of avoiding getting involved in local politics:

> In Palestine one of the kids told a story of him throwing stones at [Israeli] soldiers. This goes back to an event when the IDF [Israeli Defence Forces] raided a camp and hurt two children. We also did 3D modelling with kids 9-10 years old about how the camp should look like [in the future]: they created a high building with a swimming pool on top, and made it really beautiful. To see that there are other ways to live.
>
> (KA Int, 21/03/2018)

For a researcher coming from the outside, it is difficult to be position oneself in such a highly politicized, conflictual context. The challenge for researchers is to arrive at an adequate understanding of the situation and also to assess the positions of the different connections they mobilize for their project. In such delicate situations they may be well advised to periodically reflect on their own normative position, in which ways it may differ from those of the key stakeholders in the field, and how these differences affect their collaboration.

Not all contexts are as sensitive, but dealing adequately with a highly politicized context can be exacting. This was seen, for example, in a project that developed computer support for collaborative urban planning, where dealing with the politics of a place in which the urban prototype was to be evaluated posed considerable challenges:

> This turned out to be a highly political issue: local authorities had to be ensured that the project would not be intrusive and disrespectful of decisions already taken. Negotiating the legitimate participants proved to be highly sensitive. It was almost impossible to freely select participants according to our own criteria to include as many different voices as possible. Fears of criticism and opposing views had to be managed.
>
> (Bratteteig and Wagner, 2014: 49)

Huybrechts et al. (2017) argue that politics as a dimension may require researchers to look beyond the micro-politics of dealing with user-participants in a project and pay attention to the institutions that frame the possibilities for action:

> While we often consider our work as PD and Co-Design researchers as being 'on the ground' where citizens are involved, the work that makes this happen extends far beyond this: it requires legislation-checks, policy-checks, fund-raising, partnership-forming, reporting and assessments in relation to all parties involved.
>
> (p. 151)

The area of emergency and crisis management is a good example of this need not just to find the right partners for a project but also to understand the institutional background within which they are acting. The *Infostrom* project had to manoeuvre a highly politicized field with overlapping institutional responsibilities and multiple jurisdictions, as it involved two counties with their different institutions, one operating with professional rescue workers, the other with voluntary firefighters. As these different arrangements and interests were difficult to grasp, building an alliance that would help sustain the *SecureArena* approach in the long run turned out to be unfeasible because this

> federal level issue in Germany is that sometimes you have competing ideas, competing systems, you end up somewhere in nowhere and though you have an interesting idea and everybody says it's interesting and it would be good to have something like this, but nobody is willing to pay for it.
>
> (VP Int, 21/03/2018)

Getting a picture of the field is probably not just a question of ethnographic sensibility with respect to the forces that shape it but may require good and reliable contacts with some of the players. But even then, not all of a project's contacts may be fully aware of what is going on, due to a lack of transparency— as was the case in the *Infostrom* project, where a group of firefighters, being unaware of the work done in *Infostrom*, decided to develop a platform for emergency management on their own in parallel with the project.

ActionADE also engaged in political work that reached beyond the immediate context of the project, trying to influence the approach chosen by the provincial health authority. They did this by publishing their project agenda in influential venues early on in the project.

These project examples show that creating alliances is a practical necessity for practice-based research to succeed. They also point to the difficulties researchers may encounter when trying to find the right partners and show how challenging it can be to fully grasp the institutional and political context in which the different actors they connect with operate. Achieving sustainability of practice-based research also requires a certain level of alignment between all partners with regard to longer-term visions. In general, alliances built up during a specific project may be used for future activities, as they 'point towards technologies to be designed for later appropriation and further development [...], and not least towards how groups and individuals may be empowered to sustain their participation in later projects' (Bødker et al., 2017: 254).

11.6 Aligning stakeholder interests and perspectives

The multiplicity of stakeholders is a key feature of many practice-based projects, and at the same time, it is a potential source of tensions that undermine the quality and future-proofing of their outcomes. A project that seeks to offer users (be it individuals, a community, or an organization) new possibilities for accomplishing their work or everyday activities has the users' perspective—that is, their practices, visions for the future, and specific needs—in focus. However, achieving this may be hampered by conflicting stakeholder interests and perspectives that may not be easily or sufficiently well aligned, with consequences for the sustainability of a design outcome. The following sections describe how different categories of stakeholders—researchers, funding agencies, management, IT professionals—might have different outlooks, attitudes, and frames of mind that have an impact on sustainability as an aim, irrespective of whether these differences are openly articulated.

11.6.1 Challenges for researchers

For academic and industrial researchers that are engaged in practice-based design, the main challenge is how to create and maintain the basic conditions for sustainability to become an aim and issue in a project. In research involving work organizations, the critical conditions include: recognizing the frontend employees as knowledge workers and, consequently, focusing on their work practices as a basic way of understanding the context of any initiative; valuing the different situations that emerge from the study of the context and, consequently, conceiving the technology as a way of managing the resulting complexity. Finally, it is critical that the project has an ethical mission to empower the users and improve their working conditions in the given organizational setting. When working with groups of individuals or with communities, researchers have to view the community from the perspective of those who live in it, take account of diversity and possible conflict, and understand the context and history to be able to develop a shared strategy and mission together with community members. Since the other stakeholders in a project do not necessarily take this perspective, the researchers have to cope with the problems that emerge in this unbalanced situation. Some issues have already been mentioned, such as the 'invisible work' needed to negotiate and maintain a common understanding of the context or managing the different temporal frames stakeholders bring to a project.

A particular set of issues concerns the specific situations of senior and young researchers that both the academic and advanced industrial research ambits have in common: how best to respond to the high pressure to publish. This pressure forces researchers to be aware of what kind of work 'counts' in publishing venues, where disciplines are usually siloed. While some of these venues (like those in the fields of PD and CSCW) are open to multidisciplinary research, the majority of venues in computer science ask for a relevant and innovative technological contribution (in the academic sense) that may not be the main focus of practice- and sustainability-oriented research.

Practice-based research requires an explorative stance that seeks and is open to opportunities to introduce IT-based artifacts and practices in organizations or communities, sometimes with negative or only partial outcomes. The time needed for harvesting the results of such an engagement may be in conflict with the pressure of advancing an academic career. For example, research in the frame of Industry 4.0 (as in the projects with SMEs in manufacturing) has to deal with a complex application area that asks researchers—often young PhD students—to spend a lot of time observing and talking to people to be able to understand the work practices and fully grasp what might be a useful technological intervention. SMEs rarely have the time and resources to provide space for experimentation. They usually expect a fully operable solution that may put researchers in the position of service providers, with responsibility for security and maintenance as well as needing to be available for troubleshooting. These activities, although instrumental for a project take precious time away from writing high-quality publications. Also, they are not easily publishable as research papers in mainstream IT venues; such papers are of primary value, hence helpful in advancing an academic career.

Similar experiences are reported by researchers working in other domains. In the *ActionADE* project, it was reflected in the work needed to manoeuvre a set of complex and shifting relationships and 'invent' all kinds of new procedures to be able to move the project forward—'in one of our papers we counted all the organizations we interacted with and I mean it's a ridiculous amount of effort' (EB Int. 13/1,272,018). The same holds for the work in developing coun-tries. One of Nicola Bidwell's conclusions from her experiences is about 'the tension between academic requirements in developing countries as we try to grow a presence overseas and the long-term sustainability of projects there; a very significant tension with long-term sustaining our products and people' (NB Int, 03/06/2019).

To describe this kind of tension, Whitley and Gläser (2014) introduced the term 'protected space', which is

> [...] understood as the period of time for which scientists have control over the use of particular amounts of human and material resources, including their own time, to pursue particular problems without suffering severe rep-utational and career consequences [...] It has two dimensions: duration and access to resources, including the proportion of working time available for researchers to devote to particular problems.
>
> (Whitney et al., 2018: 112)

Unless the criteria for evaluating academic research shift towards a stronger appreciation of the work of conducting practice-based and sustainability-oriented research and its results, researchers will have to live in a situation of partially unrecognized 'double work'. This puts additional responsibility on the shoulders of senior researchers, as they are most likely to be in the position to create a 'protected space' for themselves and their young collaborators.

11.6.2 How funding schemes frame research

The funding policies underlying the cases we have discussed were rather heterogeneous due to the variety of agencies involved: international (Eu-ropean), national, regional, private funders such as NGOs, internal (in the case of industry-based research), and funded by a special university-based programme (the *WOAD* project). When building a research line, the re-searchers typically tried to arrange for different sources of funding, eventually combining them.

The diversity of funding schemes has been investigated from different perspectives, such as: how researchers adapt their strategies to the funding conditions (Laudel, 2006); the conditions for funding schemes to encourage researchers to conduct unconventional and high-risk research (Heinze, 2008; Whitley et al., 2018); the growing complexity in funding environments; and the tendency to incorporate public policy goals in funding schemes and encourage cooperation between academia and industry (Gläser and Velarde, 2018). Lepori et al. (2007) distinguish between academic instruments ('oriented to the production of academic results'), thematic instruments ('on priority subjects for policy reasons (for example social needs) or for economic development (technological programs)'), and innovation instruments (p. 250). Each agency has its own portfolio of funding instruments that combines these different goals and offers a variety of opportunities to practice-based research. However, there are several interconnected factors that can produce hurdles for sustainability-oriented research.

Goals and conditions set by funding agencies

The continuity of a research line is a basic condition for sustainability. In general, irrespective of the quality of a project's achievement, funding schemes do not envisage the possibility of a potential follow-up project allowing the completion of partial results. This creates pressure to achieve as much as possible within project time, but also compromises the robustness of a project's outcomes—for example, creating a prototype that is not yet ready to be deployed in a real work setting. The *CyberRüsten* and *Living Lab Energy and Environment* projects, both aimed at SMEs in manufacturing, faced this situation, which required the research teams to look for new funding sources. This effect can be mitigated in the case of more local funding agencies (if not companies), as it is easier to establish a relationship of mutual trust that may facilitate the renewal of the contract in a new programme. The projects in the area of emergency and crisis management (*Infostrom*, *KOKOS*) as well as firefighting (*Landmarke*, *Koordinator*) benefitted from the research team's growing familiarity with the actors in the domain, which was helpful in acquiring new funding for the next steps of the research with almost the same partners.

Achieving an outcome that is sustainable in the future depends on the extent to which the technological solution is close to the needs and potentials of its envisioned users. For programmes that explicitly involve IT-based solutions, the wider the target of the programme, the greater the request for technology-driven innovation, based on what the funding agency considers leading-edge technologies (see, for example, the Horizon 2020 programme in Europe and its expected follow-up programme, EU Horizon 21–27). Instead, programmes that focus on more local settings are more likely to espouse user-driven innovation, as they are more defined and raise more specific needs and requirements. Some funding lines, such as calls from the German Federal

Ministry of Education and Research (BMBF), have a focus on technological innovation and do not even aim at a sustainable outcome, although they may call for user-centred and participatory design. A tendency is to solve these contradictory expectations by delegating the follow-up activities of a project to the (commercial) interests of some partner(s). In any case, as most relevant funding schemes for practice-based research do not offer means for sustainable measures in the field after the project ends, the researchers that have deeply engaged with users sometimes have to mobilize additional resources, including their own working time, to compensate for the lack of continuity and achieve some degree of sustainability.

A special problem for projects in developing countries is that funding agencies that promote research with a focus on very special settings may not be aware of local conditions that could make a sustainable result next to impossible. An example of such a 'misfit' is the case of the *Computers for Kwando* project in Namibia, where the donor organization had not only ignored the fact that the computers, which had been shipped to a place in rural Africa, may need repair, but was also unaware of the existence of local repair shops and did not allow for use of these local resources. Jackson et al. (2012) see this as a more general problem in ICT4D research, pointing to

> a perennial donor handwringing around the fact that development recipients may be using the resources of donor-supplied ICT resources for 'trivial' reasons: checking football scores rather than crop prices; writing love notes rather than resumes. Regardless of inspiration, by limiting or short-circuiting the development of local repair worlds, such efforts to manage use through design and policy seem likely to undermine, rather than support, long-term goals of sustainability.
>
> (p. 115)

Some funders (especially at the national and regional levels) require partnering with user organizations, a condition that makes it easier for projects to follow a practice-based approach. Most of the projects at the University of Siegen operated under this type of funding regime. *HADex* (University of Technology of Troyes, France) was directed by the Mutualité Française Champagne Ardennes, and in the case of the *Telemedicine toolkit* project, a regional healthcare agency funded a study of the appropriation process in several nursing homes. Working with users such as patients in a hospital, very old and fragile adults in home care, or children involves ethical issues and requires a specific commitment to creating an environment in which these issues could be accounted for and handled with care.

In sum, measures that help ensure the life of a design solution beyond the end of a project are not usual in funding programmes and are difficult to create for a research team.

'Rules' that constrain

When applying for funding, a project not only needs to address the topics which the funding agencies deem relevant; it also has to adhere to particular 'rules' in order to obtain financial support. Randall et al. (2018) suggest we look at proposal writing as a political process:

> As can be seen, the first step in getting funding is to assemble a project team according to the criteria put forward by the funding agency. This process is inherently political since it involves negotiating not only the research topic, but also the distribution of financial means and tasks, the research approach as well as duties and responsibilities of each of the prospective project partners. Hence, the personal network(s) of the applicant(s) plays a crucial role.
>
> (p. 523)

This means that a strong network of relationships is useful not only during a project (indeed, as Bietz et al. (2010) suggest, this creates fruitful synergies that possibly reduce potential tensions) but also when it is conceived, to make the project proposal stronger.

Funding schemes usually require the formation of consortia that include several kinds of participants, such as (international) research partners, companies, public authorities, and institutions, whose missions are related to the content of a project (including user organizations). This is obviously positive with respect to the possibilities of attaining cross-fertilization effects across countries and research groups and increases a project's impact on the outside world, but at the same time, it may increase the levels of conflict between individual and projects goals as well as among stakeholder interests in a project. Some research activities may lack the necessary funds because their relevance is not perceived or cannot be fully anticipated, and it may be difficult to gain acceptance from the partners—and ultimately the funding agency—around changing the assignment of resources. Hence, building and managing a research consortium requires some experience and skills, especially on the side of the researchers.

International research programmes, and also some big national funding schemes, frequently require the involvement of well-known IT companies: a proposal's success may depend on having the 'right' stakeholders on board.

Strong partners can guarantee a solid engagement and support for the project but at the same time can have a negative impact. An example of the potentially detrimental effects of this presence is found in the *PICADo* project, which was dedicated to improving the quality of home care. Under pressure from the funding programme— and the partner committed to providing its technological components—to create technically innovative solutions, the consortium envisioned a complex solution which was not well accepted by the user partners, and the project could not reach its goals.

Funding schemes often impose a narrowly defined regime of milestones, deliverables, reviews, and other types of conditions which may be difficult to comply with. The *ActionADE* project is instructive in this respect, as several funding cycles were needed for the initiative to develop from a solution deployed in one hospital to one integrated in a province-wide ecosystem. Each funding agency had its own rules determining what kind of activities may be funded under which conditions. This example confirms the importance of a long-term view. But it also demonstrates the difficulties researchers might have in following up on such a view, given that the funding institutions have their own timelines and planning cycles that do not necessarily accommodate it.

Finally, funding agencies may define rules governing the ownership of the results, and as such influence how sustainability can be achieved. For example, in the series of projects in Mankosi, South Africa, the research activities were funded by several agencies, including the National Research Foundation of South Africa, which financed the initial roll-out of the rural Wi-Fi mesh network. This created some concern with respect to ownership, which was intended to be entirely in the hands of the community (Rey-Moreno et al. 2013), and also motivated the development of a business model that would make the community independent from external donors and able to more freely manage the sustainability of the initiative.

A quite different scenario characterizes industry-based research that is mostly internally funded, although sometimes such funding is complemented by external research funds. In this situation, sustainability can be hampered by the company's goals, which are usually strictly output-oriented. Moreover, industry-based research projects are much more closely monitored than those receiving public funding and can be negatively influenced by the company's internal dynamic. For example, at Xerox in Grenoble, research projects were subject to the same business model as other activities, with short reporting cycles. In the case of the *Agent Performance Indicator* project, management opposed the—in their view—slow pace of research activities, which were based on an iterative process, and the business unit increased the pressure on the research team. Shifting competences due to organizational changes or a 'project champion' in the company leaving may endanger the continuity of a research initiative. For example, at some point in the *IBM Cloud Service Analytics* project, the amount of effort needed to adapt the solution to other business units (following frequent organizational changes) was deemed too costly and the project was discontinued.

In general, funding schemes and the rules on which they are based are not supportive of practice-based research and the future-proofing of its outcomes. While a research team may find 'workarounds', funding schemes need to be redesigned to make sustainability a realistic goal.

11.6.3 Managerial strategies

In industrial/institutional projects the managerial component plays a central role. In their study of the adoption of *Lotus Notes*, Orlikowski and Gash (1994) introduced the notion of 'technological frames'

> to identify that subset of members' organizational frames that concern the assumptions, expectations, and knowledge they use to understand technology in organizations. This includes not only the nature and role of the technology itself, but the specific conditions, applications, and consequences of that technology in particular contexts.
>
> (p. 178)

When the technological frames of key actors in an organization, such as managers, IT professionals, and users are significantly different, conflicts around the type of technology and its potential uses may arise. Such a divergence of technological frames surfaced in, for example, the Xerox *Agent Performance Indicator* project. The solution proposed by the research team was rejected by the company's management not because of its technical quality; rather, 'what was being questioned was the ability and willingness of a low-skilled knowledge worker to interpret and make constructive and legitimate use of data which, from an organizational point of view, was not immediately related to ongoing call-taking activity' (Colombino et al., 2020: 8). Zuboff (1988) observed that managers were unable to accept IT that would increase workers' autonomy and decision-making authority, and hence could not 'wrest themselves from deep-seated images of managerial control' (p. 278). This was also the case in the *WOAD* project: the aim of the hospital's top management was to control complexity rather than open up to hospital staff being able to flexibly adapt a solution to their specific needs. They considered this idea to be a waste of resources. In contrast, the doctors and nurses involved thought a centralized solution based on pervasive standards was unproductive: they 'are not able to use these standards (such as the HL7 code for classifying diseases) that did not fit what they needed' (CS Int, 22/03/2018).

However, there are also examples of management taking a much more open and flexible approach to implementing IT tools that leads to completely different outcomes. Reflecting on health IT adoption, Avgar et al. (2012) point to the key role of a different management culture:

> Research specific to the healthcare setting has also documented the centrality of an organization's learning capabilities in adopting new technologies and advancing patient care [...] Without such a culture in place, the potential returns to health IT can only emerge from the limited set of uses originally conceived by those far removed from the frontlines.
>
> (p. 495)

For example, in the Norwegian *Videoconferencing* project, the hospital's management was well aware of the local conditions and practices and understood the need to carefully adapt any technological solution to the skills and competences of healthcare workers and build on their strengths. They not only took the necessary organizational measures but also did this with care, providing all kinds of support for healthcare workers (and patients) to adopt the tool. However, this was a simple, off-the-shelf tool that required limited integration with a larger system. Considerations concerning the relationship between the local and the 'global' did not particularly come into play in this case.

The projects in the area of manufacturing suggest that management in SMEs has a quite cautious attitude to systems development. Their main focus is on product innovation, since processes are usually easy to monitor and function well, although they depend on the workers' skill levels. Industry 4.0 innovations are not necessarily a priority for management. On a more general level, management in these companies is reluctant to integrate designs 'coming from academia', as they don't necessarily trust their practical relevance. This confirms the importance of initiatives such as the CC *Mittelstand 4.0*, which offers the workers and managers of SMEs in South Westphalia and the Ruhr district a place for confronting and possibly aligning different 'technological frames' through mutual learning about the possibilities and problems of process innovation (e.g. improving production planning or supply chain management). It also teaches them how to approach developing and implementing technical solutions in accordance with a practice-based approach.

This approach is in line with the funders' research interests and strategy: it is not about developing the newest AI tools for the industry, but about learning and creating awareness of new digital tools and changing managerial culture. Such an approach paves the way towards more solid future collaborations, with a focus on sustainable solutions.

11.6.4 The perspective of IT professionals

The implementation of a technology that has been envisaged and developed in a prototypal form in a project or case often involves academic and/or industrial IT professionals that are external to it. These professionals are rarely trained to understand work practices in their variability. Therefore, they adhere to a 'technological frame' that is more congruent with the top-down approach of systems development than with the principles of practice-based research. The top-down approach is typical of mainstream IT researchers and IT providers, and of the companies and organizations the latter work for. This fact has serious consequences for the sustainability of the solution. Moreover, technologies may come into play which are an outcome of a highly centralized politics of system acquisition (e.g. in healthcare, as discussed by Reidl et al., 2008). Often these legacy systems have their custodians in the company's IT department. In the *WOAD* project, the hospital's top management, backed up by its IT department, stood in the way of a flexible, adaptable solution that the end users—physicians and nurses—had chosen to support.

A well-documented example of research that was dominated by the commercial interests of a big player in the field is the Norwegian *DocuLive* project. The pressure exerted by the multinational technology partner to implement a top-down approach based on standardizing practices met the resistance of the Norwegian project consortium, with the involved hospitals progressively abandoning the project. On the other hand, when commercial interests are distributed among a variety of actors in the market, a compromise leading to a sustainable solution may be achievable. In the Norwegian *Welfare Technologies* (*WFT*) project, this situation led to a sustainable solution that limited the centralized control of the flows of data connecting the local devices and the core platform.

When researchers, who take a practice-based approach, and IT professionals, who have been trained in another world, have to collaborate in design, their different 'technological frames' make the sustainability of the solution difficult to achieve. The *Cloud Services Analytics* and *Intelligent IT Configuration* projects at the IBM Research Lab illustrate an unfortunate dynamic.

In these cases, the top-down method for adopting AI-based tools chosen by the management clashed with the efforts of the researchers to make these tools flexibly adaptable to local practices and their results understandable to users. In the second of these projects, IT professionals were confronted with the contradictions resulting from two concomitant 'technological frames': as developers, they had a strong interest in AI and in the company's success; as users they felt the need to see their work supported and enriched by the tools they were developing. A high level of technical skill on the part of the users was not a sufficient condition for the sustainability of the new (innovative) technology. Making the design artifact compatible with their practices, which is far more relevant, represents an entirely different 'technological frame'.

A critical point is reached in a project's trajectory when IT designers have to implement and deploy the 'ideas' (or prototypes) that have been conceived by researchers. This handing-over can generate a dynamic that hampers the sustainability of the final solution. This was the case in the Xerox *Turk-Bench* project, where the full sustainability of the initial idea clashed with the limited readiness of the IT professionals implementing the product. They did not understand the value of the part of the interface that they decided to drop. In the *ActionADE* project, the task of integrating the local system in support of ADE reporting with the regional *PharmaNet* system was given to a private software company. In contrast to the developers of the local system, the software company did not have the detailed knowledge of the different work practices the integrated system is supposed to support. Nevertheless, this software company was in charge of deciding how the standards agreed upon are operationalized—that is, 'what the information captured through *ActionADE* and transmitted to pharmacies looks like when a pharmacist gets an alert' (EB, additional comment).

The meeting of incongruent 'technological frames' is a general problem that becomes particularly acute when a socio-technical solution is handed over to an organization, community, or group of users. Whether the sustainability-oriented 'vision' of a project will be maintained depends on the researchers' ability to transmit this vision to software developers acting in the new context, who may have been trained in a different tradition.

11.6.5 Summing up

The different project trajectories do not allow general conclusions to be drawn concerning the role and impact of different stakeholders. Rather, they provide

Table 11.5 Overview of stakeholder interests and strategies.

Stakeholders	Interests and strategies
Researchers	• Reconcile exigencies of an academic career with the practical work needed in a project (much of it invisible and not immediately usable in research publications) • Efforts to plan for long-term engagements with a user community/organization • Consortium-building as a challenge, skill, and strategy • Clashes between different temporal rhythms: 'Taking time' for slow-paced processes in the real world versus demands for speedy academic output
Funding agencies	• Diversity of funding environments with their own particular conditions (in terms of budget rules, timelines, types of consortia, and results) • Often contradictory demands (e.g. claim for user participation but no means for supporting sustainable practices) • National and regional programmes are often more open to user-centred innovation requiring collaboration with local user organizations • Lack of attention to long-term sustainability—researchers cannot rely on options to get funding for follow-up projects
Management	• Often unable to recognize value of local practices and accept workers' expertise and autonomy • In large-scale projects, often acts top-down, driven by efforts to standardize and, hence, control complexity • In smaller-scale projects, easier to convince to support the evolution of new practices around a piece of technology • In traditional SMEs, conservatism due to economic pressure and the fear of disrupting well-established processes
IT professionals	• In large-scale projects there is often a push for a top-down approach in alliance with management • Large-scale projects are often dominated by commercial interests of software companies in selling replicable solutions • Lacking understanding of the limitations of AI-based tools in practice • Lacking appreciation of local variations of (work) practices and the need to respect and support them

a picture that is incomplete but offers valuable perspectives and insights. These are summarized in Table 11.5.

11.7 Ownership dynamics

A 'sense of ownership' is considered crucial for achieving sustainability (Ballantyne, 2003). We define ownership as the processes through which stakeholders involved in a project take control of and responsibility for the unfolding design solution and its implementation in a particular context. Ownership can mean different things to different people. On a community level, Rey-Moreno et al. (2015a) found that inhabitants of the Mankosi community

> explained their own, others' or the community's ownership of the network by pointing to their power to decide over inherent matters and to control the project advancement. Furthermore, associations between ownership and responsibility were proven, for instance: 'We are looking after it, its ours, and we are taking full responsibility of it.'
>
> (p. 10/16)

Ownership can be exercised individually or collectively. It can be practised in various ways, depending on the purposes, skills, and knowledge of people. In a practice-based project, ownership regards the formulation of desired goals, the methodology and research protocols, the division of tasks among stakeholders and their alignment, and how the conditions of collaborating with the site of a future intervention are defined and managed. Hence, in a practice-based approach, ownership is to some extent shared from the beginning, with different stakeholders having a say and exerting control over different matters. Since a project goes through various phases, ownership can move from one stakeholder to another, with varying effects on the sustainability of the project outcomes.

Funding institutions or a company's top-level management team exert ownership in the initial phase of the project when its goals are established, the general rules it has to follow are defined, and the human and financial resources are allocated. Once the project actually gets started, they control how it complies with the affordances and constraints that have been agreed upon, and have the ability to rearrange them or stop the project. For example, all academic projects that are funded by research agencies have to follow the established funding scheme and, in a more or less formal way, report on their intermediate results and react to the possible criticisms and requests. In industrial research centres, this control is enacted in a much more direct and immediate way, as demonstrated by the decision of IBM's top management to stop the *Cloud Service Analytics* project when it was unable to fulfil its expectations.

When the project enters its operational phase, ownership is concerned with choosing the approach that drives the construction of the (initial) socio-technical solution, as well as how it should be embedded in a particular context. In this phase, many stakeholders—for example, researchers, local management, IT professionals, as well as the cooperating future users—have an active role, all with their own interests and perspectives. As a consequence, in this phase ownership is the result of negotiation processes that may involve different levels of conflict.

In practice-based projects, academic researchers seek to establish particular research protocols with the intention of developing a design solution that promises to be useful in a particular context/field of activity. Hence, they exert a strong influence on the transition from the pre-study stage to the implementation and validation of the solution. Illustrations of the strength of the research approach can be found in many of the cases of academic research discussed in this book. The strong methodological cohesion of the research teams in Siegen led to solutions that proved useful in practice, even if they did not reach the stage of appropriation due to external conditions (like in the projects involving firefighters or SMEs in manufacturing). The French team at Troyes University of Technology used their work on supporting practices in homecare in different projects to establish their approach—CSCW research combined with the notion of 'Living Lab'—in the field. Although its initial plans were disrupted by a change of regional strategy, the research team were able to continue their work, establishing their approach in alliance with the new actors in the region. The *ActionADE* project, in its first phase, adopted a participatory approach that created a strong relationship with the local clinicians and the IT professionals, which ultimately led to the successful deployment and appropriation of the ADE system in a local hospital.

The situation of research groups in industry is somewhat different, as they are less independent in defining their approach and selecting projects to work on. In the IBM *Intelligent IT Configuration* project, for example, the members of the research centre only became involved after the main methodological decisions had been taken. It was difficult for them to deeply influence the content of the project; however, they were able to introduce PD principles to support the users' perspective in a situation where the future direction of the project was uncertain.

Ownership may become a serious issue in the transition from the phase in which an initial solution is constructed to the phase of its deployment or integration in a wider context. At this stage, the project team may be forced to rethink their strategies, as new stakeholders have to be involved. This was the case in the *ActionADE* and *Agent Performance Indicator* projects. In both cases, the outcomes of the first part of the project, when the researchers had been the main owners of the approach and dynamics of the project, were questioned by the new stakeholders, who became the new substantial own-ers. In the *ActionADE* project the researchers remained active, but they found themselves increasingly relegated to the role of consultants. In the *Agent Perfor-mance Indicator* project, the researchers were no longer able to follow how the application was deployed and in which ways its functionality was simplified to this purpose.

Sharing ownership with those who may make use of the design outcome in the future in all phases of a project creates good conditions for future-proofing. However, the course taken in projects that targeted strongly structured, hier-archical organizations illustrates that this is not likely to happen in these types of organizations, since top management and the involved IT professionals are generally reluctant to recognize the ability of employees to make their own decisions and the power relationships surrounding the projects play a relevant role. An exception is the *Videoconferencing* project; this was driven by the hos-pital's management, which took measures to share ownership with the users of the system.

The situation is more favourable when projects are targeted to (and also sometimes initiated by) communities. Working with very old and frail adults in a residential home in Oslo, Joshi and Bratteteig (2015) took great care to involve them in the co-construction of a new DAB radio. This example of shar-ing ownership illustrates that it is a cultural issue reflecting power relations and social values—in this case, there was respect for the experiences and skills of very old adults that under different circumstances may have been consid-ered no longer suited to participate. The ICCs are a good example of shared ownership with participants whose conditions and experiences contributed to determining the socio-technical design of the computer club as well as the actual technology set-up.

The projects in Mankosi, South Africa, started out with the aim of hav-ing the community as the main owner of the approach and the design result. Rey-Moreno et al. (2015a) offer an in-depth analysis of the development of ownership in the rural community network that was developed. They make a distinction between *personal ownership* of the network, which 'was restricted to limited areas of the project or tasks', and *collective ownership* of the network, with people entrusting selected competent members of the cooperative with the power to manage and maintain the network. They also observed how 'a sense of ownership may challenge preexisting local ways of thinking and doing' concerning, for example, young people. Here 'the project appeared to enable the emergence of local cells for decision-making and taking action, based on capacity and commitment' (p. 11). They conclude:

In the case of the community network we analysed, collective, rather than individual ownership prevailed: the network was perceived as belonging to the community. Second, the case proved that for local ownership to take effect and be conducive to an active sense of entitlement for the network, there is a need for the sense of ownership to be complemented by active local involvement in its exercise.

(p. 14)

While ownership is an issue throughout a project, it becomes critical when an IT artifact is implemented and processes of learning and appropriation have to be organized in the receiving community, institution, or other contexts. Then the question 'who owns the design result' makes a difference regarding the nature and quality of these processes.

11.8 Appropriation and learning

'In any complex environment it is clear that IT artifacts should be designed with an understanding of the variability of practices in potential fields of application and their temporal evolution in mind' (Wulf et al., 2018: 10). One might say that projects that have followed this principle have prepared the grounds for users to appropriate the designed system. But it is not always as straightforward as that. Some impediments on the way to a design result being appropriated by its users are not within the discretion of the designers, or it may not be possible to resolve them within the project duration. A system needs to be sufficiently robust to be used in a real work context; it may need to be integrated with an existing system; the context may not allow the system to 'just' be experimented with, as in the case of a high-risk situation such as firefighting or SMEs in manufacturing, where managers shy away from costly disruptions of the production process; or it may need real-time sensor data that are not made available within project time as in the case of the eco-feedback project in industry. However, learning as an important step towards appropriation can still take place: the developers may have gained insight into the usefulness of the design outcome and further steps to take; managers and/or end users may have learnt about the potential of a particular technical solution or acquired relevant insights into their own practices or new skills.

Hence, it is interesting to look at the relations between appropriation and learning from the perspective of ownership—who is in control of these processes and takes responsibility for them. The projects and cases point to different scenarios or constellations whose differences are not always clear-cut: often projects and cases move between different ownership constellations.

11.8.1 Ownership is shared between users and professional designers

The ownership of the learning process is shared between users and professional designers when they are engaged in 'mutual learning', which Bratteteig et al. (2012) describe as a two-way process: 'Users join the design project with knowledge and experience from their current practices (be they work or other activities), while the professional designers have knowledge of technological options and concrete experience with (some of) these' (p. 133).

The projects and cases provide many examples of mutual learning as an important step towards how users appropriate a (jointly) developed solution—or at least part of one. We highlight two types of projects and cases that accomplished different goals on the basis of shared ownership: (1) developing a technologically innovative solution that is tailored to a particular field of activity (e.g. firefighting); (2) using simple, off-the-shelf or ready-made technologies for community development (e.g. *Zenzeleni Networks*, *Come_IN*).

In the projects with firefighters, the researchers shared ownership of the learning process, from early explorations of design concepts to the development of the initial prototypes. They went through an intense period of learning about firefighting practices before they came up with the first design ideas (focusing on the use of landmarks), and they were only able to refine and further develop the landmarks into a communication tool as a result of the intense exchange of experiences in the regular workshops with firefighters. The participating firefighters not only learnt about technical possibilities but also contributed with their own ideas. As well as testing the prototypes, workshop discussions helped them become more aware of—and critically reflect on—their own practices. However, towards the end of this research line, the firefighters lost ownership of the development of the solution when the power to decide on its future moved to the institutional level.

Zenzeleni Networks and *Come_IN*, both aiming to use ready-made technologies for community development, were able to experience full appropriation on the basis of mutual learning. When building the wireless mesh network in the rural Mankosi community in South Africa in close collaboration with the community represented by the tribal authority, researchers needed an intimate knowledge of the community concerning the physical constraints given by the terrain. They also had to be aware of security issues in order to find an appropriate design solution. The community was actively involved in all design decisions, from the set-up of solar charging stations for mobile phones to rolling out a wireless mesh network.

Another case of appropriation based on mutual learning took place in the ICCs in different countries and locations. First of all, the participating children and their parents jointly defined the contents of the small projects they wanted to work on. This stimulated mutual learning among all participants—the researchers, the leaders and teachers of the computer clubs, and the children— about the value of the different learning experiences and also the particular cultural and social experiences that shaped them. This was the basis for the appropriation of the digital platform that was built in a PD process involving refugees and migrants, as well as their volunteer and professional helpers (see Chapter 7). From a broader perspective, the ICCs in Palestine fostered connections and learning between the inhabitants of the camps and those living outside as a way of grounding the initiative in this complex context.

Capability-building: The role of researchers

In practice-based research, researchers also have a key role in preparing the grounds for appropriation up to the point that the participating organizations, communities, or other types of participants are ready to take over. To this aim, an important set of activities is capability-building—enabling future users (or especially trained users) to set up, use, adapt, and eventually repair an IT artifact, evolving practices around it. This implies, among other things, that the technology is sufficiently flexible and malleable and easy enough to master and maintain.

The community development projects provide the strongest examples of capacity-building, shedding light on the special roles and responsibilities of researchers in projects that strive for sharing and handing over ownership. When starting to develop ICCs in different countries and areas, the researchers sought to turn them into places for social and personal learning, with the idea that this learning should be continued in the home and would manifest itself, in the long-term, as a capacity to learn. This is similar to the kind of learning that IT projects with old adults engage with, as, for example, in the *City Quarter* project (Müller et al., 2015), where the researchers invested serious effort in developing a rich set of self-learning and social learning tools that

> were intended to help the users to solve some of the problems they encountered with their tablets and smartphones, such as update alerts, problems

with sending emails or with the Internet connection, independently. This strengthened the participants' autonomy in using their mobile devices beyond the end of the project when the researchers would no longer be available.

(Meurer et al., 2018: 514).

A similar long-term type of capability-building, though on a professional level, is practised in the CC *Mittelstand 4.0*, which offers training in important digitalization issues to representatives of manufacturing SMEs with the intention of preparing the grounds for further collaboration. One of the key themes of these workshops is the centre's practice-based approach to designing tools and systems with a view to developing sustainable solutions.

In some contexts, capability-building activities are in the foreground of a project, as they are crucial to the development of a viable solution, as was the case in 'rolling out' a Wi-Fi mesh network in rural Africa (Moreno et al., 2013). In response to the different design solutions, the community allocated responsibilities for the various activities that were necessary to sustain them, building 'local control and accountability mechanisms' such as how to 'make decisions about what to do with the money collected and how to solve problems' within the community, involving all households (Rey-Moreno et al., 2015b: 8). Moreover, the community supported by the researchers accomplished steps that had been set as milestones, such as 'installation of lights in households, establishment of the cooperative, application for license exemption, a bank account for the cooperative, a billing system for break out calls and realising break out with an Internet gateway' (p. 8). The establishment of financial and legal resources, as well as the decision-making mechanisms, are institutional arrangements which Madon et al. (2009) consider as key to ensuring the long-term sustainability of (social) innovations. In addition, the project built a network of local research assistants and devised a strategy of developing local competencies around the network: 'The approach we followed was to build that capacity into the installation of the entire network, and all the other sub-systems required, as part and parcel of the training' (p. 5). Training was based on hands-on practical exercises, 'e.g. working with wood to construct custom boxes to hold the batteries, installing and dimensioning solar and storage systems, building the connection panel for the electrical installation, configuring and installing the routers, and aligning their antennae' (p. 5), with trainees gradually taking over the implementation of additional units. In this project, 'on site' capability-building was one of the main strategies to ensure sustainability (and ownership).

It is important to notice that technology projects targeted to situations characterized by limited resources must identify and acknowledge the local capacities such as the small private repair shops and repair markets in Rundu (South Africa) and Dhaka in Bangladesh as Jackson et al. (2012, 2014) describe. These projects largely depend on the existence of a local repair culture, without which technology intervention would not survive. Learning there happens through apprenticeship and collaboration and is supported by practices of sharing information (e.g. through WhatsApp) and a variety of online resources. This is an example of 'expansive-learning' (Engeström, 2001), which in this case is not only about acquiring new skills and competences but also about building an infrastructure of repair shops and the necessary support structures. It also breeds 'local innovators' (Wyche et al., 2015) that are able to flexibly mobilize resources for adapting devices and systems to local circumstances.

Ownership is in the hands of an organization's management
When the management of an organization has a prevailing role in the development of the solution, appropriation is the result of a balance of different factors. As Orlikowsi (1992) has observed in her well-known study of the adoption of *Lotus Notes*, a tool can only be successfully integrated into people's practices if this process is supported by organizational change. This perspective looks at a new tool or system as enabling organizational change. One can also turn this perspective around and look at the appropriation of a tool or system as depending on organizational responsiveness in the sense that a receiving organization needs to prepare the grounds for a new piece of technology for it to eventually be appropriated. While management may be in control, it may be prepared to share ownership to some extent with end users and leave some space of action to the involved researchers.

We can distinguish between different types of cases. The first type is projects in healthcare institutions, some of them lasting over many years, that adopt off-the-shelf technologies, seeking to make them useful throughout the organization. In these cases, (external) researchers had the limited role of observers. The *Videoconferencing* project, for example, illustrates the commitment of management in a Norwegian hospital to turn this simple technology into a much-used and useful tool to support the rehabilitation process of patients after their discharge from the hospital. Management took a series of measures in support of the appropriation process, inviting employees to participate in designing them. While some of these measures—such as the revision of discharge procedures, the installation of a 'telemedicine team', or making videoconferencing rooms freely accessible for all—were organizational, other measures had to do with preparing the staff by providing training for all, mobilizing participation through the sharing of success stories, simplifying administrative steps, and so forth. A simpler but equally successful set of measures was taken by health management in the case of the *Scanning* project, which sought to stimulate hospital departments to define their local scanning procedures, thereby ensuring the avoidance of disruption to work processes.

A more problematic example is the *Telemedicine toolkit* project that entered a series of nursing homes in the form of 'suitcases' containing equipment for performing simple measurements, all ready to be appropriated (or in this case 'domesticated'). Simply introducing this toolkit without having considered the work experiences, practices, and needs of the nurses and orderlies resulted in the tool being disregarded, since they did not understand when it would be appropriate to use the tools or how to do this without their attention being distracted from a patient in a potentially dangerous situation—a 'classic' case of misalignment. As management insisted on the suitcases being used, the users in one of the nursing homes took some unexpected actions, creating guidelines that helped orderlies and EMDC professionals to interact during an emergency, a move that resulted in the successful adoption of the suitcase. They not only decided to use the suitcase in a slightly different way but also found out how to make it applicable to unanticipated situations. This is a form of appropriation in which some particularly active users redefine, change, or extend a tool that does not fit their practices. While this project was under strong management control in the introductory and promotional phase, some users were able to see value and possibilities in tools that did not fit, evolving their practices around this potential.

The AI-based technology development projects at IBM illustrate yet another aspect of appropriation and learning. The strategy of IBM's management team to develop and adopt machine learning tools in support of the activities of sellers and IT architects resulted in misalignments between these tools and the employees' work practices. The reason for these misalignments was not an unwillingness on the side of the designers to understand the practices they sought to support. Instead, it was to do with the complexity of these practices and the difficulties of shaping data analytics in accordance with them, which resulted in users having problems engaging with the results. In the case of the *Cloud Services Analytics* project, the sellers were not motivated to appropriate the technology and 'continued to take their decision outside the system as they didn't see any advantage in using it' (JB Int, 15/12/2019). Moreover, the management did not fully anticipate the cost of adjusting the technology for frequent organizational changes and underestimated the amount of effort required to achieve the technology adoption in different contexts.

In the *IT Configuration* project, the IT architects were highly motivated by professional interests and their role was fundamental in the evolution of the solution towards a possible appropriation. An extensive field study of users' experiences with the system they tested (Wolf and Blomberg, 2019b) documented the architects' reflections on how to improve the AI-based tool to better match their practices and needs. For example, they imagined 'how algorithmic ways of data processing could be leveraged to enhance their reading practices' (p. 143) of a client's requirements document; how 'situated configuration work—matching client requirements with just the right assortment of the company's offerings'; and how 'the collaborative nature of solutioning work' (p. 11) could be supported by the tool. One might think of the architects engaging with the tool and their 'imagined relationship with algorithmic capabilities' (p. 12) as a form of appropriation that happens as part of the design process, even though 'orderly use' is not in sight due to the insufficiencies of the tool.

In these different examples from healthcare institutions and industrial research projects, management exerts ownership in rather different ways. Although in control and also in a position to stop a project, management also provided space for, and in some cases active support of, appropriation and learning, giving users the possibility of exploring and also redefining and extending tools.

11.9 Types of innovation

Every project aims at some kind of innovation that legitimizes the investment in financial, organizational, and human resources. What innovation means in a particular context can be discussed in different ways depending on the approach taken in a project, its goals, and how research outcomes are evaluated; it also depends on whether the research aims to achieve the sustainability of its outcomes. While the distinction between design-driven and user-driven innovation provides a broad orientation, much finer distinctions can be made when considering the different cases. One of the conclusions that can be drawn to begin with is: a technological innovation cannot be considered in isolation when the goal is to achieve its sustainability in a real-world context, since a small technological innovation can have far-reaching social effects and, vice versa, big technological innovations can generate troubles. On the basis of this insight, an analysis of the projects and cases, although not contributing entirely new concepts, presents different scenarios that highlight the interplay between innovation and sustainability.

11.9.1 Off-the-shelf technologies with far-reaching social innovation effects

When a consolidated (off-the-shelf) technology is adopted in a particular context, technological innovation is limited: the genuine innovation concerns the context in which it is inserted. If this technology has a circumscribed purpose, its replication in different settings makes its adoption in the new context of use easier, since it is in principle neutral with respect to the hosting organization. In any case, the adoption needs to be carefully considered and can be the source of innovative social changes. For example, in the *Scanning* and *Videoconferencing* projects, the innovative outcomes of the former include improvements in hospital procedures and the reduction of paper circulation; in the latter project, outcomes included the extension of an already familiar technology to improve communications with healthcare professionals taking care of rehabilitation services outside the hospital. The ICCs that were created in the *Come_IN* project adopted light but effective off-the-shelf technologies, allowing wide replicability of the original idea while promoting other kinds of innovation, including nurturing both the capacity to learn and intercultural learning based on mutual respect. One of the key findings is that 'the translation of cross-cultural understanding and respect as values from an overarching public discourse to a specific socio-technical initiative on the local level requires a detailed and attentive collaboration of all involved stakeholders' (Weibert et al., 2017: 730). In this case, the technologies were simple and the learning and change processes of the participants were in the foreground. In the case of the projects aiming to construct infrastructures in support of rural communities in developing countries, the well-established nature of the adopted technologies facilitated the 'genuinely' innovative aspects of the solution: its conception and appropriation by the communities themselves, made possible by their autonomy from external stakeholders that may have imposed problematic technological, organizational, or commercial constraints. The wide diffusion of a 'creative repair culture' in these contexts is one of the key factors enabling socially and financially innovative solutions that are sustainable in the long term.

When an off-the-shelf technology offers a more complex solution, achieving sustainability becomes more problematic, since the technology can be unsuited to a specific local context. This case is typical of technology-driven innovation that by definition considers 'average' situations, presupposes 'typical' user needs, and disregards contextual differences to make the solution 'widely applicable'. This strategy promises the reduction of development costs but generally increases the costs of the appropriation of the solution, as it requires more substantial social, organizational, and even technological adaptations. For example, in the *Telemedicine toolkit* project, a pre-established solution was (mistakenly) supposed to be easily replicable in various telecare settings: its adoption either failed or required a substantial effort to make it sustainable. The more complex the functionalities offered by a predefined solution, the more serious the problems that may be generated: the stories of the adoption of imported HIS—for example, the EPIC technology in Denmark (Bansler, 2019)—demonstrate the problems of the technology-driven strategy in even more substantial ways.

11.9.2   Technologies that are designed to innovate specific practices

The interplay between technological innovation and sustainability was different across the projects and cases that used technology development to respond to the needs of users in a particular context. Solutions based on (the composition of) simple components can fulfil the innovation goals of the project and support its sustainability, when the focus on users' practices leads to the identification of functionalities that fit users' needs and are easily appropriated due to their simplicity. This was the case in the IBM *RFS-D* and the Xerox *Print Awareness Tool* projects, which met their objectives, and the French research line on telecare that produced the *CARE* application. While the research line with firefighters focused on helping professionals (and volunteers) innovate their navigation and communication practices, the researchers also aimed at technological innovation with the *Landmarke* solution. Hence, design can be deeply embedded in the practices of a specific group of users and at the same time be technologically ambitious. On the other hand, these projects demonstrate that the combination of social and technological innovation can be challenged by other contextual conditions.

The projects that aimed at reducing the fragmentation of solutions in the healthcare domain provide a different perspective on innovation. These projects did not start from a study of work practices. Their aim was to improve the quality of care by ensuring informational and functional interoperability. The institutional promoters of these initiatives pushed for a standard centralized integration and, when the difficulties of reaching a satisfactory design result could no longer be ignored, had to take a more decentralized approach. In principle, a technology can be designed according to both approaches; but decentralization has been shown to lead to higher levels of innovation in the solutions, as demonstrated, for example, by the research on blockchain-based architectures (Yli-Huumo et al., 2016). The debate on centralized versus decentralized solutions is mainly focused on their ability to guarantee privacy and security—aspects that are important but do not cover all the relevant issues. The integration projects in the healthcare domain suggest that it was the opposition of some stakeholders and the strong arguments they raised that enforced a conceptual drift in the mind of the promoting institutions. Irrespective of the technical solution, the drift towards the needs of diverse and local stakeholders was the true achieved innovation that was fundamental to reaching the sustainability of the final integration.

11.9.3 When user-oriented innovation leads to complex technical solutions

While simplicity is a good, although insufficient, precondition for reaching sustainability, more complex solutions may be needed to respond to the needs of users. In this case, their sustainability is more uncertain and depends on a variety of contextual factors.

The *WOAD* project aimed to provide the malleability of a set of partially quite ambitious functionalities that had emerged from the clinicians' practices. A key observation concerns how clinicians flexibly structure the pieces of information they need to care for their patients and link them. The approach taken in *WOAD* was in response to the involved clinicians' request to be allowed to construct their own solutions. The ambition was to reflect this flexibility by setting up an interface with the underlying complex architecture that was simple and accessible for the user. However, as the functionalities of the proposed system were demanding, the project would have needed the services of a software company able to deliver a sufficiently robust solution to be experimented with in the field. Unfortunately, this collaboration was not achieved and the reuse of the solution in another context turned out to be impossible.

The story of *OpenDash* shows that the sustainability of a complex innovative application can be managed through fruitful collaboration between academic researchers, who look specifically for innovative functionalities required for the application to be able to adapt to different contexts, and the spin-off created to engineer the new versions of the application according to the needs that can emerge in those contexts. First, the adaptation to a new context requires some amount of end-user development—for example, supporting the visualization of new types of data in an interactive way (as was done, for example, in the *EKPLO* project). Second, the sustainability of the platform also depends on the ability to integrate the application with the legacy systems operating in a prospective user organization.

Researchers may opt for the adoption of a complex innovative solution, since it seems a suitable answer to complex problems. In this case, the sustainability of the solution greatly depends on the extent to which users can appropriate it, on top of the technical problems that its implementation can meet.

The projects that adopt 'intelligent' AI-based technologies to construct their solution are typical examples of this strategy. When the complexity involves the capabilities of knowledgeable workers, such as their intuition and creativity based on an experience that is difficult to formalize, this technological innovation meets serious difficulties. On the one hand, finding suitable algorithms that produce satisfactory solutions for the complex problems is not a trivial task. On the other hand, and even in the positive case, these solutions are generally not easily understandable by the users, since the more sophisticated and powerful the algorithmic machinery, the more its logic is far from the problem-solving practices of the knowledgeable workers. For example, in the *IT Configuration* project, the solution disregarded both the cooperative nature of the work needed to identify the suitable architecture and the tacit rules that the architects apply to check its completeness.

More generally, given the (recurrent yet) declining myth that an intelligent technology can substitute knowledgeable human beings, with the difficulties becoming evident, the insight that solutions that aim at exploiting intelligent machine learning capabilities have to coexist and 'cooperate' with their users gains attention. The distance between machine learning and human reasoning in complex situations is a common experience that is testified by the research efforts that try to fill in this gap by making the logic embedded in the algorithms more understandable (Miller, 2019). The question is whether this approach is the most profitable one and whether starting from the problem-solving practices of the knowledgeable workers to conceive the intelligent support could offer a more effective way of reducing this gap. This was the approach taken in Bandini et al. (2002), where a similar goal to improve the configuration of complex architectures was at stake. The intelligent solution was based on the documental artifacts and classification schemes the architects had collaboratively constructed for this purpose and on the architects' practices that keep them updated, meaningful, and reliable to support reuse of already experienced architectures. In any case, how to design intelligent technologies so that they can and will be appropriated by users as a basic step towards their sustainability will be one of the challenges that research has to face in the years to come.

The different 'innovation scenarios' discussed so far (see Table 11.6) are not exhaustive. They suggest that we should look more deeply into the

Table 11.6 Innovation scenarios and their characteristics in the respective cases.

Innovation Scenario	Characteristics	Examples
Off-the-shelf technologies	• Limited technological innovation, but potentially far-reaching social innovation effects	*Videoconferencing* project ICCs
Large-scale technical interventions	• Using a centralized top-down approach disrupts social practices	*B-EPR*
	• Barriers to innovation unless variations of practices are accounted for	*SEP*
Technologies that are designed to innovate specific practices	• Technology-driven innovation: Assumes easy adaptability but entails high cost of appropriation	*Telemedicine toolkit*
	• User-driven innovation: Robust technical solution allows focus on innovation of practices	Xerox *Print Awareness Tool*, *CARE* prototype, *Come_IN*, *Zenzeleni Networks*
But when the technical problems are complex …	• Ambitious technical solutions that require substantial resources	*OpenDash*
	• Innovation would require change of contextual conditions	Projects with firefighters *WOAD*
Start out from technical innovation (AI), see if it works …	• Technical challenges foregrounded • Complexity of work practices underestimated	IBM Request for Service Management IBM *Intelligent IT Configuration*

conditions and constellations under which researchers aim to make an innovative contribution.

11.10 The qualities of the technology

The solutions generated by the projects and cases are of a socio-technical
nature; that is, they imply various types of innovation at the technical, organizational, and/or community levels. While the organizational and community
components are deeply dependent on the local conditions, it is possible to
identify some qualities that influence the sustainability of the technological
component during and after the project ends. These qualities are considered
in any kind of software engineering approach but are discussed here from the
perspective of the users of the technology, in opposition to the traditional
perspective of its professional designers.

11.10.1 Robustness

Robustness is a basic needed quality that is not, however, easy to achieve during the limited duration of funded research projects. In fact, their time span
is very often dedicated to identifying the suitable functionalities, constructing mock-ups and prototypes, and validating them with the users involved in
the project. A certain level of robustness is necessary to make this validation
possible. An important condition is to gain the confidence of the users that may
easily be shattered by failures that depend not on the offered solution itself but
on its unreliable usability in a realistic, if not real, context. The robustness of
the technology was the leading goal of the projects in developing countries.
While the final solution was constructed incrementally, its reliable usage at
any stage was essential to allow for its scalability and functional evolution.

When the hosting organization is more structured, as in the projects
targeting SMEs in manufacturing, robustness also implies a sound integration
with the local organizational procedures and the legacy technology infrastructure. In those projects, the main impediments to the validation of the offered
functionalities were the difficulties of obtaining real-time data and the fear
of potentially costly disruptions of production. In this case, specific measures
are necessary to create the confidence of management in the usefulness of a
proposed technological solution in the near future.

When the level of integration is less complex and the hosting organization is
comparatively flat, robustness is less crucial, since the confidence of the users

is more closely related to the fact that the technological solution reflects their work practices and that they have been part of conceiving it. This was the case with, for example, the *CARE* component that was developed in the *CALIPSO* project. In the projects that have been promoted and managed by public institutions and by the top-level management of private companies, robustness is a criterion that the IT players participating in the project are supposed to ensure and as such is part of their formal contract with these promoters.

Maintainability

Another crucial quality of a technology with respect to sustainability is its maintainability: that its operativity can be preserved in the face of malfunctioning or a new technological infrastructure. A modular functional architecture is an obvious positive feature with respect to the maintenance of a solution; it is also useful for adapting a solution to new settings and needs as well as to new technological infrastructures. Nowadays, this quality is common to all good software development, especially if it aims to make the developed application open source. This was an approach explicitly taken within the *WOAD* and the *OpenDash* projects. Moreover, modularity offers a simplified identification of the components constituting the solution architecture. This is central to the repair of devices and the software accompanying them, independent of the intervention of their providers. Building and having access to 'repair worlds' was a very important achievement in the case of the projects conducted in South Africa and Namibia, and key to empowering the local communities. These projects demonstrate that one important condition for an IT-based solution to be sustainable is that low cost, ease of use, and maintainability are taken care of. Jackson et al. (2012, 2014) argue that 'distinctively different worlds of design and practice [...] appear to us when we take erosion, breakdown, and decay ("broken world thinking") rather than novelty, growth, and progress as our starting point' (p. 107). In an ethnographic study they identified the various sites—private as well as semi-public—on which the durability, stability, and sustainability of the IT infrastructure in a particular region depend.

Tailorability

Related to modularity, a given technology also needs to comply with the adoption of standards and uniform procedures to the minimum degree necessary to guarantee interoperability. The stories of the Danish and Norwegian integration projects are instructive concerning the value of interoperability and decentralization. Leaving part of the control to the 'periphery', in particular to the end users (as discussed in Chapter 2), is instrumental to the quality of tailorability (see also Wulf et al., 2008). This quality is rarely in the focus of technology design. Solutions at most offer users the possibility of setting the value of some configuration parameters, as in the case of the widely adopted mashup architectures and tools (Koschmider et al., 2009). Tailorability becomes mandatory when the users express the need to quickly and autonomously construct their technical support in relation to their specific needs and the dynamic setting in which they operate. The *WOAD* and *OpenDash* projects responded to this need, turning it into one of their main missions. To be able to achieve this, they had to manage the related complexity in the design of their solution, which is rooted in a layered and open platform supporting malleability. Layers are needed to clearly separate the users' work environment, which must reflect their practices, from the infrastructure that offers the basic services; openness is needed to make these services evolve to respond to new needs.

Companies are often subject to substantial organizational changes and can be forced to face new business models and products. When the problem that the technology has to solve is responsive to the organization, an important quality of the solution is its scalability and replicability across the organizational structure from both the technological and organizational standpoints. The IBM *Cloud Services Analytics* project showed the value that management gave to this quality. It also demonstrated how the impossibility of achieving this quality due to the complexity of the 'intelligent' solution was one of the factors that 'killed' the whole project, irrespective of the huge investment that had already been made.

11.11 Long-term measures

Some of the measures we have discussed so far require a long-term strategy that reaches beyond a particular project and may also require multidisciplinary competences that are not typical of IT education programmes. Projects can fulfil this need by involving experts with the appropriate skills in their consortia. As this may not always be possible, researchers themselves may need to invest time and effort in activities that are complementary to their core competences. Senior researchers are often in a better position to take over tasks that keep a project going, due to their experiences and greater freedom.

11.11.1 Financial and legal sustainability

Prerequisites to achieving the sustainability of a design solution that has been developed in a practice-based project and deployed in a real-life context may include ensuring financial and (sometimes) legal sustainability. This may not be a problem if the participating user organization is taking over ownership of the solution and is also willing to carry the costs. As we have seen, SMEs in manufacturing may have problems in doing so, as many of them are under enormous financial pressure and may shy away from investing in a piece of technology with unknown benefits in the future. At Xerox Grenoble, procuring the continuation of a research project beyond the accounting mechanisms of a bureaucratic organization created particular challenges. The research team had to think and efficiently argue about how to prolong research activities beyond the budget year:

> In an organization there should be a consistency between the vision for what research is, inventing the future [...] all corporations have their own way of describing long-term research and how important it is but then there is an operational reality and it is bureaucratic and it is built around layers of management and middle management who work and report on cycles, financial reports in cycles.
>
> (TC Int, 11/06/2019)

The researchers in the *ActionADE* project became actively involved in ensuring the financial viability of the provincial integration project through several funding cycles. When they found out that 'for our application to succeed meant for *Pharmanet* having to agree to pretty significant changes that required significant budget' (EB Int, 13/12/2018), the researchers themselves had to contribute towards writing a justification for a huge budget. They also engaged in drafting procedures that were in line with the legal requirements of some of the stakeholders they were involved with.

When there is no user organization or community but users are individuals living in their homes, as was the case in projects with older adults (Meurer et al., 2018), the researchers had to tackle the problem of providing support for troubleshooting and further learning beyond the end of the project. For example, in the *SehrMobil* project, researchers

> made sure that the participants could keep their smartphones after the end of the project for as long as they wished (but they had to pay the Internet

fees on their own). This solution was much more appreciated, as the relationships with the academic researchers had become part of their weekly routine. Ongoing technology support for elderly people may be difficult and also costly.

(Meurer et al., 2018: 513)

As we have seen, the projects in Mankosi, South Africa, followed the strategy to become independent of donor agencies by developing a business model that ensured affordable pricing in collaboration with community members. This was made possible as the community was able to gain the interest of some commercial clients willing to pay for the service provided by *Zenzeleni Networks*. Bidwell and Jensen (2019) describe as among the key challenges:

the lack of enabling policy and regulatory environments, shortage of financial resources and skills, as well as limited awareness of the technical options, and lack of time to plan and undertake tasks in remote and rural areas often with very limited resources.

(p. 63)

In the *Come_IN* project the need for financial support for the various ICCs was partially met by turning them into associations, a legal status that gives them more autonomy and chances to acquire resources, especially from local institutions.

Research teams need to account for these challenges if they want their initiatives to be sustainable and the communities with whom they engage to benefit from them in the long term.

Ensuring the research line: Different strategies

As the conditions for sustainable outcomes are difficult to create within the time frame of one single project, one of the key strategies of researchers was to find ways to continue the work after the project ended. This might require a managerial attitude that is often based on long-term experiences in the research field, combined with strong personal motivations.

One of the most obvious moves was to transfer a prototype and the knowledge acquired in one project to new projects. This strategy requires examining the transferability of what has been achieved in a particular context and also begs the question of 'what is to be transferred: a designed IT artifact with particular functionalities, an approach to solving particular issues (such as community-building, health, mobility), or a component of a technological infrastructure' (Meurer et al., 2018: 516). Examples are the transfer of the *CARE* prototype from the *CALIPSO* project to new projects under a different institutional regime, or the strategy taken by the researchers in the *WOAD* project to open up to other application areas when the hospital's top management refused to support the design solution. This put them in a position to continue important conceptual work and search for commercial partners. In the case of the firefighting projects, the strategy was not to directly transfer design results developed in *Landmarke* but to use the relationship of trust that had been developed for proposing follow-up research on emerging new design ideas. A part of this strategy was also to ensure the continuing support of key stakeholders and the ability to use the training facility for testing the new design ideas and prototypes with firefighters in a safe environment.

The researchers that worked on *OpenDash*, offering it to other projects in the Siegen group and extending its functionalities, took a different path with the decision to create a spin-off. This move also required consideration of financial sustainability in the longer term, of appropriate technology choices (e.g. a layered architecture, building their own middleware), and of what should be open source and what only available commercially. The CC *Mittelstand 4.0* offers an example of another, rather complex strategy to ensure the continuity of a research line. It uses a mixture of network-building with SMEs in manufacturing and training workshops to disseminate their approach and showcase prototypal designs achieved in specific projects in order to get companies interested in further small but eventually also large collaboration projects. One mission of the competence centre is to promote the distribution of the open-source technologies developed by the academic team. This far-sighted strategy aims to demonstrate that the introduction in companies of ideas and prototypal solutions developed in research can be managed in non-disruptive ways; and that technologies that had initially been developed in a particular context can be replicated in other companies while respecting the existing conditions and work practices, thereby paving the way for evolution of the SMEs towards a stronger position in the competitive market.

The strategy in the *ActionADE* project was different, as different funding cycles were needed to ensure the long-term goal of achieving a province-wide solution to documenting ADEs. One important move the research team undertook in this direction was not only to build relationships with the relevant healthcare institutions but also to establish themselves as experts in the field as well as shape the field. This was done in view of potential competitors that may offer other solutions to adverse drug reporting but most probably would not follow a practice-based approach. From an early stage, the key researchers made their approach visible in key publications, thereby influencing the requirements. Being aware of the existing alternatives to their system and their shortcomings helped them to argue convincingly for their own approach.

The series of ICCs in different places and countries follows another pattern. Here, the main motivation to continue and take the approach to other, far away contexts was 'political' in the sense of bringing a potentially beneficial learning opportunity to children and their families in troubled and deprived areas of the world. As we saw, the key challenge underlying this 'journey' towards replication was to sufficiently contextualize the approach so that it would reflect the lifeworlds, needs, and resources in places like Palestine or the mountainous areas in Morocco.

11.12 Concepts revisited

The main insights for future-proofing practice-based computing, which we gained from our 'parcours' through many different projects and cases in different fields of activity with a view to capturing variation (and possibly repetition) (Robinson, 2016), are on two levels. They call for reflections on the value of the sensitizing concepts we used in this book and how to apply them, find more precise definitions, eventually extend them, or come up with additional concepts or important interlinkages between concepts to explore. They also stimulate thinking about the possible benefits of working with a large number of cases, which motivated us to 'think with elsewheres' instead of concentrating on what is comparable in a stricter sense ('control for difference').

Our view of issues of long-term sustainability was nourished by the sensitizing concepts the literature suggests (Chapter 2). Not all project stories offered enough detail to elaborate on all the aspects we deem relevant. We would have liked to learn more about the temporal aspects of projects under different funding conditions and with different ambitions. Also, the issues of financial sustainability and institutionalization were only partially covered by the project accounts we assembled from project publications in combination with interviews with the leading researchers. This is partially to do with the fact that these issues have not been systematically researched within all contexts, since how to support long-term sustainability was often only implicitly present in the researcher's mind.

We have arrived at a new view of some of the concepts. The notion *forms of sustainability* proved practically useful for making distinctions between the future perspectives of projects as well as the impediments they met. The *discontinued* form was important to add. It does not simply indicate 'failure'. Some of the projects were stopped by management because they did not fulfil the expectations, turned out to be too risky, or were simply not compatible with the management's top-down approach. However, learnings were made on the way to this stage. In several cases it turned out to not be possible to arrive at a robust solution within project time due to the complexity of the target situation. The *discontinued* form points to the inadequacy of many funding schemes in view of achieving sustainable results. In some domains, such as firefighting, it is difficult to arrive at the stage of appropriation in real use, let alone a 'product', due to the high-risk nature of the activity and the existence of lengthy and costly certification procedures.

The other level we added, the *(still) open* level, does not just reflect the fact that the outcome of some of the projects or cases was still open. It includes cases where the ambition and/or complexity of the issues may require several funding cycles to arrive at a satisfactory solution. Scaling up a locally successful solution, integrating it with the installed base, and/or having to work on time-consuming adaptations to the new context to which a solution is to be transferred are all reasons why a research line may extend further into the future than might have been expected. In other cases, the dynamics of the ownership of the project outcomes make the information about their further development difficult to access and evaluate.

The projects and cases also provide some valuable but not entirely new insights into *temporal issues*. One is to do with the important but time-consuming activities that we summarized under 'embedding', most of them requiring skills that often remain invisible but are crucial for a project to succeed, not just in terms of publications but in terms of practical impact. Another insight is that with respect to some contexts, understanding and respecting the temporal practices and time horizons of a user community or group of users may be key to developing a design result that can be future-proofed. We also identified some research goals that point towards the future 'per se' and that are also the reasons for the uncertainty of outcomes: infrastructure development, appropriation and learning, and network-building.

In practice-based projects, the term *contextualizing* usually refers to the work of understanding the context of use so as to be able to embed a design in the local context. We broaden this concept to indicate that when designing for a sustainable result, it is necessary to do more than 'get to know the work practices'. This insight has been formulated before (see, e.g., Bødker et al., 2017). We have seen the sometimes tedious and unaccounted-for work of contextualizing in many projects. This kind of work is simply necessary in order to be able to heave a project over a blocking situation (the *discontinued* form).

Ownership is a concept that proved highly relevant to the understanding of the trajectories of the projects and cases, and needs more attention. It refers to who in a project has a voice in decision-making and shaping a project's course but also who takes responsibility. Ownership may be exercised individually or collectively, and it is something that usually changes over the course of a project. Ownership is also dependent on the distribution of resources (funds, knowledge, access to people, etc.) in a project, as well as on the method or approach (practice-based and participatory, top-down, and their variations). The notion of ownership is particularly useful for the analysis of appropriation and learning processes. First of all, appropriation and learning are strongly connected, as the possibility of integrating a design solution into a particular context presupposes learning, which in many cases is mutual, concerning both researchers/developers and users. The projects that were most successful from a future perspective systematically practised capacity-building with a view to appropriation. At some stage the learning may become expansive, as, for example, in the repair shops Jackson et al. (2012, 2014) studied, the *Videoconferencing* project, and the projects with firefighters that, although they did not reach the appropriation level, stimulated deep learning about firefighting practices.

Exploring the links between *ownership* and *appropriation* led to distinguishing between different situations. In the projects with a strong PD component, ownership was in the hands of the (community of) users from the very beginning. An impressive example of this situation is the series of projects with the Mankosi community. This, however, was only possible because the researchers engaged in systematic capacity-building, enabling future users (especially trained users) to set up, use, adapt, and eventually repair an IT artifact, evolving practices around it. In many of the practice-based projects, although researchers share ownership with users, they always play a key role as IT experts, which means that they are able to control the vision of the project and also systematically steer it towards a design result that can be appropriated in practice.

The *ActionADE* project is an example of this situation that also shows what happens when ownership is (and has to be) gradually transferred to the key institutional actors. Ownership in the hands of management is the most complicated situation, although the power of management to impose an approach and particular goals may look deceptively straightforward. The ability to, in such a situation, arrive at a design result that can be successfully appropriated depends on how much space and 'voice' management is willing to grant the researchers in a project, and whether it listens to the end users of an envisioned solution that speak from the point of view of their local practices. The example of the French home care research line indicates that a viable strategy is to focus on the players in a regional context that are 'in charge', convincing them of the value of a practice-based approach offering collaboration and support. A yet stronger way of coupling forms of ownership and appropriation is demonstrated in the *Come_IN* project, which assumes a strong community development perspective. In those settings, researchers take over a variety of additional roles. Besides being the technology experts, they act as 'facilitators' of community development that is driven by a common long-term vision and common development goals—more in the sense of local coproduction.

Our analysis has also referred to *type of innovation*, a concept that is used in the literature in different ways. The project stories have a clear message, as they show that technological innovation cannot be considered in isolation when the goal is to achieve its sustainability in a real-world context. The 'innovation scenarios' we identified link innovation and sustainability in a spectrum reaching from projects with social innovation as the main outcome to large-scale initiatives that are disruptive, as they impose a technical solution that ignores the variability and complexity of local practices. Particularly challenging are situations in which the implementation of technologically ambitious solutions in support of local practices requires considerable high-quality resources that can make achieving sustainability difficult.

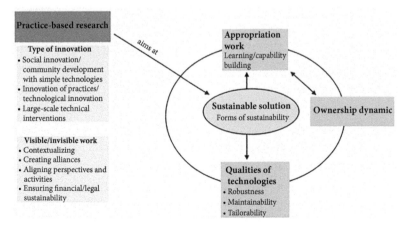

Fig. 11.1 Concepts revisited

Figure 11.1 provides an overview of the concepts we have revisited, reinterpreted, and extended. It also reflects the path we have traced from projects and cases, highlighting some of the interdependencies our comparative analysis brought to the fore.

12

The complex way to sustainability

Our journey through a rich set of projects was possible thanks to the collaboration of our colleagues, who shared their experiences and thoughts about the issue of sustainability with us. Their contribution allowed us to consider rather different projects in terms of fields of activity, funding agencies, research team composition, and contextual conditions. The conversations with these colleagues gave us the possibility of looking at the projects from the inside, getting a first-hand account of the achievements and problems they encountered, and discussing their strategies and measures for achieving sustainable results on the project. The outcomes of this challenging and stimulating journey have been analysed and compared in the light of a set of sensitizing concepts that, directly or indirectly, cover the issue of sustainability from the perspectives of diverse research areas.

The sustainability perspective is not common, even in research communities such as CSCW and PD, which focus on users and their practices and seek to empower them with IT-based solutions. Researchers may consider the sustainability perspective as valuable but still 'out of the scope' of their projects: they do not see a possibility of continuing their research after the project ends, since funding these activities is difficult due to the limitations of current funding structures. The rich empirical material that forms the backbone of this book and its analysis can inspire researchers, institutions, managers, IT professionals, and educators to promote the goal of sustainable design results and increase the overall awareness of its strategic relevance.

We are now in a position to highlight a number of issues that matter and that, in our view, should be considered when aiming to obtain sustainable results in IT-based projects and initiatives. We do this while keeping the 'big questions' formulated in the introduction in mind.

Future-proofing. Wulf et al., Oxford University Press.
© Carla Simone, Ina Wagner, Claudia Müller, Anne Weibert, and Volker Wulf (2022).
DOI: 10.1093/oso/9780198862505.003.0012

12.1 Creating environments of sustainable innovation

For a future research agenda for sustainability in practice-based computing, it seems necessary to continue thinking across projects in terms of aggregated case studies—that is, from projects to local, national, or even transnational longer-term initiatives. To achieve this, it is important to think beyond the current paradigms of IT research and development and to take a closer look at the arrangements of stakeholders and practices that need to be built for such initiatives to come to fruition. The case studies point to several strategies on different levels.

12.1.1 Embedding practice-based research in regional development initiatives

Several cases, notably those concerning Industry 4.0 in SMEs, emergency and crisis management, and the French home care projects, point to the opportunities that positioning practice-based research in a regional context may foster in terms of the long-term sustainability of its outcomes. In urban planning, regions are defined as wide areas that encompass both urban and rural territories. When thinking in terms of a region, it is important to account for 'the idea that processes and network formations take place across spatial barriers and on different levels, thus transcending administrative boundaries' (Boonstrat and Bolens, 2011: 107). A region is defined by its identity in terms of history and tradition as well as the specific resources it offers: these include people with their skills and common ways of doing things; companies with their technological know-how and entrepreneurial tradition; cultural institutions, health-related agencies, and so on.

For practice-based research, operating on a regional level offers the advantage of being able to not only adapt its vision to these local conditions but also participate in the definition of this vision. It also offers the chance to utilize already-existing networks and facilitates access to political decision-makers and funding agencies in the region. Another benefit derives from the fact that companies in a region may have developed similar approaches and common (work) practices and may already share their experiences to some extent. This increases the possibilities of leveraging a solution that has been developed in collaboration at one particular site and replicating and eventually evolving it further in other similar places.

Such a widened perspective towards regional initiatives puts a focus on new forms of local arrangements including interdisciplinary and intersectoral cooperation between academia, (local) politicians, companies, trade unions, NGOs, and communal organizations. These groups can work together to network different initiatives and shape the long-term developmental agenda of a region. The agenda should be led by a discourse between the actor groups to negotiate the question of how they wish to live and work in their region in the future. Hence, future-proofing requires academia to see itself as a facilitator of regional change processes which emerge from the perspectives held in a region, from its social relationships, and from the people living there.

There are many ways of establishing such a discourse by reaching out to important stakeholders in a region. These range from participating in key events in the region to offering specific information and training in the form of workshops, lectures, and roadshows to interested companies (see the CC *Mittelstand 4.0*, Chapter 3). Academia needs to build relationships with politicians and politically influential actors in a region. Regional living labs, such as the *Malmö Living Lab* (Hillgren et al., 2011) or the *PRAXLABS* concept (Ogonowski et al., 2018) may be a solid basis for such novel arrangements. They can serve as local innovation hubs and provide opportunities for aligning technology development and long-term appropriation support.

Gaining a foothold in large-scale systems

Practice-based research in domains such as, for example, healthcare faces enormous difficulties connected with legacy systems, large-scale infrastructures, and the prevalence of top-down approaches. These problems are difficult to avoid and create formidable obstacles to achieving a sustainable result in cases where sustainability depends on successful integration. In general, 'projects which require systemic change are difficult to sustain' (Aanestad, Chapter 13).

Several considerations may help researchers to move from discontinuing a promising design solution after a project ends to maintaining and eventually also scaling it. One future-proofing strategy that was successful in the case of the *ActionADE* project was to form strategic partnerships with the different stakeholders in the field—including software companies—to ensure that the vision of the project is shared and respected, and to also 'implant' the approach based on user participation and attention to local practices in these companies and institutions. A second strategy is to start small, within a limited space, work to implement, appropriate, and recognize a design solution, and eventually scale this up to similar sites within or beyond an organization. Both strategies involve a perspective of 'longue durée' in the sense of thinking from the start of a project or initiative about how to possibly scale, replicate, and evolve it, forging alliances and adapting to changing constellations of actors.

Transnational/cultural sharing of solutions

The projects in developing countries suggest yet another path, which is based on sharing sustainable community-based solutions across regional and national boundaries. This is a case of replicating and eventually also evolving solutions achieved by other communities. An example is community networks (CNs). Non-profit organizations, such as *AlterMundi,* provide advocacy to CNs in Latin America but also concrete assistance in the form of open-source and decentralized technologies. Bidwell (2020) uses the term 'mesh-work' to describe 'threats formed by CN members' (p. 128), stressing that these 'innovate within the life of their own CNs' (p. 132) and that all benefit from the diversity of the sites and the different technical skills of those who participate. Winschiers-Theophilus et al. (2019) provide a somewhat different example of sharing experiences and solutions across continents; they mention sites in Borneo and Namibia that, although different in many ways, 'have a number of fundamental similarities allowing for transferability of best practices and design patterns' (p. 426).

From a practice-based research perspective, these examples suggest the benefits of an incremental approach which starts from small local interventions that work and can be maintained and moves on to a much larger number of sites. This approach would not just amplify the learning opportunities at each site but would also allow the teams to capitalize on the diversity of skills made available and the power a networked initiative may accrue in negotiations about access to resources. The 'moving away' to sites in other countries and cultures may also help 'strengthen the theoretical and empirical basis of particular design results and/or insights' (Meurer et al., 2018: 516).

Future-proofing within an industrial ambit

Within the industrial ambit of IT service providers, practice-based research serves several interrelated purposes. In the cases we discuss in this book, the primary goal of the research was to improve practices within the company. This has a long tradition in companies such as Xerox. Early examples are Blomberg's (1987) critical look on machine 'reliability' (the big Xerox photocopiers), or Orr's study of the work of technicians that later shaped interventions with 'Eureka', Xerox's platform for knowledge-sharing. Within large hierarchical companies which undergo frequent organizational changes with strong internal competition, scaling a solution even within the company may not be easy. However, a major incentive and goal is to replicate solutions that have been developed, successfully deployed, and tested within the company in outside markets, selling them to clients. A third, related goal is for such a company to establish itself as an expert and possibly a forerunner in a new or emerging field of technology, such as AI or machine learning.

On a very small scale, university spin-offs use a similar strategy. For example, *OpenDash* uses the funded research projects of the research group with which it is still associated to further evolve its product, a visualization dashboard, while at the same time offering it to commercial clients with the features that they need (e.g. security) as well as integration with the existing technical infrastructure.

University spin-offs

University spin-offs are created to bring a solution to the market and devise strategies to replicate and further evolve it in a diversity of client organizations. The step from practice-based research to creating a spin-off is complicated by the fact that the ideas and artifacts that researchers hope to use as a starting point for a commercial endeavour are socio-technical by nature. What they seek to bring to the market is an assemblage of technical artifact and approach, with clients having to commit to a change process. *Ximes* has solved this problem by developing participatory techniques and a strong coaching component alongside the software it offers. From the perspective of sustainability, another challenge spin-offs face is combining the research needed to evolve a product with the practical necessities of implementing it at a particular site. Both *OpenDash* and *Ximes* have maintained strong links to academia and seek to arrange for research opportunities flexibly whenever this is possible.

12.2 Grounding future-proofing in current actions and long-term challenges

The strategies we have identified for building sustainable environments for innovation point to different possibilities for directing practice-based research beyond single projects to generate solutions with long-term societal effects. By articulating and elaborating a set of concepts beyond their original research ambit, the book offers a conceptual basis that has proved helpful in identifying and characterizing the different dimensions of sustainability, suggesting various paths towards sustainability and how to cope with the complex issues on the way. We have emphasized, for example, the link between various forms of learning with different degrees of appropriation; the link between appropriation and the dynamics of ownership during the various phases of a project; and, finally, the distinction between forms of sustainability as a useful means of integrating the findings in a unique parameter that captures the effects and transferability of the project outcomes and supports a comparative analysis of the different experiences gained during the projects. The resulting conceptual basis helps to identify a set of 'here and now' design principles and some more long-term challenges.

12.2.1 'Here and now' design principles

Some principles can be applied by the designers without significant changes to the context surrounding the projects they are involved in: these principles mainly concern their own approach to IT design.

Taking a wide ethical perspective
A fundamental principle of a sustainable design is focusing on the local dimension, anticipating and caring about how to enrich it while avoiding possible disruptions. At the user level, this implies that value is added to the local knowledge and the practices that are based on it. According to Schmidt (2018), practice

> not only points to a regularly recurring activity [...] but also points to the ways in which skills are acquired through learning and training; the ways in which techniques are adopted, acquired, adapted, and applied; and the ways in which performance standards are developed, negotiated, and brought to bear in actual situations.
>
> (p. 52)

At a higher strategic level, focusing on the local dimension means recognizing the different value paths that characterize the lower organizational levels where a design result has to be appropriated and implemented and also thinking about the best way to integrate it in the high-level view. In both cases, a design that has been based on an awareness of the complexity of the local dimension supports a view of technology that helps manage this complexity and does not take the opportunity to unduly simplify and, hence, discount it. If not, complexity will surely emerge in another form, with unpredictable consequences. This means taking an *a priori* perspective and planning the related actions, instead of reacting *a posteriori* when faced with conflicts and resistance that have a negative economic value in terms of the costs of time and resources.

To aim at sustainability, designers must take a wide ethical perspective: towards the users by empowering them, improving their work/life in substantial ways, and preserving the skilled parts of work (Blomberg and Suchman, 1996; Bannon et al., 2011); but also towards the organization or community hosting the initiative and, more broadly, towards society. For this to happen, as already emphasized in Blomberg et al. (1996), the local dimension has to be understood in the frame of broader contexts: 'Assume that change is already and always in progress. Understand the politics of change and where you stand within them' (p. 260). Navigating responsibly within broader contexts requires researchers to be aware of their own values and their commitments with respect to them:

> *Understand how extended contexts (e.g., institutional and global) constrain the scope of what can be accomplished in a given setting, and attempt to question or take advantage of those contexts as appropriate* [...] the constrained conditions of product development, and the movement toward increased outsourcing [...] brought us into contact with intensification and shifting configurations of work within and among organizations locally, regionally, and worldwide [...]. To some extent we were required to incorporate these conditions, as given but also problematic, in the direction of our own research.
> (Blomberg et al., 1996: 260–1) (original emphasis)

The important point is that researchers working in academia need to reckon with the complexities of real-world contexts. Knowing the context is more than just understanding the everyday life or work practices; it is also about knowing the politics, the conflicts, and the resources (people, funding, etc.) that may be mobilized.

The socio-technical nature of innovation

Taking the view of long-term sustainability is an ethical imperative that also affects what is meant by innovation. This is a crucial issue for research initiatives that are rewarded by scientific publications, where innovation usually means unprecedented technology or novel application domain. This definition is based on a narrow idea of what constitutes an innovation. Technologies that prove useful but are simple (not cutting edge) as well as already well-researched domains may require innovative approaches and strategies to be successful from the sustainability perspective; they may have a positive impact in a social context that is unique and, hence, raise unique challenges.

Going beyond the purely technical perspective of innovation entails the ethical choice taking care of prospective users and of their specific context in the given application domain. While some of this care-taking involves serious attention to practices and community-related and organizational life (which may result in academic publications), other aspects of this work are considered non-academic. They often remain invisible and unsupported and may become a source of conflict with stakeholders that have different goals, such as commercial or productivity expectations. Nevertheless, designers that share this ethical perspective on innovation struggle to create the space for the invisible work it requires, as they consider achieving results that are sustainable in the long term as a fundamental part of innovation. In so doing, they accept the risk of slowing down the pace of what is officially considered innovation by the academic reward system: we will come back to this issue.

In any case, their experiences are valuable and constitute progress in the research field: they have to be properly documented and shared in the scientific community to become part of its store of knowledge and be leveraged and enriched in new initiatives. There is a need to change the academic recognition culture, which is primarily defined by the scientific publication list, by giving merit to the work done by researchers to create a sustainable social impact for an organization, community, and/or region.

Early focus on technology integration and maintenance

Any technical solution has to be integrated with the legacy technological infrastructure, from the available communication system up to the constellation of applications in use. A design oriented to sustainability has to create the conditions for this integration to be achieved, even by different IT professionals at a later date. These conditions presuppose the specification of suitable interfaces that preserve the design properties of the solution and respect those constraints of the legacy systems that cannot be modified: for example, the identification and availability of the sources of required input data and the specification of how they can actually be provided; or the identification of organizational procedures or technological interfaces to reduce the friction with legacy systems conceived with a different philosophy, typically based on a distributed versus a centralized approach; or adopting a top-down standardization versus a practice-based definition of data structures and procedures.

The long-term maintenance and repair of the software and hardware components of the solution also have to be considered through an ethical design practice that takes responsibility for the social and ecological aspects of its design outcome. Long-term maintenance and repair could require ad hoc strategies such as excluding more innovative components that are not sufficiently stable and robust to be used in real-world contexts, are difficult to procure, or may quickly become obsolete as they respond to a throwaway philosophy or have poorly defined upgrading policies.

An ethical commitment to empowering the users looks to increase their autonomy in managing the technology and its adaptation to new needs and situations. Technological tailorability and malleability are important design approaches towards this goal. However, they should not be considered pure technical problems. On the one hand, they have to be conceived with a view to the practices of users—that is, on the basis of data structures and procedures the users consider as effective and not according to an abstract and disembodied notion of modularity and effectiveness. On the other hand, the technology has to support adoption and appropriation in an incremental way, mindful of the different initial skills of the users, their attitude towards the technology, and their possibly different learning curves.

Early consideration of ownership

Project ownership plays a relevant role in the process of users learning about a new technology and appropriating it—two cornerstones of sustainability during a project and after it ends. Ownership plays a fundamental role, especially in the delicate transition of a project from a more prototypical/academic stage to the handover of the initial solution to the participating (community of) users or the target organization. In this transition, the vision guiding the project can be lost or converted—with unpredictable, often problematic, consequences for its long-term sustainability—due to a change of the composition of the project team. Perhaps previous stakeholders, typically researchers, have to leave and new stakeholders, with their own strategies and interests, take over the project's governance. Ownership also plays a fundamental role when the conditions for a project to start are defined or a research line in academia needs to be reinforced, or when it is important to convince non-academic players of the value and positive social impact of a research initiative and obtain their support.

Planning the ownership of the project and how it should be shared and passed on in all its stages (pre, during, and post) should already be part of proposal writing, to avoid it becoming an issue later when problems emerge and finding a solution may become difficult, if not impossible. We may think of such a plan as a sort of 'contract' that commits all involved stakeholders to accepting the project vision and exerting their ownership according to the roles they consented to assume in the different stages of the project. The contract may be revised at any time under the condition that the ethical stance of the project is maintained or at least renegotiated. If the stakeholders do not want to commit themselves to such a process, the sustainability of the project outcomes is uncertain and potentially not achievable. The inclusion of regional organizations and community partners already at the application stage points to the possibility of sharing ownership from the beginning. This would also give the non-academic partners more confidence that the researchers will allow sufficient space for bottom-up processes and that they will engage with local needs.

This endeavour can be made easier by adopting strategies oriented towards preventing possible conflicts and generating a positive synergy between the members of the research team. One strategy is to involve not only all the stakeholders in a consortium in developing a long-term perspective, but also institutional actors outside the project team that may be able to create the conditions for a sustainable project outcome and guarantee the management of a new socio-technical situation from the administrative viewpoint. This may include providing the necessary logistics and the appropriate human and financial resources as well as monitoring organizational changes, depending on the nature of the project.

From a more research-oriented perspective, a fruitful strategy is to build a stable research team based on mutual trust and capable of developing a shared vision of research and their specific role in it. Such teams often grow when researchers have the opportunity to collaborate in several projects over longer periods of time, but they have to be nurtured. It is important that they remain open to new members, in particular younger researchers, as part of an educational strategy both in academia and in industrial settings.

12.3 More long-term challenges

Research teams that want to pursue a long-term perspective in their projects have to work on building a culture of sustainability in IT-based initiatives. We identify four ambits where a change of perspective can contribute to making sustainability a goal that is more naturally achievable.

12.3.1 Extending the nature of the computing discipline

Irrespective of several decades of experience with the challenges of integrating IT-based technologies in almost all areas of people's life, the computing field still sees its realm as mainly in technical artifacts and their mathematical foundations, a view that tends to ignore the social practices these artifacts are embedded in. Some emerging trends such as 'value-based computing' try to introduce ethical principles to IT design (Friedman and Hendry, 2019). They are, however, not able to significantly change the traditional perspective of computer science, for which the notion of innovation is still confined to original artifacts and technical design methods. Within this perspective, maintainability and flexibility refer to the technical qualities of a technology.

A claim to sustainability challenges the academic tradition of a disciplinary division of labour, as the future-proofing of the technical artifact and the social practices it supports asks researchers to go beyond the current 'siloed' disciplines. The identity of the computing discipline has to be extended so that the understanding of the social practices that are related to the evolving appropriation of IT artifacts becomes an integral part of its (long-term) research practices, with a corresponding programme. In this sense, computing needs to open up to play a role as one of the partners in multidisciplinary action research initiatives that include change agents with a variety of different disciplinary backgrounds, collaborating and contributing from different disciplinary angles. One could imagine the emergence of a post-disciplinary organization of academic work, both in research and educational settings.

A first tangible step towards this evolution could be to give more value and recognition to scientific publications that are written in a long-term and multidisciplinary perspective and that make visible aspects of research that are traditionally not considered reportable.

12.3.2 Changing the managerial culture

The failure of top-down initiatives that disregard local practices is not a new insight but needs to be emphasized, given the numerous large-scale projects that fail. Several issues stand out, which should be considered in the education of managers.

First, the importance of management being aware of variations of local practices within and across organizations contrasts the intention to manage complexity through standardization. As Balka et al. (2008) suggest, the diverse typology of sources of variations is to be found not only at the work practice level but also at the institutional, organizational, political, and policy-making levels (see also Gärtner and Wagner, 1996). The successful management of large-scale projects requires a high level of sensitivity not only to 'the local' in its complexity and variability but also the knowledge and tools to analyse the different levels of organizational life that affect it. Apart from a need for such knowledge and tools, management's 'technological frames' have to be reconsidered on three levels, as Orlikowski and Gash (1994) propose:

> (i) *Nature of Technology*—refers to people's images of the technology and their understanding of its capabilities and functionality. (ii) *Technology Strategy*— refers to people's views of why their organization acquired and implemented the technology. It includes their understanding of the motivation or vision behind the adoption decision and its likely value to the organization. (iii) *Technology in Use*—refers to people's understanding of how the technology will be used on a day-to-day basis and the likely or actual conditions and consequences associated with such use.
>
> (p. 183)

Second, management should acknowledge the work needed to construct systems that are actually useful on a 'day-to-day basis' in the long term; it should recognize the step-by-step incremental nature of this process and pay attention to the many details that make work 'work'. This implies a future-oriented temporality that also accounts for slow-paced activities that 'take time'.

Finally, management should be aware of the consequences of selecting IT researchers and technology providers to work with. They are not necessarily supportive of the practitioners they should serve. On the contrary, they may increase pressure in support of their own agenda, which may be short-term economic or longer-term strategic (e.g. they may seek to be part of the definition of standards). These goals are often at variance with the commitment to reach a design result that can and will be appropriated and found useful in practice.

12.3.3 Reorienting the perspective of funding agencies

Future-proofing requires new research funding strategies and instruments. In practice-based IT research, funding should not be directed towards merely technological innovation but towards innovative technologically supported social practices with a view to achieving sustainability. However, a clear commitment to the sustainability of project outcomes in practice cannot be found in any research programme, and no specific funding scheme is proposed for this aim.

Under the current funding conditions, sustainable outcomes cannot always be reached during the lifetime of a single project. So, researchers are forced to seek funding for sustaining their research lines and struggle to obtain it. In fact, when a project ends, there is no guarantee that its continuation to explore more stable and complete results will be funded, even if its outcomes are positively evaluated by the funding agency. One of the main obstacles is that funding schemes promoting academic research in the IT domain are not conceived with the sustainability of project outcomes as one of their main concerns. On the contrary, the rather conservative academic view of technological innovation prevails as an evaluation criterion for choosing new projects.

The projects and cases suggest various routes to take. One concerns the time horizon of funding. Funding schemes should account for the main phases practice-based research has to complete in order to achieve sustainability and support them with dedicated resources: an initial phase to start the research, define a shared vision and possible outcome, and create the contextual conditions for technologies and practices to become sustainable in the future; a second phase to reach a robust design result through the implementation of the detailed and agreed-upon work plan; a third phase to monitor and assist the deployment and appropriation of the results in the target setting, as well as take measures to reach the *maintain* and possibly also the *evolve* form of sustainability. This would offer practice-based IT projects a broader time horizon. It would also require funders to flexibly adjust deadlines and criteria to the different activities that each of these phases entails.

A second strategy is to set up funding for community-based research partnerships (see, e.g., Thomas-Hughes and Barke (2018) for the United Kingdom's Connected Communities programme). This would provide communities with a framework for addressing their questions to a research team which makes its expertise available, assisting the community in codeveloping a socio-technical solution. This approach can be found in healthcare, where 'certain funding bodies are providing the push on academic researchers to engage their subjects more actively; communities are providing the pull' (Green and Mercer, 2001: 1928). It often involves indigenous or marginalized communities. It is much less common in IT projects, with some exceptions (e.g. Karasti and Baker, 2008).

12.3.4 The future-proofing turn

In this book, we have elaborated on the concept of future-proofing in practice-based research. Looking at innovations in both organizational and community contexts, we identified the importance of interlinking the different social arenas in which practice-based design is embedded: the arena of technology design and social practices, the arena of organization or community development, and the political and policy-making context. The sustainability of research requires an expansion of the current perspective—from project-based towards longer-term engagements and responsibilities.

Future-proofing imposes new directions on the design of technical artifacts, specifically for their technical maintainability in practice, and their interpretative and technical flexibility. So, future-proofing argues for a new direction in IT research as well as for the software industries. We need to link IT artifacts and technological competencies more closely to the organizations and communities whose development increasingly depends on future-proof IT infrastructures. On the other hand, organizations and communities should become aware that future-proofing of IT-based solutions is an unavoidable requirement to enhance their performance and the quality of the (working) lives of their members.

From the side of the IT producers, future-proofing requires a technology that is open to reuse, adaptation, evolution, and tailoring, possibly by IT professionals different from the original developers of the artifact. Communal property and open-source code are policies going in this direction, but with some problematic aspects. Both academic and commercial IT designers should produce high-quality software components and documentation to make sharing productive, but the time pressures under which they operate, for different reasons, makes this difficult. On the other hand, IT providers should reconsider their business, which usually adopts a closed-source code policy that presupposes market-based relationships between software producers and their clients: this policy creates strong dependencies, which may result in users having little influence on the technical developments when artifacts are replicated or expanded.

In the face of the evidence gathered, we suggest that the software industry should not only aim at maximizing market shares, company values, and profits but also take responsibility for building and maintaining IT infrastructures understood as a public good that enhances the quality of life. On a more general level, future-proofing in practice-based computing may make a post-capitalist turn in the software industry desirable.

SECTION IV
EPILOGUE

13

Personal experiences and reflections

Four researchers take the opportunity to reflect on their personal experiences with the cases they contributed. They look back at the ambitions and achievements of the research lines they were involved in, providing their own accounts of how the research evolved, which types of barriers they encountered, and which strategies they devised to future-proof their research. Hence, while the overall picture that emerged from writing the book was influenced by our understanding and interpretation of the collected material, the epilogue offers the original points of view of the researchers, providing a space for them to express their feelings and opinions about their research experiences.

Reflecting on her work in developing countries, Nicola Bidwell adopts the notion of 'meshwork' to characterize 'inhabitant' and 'occupant' knowledge and to discuss their differences and mutual interplay, as well as the different temporalities they follow. She is concerned with better understanding how to reconcile local temporalities with the exigencies of setting up and running a technology project and how to let the 'inhabitants' gain autonomy in its management and evolution.

Ellen Balka provides a report on some of the most difficult moments in the evolution of the *ActionADE* project when it entered the phase of integrating the solution with the provincial healthcare ecosystem, a step that entailed scaling and replicating the initial results that had been obtained in a local hospital in different locations and institutions. The experiences the research team gained during this phase raise the issue of how standardization and appropriation can be achieved in such a complex scenario involving both new technical issues and new stakeholders with different roles. Ellen Balka also raises the question of how to reconcile working in a complex institutional environment with the exigencies of an academic career.

Myriam Lewkowicz emphasizes her continual focus on research outcomes that have a sustainable impact on the local and regional healthcare communities, connecting it with regional development. One of her strategies is to seek

Future-proofing. Wulf et al., Oxford University Press.
© Carla Simone, Ina Wagner, Claudia Müller, Anne Weibert, and Volker Wulf (2022).
DOI: 10.1093/oso/9780198862505.003.0013

the political support of influential authorities so as to be able to valorize her team's practice-based approach to design in different applications. She also describes a recent change of health policy in the region and her efforts to adapt the evolution of her research line in telemedicine to these changing conditions. Her message is about the need for researchers to be flexible in defining their strategies to achieve sustainable results.

Margunn Aanestad presents her long-term experiences as an 'observer and analyst' of projects in various field of activity, which complements the 'designer-researcher' perspective characterizing the other contributions. In this role she has observed the many ways in which 'users encounter new technologies' when dealing with problems at the organizational level as well as at the level of national public institutions. Her experiences point to many issues discussed in the book, including the relevance of ownership and of taking an ethical stance in design, and the continuous care that is needed to make the outcomes of a project sustainable.

13.1 Nicola Bidwell: Meshworking temporalities in technologies that sustain

It's six-and-a-half years since I packed my car with the belongings from my room in Mankosi and drove that rugged, twisting gravel road away from a place I had called home for over four years. I've returned thrice, though only once for research, and keep up with news, such as about new babies and how inhabitants fared in the pandemic. Maintaining my connection is largely possible because of the achievements of the Zenzeleni community network; in fact, the network significantly supported inhabitants as the COVID-19 lockdown ensued. It added network infrastructure to extend community Wi-Fi access points, which permitted people who returned to their rural family homes from urban areas to continue to study and work and made health information locally accessible (Bidwell and Luca de Tena, 2021). Living locally and maintaining connections—for more than thirteen years with some inhabitants—has given me a particular perspective on relationships between knowledge and time in rural technology design. Thus, my reflection considers how some of these relationships shape what is sustained.

I've found Tim Ingold's analyses helpful in considering relationships between inhabitant knowledge and sustainability. Inhabitant knowledge, Ingold (2007, 2011) explains, is forged as we move through the world along paths of life and travel. Unlike generating data at separate sites of observation and then integrating it vertically, in scientific studies, or laterally, in installing and maintaining network infrastructure, inhabitant knowledge is integrated *alongly*. We all embody inhabitant knowledge as we move through and make the social and physical fabric of our environments. Our knowledge emerges in exchanges between our bodies and the fabric in which we move and of which we are part. This knowledge, Ingold (2008) explains, is not abstracted, classified, or networked but *meshworked*. A *meshwork*, he proposes, knots together many threads created by the movement and growth of life. I applied Ingold's concept of the meshwork to describe how the paths of life create and sustain an Argentine community network, looped through and between each other, binding together as they went along (Bidwell, 2020a). By sharing resources, community network members accrue the type of relational assets that Light and Miskelly (2019) show can contribute to an ecology of mutually supportive systems that enable social innovations to be sustained. Thus, I begin by describing some relationships in the meshwork in which the Zenzeleni community network emerged and the role of supporting inhabitant knowledge. Then, I link meshworking knowledge to the ways in which time becomes embedded in technology and technology projects, and what this means for sustainability.

13.1.1 A meshwork across time

As I reflect on *Zenzeleni Networks*, I realise that a wide array of people participated in the meshwork of relations: some before me and many after, some I know and many I do not. In 2008, I lived for three months in the headman's house in Lwandile, 8 km along the coast from, and an hour's drive from, Mankosi. My stay was made possible by Bill Tucker, an academic in Cape Town, and Arjan van der Sar, an IT volunteer at a rural hospital a 1.5-hour drive away, who had installed Wi-Fi to connect Lwandile's clinic to the hospital, and the headman's house to the internet. The relationships and knowledge forged during my stay prompted Bill and Arjan to install Wi-Fi between three villages much further along the coast and in the opposite direction to Mankosi. Around the same time, I met Paula Kotze, a research director at South Africa's Council for Scientific and Industrial Research (CSIR), at a workshop that Gary Marsden and Matt Jones hosted in Cape Town; the following year we applied for a fellowship for me at CSIR and for funding for technology research in rural Eastern Cape from the United Kingdom's Engineering and Physical Sciences Research Council (EPSRC). Meanwhile, I undertook participatory design of a mobile digital storytelling app in Mankosi, where electricity was available in a backpackers' hostel. The EPSRC project sought to enable inhabitants to use mobile phones and a shared repository to communicate asynchronously without the prohibitive costs of access to the services of mobile network operators (MNOs). When we launched in 2010, we discussed Wi-Fi links to connect shared repositories between the villages; however, I was unaware of the term 'community network', and it would take another three years, in which my life entwined with even more people's lives, before Wi-Fi was installed. Inhabitants and I learnt together by redesigning and operating communal cell-phone solar charging stations and asynchronous media-sharing systems.

The EPSRC project, originally conceived externally, would not have been launched, not least sustained, without being bound into the everyday life going along in Mankosi. Thus, in March 2012, when Carlos Rey-Moreno posed his intention to set up Wi-Fi as part of his PhD project with Bill, I stubbornly asserted that he must live locally. The Wi-Fi that Bill and Arjan had installed between villages along the coast in 2008 did not last long, unlike the solar charging stations in Mankosi, because we could not maintain frequent contact to mesh with the inhabitants' local knowledge. With experience on telecommunications networks in Peru and contacts in Guifi.net, a vast community network in the Iberian Peninsula, Carlos entangled other threads into the meshwork in which *Zenzeleni Networks* emerged; as the community network emerged, other threads also became entwined. For instance, the launch of the African Community Network Summit, at AfriCHI 2016 in Nairobi, enabled Zenzeleni to interconnect with other community networks across the continent.

13.1.2 Recognizing and supporting inhabitant knowledge

In those early discussions about a Wi-Fi network with Carlos and Bill, I was similarly adamant that research must concretely acknowledge the value of *alongly integrated inhabitant* knowledge. The institutions in which technology research is embedded privilege an *occupant* epistemology that integrates data that is discretely sampled at times or locations, *upwardly* in scientific studies or *laterally* in technology implementations. Such privileging is reproduced in the distinct ways in which *researchers*, *participants*, and *project beneficiaries* are named and recompensed. For instance, in the EPSRC grant proposal only post-doctoral staff were considered 'salaried'; however, since I received a small stipend from the CSIR and living in Mankosi was relatively inexpensive, we used the budget in the EPSRC grant for my support for small salaries for a team of eight 'Local Researchers' (LRs). While not all the LRs had completed high school, and only two had or were undertaking university degrees, their inhabitant knowledge was vital to gathering data, contributing to design, and linguistically and culturally translating between local and non-local meanings. Material recognition of this knowledge, by payment, set a precedent for local technology endeavours and enabled Masbulele Jay Siya to work full-time on the Wi-Fi project and subsequently co-found *Zenzeleni Networks*.

The LRs and I also contributed to setting a precedent in the field of HCI for respecting inhabitant knowledge in the authorship of nine academic publications resulting from the asynchronous media-sharing and solar cell-phone charging stations project. Not all of those named as co-authors (e.g. Bidwell et al., 2011, 2013) directly benefited from publication authorship, although one LR did go on to complete her masters and PhD. Nor was it possible to individually name all of Mankosi's inhabitants who participated in the social production of knowledge. Yet, despite its imperfections, signalling the fundamental importance of this knowledge is preferable to privileging certain categories of knowledge by limiting authorship to researchers in certain institutions. Indeed, Masbulele Jay, co-founder of *Zenzeleni Networks*, was a recipient of the International Federation of Information Processing's inaugural award for 'Best Contribution to Social and Economic Development' at INTERACT 2013, for a paper that we co-authored (see: Bidwell and Siya, 2013).

Of equal importance to explicitly acknowledging inhabitant knowledge is removing the barriers, created by occupant epistemologies, to inhabitants extending their meshworks themselves. An important outcome of Carlos's work on *Zenzeleni Networks* was facilitating interconnections between community networks in Africa and globally, such as through the Association for Progressive Communications' peer community networks (APC, 2020) and the African Community Network Summit (organized by ISOC (Internet Society), 2020). In October 2019, for instance, I sat next to Nontsokolo Gladys Sigcau, director of Zenzeleni Mankosi Cooperative (*Zenzeleni Networks*) on a bus taking participants in the Fourth African Summit from all over the continent to the Kondoa community network in Tanzania. I certainly had not imagined when I used to drop in to chat to Mama Sigcau about our solar charging station that eight years later we would both be in Tanzania. Indeed, I did not have any destination in mind in those early years, nor did I consider how rural communities might forge their own paths in extending their meshwork. I simply focused on our mutual learning as we went along.

13.1.3 Temporalities embedded in technology and technology projects

The knowledge involved in decisions about design and technology projects is always shaped by many temporal relations, whether that knowledge is alongly or upwardly integrated. I have written about how the rhythms of daily routines, like collecting water or taking cattle to graze, tuned the design and operation of the solar charging stations in Mankosi (Bidwell et al., 2013) and how seasonal rhythms influence the trajectories of rural community networks in Argentina (Bidwell, 2020a). Experiences of time, however, are multiple. Even in a rural village, where people's lives may be more homogeneous than in urban areas, temporalities are differential. Indeed, the different everyday routines of women and men in Mankosi shaped their perspectives on the meaning of operation of, use of, and access to the solar charging stations (Bidwell et al., 2013) and the labour involved in the community network (Shewarga-Hussen et al., 2016). Occupant knowledge cannot depict the detail of local temporal differentiations, and yet, as I describe next, it often influences technology projects and design.

The practices that sustained the solar cell-phone charging stations in Mankosi would have been invisible had I upwardly integrated data about operation and use, as most technology research does. Realizing this, I wrote about the tensions between occupant knowledge and locally sustainable technology research and design (Bidwell et al., 2013). However, the temporalities of local practices, project funding, and device longevity often do not reconcile. For instance, consider a difficulty produced by our trial of prototype asynchronous media-sharing systems. At the end of the trial, inhabitants had copies of content they stored on the shared repository and we explained that, while all the equipment was theirs to keep, our ability to back up further content was limited. Thus, three years after I left, inhabitants who had continued to use the prototype (e.g. Bidwell and Siya, 2013) lost content when the tablet eventually failed.

In the years since I first noticed tensions between occupant knowledge and locally sustainable technology research and design, I have become aware of the role of policy and regulation in technology design (e.g. Jackson et al., 2014) and how this, too, implicates occupant knowledge. From the end of 2017, I engaged with advocates for policy and regulatory environments that better enable community networks. The activists lobby policy-makers to reduce the administrative and financial barriers to obtain licenses for networks so that they can use the electromagnetic spectrum and extend the range of frequencies that do not require licences. I observed the stark contrast in spatial and temporal scales between international advocacy and rural operations of local community networks. Huge spatial scales, such as the vast territories of MNOs, frame telecommunications policy discussions and activists seek to exert as much influence as possible in the short periods in which they have funding. Thus, activists move rapidly between highly connected spaces of telecommunications decision-making around the world and justify the viability of community networks according to measures that align with these scales (Bidwell, 2019). The occupant knowledge, that regulatory and policy discussions draw on, masks the temporal differentiation that shapes the meaning of access to inhabitants of community networks.

Advocacy for regulations that better enable community networks tends to treat Wi-Fi technology as neutral. Yet women, more often than men, in four rural community networks that I studied in the Global South, spoke of the incompatibility of Wi-Fi access with the routines of their agricultural and domestic work (Bidwell, 2020b). Decisions in these rural community networks are more often made by men, even when women comprise the majority in local populations. This illustrates how technologies are appropriated through power relations that interact with local temporalities, and tensions emerge that can undermine the sustainability (e.g. Bidwell, 2020b).

13.1.4 Vigilance to temporal integrations and differentiations

The organizational structures involved in *Zenzeleni Networks* contribute to a meshwork that ensures that inhabitant knowledge sensitizes decisions to local temporal differentiations, yet reconciling local temporalities and those of prevalent technology regimes remains difficult. Zenzeleni Mankosi Cooperative includes women and men of varied ages and is supported by *Zenzeleni Networks*, a non-profit cooperative (NPC) which facilitates engagements with regulatory authorities, funding sources, and telecommunications research and expertise. The staff of the NPC find themselves brokering between the temporalities lived in Mankosi and those associated with quality standards for 24/7 internet provision, milestones for funding, and deadlines for legal compliance. Having experienced the difficulties of managing international deadlines while living in Mankosi (Bidwell et al., 2013), I have great sympathy for the enormity of the NPC's task. Thus, while fostering meshworks to integrate policy, design, and appropriation are essential to sustaining technology, we still need to identify ways that we can better respond to the differential and relational nature of time.

13.2 Ellen Balka: Persistence and patience and relations—*ActionADE* at eight

Nearly twenty years ago, I began a paper about theoretical and practical considerations related to women's participation in technology design with the following two quotes:

> Researching participation, then, is no easy matter. It is beset with problems of both a technical and an interpretive nature. This is not to argue, however, that it should not be undertaken. If there is to be any evidence with which to assess the impact of participation, some studies must be carried out. ... There is a need for greater information about outcomes, and what people feel about them, in order to understand what participation means in practice.
> (Richardson, 1983: 125)

> The best way to understand something is to try to change it.
> (Kurt Lewin, cited in Greenwood and Levin, 1998: 19)

I've always been interested in how we evaluate the efforts of participatory design projects. And, while I am aware that it is difficult, if not impossible, to assess the impact of participation, and agree with Richardson (1983) that some studies should be carried out (and in the case of *ActionADE*, some are ongoing and others are planned), although *ActionADE* is not completed, I can say some things about the results—or outcomes—we have achieved to date, as well as what we have learnt so far.

Here, I'll reflect on these two points in relation to some of the ideas that are raised in the first and second chapters in this book. I'll begin by recounting some of the changes which have occurred with *ActionADE* since I was interviewed. I'll then reflect on the two quotes above in relation to one of the key themes in this book—how IT research projects achieve lasting effects within their target settings.

13.2.1 *ActionADE* now

As I write this piece, the integration of *ActionADE* in the provincial ecosystem has progressed along three main phases.

After the definitive processes were laid out for moving from symbolic cooperation to real cooperation (a process which spanned several years) and *ActionADE* went through the province's budgeting office successfully, conformance specifications for integration were developed, tested, and implemented—a process our team participated in. *ActionADE* received patients' prior dispensed medication history from *PharmaNet*, which prepopulated a patient's record within *ActionADE*, and became the starting point for the work required to arrive at a diagnostic conclusion that an ADE had occurred.

The second phase of integration involved sending *ActionADE* reports to *PharmaNet*, where they were incorporated into a patient's medication dispensing history.

The third phase involves sending those reports out to community pharmacies, where their software parses ADE report data, displays it, and issues an alert in the event that a pharmacist attempts to dispense a drug which has previously caused harm to the patient filling a prescription.

This will be possible as one of the community pharmacy software companies (which has a significant market share in the province) will be releasing its newest software version, which includes functionality allowing the company to parse *ActionADE* data, to five beta test sites. Until the software vendor that is beta testing releases its new version to all of its client pharmacies, and other community pharmacy software companies release their updated versions which support parsing and proper display of *ActionADE* data (two additional vendors are working on it), community pharmacies (and other *PharmaNet* users) will simply receive a notification that an ADE report generated through *ActionADE* is on file. If the Ministry of Health does its communications job well at that point, people working in community pharmacies where our unparsed reports may appear will know that a patient-specific alert (as opposed to a generic alert unrelated to a specific patient) has occurred and that further detail about a past ADE can be found elsewhere.

After a period of monitoring and change management at the beta site community pharmacies, our end-to-end implementation of *ActionADE* will, in a technical sense, be complete. All the pieces of the *ActionADE* solution we have had control over will have moved from idea through participatory design, informed by research (which supported numerous decisions including when, where, and how to support standardization), to prototype testing, first into stand-alone software and, finally, into software which shares data across multiple software products—some developed through public funds and others developed by private-sector entrepreneurs.

While conformance testing was ongoing, we began rolling out *ActionADE* to other units within our initial hospital; more recently, we have been rolling out *ActionADE* to other hospitals in the province. In addition, our request to create a hyperlink from *ActionADE* to the best-in-breed acute care clinical information system which is now being widely implemented throughout the province has been approved by the Core Clinical and Operations Advisory Team (CCOAT), a key decision-making and governance group in the *Clinical Systems Transformation (CST)* project. This was an important milestone for us, as the journey to first identify how decisions were made in relation to the multiple health authority CST project proved a long and winding path which, among other things, included an initial CST project launch, contractual problems (followed eventually by an exit form the original CST project management contract), and a project reboot (to CST 2.0) with new project operations groups and senior project staffing.

13.2.2 Project outcomes, outcomes of participation, and achieving lasting effects

Project outcomes, outcomes of participation, and achieving lasting outcomes are not one and the same, yet can be hard to separate.

Project outcomes

In the context of *ActionADE*, the health outcome we are trying to achieve is a reduction in preventable repeat ADEs by closing the informational continuity-of-care gaps between the location where ADEs are diagnosed (emergency departments), and the location where redispensing of previously harmful medications has occurred (community pharmacies). We are also trying to increase the frequency of ADE reporting by clinical care providers without adding to documentation burden. Finally, we have learnt through ethnographic observations that there was no place for ADE records to easily reside in patient charts, and we hope that *ActionADE* will support clinicians by bringing the information necessary for arriving at a definitive diagnosis into a single place in a patient's record.

A randomized control trial ((RCT)—a condition of funding, as well as the gold standard of clinical studies) is planned, but cannot be carried out until after ADE reports are pushed to community pharmacies and some time elapses. However, we do know that *ActionADE* is being used (mostly by pharmacists—at least in our initial location). As we implement *Action-ADE* beyond emergency departments and to additional hospitals, we are also expanding use beyond physicians and pharmacists to other groups legally permitted to view patient data (e.g. nurse practitioners).

Outcomes of participation

We know that the number of ADEs reported in sites where *ActionADE* is used increased significantly, which we attribute to the care and attention given to listening to participants' voices through allowing them to participate in our project's design activities, participants' commitment to the goal of preventing ADEs, and their continued engagement with the project. We also brought a research focus to system development, which included, for example, an awareness of the work that standards do and the roles they play within information systems—an area our team paid particular attention to.

Finally, we also know that the number of requests for changes from users has slowed to a halt, and we are seldom hearing about problems from users. So, while we cannot say that we have reduced the number of preventable repeat ADEs, we can say with significant confidence that we have closed the gap in informational continuity of care between the locations where ADEs are identified and (once data are pushed to the community pharmacies) the location where prescriptions are refilled. If we consider use and the creation of ADE reports as a proxy outcome for reduction in preventable ADEs, we have succeeded.

Adoption and extending use: Achieving lasting effects

The introduction to this book suggests that results should enrich users' work and help the organizations improve their services, as well as the working conditions of users. Though thus far we lack rigorous data to suggest this is the case, we are quite confident that we have achieved this. But what about another point that was raised? Can *ActionADE* be adapted and further developed by other users who are interested in changing their practices? With respect to *ActionADE*, we can point to one concrete case in which this has happened and two other situations which suggest that further uptake is likely.

When COVID-19 hit, *ActionADE* emerged as a ready-to-hand and easily scalable tool for tracking ADEs that occurred in relation to COVID-19 treatments. This was done in an effort to lower the morbidity and mortality of COVID-19 at a time where numerous unproven and, in many cases, harmful treatments needed to be both sanctioned and cautioned against. The COVID-19 registry team sought and received ethical approval to use *ActionADE* for ADE tracking. However, they found the use case they thought *ActionADE* would support did not emerge in a Canadian context. So, while the adoption of *ActionADE* was envisioned, ultimately it was not needed and hence not used in that context.

At around the time that most of the work was completed for our initial end-to-end deployment to *PharmaNet* and out to community pharmacy systems, our developer began a conversation with us about the possibility of using a key element of our design in other applications his team was working on, which required a medication dispensing history, medication reconciliation functionality, or both. *ActionADE* seems ripe to be adapted and further developed for different usages.

Once the development of *ActionADE* was well underway, Vanessa's Law was passed, which (eventually) made patient-specific ADE reporting of serious ADEs to the federal government mandatory, beginning in December 2019. Our team has closely followed the development and implementation of this policy change and (again), after a prolonged negotiation, we recently learnt that *ActionADE* will be the means through which the ADE data that must now be reported to the federal government will be captured, and sent on its way to the federal Ministry of Health.

All of these uses will constitute either new or changed practices which should enrich users' work and help the organizations improve their services and the working conditions of users. In many senses, we have succeeded. However, in my initial conversation with our developer about incorporating *ActionADE* into other software, I reminded him that reusing the software was the easy part. The permission to introduce new software into the hospital in an above-board manner (rather than doing it 'under the radar' as many teams before us had) to receive data from the Ministry and send documented ADEs to the Ministry of Health (which involved writing business plans and conducting privacy impact assessments and strength, threat, and risk analyses (STRAs)) had taken our team years. While each new project that sought to build on our team's work might have been able to leverage our team's design and the defined conformance standards to support a two-way flow of data between our application and the Ministry of Health about something other than billing (which had not existed prior to *ActionADE*), all the relationship-building, negotiations, and meeting privacy regulations would still need to be undertaken afresh by each new project team.

ActionADE was designed and implemented incrementally, and hence could prove a useful building block for other teams that need to demonstrate that a software application works as a stand-alone application before stakeholders buy in to full integration.

Achieving lasting effects in target settings

Having just formally received approval to create access to *ActionADE* from the best-in-breed clinical information system being implemented provincially, I'm quite optimistic (today at least) that *ActionADE* will create a lasting effect, and will enable 'people, communities, and/or organizations to self-develop' (as mentioned in the introduction to this book). I remain optimistic that the infrastructures we have built and pushed others to build, and particularly the *ActionADE* software, its connection to the Ministry of Health, and its connection to pharmacies and emergency departments, will remain, along with a linkage between *ActionADE* and the best-in-breed acute care clinical information system currently being implemented. But only time will tell if *ActionADE* is 'future-proofed'.

Because our project has involved integration with such large systems and interaction with the involved stakeholders and because moving the project forward with the Ministry of Health required such a huge investment of their time and human resources, it seems unlikely that our project will wither. But more importantly, a core connecting piece of the infrastructure—*PharmaNet*—has been changed to support *ActionADE*. This bodes well for our future.

Having said that, for a variety of reasons, the Ministry has implemented a minimally viable product (MVP) on their end to support *ActionADE* integration. *PharmaNet* is due for modernization, and of course we don't know what will happen to *ActionADE* if and when that modernization occurs. While we have been successful in altering the backend database(s) that together form the core of *PharmaNet* to receive data from *ActionADE* reports, the legacy systems upon which *PharmaNet* is built posed limitations (such as storage limitations) that may (for example) limit the use of elements of *ActionADE* by other groups; in these cases we would be able to respond to such requests directed to us from our developer. While it has not been our goal to have others adapt our software (other than for filling the informational continuity-of-care gap with community pharmacies and for mandatory reporting under Vanessa's Law), the use of *ActionADE* by other stakeholders would certainly contribute to the sustainability of *ActionADE*.

We did, however, build the software in a way that allows it to be implemented incrementally. Although we consider prepopulation of a patient's medication history a key component of *ActionADE* (as this saves frontline care providers a significant amount of time when taking and reviewing a patient's medication history), *ActionADE* can be run in the absence of a connection to *PharmaNet*. Although this makes the software more time-consuming to use, it also means that, if need be, the software can be implemented without *PharmaNet* integration, which could hasten its uptake in other provinces.

13.2.3 Participation in large-scale system integration projects

Perhaps the biggest challenge our project faces—both in terms of participatory design and how future-proof it is—relates to the project's number of stakeholders and the complexity of their relationships with one another. During the second grant, we attempted to build relationships directly with community pharmacy software companies, but we did not succeed in bringing any of them onto our team as project partners, collaborators, or sponsors. This was not surprising, in that they all had existing products which they assumed (incorrectly) achieved what *ActionADE* sought to. Additionally, the companies whose software is widely used in British Columbia in community pharmacies understood that our software would not have 'legs' until *PharmaNet* had not only signed up to supporting *ActionADE*, but also revised the related conformance standards. We hoped to interest a community pharmacy software company in our project so we could play an active role in determining what the data originating through *ActionADE* would look like at the end where one of our target user groups—community pharmacists—used that information to avoid medication errors. In spite of our numerous efforts, we were unable to engage any of the community pharmacy software companies at that point.

As work with *PharmaNet* and the Ministry of Health progressed, we again sought to meet directly with the community pharmacy vendors. By this time, we were into our third funding cycle, which included a series of agreements specifying which stakeholders were to assume responsibility for each aspect of the project. Responsibility for communicating with community pharmacy software companies was the responsibility of the Ministry of Health. A gatekeeper there decided that we should not have direct contact with the community software vendors, which presented our team with significant challenges. We were not shown what the parsed *ActionADE* data would look like in community pharmacy software until it was implemented. Although one of the first two companies to implement parsing of our data so *ActionADE* reports would be visible in their software did a stellar job from what we have been able to see, another company's efforts left our team (and some members of the Ministry) wondering if their implementation might increase rather than decrease medication-related errors.

For the last few weeks, our team has been working on strategies for having input into what our data will look like in varied community pharmacy systems in use in our province. Through our engagement in the process of developing conformance standards with the Ministry, we have been able to advocate for which ADE data are transmitted and stored in *PharmaNet* on the basis of our empirical work with the users. But we have not yet figured out how our team can have any influence over how the data are ultimately displayed to pharmacists in the community or how, as a group, those users can participate in how they see or work with our data. Yet we hope that the user group will act on the data contained in our reports. Although we have not yet figured this piece out, it was not for lack of trying (during our earlier project stage), and we have not abandoned our goal of engaging users in designing the interfaces through which our reports will be viewed.

Finding ways to influence software products which are integrated with other systems, but over which a research team has little or no control, will increasingly be a challenge both in terms of participatory design and sustainability. I find myself pondering what sorts of things might alter the current situation. In Canada, we have funding programmes which subsidize businesses to hire graduate students to bring a greater research focus to the company's work. Should we pursue such a fellowship in hopes that a jointly supervised senior research trainee might be able to influence change if required in a community pharmacy vendor's software? Perhaps. However, this is essentially what we tried to do when writing our second grant proposal, and we were unable to bring the community pharmacy software companies onside then. Will we be more successful now that integration has occurred? Perhaps.

13.2.4 Sustaining participation and sustaining software in an era of large-scale systems integration

Each time we are able to successfully build a set of relationships which ultimately lead to greater technical integration of *ActionADE* into the province's health information technology infrastructure, the software becomes more sustainable. The more each stakeholder makes changes to their infrastructure that support the movement of *ActionADE* data across previously discrete systems, the greater the coupling and integration of previously discrete software systems and the more effective the sustainability of *ActionADE* in the future.

But coupling and integration are not the same as participation in design or shared decision-making, and this, indeed, may be one of the greatest challenges to sustaining participatory projects in an era of large-scale system integration. In contemplating this problem, two different strands of thought emerge. On the one hand, we may need to reconceptualize participatory design activities to include the formation of strategic partnerships between companies as a way to improve the likelihood that participation in design extends across previously discrete software applications, once integrated. On the other hand, if participatory approaches to system design were more widely accepted, we would not have to worry about whether an application that is used to display data which originated in our system was designed with user participation. If as a culture we truly valued users and understood and respected their work practices, we would not have to worry as much about whether or not they would be called upon to participate in design activities.

At time of the writing, we learnt that the Ministry of Health's communication and change management materials developed to support community pharmacies were really good. Although the quality of the materials is important, it is arguably more important that the Ministry of Health has invested in the project, as this type of project buy-in will be essential to the project extending beyond its funding.

At the same time as remaining optimistic that *ActionADE* will outlive our research funding and that my co-investigator and I will be able to handle the challenges that are sure to come and being certain that *ActionADE* will be the most impactful project I have worked on, I am also more confused than ever about what participation means in the current software and academic environments.

Much remains unknown about sustainable participation in an era of large-scale system integration. One of the few things I can say with certainty about the extent to which we have been able to move our project forward is that the success we have achieved has been partly a reflection of our grit, determination, and success in competing for research grants.

13.2.5 Building conditions for sustainable research

We have been fortunate to have been through three significant funding cycles. This has allowed us to continue work on *ActionADE* over almost a decade (so far). The funding allowed us to move beyond a pilot to a system in which multiple stakeholders have made a significant investment, and the magnitude of human and capital investment which has gone into supporting *ActionADE*—particularly on the part of the provincial Ministry of Health in relation to our linkage with *PharmaNet*—is likely to keep our minimal viable product afloat for at least the duration of this iteration of *PharmaNet*.

Building conditions for sustainable research requires money and time, which in academia are closely intertwined. One needs time to build a record that allows one to compete successfully for large grants and, once large grants are in hand, the time and skills to manage teams (with staffing often supplied by fairly junior entrants to the paid labour force), large projects, stakeholder relationships, and more. My co-investigator and I began working together in 2012. Out of eighteen person years of co-leading this project, we have had sixteen person years of protected time between us, for research. The fact that I had time and that at the point where I began working with my co-investigator I had already spent several years as a researcher embedded in the healthcare system (during which time I had built relationships with health-sector stakeholders and developed significant insights into how the health system worked) laid the groundwork for the role I have filled as a co-investigator of *ActionADE*. We have been incredibly successful in securing successive grants for our project, and this, too, has helped us create a fairly stable team within an academic setting, where emphasis is placed on hiring students. Many of our staff members began working with us as master's students, then worked with us full-time for a period, and subsequently went on to complete PhDs.

Growing our team as our project grew was not an easy process at all. In addition to some of the 'normal' parts of academic life which occur according to a rhythm unrelated to a research project's rhythm, we also had to accommodate numerous other tempos. In addition to funding cycles, student schedules, and scheduling around practitioner schedules, as our engagement with our stakeholders intensified, we increasingly had to deal with expectations in the world of business, government, and in one instance, consultants. The idea that you can't turn something around with little notice because you have classes to teach or papers to grade, or that you can't make a meeting because you are in the classroom all day, doesn't really matter. The expectation is that you will be available when stakeholders call meetings.

At one particularly demanding point, one of our project partners and funders required that we hire a consultant of their choosing. Work got done—though, as my co-investigator frequently reminded me, it was work that we either didn't want to do or didn't have time to do—but the process was wearing for everyone, and project morale plummeted. We weathered that challenge (some of us with some scars) and kept going, eventually replacing the consultant we had relied on for a certain skill set with a team member more accustomed to working in an academic setting. My protected time for research ran out and I had to go back to my full-time university position, and this too presented challenges. I found myself increasingly unable to meet the demands of my participation in *ActionADE* and my university job, much of which I had previously been relieved from through research fellowships that had ended over the course of the project and which had left me too senior to qualify for existing funding streams. Very few, if any, opportunities exist for senior faculty members to access time protected for research without moving to another university: a significant failing of the Canadian university system.

As the project has continued, as a team we've constantly had to respond to operational needs, and time for self-reflection and the completion of research papers is sparse and often relegated to times where we are dealing with fewer operational demands. We are now moving forward with rolling out to new sites within the province at the same time that our reports will be visible in community pharmacies (where we still hope to carry out some kinds of observations and/or interviews, in the hope of influencing design of the community pharmacy interface through which our reports will be viewed). And, finally, we're now beginning the process of linking to the acute care best-in-breed clinical information system. It is hard to see when we'll be able to focus on our research outputs amid such a demanding operations schedule, particularly in the middle of a pandemic. But we've worked together for years and have developed some expertise along the way; no doubt we will get through this as we have gotten through other challenges.

Temporal frames have presented challenges, and continue to. At the moment we are waiting for our second community pharmacy software company to implement the version which will allow them to parse our data. We still have much work to do, and as our work progresses, we will need to address a host of new issues.

We have also done a lot of things well. For example, early on, our team developed processes such as tracking the actors/stakeholders we interacted with. We also developed and have maintained decision logs which allow us to go back and reconstruct (for example) why we made certain design decisions, and how those decisions related to specific participatory activities or research undertaken by the team (what Pipek and Wulf (2009) have called 'historicity support'). These strategies and others (e.g. formal minutes of every meeting) will position us well to look back. *ActionADE* has proven to be easily implementable across a range of legacy as well as emergent systems. And yet we also face challenges as we move forward. More users means a potentially greater need for support, and with each facility we bring online there is usually one peculiar problem. Although we had developed and been using varied methods to onboard users, we have had to work to establish new strategies for onboarding users during COVID-19, and to find new incentives to get them to training—food is a great incentive in healthcare, but during COVID-19, only individual boxed lunches are allowed, in rooms with fewer people. Our approach, which could be characterized as 'sustained PD', as articulated by Simonsen and Hertzum (2012), may not continue to be practical as the number of sites we onboard increases, together with the geographic scope of those sites.

Returning to the two quotations included in the opening section, our team is looking forward to continuing to write about our project processes and outcomes as the project continues to unfold over time. We have developed an implementation protocol to guide our 'process' research alongside our randomized control trial. On a personal level, I find myself thinking about Lewin's suggestion that 'the best way to understand something is to try to change it', and I wonder how educational and research systems might better support researchers in following this advice.

13.3 Myriam Lewkowicz: Strategic thinking for sustainable practice-centred computing

This book was a trigger for me to reflect on all the projects we have conducted at the local, regional, national, and European levels around healthcare, addressing the social isolation of elderly people, social support among caregivers, and the coordination issues of professionals willing to take care of patients in their homes. Since Ina Wagner interviewed me in Paris, the situation evolved in France as a new healthcare law was passed which emphasizes the importance of cooperation among healthcare practitioners, the need for IT support, and the key role of local territories (this latter is not obvious in France, which is a very centralized country). The reflection that started with this book definitely helped me to make decisions in this evolving context, and I am grateful to Claudia Müller who, through an interview, helped me realize what are, from my experience, the main issues that have to be dealt with when aiming to ensure a sustainable, practice-based computing approach. In this epilogue, I briefly list and illustrate these main issues in the hope they can support other sustainable experiences.

13.3.1 Following topics

One of the most important and obvious things to do when planning out a research project is to identify research questions that are independent of a case, and to ensure that projects can follow-up on these questions. For instance, I studied knotworking (Engeström, 2008) with Khuloud Abou Amsha in different settings. In *PiCADO*, a three-year-long inter-ministerially funded project, we studied the collaborative practices of self-employed healthcare professionals (self-employed workers in charge of the economics of their practice: general practitioners, nurses, speech-language pathologists, physiotherapists, occupational therapists, dieticians, etc.) taking care of patients at home (Abou Amsha and Lewkowicz, 2018). In *HADex*, a year-long regionally funded project, we studied the coordination among salaried healthcare professionals of the 'hospital at home' organization. Finally, in *CALIPSO*, a two-year-long regionally funded project, we studied the coordination between the different healthcare actors for the whole trajectory of a patient, from hospital to home and vice versa, addressing the sharing of information and the communication between two very different healthcare systems (at least in France): in the city and at the hospital (Berthou, in print). By adopting the design case study framework (Wulf et al., 2011), we were able to develop a conceptual reflection on knotworking and how to design to support it (Abou Amsha et al., 2021), reflection that led us to develop a discourse involving the local and regional healthcare actors in France so that our research could impact local communities.

13.3.2 Getting political support

Having an impact on local communities is one important aspect of socio-informatics that we embrace, ensuring that the research questions that we tackle are those that are 'important, meaningful, and impactful for the communities' with whom we are working (Hayes, 2018: 308). Created by decree on 14 September 1994, Troyes University of Technology was born out of a strong political will. The general council of Aube—and more precisely its president, Senator Philippe Adnot—bet on technological development and innovation to save the economy of the department, which was highly industrialized (fourth French department) but suffering from the crisis in the textile and the mechanical industries (Moraux & Balme, 2007). This favourable political context encouraged us to interact regularly with the senator, who then became aware of the research we were conducting and was convinced of the positive impact it could have for citizens, local companies, students, and research groups. He and his team then regularly invited us to lunches at the Senate to introduce us to major actors of companies in the healthcare sector (insurances, IT, transportation), envisioning our research as a way of attracting diverse economic players in the department. He also invited us to national events and discussed policies debated in the French Senate. This political support has definitely opened up prospects to us and given me a complementary vision that was very useful in making strategic decisions.

13.3.3 Being flexible

Something that I have learnt over fifteen years of research within healthcare is that flexibility, in the sense of being able to adapt and change strategies as the context evolves, is another important aspect of sustainability. I will illustrate this aspect with a journey through a major evolution of our ecosystem.

When we defined the *CALIPSO* project as a follow-up project of *PiCADO*, our objective was to build upon *CARE* (Amsha & Lewkowicz, 2015), the prototype that was developed to support knotworking. For so doing, we involved a local software company in the project (based in Troyes) that was used to working with the local hospital. The goal was both to deliver a robust product and to ensure its maintenance, which would ensure the sustainability of the whole approach. However, this initial plan was disrupted.

The disruption started with the French territorial reform in 2016, which reduced the number of regions from twenty-two to thirteen. Before this reform, our research group was one of the few working on coordination among healthcare practitioners in our region (Champagne-Ardenne). The new region, called Grand-Est, includes Lorraine and Alsace, previously two stand-alone regions, which contain major research centres, big hospitals, and well-organized associations. A regional agency named Pulsy (www.pulsy.fr) was created to be the preferred operator of the Grand-Est regional health agency for the development and implementation of the regional e-health strategy. It aims first to support and promote the use of digital health services in the territories to health professionals, health establishments, social and medico-social structures, and users. Its objective is also to facilitate the sharing and exchange of data in a standardized and secure framework, to coordinate care and life paths, to support its members in the implementation of regulatory obligations and standards of good practice, and to promote innovation and territorial initiatives in the field of e-health. Therefore, Pulsy proposes a catalogue of systems and related services that interferes with potential local developments. Indeed, in the French healthcare system, a hospital cannot fully decide which information systems they may use; if they decide to use a system that is not 'prescribed' by their regional health agency, they are not financially supported for its acquisition, its customization, or its deployment.

We were then confronted with a difficult situation: should we go on working with the local software company and end up with a system that fits our research results but that would not be deployed by the local hospital anymore? We faced a dilemma, as supporting a practice-centred approach at the regional level would mean losing the system that we had helped develop as part of two design case studies. Keeping in mind a long-term perspective, we decided not to fight against the regional e-health agency and instead to follow the national strategy, applied at the local level. The decision was not easy, as the software company was also at risk of losing an important market, which could lead to an economic lay-off. The system that was supposed to be developed during *CALIPSO* was then never finished, but we are now involved with the local hospital in the deployment of Parcéo, a system supported by Pulsy, which calls it 'the WhatsApp for the nurses and the doctors'. By making the point that we have expertise in this domain, we managed to be integrated into the project and to have a say in the customization and deployment process. A PhD student from our research group (paid by the university) is now following the whole process, aiming to encourage a practice-centred point of view.

13.3.4 Ensuring independence through diverse sources of funding

Another important aspect of sustainability is the balancing of financial and intellectual independence. After fifteen years of responding to calls for projects, I have now learnt to adopt a portfolio approach, mixing short and longer projects and those funded by companies, administrations (hospital, healthcare agencies), and public authorities. Indeed, public funding ensures intellectual independence but also means more bureaucracy and more time spent on deliverables (and less on writing manuscripts), whereas direct contracting with companies or administration means money can be spent exactly as we want (without having to respect a budget plan defined three or four years ago). I adopt the same approach for funding PhDs; it is interesting to have a company funding a PhD (in France there is a financial incentive scheme), as the company becomes interested in the success of the research, the PhD student gains work experience, and the research group is financially supported for the supervision of the student. On the other hand, it becomes more difficult to ensure fully critical thinking in this framework. Therefore, it is important to decide which topic to address under which framework.

For instance, in the current context, it is crucial to start interacting closely with Pulsy, the new e-health regional agency presented above. Therefore, I joined forces with a colleague based in Strasbourg (where the headquarters of Pulsy are) and negotiated a PhD there for studying the regional version of the national e-health strategy. However, as mentioned above, when following the deployment of Parcéo (the system supposed to support cooperation among all the care actors), it is important to ensure that a publicly funded PhD student is working on the case. This will guarantee that we are able to raise concerns about the system and its deployment and publish about that.

13.3.5 Postponing and pausing activities

Even if following topics is an important factor for sustainability, as we mentioned first, it goes hand in hand with being able to postpone and pause activities. Indeed, what is important is to keep track of open research questions, and to be opportunistic when deciding to address them.

For instance, we started to work on teleconsultation in 2015, as both the head of the emergency medical dispatch centre in Troyes and the head of a company offering a telemedicine toolkit contacted us to assess the deployment of this telemedicine toolkit in ten nursing homes. While conducting this assessment, our findings were interesting (Gaglio et al., 2016) but we did not have time to explore them in detail, partly because our sociologist colleague who led the study, Gérald Gaglio, was given a full professorship in another university. However, I kept that in mind, and when in 2019 I got some funding through one of the sponsors of the 'SilverTech Chair' of our university, I took this opportunity to reopen the topic and went back to the doctor in charge of putting in place teleconsultation between the local hospital and nursing homes. I suggested he take on a master's student to study what they have put in place, which he accepted. The study (Cormi et al., 2020) really interested the hospital, the Director of which decided to hire the master's student for a PhD.

13.3.6 Building a team

Last but not least in terms of sustainability is to hire the right people and encourage them to network with local and regional institutions. Indeed, key to the development of our research in the last ten years was the possibility of hiring two assistant professors: firstly Matthieu Tixier, in 2013, and then Khuloud Abou Amsha four years after. Historically, and until recently, they both would work with me, but not with each other. So, when I had the occasion to reopen the teleconsultation topic as described above, I suggested that they supervise the student together. It went well, and I supported them by interacting with the head of the hospital when they were defining the PhD project for the master's student that they are now supervising together.

I envisioned my role as a mentor, positioning them on some topics, supporting them in finding the funding, and letting them grow, while being present if they needed any advice. Using this strategy, I can also share responsibilities with Khuloud and Matthieu and do not have to carry everything by myself; having more people involved at the university is definitely a matter of sustainability.

We have also recently hired an assistant professor in management science, Loubna Echajari, who conducts research related to crisis management in industry. As the pandemic started, she asked if I could put her in contact with the hospital. I did so, asking them if they were interested by a study that our research group would fund. They accepted, her presence and her work (Sanchez et al., 2020) were really appreciated, and this played an important role in how the hospital views our research group. In comparison to other research groups from our university that they are working with on projects related to optimization and data management, they consider our team highly relevant.

13.3.7 Concluding remarks

Finally, looking back at fifteen years of research applied in the healthcare domain conducted at the Troyes University of Technology, trying to have a positive impact on patients, their informal caregivers, and the professionals, I would say that the strategy that has been developed and followed is aligned with the strategy that was envisioned in 1994, when the university was created thanks to the strong political will of Senator Philippe Adnot. All the activities described in Chapter 5, analysed in Chapter 11, and reflected in this epilogue demonstrate some of the 'lived practices' in executing this overall strategy. Through these activities, we took part in the development of the local associations and in the positioning of the local hospital, and there is more to come.

Indeed, last year, the department was chosen as one of the five departments in France (out of a total of 101 departments) to experiment with what has been called 'population responsibility'. It corresponds to the 'triple aim' approach put in place in North America (Berwick et al., 2008): a better care experience for the patient, a better health for the population, and a lower cost for society. It also involves going beyond city–hospital oppositions and focusing on prevention. By taking part in this initiative, which entails ambitious improvement at all levels of the healthcare system, we are pursuing our strategy in favour of sustainable, practice-centred computing that, as we have shown, must be envisioned as a local cooperative endeavour, with all its struggles, but also new kinds of opportunities.

13.4 Margunn Aanestad: Sustainability and user-driven IT projects

The future-proofing of practice-based IT design is an important topic. The efforts and resources that go into a project should ideally result in valuable outcomes. At the very least, it should generate learning; at best, it would lead to the improvement of the situation at hand. This book, which shines a light on various experiences from IT design projects in different settings, is, therefore, a valuable addition to our body of knowledge on practice-based IT design processes.

Many of the cases in the book describe how researchers brought design- and technology-related competence into a usage context, and the focus is on how such research-stimulated projects can survive and take hold once the project ends and the researchers leave. In my own research, I have not entered the site as a 'designer-researcher'—I haven't organized projects to design, develop, and implement IT solutions. Rather, my role has been that of an observer—I have observed other people who design, develop, and implement IT solutions.

They have usually been employees in the organization where the project is run. These user-driven IT projects may have avoided some challenges that externally driven, researcher-led projects encounter. For instance, ownership was found to be a crucial dimension relating to sustainability. In the user-driven projects, the responsibility and decision-making power rests with users. This increases the likelihood that there will be continued maintenance and extension of the solution. However, there are also sustainability challenges with such projects. In the following, I would like to share some reflections around the category of user-driven IT projects and possibilities for researcher engagement that may support their sustainability.

What has drawn me to taking the 'observer and analyst' role in my research is a deep curiosity about how people encounter novel technologies. In my first job after I finished my engineering training, I worked as a service engineer in a hospital. I assisted users of medical equipment with, for instance, acute and preventive maintenance, procurement processes, and organized user training. In situations of equipment breakdown that required immediate problem-solving and emergency repairs, I observed a wide variety of approaches from the end users. Some would call for assistance as soon as an alarm sounded, fearing that something bad might happen. Others were fully cognizant of what had caused the alarm and what risks they took in ignoring it. Some trusted the numbers on the screen, other needed to also use their eyes, nose, and fingertips. I found this variability of 'stances' or 'positions' that a user could take towards the technical tools used in their work practices deeply fascinating. I have also observed a similar variability in users' approaches to IT projects, and have been fascinated by the resourcefulness of the proactive users.

In many of my studies I have observed users who have either developed their own digital tools, commissioned development, or just purchased available consumer technologies and set them up to support work. I have studied their trial-and-error learning processes, their circumspection and testing of the technology, and their assessment of its strengths and weaknesses. These users haven't needed me or my expertise in this process; they made sound judgements themselves about what was required and how to go about it. They were the designers—perhaps not of the technology itself, but at least of the specific *configuration* of work, roles, tools, and procedures in which the technology would be rooted. Let me give you an example.

In my PhD project I observed experimentation with communication technology in a medical research and development department. Novel broadband connectivity and high-end video codecs allowed for new usages of video communication between surgeons. These users relied on high-quality video to be able to distinguish between subtle colour nuances in tissue and organs, and they had tried and rejected other available videoconferencing solutions. With this technology, image quality was no longer a concern. The process of practically implementing the necessary equipment and starting to use it for real transmissions required several questions to be asked: where in the surgical theatre should the microphones and cameras be placed? Who should be responsible for turning on, connecting, and testing the equipment before a session, and, for example, selecting which image to transmit? How do we deal with the staff's apprehension about being watched when they are in the room? Over an extended period, the experiences gained from actually using this infrastructure revealed novel issues that needed handling, as well as opportunities that could be exploited. In one of the articles from this study, I described this process as design work—more concretely as 'design of configurations; the creation of a well-working mix of people, practices and artefacts' (Aanestad, 2003: 1). Arriving at a configuration that works well is key for sustained usage and spreading. This is design-in-use, not design-before-use. Over time, the novel technology gets 'woven' into the existing socio-technical arrangements of the organization. The main determinant for sustainability here is the organizational and financial possibility of going through such an extended, trial-and-error based process of adapting the technology, the practice, and the organization of work. An IT solution of some complexity cannot just be developed and 'dropped' into a new setting; there needs to be support for it to go through a 'rooting' process, or else it withers and dies. A role for a researcher oriented to sustainability may be to assist this process by providing expertise in the application or technology domain, in implementation processes, or as reflection partner, sounding board, or critic. Specifically, one of the modes in which my research may have contributed to the sustainability of such projects may have been in making visible the invisible work associated with the novel work practices.

The rooting process does not always go smoothly or swiftly. The case described in section 5.2.2 (the *Videoconferencing* project) shows that we may have to expect technological rooting processes to take decades, rather than years. This is another case of a hospital starting to use telemedicine technology, but this time based on standard videoconferencing technology available on the market. What started as a sequence of disparate projects and trials by individual champions was not abandoned when the projects ended or when these people changed jobs. Rather, a 'kernel' of activities was kept alive, initially with minimal use of resources—securing a few resources here and there. After a while, the hospital managed to establish more concerted efforts where the technology and new telemedicine practices were deliberately spread and implemented across the whole organization. In this case, the step from champion-driven, shop-floor level activities to a management-backed, deliberate, and systematic organizational change process was crucial for its sustainability. We may also find multiple examples of projects where the initiative initially struggles because it is not aligned with the strategic direction of the higher levels of the organization. In these cases, the initiative may die out. In other cases, we have seen that the user-driven innovation projects managed to succeed because they had access to a minimal but sufficient set of resources, and there was enough leeway to continue to work and keep 'under the radar' of management. If they can do this for enough time to produce results that it is not possible to neglect or reject, they may convince management to start to support the initiative (see, e.g., Grisot et al., 2013). In such situations, the presence of a researcher may strengthen the activity's legitimacy or status, and as such may support the users lobbying management.

Few IT projects emerge as a result of end users' choices. Organizational IT projects are most often initiated by management as either procurement or upgrading of a system already in use. Stories of how top-down controlled change initiatives may fail abound (see, for example, Ciborra, 2000), with failure often caused by a lack of alignment with the local work practices. This may lead to processes of resistance and suboptimal outcomes, or to actual disruption of work and a necessary roll-back of the initiative. The case described in section 5.2.1 (the *Scanning* project) describes a group of workers who had to respond to a system change that was 'dumped on' them, without adequate preparations and resources. Still, they arranged to take care of the process of redesigning their work processes and tools. This required a collective process of making sense and implementing the necessary changes. In other words, the sustainability of the top-down project required creative appropriation (including expansive learning processes) to be conducted and organized by the end users (Gasser, 1986). Projects that the organization commissions are usually financially sustained, while initiatives driven by user champions often have to struggle to be recognized by managers and included in budgetary processes.

While researcher-driven projects are often motivated by the potential of the technology to resolve challenges, user-driven innovation processes may start for different reasons. For instance, challenges, constraints, and problematic situations can initiate and drive design and innovation processes. Real-life constraints may instigate a stronger focus on sustainability from the start of these processes. For instance, in describing the local development of an open-source electronic health record system in an Indian state, Mukherjee et al. (2012) articulate an approach called 'judicious design', which points to an incremental, modular, and flexibly scalable approach. The approach was fundamentally context-sensitive to the paper–computer hybrid as well as the work practices of the hospital staff, and sought to reduce the initial complexity of an undertaking by sequencing tasks, as well as to scale with an evolutionary rather than revolutionary approach. This case describes the emergence of an extended, state-wide information infrastructure built upon the open-source electronic health record system. Such broad, scaled-up, and systemic changes are often difficult, since the changes go beyond a certain local context and encompass the relations of actors within the larger system. This is a defining quality of information infrastructures, which are characterized by spatial and temporal reach: 'infrastructure has reach beyond a single event or one-site practice' (Star and Ruhleder, 1996). Such infrastructural projects require systemic changes; local appropriation is a necessary condition, but not a sufficient one. Such projects are complex because of the multiplicity of needs, interests, and agendas of the various involved actors, leading to drawn-out processes of negotiation and change (ref. Kempton et al., 2020, discussing the case which is described in section 6.2.3). If the relation between collaborating organizations must be reconfigured or the whole sector needs to shift to a new service model, a lot of challenging coordination work is necessary. Another source of complexity (and threat to sustainability) relates to the impact of surrounding institutions. An innovative health service model may not fit with the existing legal or financial regulatory structures in the public sector. Still, a single actor (such as the innovating organization) cannot change these institutions; this requires long-term and formal political processes. Resourceful, sustained, and innovative actions within limited action spaces are required for a successful innovation to spread, scale up, and be recognized and adopted. The navigation of such challenges may benefit from recognition of what complexity means and ongoing reflections on any feasible leverage points. Assisting in this reflection among the actors has been my own preferred mode of intervening in these design processes.

Here I have emphasized the role of user-driven, IT-based change initiatives. Novel digital technologies are available to user-driven innovative activities in a different way than they used to be; thus I believe it has become increasingly important to understand this category of changes. My emphasis on the agency of the end user also has its fundament in a practice-based view which sees the end users and their work situations as a crucial site of learning and innovation (Brown and Duguid, 1991) and which sees human agents as capable of deliberate work to change things that have been 'taken for granted' and to 'disclose new worlds' (Spinosa et al., 1997).

It is exactly the promise of creating new worlds through design activities that makes this book's theme so important. All of us who participate in real-world activities involving the design of digital technologies need to reflect on what we design, how we design, and whether the design activities and outcomes are sustainable. Design is an activity with moral implications (Aanestad et al., 2018), and therefore we should be concerned with future-proofing the technologies that we (help to) develop. One side of this is to ask how the initiatives can be sustained beyond the project. In addition, we should also ask whether the resulting initiative or technology does contribute to environmental, social, and economic sustainability. To engage with this, we also need to consider where our responsibility as researcher lies and where it ends. All researchers of practice-based IT design projects, regardless of whether we take on the 'designer' or the 'observer' role, share the responsibility for the novel in this world. Our responsibilities include assessing whether it is good and desirable, and nurturing it if so, all while we continuously attend to the implications of what we have made. A stance of *continued care* is crucial to help design outcomes survive the transition between research project and 'real life', and for it to be beneficial in the bigger picture.

References

Aal, Konstantin, Rekowski, Thomas Von, Yerousis, George, Wulf, Volker, and Weibert, Anne (2015), 'Bridging (gender-related) barriers: A comparative study of intercultural computer clubs', GenderIT '15: The 3rd Conference on GenderIT, 24 April 2015, Philadelphia, PA (New York: ACM Press), 17–23.

Aal, Konstantin, Rüller, Sarah, Holdermann, Simon, Tolmie, Peter, Rohde, Markus, Zillinger, Martin, and Wulf, Volker (2018), 'Challenges of an educational ICT intervention: The establishment of a MediaSpace in the High Atlas', *International Reports on Socio-Informatics*, 15 (2) (IISI: International Institute for Socio-Informatics), 3–20.

Aal, Konstantin, Yerousis, George, Schubert, Kai, Hornung, Dominik, Stickel, Oliver, and Wulf, Volker (2014), 'Come_in@palestine: Adapting a German computer club concept to a Palestinian refugee camp', Proceedings of the 5th ACM International Conference on Collaboration across Boundaries: Culture, distance & technology, CABS '14, August 2014, Kyoto, Japan (New York: ACM Press), 111–20.

Aanestad, Margunn (2003), 'The camera as an actor: Design-in-use of telemedicine infrastructure in surgery', *Computer-supported Cooperative Work (CSCW)*, 12 (1), 1–20.

Aanestad, Margunn, Driveklepp, Anne Merete, Sørli, Hilde, and Hertzum, Morten (2017a), 'Participatory continuing design: "Living with" videoconferencing in rehabilitation', *Studies in Health Technology and Informatics*, 233, 45–59.

Aanestad, Margunn, Grisot, Miria, Hanseth, Ole, and Vassilakopoulou, Polyxeni (2017b), 'Information infrastructures and the challenge of the installed base', in Margunn Aanestad, Miria Grisot, Ole Hanseth, and Polyxeni Vassilakopoulou (eds), *Information Infrastructures within European Health Care: Working with the installed base* (Cham, Switzerland: Springer), 25–33.

Aanestad, Margunn and Hanseth, Ole (2003), 'Design as Bootstrapping: On the evolution of ICT networks in health care', *Methods of Information in Medicine*, 42, 385–91.

Aanestad, Margunn and Jensen, Tina Blegind (2011), 'Building nation-wide information infrastructures in healthcare through modular implementation strategies', *Journal of Strategic Information Systems*, 20, 161–76.

Aanestad, Margunn and Jensen, Tina Blegind (2016), 'Collective mindfulness in post-implementation IS adaptation processes', *Information and Organization*, 26 (1–2), 13–27.

Aanestad, Margunn, Mähring, Magnus, Østerlund, Carsten, Riemer, Kai, and Schuktze, Ulrike (2018), 'Living with monsters?', in Ulrike Schultze, Margunn Aanestad, Magnus Mähring, Carsten Østerlund, and Kai Riemer (eds), *Living with Monsters? Social Implications of Algorithmic Phenomena, Hybrid Agency, and the Performativity of Technology* (Cham, Switzerland: Springer International Publishing), 3–12.

Abele, Nils Darwin, Hoffmann, Sven, Kuhnhen, Christopher, Ludwig, Thomas, Schäfer, Walter, Schweitzer, Markus, and Wulf, Volker (2016), 'Supporting the set-up processes by cyber elements based on the example of tube bending', in Heinrich C. Mayr and Martin Pinzger (eds), *Informatik 2016, Lecture Notes in Informatics (LNI)* (Bonn: Gesellschaft für Informatik), 1627–36.

Abou Amsha, Khuloud and Lewkowicz, Myriam (2014), 'Observing the work practices of an inter-professional home care team: Supporting a dynamic approach for quality home care delivery', in C. Rossitto, L. Ciolfi, D. Martin, and B. Conein (eds), COOP '14: Proceedings of the 11th International Conference on the Design of Cooperative Systems, 27–30 May 2014, Nice, France (Cham: Springer).

Abou Amsha, Khuloud and Lewkowicz, Myriam (2015), 'CARE: An application to support the collective management of patients at home', CSCI '15: The 2015 International Conference on Computational Science and Computational Intelligence, 7–9 December 2015, Las Vegas, NV, 743–8.

Abou Amsha, Khuloud and Lewkowicz, Myriam (2018), 'Supporting collaboration to preserve the quality of life of patients at home: A design case study', in Mark Ackerman, Michael Prilla, Christian Stary, Thomas Herrmann, and Sean Goggins (eds), *Designing Healthcare That Works: A Sociotechnical Approach* (Cambridge, MA: Academic Press), 39–57.

Abou Amsha, Khuloud, Bossen, Claus, Grönvall, Erik, and Lewkowicz, Myriam, 'Computer-Supported Knotworking: Design Guidelines Based on Two Case Studies from the Healthcare Domain in Europe', CSCW1 '21: Proceedings of the ACM on Human-Computer Interaction, 5, 1–26.

Ahmadi, Michael, Eilert, Rebecca, Weibert, Anne, Wulf, Volker, and Marsden, Nicola (2020), 'Feminist living labs as research infrastructures for HCI: The case of a video game company', CHI '20: Proceedings of the 2020 CHI Conference on Human Factors in Computing Systems, 25–30 April 2020, Honolulu, HI (New York: ACM Press), 1–15.

Ahmed, Syed Ishtiaque, Jackson, Steven, and Rashidujjaman, Rifat (2015), 'Learning to fix: Knowledge, collaboration and mobile phone repair in Dhaka, Bangladesh', ICTD '15: Proceedings of the 7th International Conference on Information and Communication Technologies and Development, 15–18 May 2015, Singapore (New York: ACM Press), article no. 4, 1–10.

Akrich, Madeleine, Callon, Michel, Latour, Bruno, and Monaghan, Adrian (2002), 'The key to success in innovation part I: The art of interessement', *International Journal of Innovation Management*, 6 (2), 187–206.

Akrich, Madeleine and Rabeharisoa, Vololona (2016), 'Pulling oneself out of the traps of comparison: An autoethnography of a European project', in Joe Deville, Michael Guggenheim, and Zuzana Hrdličková (eds), *Practising Comparison: Logics, Relations, Collaborations* (Manchester, UK: Mattering Press), 130–165.

Ali, Maryam, and Savita Bailur (2007), 'The challenge of "sustainability" in ICT4D: Is bricolage the answer?' Proceedings of the 9th International Conference on Social Implications of Computers in Developing Countries, May 2007, São Paulo, Brazil, 19p.

Altman, David G. (1995), 'Sustaining interventions in community systems: On the relationship between researchers and communities', *Health Psychology*, 14 (6), 526–36.

Anderson, David J. (2010), *Kanban: Successful Evolutionary Change for Your Technology Business* (n.p.: Blue Hole Press).

Anderson, Neil, De Dreu, Carsten Kw, and Nijstad, Bernard (2004), 'The routinization of innovation research: A constructively critical review of the state-of-the-science', *Journal of Organizational Behavior*, 25 (2), 147–73.

Andreu, Rafael and Ciborra, Claudio (1996), 'Organisational learning and core capabilities development: The role of IT', *Journal of Strategic Information Systems*, 5 (2),111–27.

Angst, Corey, Devaraj, Sarv, Queenan, Carrie, and Greenwood, Brad (2011), 'Performance effects related to the sequence of integration of healthcare technologies', *Production and Operations Management*, 20 (3), 319–33.

Arundel, Anthony (2001), 'The relative effectiveness of patents and secrecy for appropriation', *Research Policy*, 30 (4), 611–24.

Auschra, Carolin (2018), 'Barriers to the integration of care in Inter-organisational settings: A literature review', *International Journal of Integrated Care*, 18 (1), 5.

Avgar, Ariel, Litwin, Adam Seth, and Pronovost, Peter (2012), 'Drivers and barriers in health IT adoption', *Applied Clinical Informatics*, 3 (4), 488–500.

Baacke, Dieter (1996), 'Medienkompetenz: Begrifflichkeit und sozialer Wandel', in A. Rein (ed.), *Medien-kompetenz als Schlüsselbegriff* (Bad Heilbrunn, Germany: Klinkhardt), 112–24.

Balka, Ellen, Bjørn, Pernille, and Wagner, Ina (2008), 'Steps toward a typology for health informatics', CSCW '08: Proceedings of the 2008 ACM Conference on Computer-supported Cooperative Work, November 2008, San Diego, CA (ACM Press), 515–24.

Balka, Ellen, Peddie, David, Small, Serena, Ackerley, Christine, Trimble, Johanna, and Hohl, Corinne (2018), 'Barriers to scaling up participatory design interventions in health IT: A case study', PDC '18: Proceedings of the 15th Participatory Design Conference 2018: Short Papers, Situated Actions, Workshops and Tutorial—Volume 2, Article 11, August 2018, Hasselt and Genk, Belgium (New York: ACM Press), 1–5.

Balka, Ellen and Wagner, Ina (2006), 'Making things work: Dimensions of configurability as appropriation work', CSCW '06: Proceedings of the 2006 20th anniversary conference on Computer-supported cooperative work, 4–8 November 2006, Banff, Canada (New York: ACM Press), 229–38.

Balka, Ellen, and Wagner, Ina (2021), 'A historical view of studies of women's work', *Computer-supported Cooperative Work (CSCW)* 30 (2), 251–305.

Ballantyne, Peter (2003), *Ownership and Partnership: Keys to Sustaining ICT-enabled Development Activities*, IICD Research Brief (8) (The Hague, Netherlands: International Institute for Communication and Development).

Ballegaard, Stinne Aaløkke, Bunde-Pedersen, Jonathan, and Bardram, Jakob E. (2006), 'Where to, Roberta?: Reflecting on the role of technology in assisted living roles', NordiCHI '06: Proceedings of the 4th Nordic conference on Human-computer interaction: Changing, 14–18 October 2006, Oslo, Norway (New York: ACM Press), 373–6.

Bandini, Stefania, De Paoli, Flavio, Manzoni, Sara, and Mereghetti, Paolo (2002), 'A support system to COTS-based software development for business services', SEKE '02: Proceedings of the 14th International Conference on Software Engineering and Knowledge Engineering, 15–19 July 2002, Ischia, Italy (New York: ACM Press), 307–14.

Bannon, Liam, Schmidt, Kjeld, and Wagner, Ina (2011), 'Lest we forget', CSCW '11: Proceedings of the 12th European Conference on Computer-supported Cooperative Work, 24–8 September 2011, Aarhus, Denmark (London: Springer), 213–32.

Bansler, Jørgen (2019), 'Adaptation of clinical information infrastructures by and for users', Infrahealth 2019: Proceedings of the 7th International Workshop on Infrastructure in Healthcare 2019, 30–1 May 2019, Vienna, Austria (European Society for Socially Embedded Technologies (EUSSET)).

Bansler, Jørgen and Havn, Erling (2010), 'Pilot implementation of health information systems: Issues and challenges', *International Journal of Medical Informatics*, 79 (9), 637–48.

Bardram, Jakob, Bossen, Claus, Lykke-Olesen, Andreas, Nielsen, Rune, and Madsen, Kim Halskov (2002), 'Virtual video prototyping of pervasive healthcare systems', DIS '02: Proceedings of the 4th Conference on Designing Interactive Systems: Processes, Practices, Methods, and Techniques, 25–8 June 2002, London (London: ACM Press).

Barley, Stephen R. (1996), 'Technicians in the workplace: Ethnographic evidence for bringing work into organizational studies', *Administrative Science Quarterly*, 41 (3), 404–41.

Barricelli, Barbara Rita, Rekowski, Thomas Von, Sprenger, Mary-Ann, and Weibert, Anne (2011), 'Supporting collaborative project work in intercultural computer clubs', *International Journal of e-Education, e-Business, e-Management and e-Learning*, 1 (1), 35.

Begoyan, A. (2007), 'An overview of interoperability standards for electronic health records', *Integrated Design and Process Technology*, IDPT-2007 (Society for Design and Process Science).

Berg, Marc (1999), 'Accumulating and coordinating: Occasions for information technologies in medical work', *Computer-supported Cooperative Work (CSCW)*, 8 (4), 373–401.

Berthou, Valentin (2021), 'Un carnet de santé pour mieux coordonner? Une analyse sociologique de la dynamique organisationnelle du projet Calipso', in Grenier C., Rizoulières R., and Béranger J. (eds), *La révolution digitale en santé—Comment innover et agir en faveur de la mutation du système de santé?* (Lonon: ISTE Editions), 65–88.

Berwick, Donald M., Nolan, Thomas W., and Whittington, John (2008), 'The triple aim: care, health, and cost', *Health Affairs* 27 (3): 759–69.

Betz, Matthias and Wulf, Volker (2018), 'Toward transferability in grounded design: Comparing two design case studies in firefighting', in Volker Wulf, Volkmar Pipek, Dave Randall, Markus Rohde, Kjeld Schmidt, and Gunnar Stevens (eds), *Socio-informatics: A Practice-based Perspective on the Design and Use of IT Artifacts* (Oxford: Oxford University Press), 459–88.

Bidwell, Nicola (2016), 'Moving the centre to design social media in rural Africa', *AI & Society: Journal of Culture, Communication & Knowledge*, 31 (1), 51–77.

Bidwell, Nicola (2019), 'Women and the spatial politics of community networks: Invisible in the sociotechnical imaginary of wireless connectivity', OzCHI '19: Proceedings of the 13th Australasian Conference for Human Computer Interaction, 2–5 December 2019, Fremantle, WA, Australia (New York: ACM Press), 197–208.

Bidwell, Nicola (2020a), 'Wireless in the weather-world and community networks made to last', PDC '20: Proceedings of the 16th Participatory Design Conference, June 2020, Manzanales, Colombia (New York: ACM Press), 126–36.

Bidwell, Nicola (2020b), 'Women and the sustainability of rural community networks in the Global South', ICTD '20: Proceedings of the International Conference on Information and Communication Technologies and Development, 17–20 June 2020, Guayaquil, Ecuador (New York: ACM Press), 1–13.

Bidwell, Nicola, Densmore, Melissa, Van Zyl, André, Belur, Sarbani Banerjee, and Pace, Nicolas (2019), 'Artful integrations of infrastructures by community-based telecoms', C&T '19: Proceedings of the 9th International Conference on Communities & Technologies—Transforming Communities, 3–7 June 2019, Vienna, Austria (New York: ACM Press), 331–5.

Bidwell, Nicola and Luca De Tena, Sol (2021), 'Alternative perspectives on relationality, people and technology during a pandemic: Zenzeleni Networks in South Africa', in Stefania Milan, Emiliano Treré, and Silvia Masiero (eds), *COVID-19 from the Margins: Pandemic Invisibilities, Policies and Resistance in the Datafied Society* (Amsterdam: Institute of Network Cultures), 331–5.

Bidwell, Nicola and Jensen, Michael (2019), *Bottom-up Connectivity Strategies: Community-led Small-scale Telecommunication Infrastructure Networks in the Global South* (APC (Association for Progressive Communications)).

Bidwell, Nicola, Lalmas, Mounia, Marsden, Gary, Dlutu, Bongiwe, Ntlangano, Senzo, Manjingolo, Azola, Tucker, William D., Jones, Matt, Robinson, Simon, and Vartiainen, Elina

(2011), 'Please call ME.N.U.4EVER: Designing for "callback" in rural Africa', IWIPS '11: The International Workshop on Internationalisation of Products and Systems, 11–14 July 2011, Kuching, Malaysia, 117–37.

Bidwell, Nicola, Reitmaier, Thomas, and Jampo, Kululwa (2014), 'Orality, gender and social audio in rural Africa', COOP '14: Proceedings of the 11th International Conference on the Design of Cooperative Systems, 27–30 May 2014, Nice, France (Cham: Springer), 225–41.

Bidwell, Nicola, Reitmaier, Thomas, Marsden, Gary, and Hansen, Susan (2010), 'Designing with mobile digital storytelling in rural Africa', CHI '10: Proceedings of the SIGCHI Conference on Human Factors in Computing Systems, 10–15 April 2010, Atlanta, GA (New York: ACM Press), 1593–602.

Bidwell, Nicola, Reitmaier, Thomas, Roro, Rey-Moreno, Carlos, Masbulele, Zukile, Siya, Jay, and Dlutu, Bongiwe (2013a), 'Timely relations in rural Africa', IFIP WG9.4: Proceedings of the 12th International Conference on Social Implications of Computers in Developing Countries, 19–22 May 2013, Ocho Rios, Jamaica, 92–106.

Bidwell, Nicola, Siya, Masbulele, Marsden, Gary, Tucker, William, Tshemese, M., Gaven, Ntlangano, Senzo, Robinson, Simon, and Eglinton, Kristen Ali (2013b), 'Walking and the social life of solar charging in rural Africa', ACM Transactions on Computer-human Interaction (TOCHI), 20 (4), 22.

Bidwell, Nicola and Siya, Masbulele J (2013), 'Situating asynchronous voice in rural Africa', Proceedings of INTERACT'13, 3–6 September 2013, Cape Town, South Africa (Lecture Notes in Computer Science: International Federation for Information Processing IFIP & Springer-Verlag), 36–53.

Bietz, Matthew, Baumer, Eric, and Lee, Charlotte (2010), 'Synergizing in cyberinfrastructure development', Computer-supported Cooperative Work (CSCW), 19 (3–4), 245–281.

Blevis, Eli (2007), 'Sustainable interaction design: invention and disposal, renewal and reuse', CHI '07: Proceedings of the 2007 SIGCHI Conference on Human Factors in Computing Systems, 28 April–3 May 2007, San Jose, CA (New York: ACM Press), 503–12.

Blomberg, Jeanette (1987), 'Social interaction and office communication: effects on user's evaluation of new technologies', in R. Kraut (ed.), Technology and the Transformation of White-Collar Work (Hillsdale, NJ: Erlbaum Associates), 195–210.

Blomberg, Jeanette (2016), Creating a Virtuous Cycle from Data Production to Business Outcome: The Case of Request for Service (RFS) Management (Almaden, CA: IBM Research).

Blomberg, Jeanette, Suchman, Lucy, and Trigg, Randall (1996), 'Reflections on a work-oriented design project', Human–Computer Interaction, 11 (3), 237–65.

Blomberg, Jeanette, Megahed, Aly, and Strong, Ray (2018), 'Acting on Analytics: Accuracy, Precision, Interpretation, and Performativity', EPIC '18: Proceedings of Ethnographic Praxis in Industry, 10–12 September 2018, Honolulu, HI (1), 281–300.

Blumer, Herbert (1954), 'What's wrong with social theory?', American Sociological Review, 19 (1), 3–10.

Bødker, Susanne (1994), Creating Conditions for Participation: Conflicts and Resources in Systems Design, DAIMI Report Series, 13 (479) (Aarhus, Denmark: Aarhus University).

Bødker, Susanne, Dindler, Christian, and Iversen, Ole Sejer (2017), 'Tying knots: Participatory infrastructuring at work', Computer-supported Cooperative Work (CSCW) 26 (1–2), 245–73.

Boonstrat, Beitske, and Boelens, Luuk (2011), 'Self-organization in urban development: Towards a new perspective on spatial planning', Urban Research & Practice, 4 (2), 99–122.

Bossen, Claus and Dalsgaard, Peter (2005), 'Conceptualization and appropriation: The evolving use of a collaborative knowledge management system', Proceedings of the 4th Decennial Conference on Critical Computing: Between Sense and Sensibility, 21—25 August 2005, Aarhus, Denmark (New York: ACM Press), 99–108.

Bossen, Claus, Dindler, Christian, and Iversen, Ole Sejer (2010), 'User gains and PD aims: Assessment from a participatory design project', PDC '10: Proceedings of the 11th Biennial Participatory Design Conference, 29 November—3 December 2010, Sydney, Australia (New York: ACM Press), 141–50.

Boulton-Lewis, Gillian, Buys, Laurie, Lovie-Kitchin, Jan, Barnett, Karen, and David, L. Nikki (2007), 'Ageing, learning, and computer technology in Australia', Educational Gerontology, 33 (3), 253–70.

Boutellier, Roman, Gassmann, Oliver, and Von Zedtwitz, Maximilian (2013), Managing Global Innovation: Uncovering the Secrets of Future Competitiveness (Berlin-Heidelberg: Springer).

Bowers, John, Button, Graham, and Sharrock, Wes (1995), 'Workflow from within and without: technology and cooperative work on the print industry shopfloor', in Hans Marmolin, Yngve Sundblad, and Kjeld Schmidt (eds), ECSCW '95: Proceedings of the 4th European Conference on Computer-supported Cooperative Work, 11–15 September, 1995, Stockholm, Sweden (Kluwer Academic Publishers), 51–66.

Bowker, Geoffrey C., Timmermans, Stefan, and Star, Susan Leigh, 'Infrastructure and organizational transformation: Classifying nurses' work', in W. J. Orlikowski, G. Walsham, M. R. Jones, and J. DeGross (eds), Information Technology and Changes in Organizational Work (Boston, MA: Springer), 344–70.

Braa, Jørn, Monteiro, Eric, and Sahay, Sundeep (2004), 'Networks of action: Sustainable health information systems across developing countries', MIS Quarterly, 28 (3 (Special Issue on Action Research in Information Systems)), 337–62.

Bratteteig, Tone, Bødker, Keld, Dittrich, Yvonne, Mogensen, Preben, and Simonsen, Jesper (2012), 'Methods: Organising principles and general guidelines for Participatory Design projects', in J. Simonsen and T Robertson (eds), Routledge International Handbook of Participatory Design (London/New York: Routledge), 137–64.

Bratteteig, Tone, and Wagner, Ina (2014), Disentangling Participation: Power And Decision-Making In Participatory Design (Cham, Switzerland: Springer).

Bratteteig, Tone and Wagner, Ina (2016), 'Unpacking the notion of participation in Participatory Design', Computer-supported Cooperative Work (CSCW), 25 (6), 425–75.

Brettel, Malte, Friederichsen, Niklas, Keller, Michael, and Rosenberg, Marius (2014), 'How virtualization, decentralization and network building change the manufacturing landscape: An Industry 4.0 Perspective', International journal of Mechanical, Industrial Science and Engineering, 8 (1), 37–44.

Brown, John Seely and Duguid, Paul (1991), 'Organizational learning and communities-of-practice: Toward a unified view of working, learning, and innovation', Organization Science, 2 (1), 40–57.

Bullen, Christine and Bennett, John (1990), 'Learning from user experience with groupware', CSCW '90: Proceedings of the 1990 ACM Conference on Computer-supported Cooperative Work, 7–10 October 1990, Los Angeles, CA (New York: ACM Press), 291–302.

Buscher, Monika, Kristensen, Margit, and Mogensen, Preben (2008), 'Making the future palpable: Notes from a major incidents future laboratory', International Journal of Emergency Management, 5 (1–2), 145–63.

Buur, Jacob and Matthews, Ben (2008), 'Participatory innovation', *International Journal of Innovation Management*, 12 (3), 255–73.

Cabitza, Federico (2011), '"Remain faithful to the Earth!"*: Reporting experiences of artifact-centered design in healthcare', *Computer-supported Cooperative Work (CSCW)*, 20 (4–5), 231–63.

Cabitza, Federico, Ellingsen, Gunnar, Locoro, Angela, and Simone, Carla (2019), 'Repetita Iuvant: Exploring and supporting redundancy in hospital practices', *Computer-supported Cooperative Work (CSCW)*, 28 (1–2), 61–94.

Cabitza, Federico and Simone, Carla (2013), 'Computational coordination mechanisms: A tale of a struggle for flexibility', *Computer-supported Cooperative Work (CSCW)* 22 (4–6), 475–529.

Cabitza, Federico and Simone, Carla (2015), 'Building socially embedded technologies: Implications about design', in Volker Wulf, Kjeld Schmidt, and Dave Randall (eds), *Designing Socially Embedded Technologies in the Real-world* (London: Springer), 217–70.

Cabitza, Federico and Simone, Carla (2017), 'Malleability in the hand of end-users', in Fabio Paternò and Volker Wulf (eds.), *New Perspectives in End-user Development* (Cham, Switzerland: Springer International), 137–64.

Carroll, Jennie (2004), 'Completing design in use: closing the appropriation cycle', ECIS '04: Proceedings of the 12th European Conference on Information Systems, 14–16 June 2004, Turku, Finland (AIS Electronic Library), 337–47.

Carroll, John M. and Rosson, Mary Beth (2007), 'Participatory design in community informatics', *Design Studies*, 28 (3), 243–61.

Castelli, Nico, Ogonowski, Corinna, Jakobi, Timo, Stein, Martin, Stevens, Gunnar, and Wulf, Volker (2017), 'What Happened in my home? An end-user development approach for smart home data visualization', CHI '17: Proceedings of the 2017 CHI Conference on Human Factors in Computing Systems, 6–11 May 2017, Denver, CO (New York: ACM Press), 853–66.

Castelli, Nico, Schönau, Niko, Stevens, Gunnar, Schwartz, Tobias, and Jakobi, Timo (2015), 'Role-based eco-info systems: An organizational theoretical view of sustainable HCI at work', ECIS '15: 23rd European Conference on Information Systems Completed Research Papers, 26–9 May 2015, Münster, Germany, 1–16.

Cecez-Kecmanovic, Dubravka, Kautz, Karlheinz, and Abrahall, Rebecca (2014), 'Reframing success and failure of information systems: A performative perspective', *MIS Quarterly*, 38 (2), 561–88.

Cerratto-Pargman, Teresa and Joshi, Somya (2015), 'Understanding limits from a social-ecological perspective', *First Monday*, 20 (8).

Chipidza, Wallace and Leidner, Dorothy (2017), 'ICT4D research: Literature review and conflict perspective', AMCIS '17: 23rd Americas Conference on Information Systems, 10–12 August 2017, Boston, MA.

Chipidza, Wallace and Leidner, Dorothy (2019), 'A review of the ICT-enabled development literature: Towards a power parity theory of ICT4D', *Journal of Strategic Information Systems*, 28, 145–74.

Chruscicki, Adam, Badke, Katherin, Peddie, David, Small, Serena, Balka, Ellen, and Hohl, Corinne (2016), 'Pilot-testing an adverse drug event reporting form prior to its implementation in an electronic health record', Springerplus 1 (9), 1–9.

Ciborra, Claudio (2000), 'From alignment to loose coupling: from MedNet to www. roche. com', in C. Ciborra, K. Braa, A. Cordella, B. Dahlbom, V. Hepsø, A. Failla, O. Hanseth, J. Ljungberg, and E. Monteiro (eds), *From Control to Drift: The Dynamics Of Corporate Information Infrastructures* (Oxford: Oxford University Press), 193–212.

Clarke, Adele (1991), 'Social worlds/arena theory as organizational theory', in David Maines (ed.), *Social Organization and Social Processes: Essays in Honor of Anselm Strauss* (Edison, NJ: Aldine Transaction), 119–58.

Clarysse, Bart, Wright, Mike, and Van De Velde, Els (2011), 'Entrepreneurial origin, technological knowledge, and the growth of spin-off companies', *Journal of Management Studies*, 48 (6), 1420–42.

Clement, Andrew and Wagner, Ina (1995), 'Fragmented exchange: Disarticulation and the need for regionalized communication spaces', ECSCW '95: Proceedings of 4th European Conference on Computer-supported Cooperative Work, September 1995, Stockholm, Sweden, 33–49.

Cohen, Wesley, Nelson, Richard, and Walsh, John (2002), 'Links and impacts: The influence of public research on industrial R&D', *Management Science*, 48 (1), 1–23.

Colombino, Tommaso, Hanrahan, Benjamin, and Castellani, Stefania (2014), 'Lessons learnt working with performance data in call centres', COOP '14: Proceedings of the 11th International Conference on the Design of Cooperative Systems, 27–30 May 2014, Nice, France (Cham, Switzerland: Springer), 277–92.

Colombino, Tommaso, Willamowski, Jutta, Grasso, Antonietta, and Hanrahan, Benjamin (2020), 'Deeper into the wild: Technology co-creation across corporate boundaries', in Alan Chamberlain and Andy Crabtree (eds), *Into the Wild: Beyond the Design Research Lab* (Cham, Switzerland: Springer), 55–71.

Cormi, Clément, Abou Amsha, Khuloud, Tixier, Matthieu, and Lewkowicz, Myriam (2020), 'How the local domestication of a teleconsultation solution is influenced by the adoption of a national policy?', ECSCW '20: Proceedings of the 18th European Conference on Computer-supported Cooperative Work, 13–17 June 2020, Siegen, Germany (EC-SCW 2020 Exploratory Papers and Notes: European Society for Socially Embedded Technologies (EUSSET)).

Dalsgaard, Peter and Halskov, Kim (2012), 'Reflective design documentation', DIS '12: Proceedings of the Designing Interactive Systems Conference, 11–15 June 2012, Newcastle upon Tyne, UK (New York: ACM Press), 428–37.

Davis, John-Michael, Akese, Grace, and Garb, Yaakov (2019), 'Beyond the pollution haven hypothesis: Where and why do e-waste hubs emerge and what does this mean for policies and interventions?', *Geoforum*, 98, 36–45.

De Carvalho, Aparecido Fabiano Pinatti, Hoffmann, Sven, Abele, Darwin, Schweitzer, Marcus, Tolmie, Peter, Randall, Dave, and Wulf, Volker (2018), 'Of embodied action and sensors: Knowledge and expertise sharing in industrial set-up', *Computer-supported Cooperative Work (CSCW)* 27 (3–6), 875–916.

Deery, Stephen and Kinnie, Nicholas (2004), 'Introduction: The nature and management of call centre work', in Stephen Deery and Nicholas Kinnie (eds), *Call Centres and Human Resource Management: A Cross-national Perspective* (London: Palgrave Macmillan), 1–22.

Disalvo, Carl, Sengers, Phoebe, and Brynjarsdóttir, Hrönn (2010), 'Mapping the landscape of sustainable HCI', CHI '10: Proceedings of the SIGCHI Conference on Human Factors in Computing Systems, 10–15 April 2010, Atlanta, GA (New York: ACM Press), 1975–84.

Dittrich, Yvonne, Eriksén, Sara, and Wessels, Bridgette (2014), 'Learning through situated innovation. Why the specific is crucial for Participatory Design research', *Scandinavian Journal of Information Systems*, 26 (1), 29–56.

Doherty, Neil, Coombs, Crispin, and Loan-Clarke, John (2006), 'A re-conceptualization of the interpretive flexibility of information technologies: Redressing the balance between the social and the technical', *European Journal of Information Systems*, 15 (6), 569–82.

Dourish, Paul (2003), 'The appropriation of interactive technologies: Some lessons from placeless documents', *Computer-supported Cooperative Work (CSCW)*, 12 (4), 465–90.

Doyle, Lynn H. (2003), 'Synthesis through meta-ethnography: Paradoxes, enhancements, and possibilities', *Qualitative Research*, 3 (3), 321–44.

Dunbar-Hester, Christina (2008), 'Geeks, meta-geeks, and gender trouble: Activism, identity, and low-power FM radio', *Social Studies of Science*, 38 (2), 201–32.

Egger, Edeltraut and Wagner, Ina (1992), 'Negotiating temporal orders: the case of collaborative time-management in a surgery clinic', *Computer-supported Cooperative Work (CSCW)*, (1), 255–75.

Ehn, Pelle, Nilsson, Elisabet, and Topgaard, Richard (2014), 'Introduction', in *Making Futures: Marginal Notes on Innovation, Design, and Democracy* (Cambridge, MA: MIT Press), 2–13.

Ellström, Per-Erik (2001), 'Integrating learning and work: Problems and prospects', *Human Resource Development Quarterly*, 12 (4), 421–35.

Engeström, Yrjö (2001), 'Expansive learning at work: Toward an activity theoretical reconceptualization', *Journal of Education and Work*, 14 (1), 133–56.

Engeström, Yrjö (2008), *From Teams to Knots: Activity-Theoretical Studies of Collaboration And Learning At Work* (Cambridge: Cambridge University Press).

Engeström, Yrjö, Engeström, Ritva, and Vähäaho, Tarja (1999), 'When the center does not hold: The importance of knotworking', in Seth Chaiklin, Mariane Hedegaard, and Uffe Juul Jensen (eds), *Activity Theory and Social Practice: Cultural-historical Approaches* (Aarhus, Denmark: Aarhus University Press), 345–74.

Farooq, Umer, Ganoe, Craig, Xiao, Lu, Merkel, Cecelia, Rosson, Mary Beth, and Carroll, John (2007), 'Supporting community-based learning: Case study of a geographical community organization designing its website', *Behaviour & Information Technology*, 26 (1), 5–21.

Fischer, Gerhard (2001), 'Communities of interest: Learning through the interaction of multiple knowledge systems', IRIS '24: Proceedings of the 24th IRIS Conference, 11–14 August 2001, Ulvik, Norway, (1), 1–13.

Fischer, Gerhard, Fogli, Daniela, and Piccinno, Antonio (2017), 'Revisiting and broadening the meta-design framework for end-user development', in Fabio Paternò and Volker Wulf (eds), *New Perspectives in End-user Development* (Cham: Springer), 61–97.

Fitzpatrick, Geraldine (2004), 'Integrated care and the working record', *Health Informatics Journal*, 10 (4), 291–302.

Fitzpatrick, Geraldine and Ellingsen, Gunnar (2013), 'A review of 25 years of CSCW research in healthcare: Contributions, challenges and future agendas', *Computer-supported Cooperative Work (CSCW)*, 22 (4–6), 609–65.

Friedman, Batya and Hendry, David (2019), Value Sensitive Design: Shaping Technology with Moral Imagination (Cambridge, MA: MIT Press).

Furuholt, Bjørn and Sæbø, Øystein (2018), 'The role telecentres play in providing e-government services in rural areas: A longitudinal study of Internet access and e-government services in Tanzania', *The Electronic Journal of Information Systems in Developing Countries*, 84 (1), 1–14.

Gabriel, Magdalena and Pessl, Ernst (2016), 'Industry 4.0 and sustainability impacts: Critical discussion of sustainability aspects with a special focus on future of work and ecological consequences', *Annals of the Faculty of Engineering Hunedoara*, 14 (2), 131–6.

Gaglio, Gérald, Lewkowicz, Myriam, and Tixier, Matthieu (2016), '"It is not because you have tools that you must use them": The difficult domestication of a telemedicine toolkit to manage emergencies in nursing homes', GROUP '16: Proceedings of the 19th International Conference on Supporting Group Work, 13–16 November 2016, Sanibel Island, FL (New York: ACM Press), 222–33.

Gantt, M. and Nardi, B. A. (1992), 'Gardeners and Gurus: Cooperation Among CAD Users', CHI '92: Proceedings of the ACM Human Factors in Computing Systems Conference, 3–7 June 1992, Monterey, CA (New York: ACM Press), 107–17.

Gärtner, Johannes (1996), 'Schichtarbeitszeitplanung zwischen Interessensausgleich und Komplexitätsbewältigung', in Jörg Flecker and Johanna Hofbauer (eds), Vernetzung und Vereinnahmung—Arbeit zwischen Internationalisierung und neuen Managementkonzepten (Opladen, Germany: Westdeutscher Verlag).

Gärtner, Johannes and Wagner, Ina (1996), 'Mapping actors and agenda. political frameworks of design & participation', Human–Computer Interaction, (11), 187–214.

Gärtner, Johannes and Wahl, Sabine (1998), 'Design tools for shift schedules: Empowering assistance for skilled designers & groups', International Journal of Industrial Ergonomics, 21 (3–4), 221–32.

Gasser, Les (1986), 'The integration of computing and routine work', ACM Transactions on Information Systems (TOIS), 4 (3), 205–25.

Gilchrist, Alasdair (2016), Industry 4.0: The Industrial Internet of Things (New York: Apress).

Gläser, Jochen and Laudel, Grit (2016), 'Governing science: How science policy shapes research content', European Journal of Sociology, 57 (1), 117–68.

Gläser, Jochen and Velarde, Kathia Serrano (2018), 'Changing funding arrangements and the production of scientific knowledge: Introduction to the special issue', Minerva, 56, 1–10.

Gökalp, Ebru, Şener, Umut, and Eren, P. Erhan (2017), 'Development of an assessment model for industry 4.0: Industry 4.0-MM', SPICE '17: Proceedings of the 17th International Conference on Process Improvement and Capability Determination in Software, Systems Engineering and Service Management, 4–5 October 2017, Palma de Mallorca, Spain (Cham, Switzerland: Springer), 128–42.

Graham, Stephen (2010), Disrupted Cities: When Infrastructure Fails (Milton Park, UK: Routledge).

Graham, Stephen and Thrift, Nigel (2007), 'Out of order: Understanding repair and maintenance', Theory, Culture & Society, 24 (3), 1–25.

Green, Lawrence and Mercer, Shawna (2001), 'Can public health researchers and agencies reconcile the push from funding bodies and the pull from communities?', American Journal of Public Health, 91 (12), 1926–9.

Greenhalgh, Trisha, Potts, Henry W., Wong, Geoff, Bark, Pippa, and Swinglehurst, Deborah (2009), 'Tensions and paradoxes in electronic patient record research: A systematic literature review using the meta-narrative method', The Milbank Quarterly, 87 (4), 729–88.

Greenwood, Davydd J. and Levin, Morten (1998), Introduction to Action Research: Social Research for Social Change (Newbury Park, CA: Sage).

Grisot, Miria, Kempton, Alexander Moltubakk, Hagen, Laila, and Aanestad, Margunn (2019), 'Data-work for personalized care: Examining nurses' practices in remote monitoring of chronic patients', Health Informatics Journal, 25 (3), 608–16.

Grisot, Miria, Thorseng, Anne, and Hanseth, Ole (2013), 'Staying under the radar: Innovation strategy in information infrastructures for health', ECIS '13: Proceedings of the 21st European Conference of Information Systems, 5–8 June 2013, Utrecht, The Netherlands.

Gurvitch, Georges (1964), The Spectrum of Social Time (Dordrecht, Holland: D. Reidel Publishing Company).

Haddon, Leslie (2003), 'Domestication and mobile telephony', in James Katz (ed.), *Machines That Become Us: The Social Context of Personal Communication Technology* (New Brunswick, NJ: Transaction Publishers), 43–56.

Haddow, George, Bullock, Jane, and Haddow, Kim (eds) (2017), *Global Warming, Natural Hazards, and Emergency Management* (Boca Raton, FA: CRC Press).

Handel, Mark J. and Poltrock, Steven (2011), 'Working around official applications: experiences from a large engineering project', CSCW '11: Proceedings of the ACM 2011 conference on Computer-supported cooperative work, 19–23 March 2011, Hangzhou, China, 309–12.

Hanrahan, Benjamin V., Martin, David, Willamowski, Jutta, and Carroll, John M. (2019), 'Investigating the Amazon Mechanical Turk market through tool design', *Computer-supported Cooperative Work (CSCW)*, 28 (5), 795–814.

Hanseth, Ole (1996), 'Information infrastructure development: Cultivating the installed base', *Studies in the Use of Information Technologies*, 16, 4–16.

Hanseth, Ole and Aanestad, Margunn (2003), 'Design as bootstrapping: On the evolution of ICT networks in health care', *Methods of Information in Medicine*, 42 (4), 385–91.

Hanseth, Ole, Jacucci, Edoardo, Grisot, Miria, and Aanestad, Margunn (2007), 'Reflexive integration in the development and integration of an Electronic Patient Record System', in Ole Hanseth and Claudio Ciborra (eds), *Risk, Complexity and ICT* (Cheltenham, UK: Edward Elgar Publishing), 118–35.

Harrison, Richard T., and Leitch, Claire (2010), 'Voodoo institution or entrepreneurial university? Spin-off companies, the entrepreneurial system and regional development in the UK', *Regional Studies* 44 (9): 1241–62.

Haskel, Lisa and Graham, Paula (2016), 'Whats GNU got to do with it? Participatory design, infrastructuring and free/open source software', PDC '16: Proceedings of the 14th Participatory Design Conference, 15–19 August 2016, Aarhus, Denmark (2) (New: ACM Press), 17–20.

Hayes, Gillian R. (2018), 'Design, action, and practice: Three branches of the same tree', in Volker Wulf, Volkmar Pipek, Dave Randall, Markus Rohde, Kjeld Schmidt, and Gunnar Stevens (eds), *Socio-informatics: A Practice-based Perspective on the Design and Use of IT Artifacts* (Oxford: Oxford University Press), 303–18.

Heeks, Richard (2008), 'ICT4D 2.0: The next phase of applying ICT for international development', *Computer*, 41 (6), 26–33.

Heinze, Thomas (2008), 'How to sponsor ground-breaking research: A comparison of funding schemes', *Science and Public Policy*, 35 (5), 302–18.

Henderson, Austin and Kyng, Morten (1991), 'There's no place like home: Continuing design in use', in J. Greenbaum and M. Kyng (eds), *Design at Work: Cooperative Design of Computer Systems* (Hillsdale, NJ: Lawrence Erlbaum Associates), 219–40.

Henke, Christopher (1999), 'The mechanics of workplace order: Toward a sociology of repair', *Berkeley Journal of Sociology*, 44, 55–81.

Hillgren, Per-Anders, Seravalli, Anna, and Emilson, Anders (2011), 'Prototyping and infrastructuring in design for social innovation', *CoDesign*, 7(3–4), 169–83.

Hippel, Eric von (2005), *Democratizing Innovation: Users Take Center Stage* (Cambridge, MA: MIT Press).

Hoeve, Aimée and Nieuwenhuis, Loek F. M. (2006), 'Learning routines in innovation processes', *Journal of Workplace Learning*, 18 (3), 171–85.

Hoffmann, Sven, De Carvalho, Aparecido Fabiano, Abele, Darwin, Schweitzer, Marcus, Tolmie, Peter, and Wulf, Volker (2019), 'Cyber-physical systems for knowledge and expertise sharing in manufacturing contexts: Towards a model enabling design', *Computer-supported Cooperative Work (CSCW)*, 28 (3–4), 469–509.

Hohl, Corinne M., Lexchin, Joel, and Balka, Ellen (2015), 'Can adverse drug reaction reporting create safer systems while improving health data? The devil is in the detail', *Canadian Medical Association Journal (CMAJ)*, 187 (11), 789–90.

Hohl, Corinne, Small, Serena, Peddie, David, Badke, Katherin, Bailey, Chantelle, and Balka, Ellen (2018), 'Why clinicians don't report adverse drug events: qualitative study', *JMIR Public Health And Surveillance*, 4 (1), e21.

Honkaniemi, Hasu Mervi, Saari, Laura Eveliina, Mattelmäki, Tuuli, and Koponen, Leena (2014), 'Learning employee-driven innovating: Towards sustained practice through multi-method evaluation', *Journal of Workplace Learning*, 26 (5), 310–30.

Hosman, Laura and Armey, Laura (2017), 'Taking technology to the field: Hardware challenges in developing countries', *Information Technology for Development*, 23 (4), 648–67.

Houlihan, Maeve (2004), 'Tensions and variations in call centre management strategies', in Stephen Deery and Nicholas Kinnie (eds), *Call Centres and Human Resource Management: A Cross-national Perspective* (London: Palgrave Macmillan), 75–101.

Houston, Lara and Jackson, Steven (2017), 'Caring for the "next billion" mobile handsets: Proprietary closures and the work of repair', *Information Technologies & International Development*, 13, 200–14.

Houston, Lara (2019), 'Mobile phone repair knowledge in downtown Kampala: Local and trans-local circulations', in Ignaz Strebel, Alain Bovet, and Philippe Sormani (eds), *Repair Work Ethnographies* (Singapore: Palgrave Macmillan), 129–60.

Hughes, John, Randall, Dave, Shapiro, Dan (1992), 'Faltering from ethnography to design', CSCW '92: Proceedings of the 1992 ACM Conference on Computer-supported Cooperative Work, 1–4 November 1992, Toronto, Canada, 115–22.

Hussen, Tigist Shewarega, Bidwell, Nicola, Rey-Moreno, Carlos, and Tucker, William (2016), 'Gender and participation: Critical reflection on Zenzeleni networks in Mankosi, South Africa', AfriCHI'16: Proceedings of the 1st African Conference on Human Computer Interaction, 21–5 November 2016, Nairobi, Kenya, 12–23.

Huybrechts, Liesbeth, Benesch, Henric, and Geib, Jon (2017), 'Institutioning: Participatory design, co-design and the public realm', *CoDesign*, 13 (3), 148–59.

Huybrechts, Liesbeth, Hendriks, Niels, Yndigegn, Signe Louise, and Malmborg, Lone (2018), 'Scripting: An exploration of designing for participation over time with communities', *CoDesign*, 14 (1), 17–31.

Hyysalo, Sampsa (2004), 'Technology nurtured-collectives in maintaining and implementing technology for elderly care', *Science & Technology Studies*, 17 (2), 23–43.

Ibrahim, Rouba, L'ecuyer, Pierre, Shen, Haipeg, and Thiongane, Mamadou (2016), 'Interdependent, heterogeneous, and time-varying service-time distributions in call centers', *European Journal of Operational Research*, 250 (2), 480–92.

Ingold, Tim (2007), *Lines: A Brief History* (London: Routledge).

Ingold, Tim (2008), 'Bindings against boundaries: Entanglements of life in an open world. Environment and planning', *Environment and Planning A*, 40 (8), 1796–810.

Ingold, Tim (2011), *Being Alive: Essays on Movement, Knowledge and Description* (London: Routledge).

Irani, Lilly, Vertesi, Janet, Dourish, Paul, Philip, Kavita, and Grinter, Rebecca (2010), 'Postcolonial computing: A lens on design and development', CHI '10: Proceedings of the SIGCHI Conference on Human Factors in Computing Systems, 10–15 April 2010, Atlanta, GA, 1311–20.

Iversen, Ole Sejer and Dindler, Christian (2014), 'Sustaining participatory design initiatives', *CoDesign*, 10 (3–4), 153–70.

Jackson, Steven, Gillespie, Tarleton, and Payette, Sandy (2014), 'The policy knot: Re-integrating policy, practice and design in CSCW studies of social computing', CSCW '14: Proceedings of the 17th ACM Conference on Computer-supported Cooperative Work & Social Computing, 15–19 February 2014, Baltimore, MD, 588–602.

Jackson, Steven, Pompe, Alex, and Krieshok, Gabriel (2012), 'Repair worlds: Maintenance, repair, and ICT for development in rural Namibia', CSCW '12: Proceedings of the ACM 2012 Conference on Computer-supported Cooperative Work, 11–15 February 2012, Seattle, WA (ACM Press), 107–16.

Jackson, Steven, Syed Ishtiaque, Ahmed, and Rashidujjaman, Rifat (2014), DIS '14: 'Learning, innovation, and sustainability among mobile phone repairers in Dhaka, Bangladesh', Proceedings of the Designing Interactive Systems Conference, 21–25 June 2014 Vancouver, BC (ACM Press), 905–14.

Jha, Ashish, Orav, John, Zheng, Jie, and Epstein, Arnold (2008), 'Patients' perception of hospital care in the United States', *New England Journal of Medicine*, 359 (18), 1921–31.

Joshi, Suhas Govind and Bratteteig, Tone (2015), 'Assembling fragments into continuous design: On participatory design with old people', in H. Oinas-Kukkonen et al. (eds), SCIS '15: The 6th Scandinavian Conference on Information Systems, 9–12 August 2015 Oulu, Finland (Springer International Publishing), 13–21.

Joshi, Suhas Govind, and Bratteteig, Tone (2016), 'Designing for prolonged mastery: On involving old people in participatory design', *Scandinavian Journal of Information Systems*, 28 (1), 3–36.

Kafai, Yasmin, Peppler, Kylie, and Robbin, Chapman (eds) (2009), *The Computer Clubhouse: Constructionism and Creativity in Youth Communities* (New York: Teachers College Press).

Karasti, Helena and Baker, Karen (2008), 'Community design: Growing one's own information infrastructure', PDC '08: Proceedings of the 10th Anniversary Conference on Participatory Design, 1–4 October 2008, Bloomington, IN (New York: ACM Press), 217–20.

Karasti, Helena, Baker, Karen, and Millerand, Florence (2010), 'Infrastructure time: Long-term matters in collaborative development', *Computer-supported Cooperative Work (CSCW)*, 19 (3–4), 377–415.

Kaschula, Russell and Dlutu, Bongiwe (2015), 'Reinventing the oral word and returning it to the community via technauriture', in Nicola Bidwell and Heike Winschiers-Theophilus (eds), *At the Intersection of Indigenous and Traditional Knowledge and Technology Design* (Santa Rosa, CA: Informing Science Press), 377–90.

Kempton, Alexander Moltubakk, Miria Grisot, Kristin Brænden, and Margunn Aanestad (2020), 'Infrastructural tuning in public-private partnerships', ECIS '20: Proceedings of the 28th European Conference on Information Systems, An Online AIS Conference, 15–17 June 2020.

Kimaro, Honest (2006), 'Strategies for developing human resource capacity to support sustainability of ICT based health information systems: A case study from Tanzania', *The Electronic Journal of Information Systems in Developing Countries*, 26 (1), 1–23.

Kleine, Dorothea and Unwin, Tim (2009), 'Technological revolution, evolution and new dependencies: What's new about ict4d?', *Third World Quarterly*, 30 (5), 1045–67.

Koschmider, Agnes, Torres, Victoria, and Pelechano, Vicente (2009), 'Elucidating the mashup hype: Definition, challenges, methodical guide and tools for mashups', Proceedings of the 2nd Workshop on Mashups, Enterprise Mashups and Lightweight

Composition on the Web at WWW, 20 April 2009, Madrid, Spain (New York: ACM Press), 1–9.

Kuutti, Kari and Bannon, Liam (2014), 'The turn to practice in HCI: Towards a research agenda', CHI '14: Proceedings of the SIGCHI Conference on Human Factors in Computing Systems, 26 April —1 May 2014, Toronto, Canada (New York: ACM Press), 3543–52.

Laudel, Grit (2006), 'The art of getting funded: How scientists adapt to their funding conditions', Science and Public Policy, 33 (7), 489–504.

Lave, Jean and Wenger, Etienne (1991), Situated Learning: Legitimate Peripheral Participation (Cambridge, MA: Cambridge University Press).

Lee, Charlotte and Schmidt, Kjeld (2018), 'A bridge too far? Critical remarks on the concept of 'infrastructure' in CSCW and IS', in Volker Wulf, Volkmar Pipek, Dave Randall, Markus Rohde, Kjeld Schmidt, and Gunnar Stevens (eds), Socio-informatics: A Practice-based Perspective on the Design and Use of IT Artifacts (Oxford: Oxford University Press), 177–218.

Lepori, Benedetto, Van Den Besselaar, Peter, Dinges, Michael, Van Der Meulen, Barend, Potì, Bianca, Reale, Emanuela, Slipersaeter, Stig, and Theves, Jean (2007), 'Indicators for comparative analysis of public project funding: Concepts, implementation and evaluation', Research Evaluation, 16 (4), 243–55.

Lévi, Francis and Saguez, Christian (2008), Le patient, les technologies et la médecine ambulatoire. Académie des technologies (Rapport de l'Academie Des Technologies).

Ley, Benedikt, Ogonowski, Corinna, Mu, Mu, Hess, Jan, Race, Nicholas, Randall, Dave, Rouncefield, Mark, and Wulf, Volker (2014), 'At home with users: A comparative view of living labs', Interacting with Computers, 27 (1), 21–35.

Ley, Benedikt, Pipek, Volkmar, Reuter, Christian, and Wiedenhoefer, Torben (2012), 'Supporting improvisation work in inter-organizational crisis management', CHI '12: Proceedings of the SIGCHI Conference on Human Factors in Computing Systems, 5–10 May 2012, Austin, TX (New York: ACM Press), 1529–38.

Lieberman, Henry, Paternò, Fabio, Klann, Markus, and Wulf, Volker (2006), End-user Development: An Emerging Paradigm (Cham, Swizterland: Springer International Publishing).

Light, Ann and Miskelly, Clodagh (2019), 'Platforms, scales and networks: Meshing a local sustainable sharing economy', Computer-supported Cooperative Work (CSCW), 28 (3–4), 591–626.

Ludwig, Thomas, Boden, Alexander, and Pipek, Volkmar (2017a), '3D printers as sociable technologies: Taking appropriation infrastructures to the internet of things', ACM Transactions on Computer-human Interaction (TOCHI), 24 (2), 17.

Ludwig, Thomas, Kotthaus, Christoph, and Pipek, Volkmar (2015), 'Should I try turning it off and on again? Outlining HCI challenges for cyber-physical production systems', International Journal of Information Systems for Crisis Response and Management (IJISCRAM), 7 (3), 55–68.

Ludwig, Thomas, Kotthaus, Christoph, and Pipek, Volkmar (2016), 'Situated and ubiquitous crowdsourcing with volunteers during disasters', Proceedings of the 2016 ACM International Joint Conference on Pervasive and Ubiquitous Computing: Adjunct, 12–16 September 2016, Heidelberg, Germany (New York: ACM Press), 1441–7.

Ludwig, Thomas, Kotthaus, Christoph, Reuter, Christian, Van Dongen, Sören, and Pipek, Volkmar (2017b), 'Situated crowdsourcing during disasters: Managing the tasks of spontaneous volunteers through public displays', International Journal of Human-computer Studies, 102, 103–21.

Ludwig, Thomas, Stickel, Oliver, Boden, Alexander, and Pipek, Volkmar (2014), 'Towards sociable technologies: An empirical study on designing appropriation infrastructures for 3D printing', DIS '14: Proceedings of the Designing Interactive Systems Conference, 21–5 June 2014, Vancouver, BC, (ACM Press), 835–44.

Lutz, Peter (2016), 'Comparative tinkering with care moves', in Joe Deville, Michael Guggenheim, and Zuzana Hrdličková (eds), *Practising Comparison. Logics, Relations, Collaborations* (Manchester: Mattering Press), 220–50.

Mackay, Wendy (1990), 'Patterns of sharing customizable software', CSCW '90: Proceedings of the 1990 ACM Conference on Computer-supported Cooperative Work, 7–10 October 1990, Los Angeles, CA, 209–21.

Mackenzie, Catriona and Stoljar, Natalie (2000), 'Introduction: Autonomy Reconfigured', in Catriona Mackenzie and Natalie Stoljar (eds), *Relational Autonomy: Feminist Perspectives on Autonomy, Agency and the Social Self* (New York: Oxford University Press), 3–34.

Madon, Shirin, Reinhard, Nicolau, Roode, Dewald, and Walsham, Geoff (2009), 'Digital inclusion projects in developing countries: Processes of institutionalization', *Information Technology for Development*, 15 (2), 95–107.

Mann, Samuel, Smith, Lesley, and Muller, Logan (2008), 'Computing education for sustainability', *ACM SIGCSE Bulletin*, 40 (4), 183–93.

Martin, David, Hanrahan, Benjamin, O'Neill, Jacki, and Guota, Neha (2014), 'Being a turker', CSCW '14: Proceedings of the 17th ACM Conference on Computer-supported Cooperative Work & Social Computing, 15–19 February 2014, Baltimore, MD, 224–35.

Martin, David, Mariani, John, and Rouncefield, Mark (2009), 'Practicalities of participation: Stakeholder involvement in an electronic patient records project', in Alex Voss, Mark Hartswood, Rob Procter, Mark Rouncefield, R. Slack, and Monika Büscher (eds), *Configuring User-Designer Relations* (London: Springer), 133–155.

Martin, David, O'Neill, Jacki, Randall, Dave, and Rouncefield, Mark (2007), 'How can I help you? Call centres, classification work and coordination', *Computer-supported Cooperative Work (CSCW)*, 16 (3), 231–64.

Mats-Åke, Hugoson (2007), 'Centralized versus Decentralized Information Systems', Proceedings of the 2nd IFIP Conference on History of Nordic Computing, 21–23 August, Turku, Finland (Heidelberg: Springer), 106–15.

Mehrotra, Vijay and Fama, Jason (2003), 'Call center simulation modeling: methods, challenges, and opportunities', Proceedings of the 35th Conference on Winter Simulation: Driving Innovation, 135–43.

Mendoza, Antonette, Stern, Linda, and Carroll, Jennie (2007), 'Plateaus in long-term appropriation of an information system', ACIS '07: Proceedings of the 18th Australasian Conference on Information Systems, 5–7 Dec 2007, Toowoomba, Australia (University of Southern Queensland), 189–98.

Merkel, Cecelia B., Xiao, Lu, Farooq, Umer, Ganoe, Craig H., Lee, Roderick, Carroll, John M., and Rosson, Mary Beth (2004), 'Participatory design in community computing contexts: Tales from the field', PDC '04: Proceedings of the 8th Conference on Participatory Design: Artful Integration: Interweaving Media, Materials and Practices, 27–31 July 2004, Toronto, Canada (ACM Press), 1–10.

Meurer, Johanna, Müller, Claudia, Simone, Carla, Wagner, Ina, and Wulf, Volker (2018), 'Designing for sustainability: key issues of ICT projects for ageing at home', *Computer-supported Cooperative Work (CSCW)* 27 (3–6), 495–537.

Miller, Tim (2019), 'Explanation in artificial intelligence: Insights from the social sciences', *Artificial Intelligence*, 267, 1–38.

Mishra, Jyoti Laxmi, Allen, David, and Pearman, Alan (2011), 'Activity theory as a method-ological and analytical framework for information practices in emergency management', Proceedings of the 8th International ISCRAM Conference, 8–11 May 2011, Lisbon, Portugal.

Mohr, Catherine (2010, February), *Sustainability by Design* (video). TED Conferences. https://www.ted.com/talks/catherine_mohr_the_tradeoffs_of_building_green? referrer=playlist-sustainability_by_design

Moraux, Marie-France and Balme, Pierre (2007), 'Université de Technologie de Troyes', (Paris: Inspection générale de l'administration de l'Éducation nationale et de la Recherche).

Mukherjee, Arunima, Aanestad, Margunn, and Sahay, Sundeep (2012), 'Judicious design of electronic health records: Case from public health system in India', *Health Policy and Technology*, 1 (1), 22–7.

Müller, Claudia, Hornung, Dominik, Hamm, Theodor, and Wulf, Volker (2015), 'Practice-based design of a neighborhood portal: Focusing on elderly tenants in a city quarter living lab', in Proceedings of the 33rd Annual ACM Conference on Human Factors in Computing Systems (New York: ACM Press), 2295–304.

Mumtaz, Shazia (2001), 'Children's enjoyment and perception of computer use in the home and the school', *Computers & Education*, 36 (4), 347–62.

Mykkänen, Minna, Miettinen, Merja, and Saranto, Kaija (2016), 'Standardized nursing doc-umentation supports evidence-based nursing management', *Nursing Informatics*, 225, 466–70.

Nardi, Bonnie A. and Miller, James R. (1991), 'Twinkling lights and nested loops: Dis-tributed problem solving and spreadsheet development', *International Journal of Man-Machine Studies*, 34 (2), 161–84.

Nations, United (1987), *Report of the World Commission on Environment and Development, 'Our Common Future'* (United Nations, General Assembly).

Nicolaou, Nicos and Birley, Sue (2003), 'Academic networks in a trichotomous categorisa-tion of university spinouts', *Journal of Business Venturing*, 18 (3), 333–59.

Noblit, George and Hare, R. Dwight (1988), *Meta-ethnography: Synthesizing Qualitative Studies (Qualitative Research Methods Series* (Newbury Park, CA: Sage Publications).

Nussbaum, Martha (2003), 'Capabilities as fundamental entitlements: Sen and social justice', Feminist economics, 9 (2–3), 33–59.

Obendorf, Hartmut, Monique Janneck, and Matthias Finck (2009), 'Inter-contextual dis-tributed participatory design', *Scandinavian Journal of Information Systems*, 21 (1), 51–76.

Oghia, Michael J. (2017), 'Community networks as a key enabler of sustainable access', in Luca Belli, Sarbani Banerjee Belur, Peter Bloom, Anriette Esterhuysen, Nathalia Foditsch, Maureen Hernandez, and Erik Huerta (eds), *Community Networks: The Internet by the People, for the People. Official Outcome of the UN IGF Dynamic Coalition on Community Connectivity* (Rio de Janeiro, Brazil: Escola de Direito do Roi de Janeiro da Fundação Getulio Vargas), 77–102.

Ogonowski, Corinna, Jakobi, Timo, Müller, Claudia, and Hess, Jan (2018), 'PRAXLABS: A sustainable framework for user-centered ICT development. Cultivating research ex-periences from living labs in the home', in Volker Wulf, Volkmar Pipek, Dave Randall, Markus Rohde, Kjeld Schmidt, and Gunnar Stevens (eds), *Socio-informatics: A Practice-based Perspective on the Design and Use of IT Artifacts* (Oxford: Oxford University Press), 319–60.

Ogonowski, Corinna, Stevens, Gunnar, Hess, Jan, Randall, Dave, and Wulf, Volker (2018), 'Managing viewpoints: Maintenance Work in Sustainable Living Lab Research', in Volkmar Pipek and Markus Rohde (eds), *International Reports on Socio-informatics*, 15 (Bonn: IISI: International Institute for Socio-Informatics), 37.

Orlikowski, Wanda J. (1992a), 'The duality of technology: Rethinking the concept of technology in organizations', *Organization Science*, 3 (3), 398–427.

Orlikowski, Wanda J. (1992b), 'Learning from notes: Organizational issues in groupware implementation', CSCW '92: ACM Conference on Computer-supported Cooperative Work, November 1992, Toronto, Canada (ACM Press), 362–69.

Orlikowski, Wanda. J. and Gash, Debra C. (1994), 'Technological frames: making sense of information technology in organizations', *ACM Transactions on Information Systems (TOIS)*, 12 (2), 174–207.

Orlikowski, Wanda J. and Hofman, J. Debra (1997), 'An improvisational model for change management: The case of groupware technologies', *Sloan Management Review*, 38 (2), 11–22.

Orr, Julian E. (1986), 'Narratives at work: Story telling as cooperative diagnostic activity', CSCW '86: Proceedings of the 1986 ACM Conference on Computer-supported Cooperative Work, 3–5 December 1986, Austin, TX (ACM Press), 62–72.

Pade-Khene, Caroline, Mallinson, Brenda, and Sewry, Dave (2011), 'Sustainable rural ICT project management practice for developing countries: Investigating the Dwesa and RUMEP projects', *Information Technology for Development*, 17 (3), 187–212.

Palen, Leysia and Aaløkke, Stinne (2006), 'Of pill boxes and piano benches: home-made methods for managing medication', CSCW '06: 20th Anniversary Conference on Computer-supported Cooperative Work, 4–8 November 2006, Banff, Canada (New York: ACM), 79–88.

Palen, Leysia, Anderson, Kenneth M., Mark, Gloria, Martin, James, Sicker, Douglas, Palmer, Martha, and Grunwald, Dirk (2010), 'A vision for technology-mediated support for public participation & assistance in mass emergencies & disasters', *ACM-BCS Visions of Computer Science 2010*, 13–16 April 2010, Edinburgh, UK, 1–12.

Pantidi, Nadia, Ferreira, Jennifer, Balestrini, Mara, Perry, Mark, Marshall, Paul, and McCarthy, John (2015), 'Connected sustainability: Connecting sustainability-driven, grass-roots communities through technology', C&T '15: Proceedings of the 7th International Conference on Communities and Technologies, 27–30 June 2015, Limerick, Ireland (New York: ACM Press), 161–3.

Paternò, Fabio and Wulf, Volker (eds) (2017), *New Perspectives in End-user Development* (Cham, Switzerland: Springer International Publishing).

Paternò, Fabio and Volker Wulf (2017), 'Malleability in the hands of end-users', in Fabio Paternò and Volker Wulf (eds), *New Perspectives in End-user Development* (Cham: Springer), 137–63.

Peddie, David, Small, Serena, Badke, Katherin, Wickham, Maeve E., Bailey, Chantelle, Chruscicki, Adam, Ackerley, Christine, Balka, Ellen, and Hohl, Corinne M. (2016), 'Designing an adverse drug event reporting system to prevent unintentional reexposures to harmful drugs: Study protocol for a multiple methods design', JMIR Research Protocols 5 (3), e169.

Pedersen, Jens (2007), 'Protocols of research and design. Reflections on a participatory design project (sort of)', PhD thesis (IT University).

Philip, Kavita, Irani, Lilly, and Dourish, Paul (2012), 'Postcolonial computing: A tactical survey', *Science, Technology, & Human Values*, 37 (1), 3–29.

Piirainen, Kalle, Gonzalez, Rafael A., and Kolfschoten, Gwendolyn (2010), 'Quo vadis, design science?: A survey of literature', DESRIST '10: International Conference on Design Science Research in Information Systems, 4–5 June 2010, St Gallen, Switzerland (Berlin/Heidelberg: Springer), 93–108.

Pinch, Trevor and Bijker, Wiebe E. (1987), 'The social construction of facts and artefacts: Or how the sociology of science and sociology of technology might benefit each other', in Wiebe E. Bijker, Thomas P. Hughes, and Trevor Pinch (eds), *The Social Construction of Technological Systems* (Cambridge, MA: MIT Press), 159–87.

Pipek, Volkmar (2005), 'From tailoring to appropriation support: Negotiating groupware usage', PhD thesis (University of Oulu).

Pipek, Volkmar, Liu, Sophia B., and Kerne, Andruid (2014), 'Crisis informatics and collaboration: A brief introduction.', *Computer-supported Cooperative Work (CSCW)*, 23 (4–6), 339–45.

Pipek, Volkmar, Reuter, Christian, Ley, Benedikt, Ludwig, Thomas, and Wiedenhoefer, Torben (2013), 'Sicherheitsarena: Ein Ansatz zur Verbesserung des Krisenmanagements durch Kooperation und Vernetzung', *Crisis Prevention*, 1, 1–3.

Pipek, Volkmar, Stevens, Gunnar, Müller, Claudia, Veith, Michael, and Draxler, Sebastian (2008), 'Towards an appropriation infrastructure: Supporting user creativity in IT adoption', ECIS '08: Proceedings of the European Conference on Information Systems, 9–11 June 2008, Galway, Ireland, 1165–77.

Pipek, Volkmar and Wulf, Volker (1999), 'A groupware's life', in Susanne BØdker, Morten Kyng, and K. Schmidt (eds), ECSCW '99: Proceedings of the 6th European Conference on Computer-supported Cooperative Work, 12–16 September 1999, Copenhagen, Denmark (Dordrecht: Springer), 199–218.

Pipek, Volkmar and Wulf, Volker (2009), 'Infrastructuring: Toward an integrated perspective on the design and use of information technology', *Journal of the Association for Information Systems*, 10 (5), 447–73.

Pirnay, Fabrice, and Surlemont, Bernard (2003), 'Toward a typology of university spin-offs', *Small Business Economics*, 21 (4), 355–69.

Prinz, Wolfgang, Mark, Gloria, and Pankoke-Babatz, Uta (1998), 'Designing groupware for congruency in use', CSCW '98, Proceedings of the 1998 ACM Conference on Computer-supported Cooperative Work, 14–18 November 1998, Seattle, Washington, 373–82.

Procter, Rob, Wherton, Joe, Greenhalgh, Trish, Sugarhood, Paul, Rouncefield, Mark, and Hinder, Sue (2016), 'Telecare call centre work and ageing in place', *Computer-supported Cooperative Work (CSCW)*, 25 (1), 79–105.

Purvis, Ben, Mao, Yong, and Robinson, Darren (2019), 'Three pillars of sustainability: In search of conceptual origins', *Sustainability Science*, 14 (3), 681–95.

Quinones, Pablo-Alejandro (2014), 'Cultivating practice & shepherding technology use: Supporting appropriation among unanticipated users', CSCW '14: Proceedings of the 17th ACM Conference on Computer-supported Cooperative Work & Social Computing, 15–19 February 2014, Baltimore, MD, USA (ACM Press), 305–18.

Ramirez, Leonardo, Dyrks, Tobias, Gerwinski, Jan, Betz, Matthias, Scholz, Markus, and Wulf, Volker (2012), 'Landmarke: An ad hoc deployable ubicomp infrastructure to support indoor navigation of firefighters', *Personal and Ubiquitous Computing*, 16 (8), 1025–38.

Randall, Dave (2018), 'Investigation and design', in Volker Wulf, Volkmar Pipek, Dave Randall, Markus Rohde, Kjeld Schmidt, and Gunnar Stevens (eds), *Socio-informatics: A Practice-based Perspective on the Design and Use of IT Artifacts* (Oxford: Oxford University Press), 221–42.

Randall, Dave, Dyrks, Tobias, Nett, Bernhard, Pipek, Volkmar, Ramirez, Leonardo, Stevens, Gunnar, Wagner, Ina, and Wulf, Volker (2018), 'Research into design research practices: Supporting an agenda towards self-reflectivity and transferability', in Volker Wulf, Volkmar Pipek, Dave Randall, Markus Rohde, Kjeld Schmidt, and Gunnar Stevens (eds), *Socio-informatics: A Practice-based Perspective on the Design and Use of IT Artifacts* (Oxford: Oxford University Press), 491–540.

Reidl, Christine, Tolar, Marianne, and Wagner, Ina (2008), 'Impediments to change: The case of implementing an electronic patient record in three oncology clinics', PDC '08: Proceedings of the 10th Anniversary Conference on Participatory Design, 1–4 October 2008, Bloomington, IN (New York: ACM Press), 21–30.

Reitmaier, Thomas, Bidwell, Nicola J., and Marsden, Gary (2010), 'field testing mobile digital storytelling software in rural Kenya', MobileHCI 12th International Conference on Human–Computer Interaction with Mobile Devices and Services, 7–10 September 2010, Lisbon, Portugal (ACM Press), 283–6.

Reitmaier, Thomas, Bidwell, Nicola, Siya, Masbulele J., Marsden, Gary, and Tucker, William D. (2012), 'Communicating in designing an oral repository for rural African villages', Information Society Technologies—Africa IST-Africa, 9–11 May 2012, Dar es Salaam, Tanzania.

Resnick, Mitchel, Rusk, Natalie, and Cooke, Stina (1998), 'The computer clubhouse: Technological fluency in the inner city', in D. Schon, B. Sanyal, and W. Mitchell (eds), *High Technology and Low-income Communities* (Cambridge, MA: MIT Press), 263–86.

Reuter, Christian, Ludwig, Thomas, Kaufhold, Marc-André, and Pipek, Volkmar (2015), 'XHELP: Design of a cross-platform social-media application to support volunteer moderators in disasters', Proceedings of the 33rd Annual ACM Conference on Human Factors in Computing Systems (New York: ACM Press), 4093–102.

Reuter, Christian, Marx, Alexandra, Pipek, Volkmar (2012), 'Crisis management 2.0: Towards a systematization of social software use in crisis situations', *International Journal of Information Systems for Crisis Response and Management* (*IJISCRAM*), 4 (1), 1–16.

Reuter, Christian, Pipek, Volkmar, and Müller, Claudia (2009), 'Avoiding crisis in communication: A computer-supported training approach for emergency management', *International Journal of Emergency Management*, 6 (3–4), 356–68.

Reuter, Christian and Spielhofer, Thomas (2017), 'Towards social resilience: A quantitative and qualitative survey on citizens' perception of social media in emergencies in Europe', *Technological Forecasting and Social Change*, 121, 168–80.

Rey-Moreno, Carlos (2017), 'Supporting the Creation and Scalability of Affordable Access Solutions: Understanding Community Networks in Africa' (The Internet Society).

Rey-Moreno, Carlos, Amalia Sabiescu, Masbulele Jay Siya, and William David Tucker (2015), 'Local ownership, exercise of ownership and moving from passive to active entitlement: A practice-led inquiry on a rural community network', *The Journal of Community Informatics*, 11 (2), 1–16.

Rey-Moreno, Carlos, Blignaut, Renette, Tucker, William, and May, Julian (2016), 'An in-depth study of the ICT ecosystem in a South African rural community: Unveiling expenditure and communication patterns', *Information Technology for Development*, 22 (sup 1), 101–20.

Rey-Moreno, Carlos, Roro, Zukile, Siya, Masbulele Jay, Simo-Reigadas, Javier, Bidwell, Nicola J., and Tucker, William David (2012), 'Towards a sustainable business model for rural telephony', 3rd International Workshop on Research on ICT for Human Development, Pisac.

Rey-Moreno, Carlos, Roro, Zukile, Tucker, William D., Siya, Masbulele Jay, Bidwell, Nicola J., and Simo-Reigadas, Javier (2013), 'Experiences, challenges and lessons from rolling out a rural WiFi mesh network', DEV '13: Proceedings of the 3rd ACM Symposium on Computing for Development ACM, 11–12 January 2013, Bangalore, India (ACM Press).

Rey-Moreno, Carlos, Sabiescu, Amalia, Siya, Masbulele Jay, and Tucker, William D. (2015a), 'Local ownership, exercise of ownership and moving from passive to active entitlement: A practice-led inquiry on a rural community network', *The Journal of Community Informatics*, 11 (10), 1–16.

Rey-Moreno, Carlos, Tucker, William, Cull, Domonic, and Blom, R. (2015b), 'Making a community network legal within the South African regulatory framework', Proceedings of the 7th International Conference on Information and Communication Technologies and Development, 15–18 May 2015, Singapore (New York: ACM), 57.

Ribes, David (2014), 'Ethnography of scaling, or, how to a fit a national research infrastructure in the room', CSCW '14: Proceedings of the 17th ACM Conference on Computer-supported Cooperative Work & Social Computing, 15–19 February 2014, Baltimore, MD (New York: ACM Press), 574–87.

Ribes, David and Finholt, Thomas (2009), 'The long now of technology infrastructure: articulating tensions in development', *Journal of the Association for Information Systems*, 10 (5), 375–98.

Richardson, Ann (1983), *Participation* (London: Routledge and Kegan Paul).

Rittel, Horst W. J. and Webber, Melvin (1973), 'Dilemmas in a general theory of planning', *Policy Sciences*, 4 (2), 155–69.

Robertson, Toni and Wagner, Ina (2012), 'Ethics: Engagement, representation and politics-in-action', in J. Simonsen and T Robertson (eds), *Routledge International Handbook of Participatory Design* (London/New York: Routledge), 64–85.

Robinson, Jennifer (2016), 'Comparative urbanism: New geographies and cultures of theorizing the urban', *International Journal of Urban and Regional Research*, 40 (1), 187–99.

Robinson, Mike (1993), 'Design for unanticipated use....', ECSCW '93: Proceedings of the 3rd European Conference on Computer-supported Cooperative Work, 13–17 September 1993, Milan, Italy (Dordrecht, The Netherlands: Springer), 187–202.

Robinson, Mike and Bannon, Liam (1991), 'Questioning representations', in Liam Bannon, Mike Robinson, K. Schmidt, (eds), ECSCW '91: Proceedings of the 2nd European Conference on Computer-supported Cooperative Work, 24–27 September 1991, Amsterdam, The Netherlands (Dordrecht, The Netherlands: Springer).

Rosner, Daniela K. and Ames, Morgan (2014), 'Designing for repair? Infrastructures and materialities of breakdown', CSCW '14: Proceedings of the 17th ACM Conference on Computer-supported Cooperative Work & Social Computing, 15–19 February 2014, Baltimore, MD, 319–31.

Rüller, Sarah, Aal, Konstantin, and Holdermann, Simon (2019), 'Reflections on a design case study: (Educational) ICT intervention with Imazighen in Morocco', C&T '19: Proceedings of the 9th International Conference on Communities & Technologies—Transforming Communities, 3–7 June 2019, Vienna, Austria, 172–7.

Saad-Sulonen, Joanna, Eriksson, Eva, Halskov, Kim, Karasti, Helena, and Vines, John (2018), 'Unfolding participation over time: Temporal lenses in participatory design', *CoDesign*, 14 (1), 4–16.

Saeed, K. A., Grover, V., Kettinger, W. J., & Guha, S. (2011), 'The successful implementation of customer relationship management (CRM) system projects', *ACM SIGMIS Database: The DATABASE for Advances in Information Systems*, 42 (2), 9–31.

Saeed, Saqib, Rohde, Markus, and Wulf, Volker (2008), 'A framework towards IT appropriation in voluntary organisations', *International Journal of Knowledge and Learning*, 4 (5), 438–51.

Sahay, Sundeep and Walsham, Geoff (2006), 'Scaling of health information systems in India: Challenges and approaches', *Information Technology for Development*, 12 (3), 185–200.

Sanchez, Stéphane, Echajari, Loubna, Friot-Guichard, Valérie, Blua, Philippe, and Laplanche, David (2020), 'L'évolution des routines comme levier de l'innovation organisationnelle: Le cas du Département d'Information Médicale du Centre Hospitalier de Troyes face à la crise Covid-19', 8e Congrès Aramos, 13–14 October 2020, Paris, France.

Scheirer, Mary Ann (2005), 'Is sustainability possible? A review and commentary on empirical studies of program sustainability', *American Journal of Evaluation*, 26 (3), 320–47.

Schmidt, Kjeld and Kaavé, Bjarne (1991), *Cooperative Production Control in Manufacturing* (Roskilde, Denmark: Risø National Laboratory).

Schmidt, Kjeld and Simone, Carla (1996), 'Coordination mechanisms: Towards a conceptual foundation of CSCW systems design', *Computer-supported Cooperative Work (CSCW)*, 5 (2–3), 155–200.

Schmidt, Kjeld, Wagner, Ina, and Tolar, Marianne (2007), 'Permutations of Cooperative work practices: A study of two oncology clinics', International Conference on Supporting Group Work (GROUP 2007), 4–7 November 2007, Sanibel Island, FL (ACM Press), 1–10.

Schmidt, Robert (2008), 'Gaining insight from incomparability: Exploratory comparison in studies of social practices', *Comparative Sociology*, 7 (3), 338–61.

Schubert, Kai, Weibert, Anne, and Wulf, Volker (2011), 'Locating computer clubs in multicultural neighborhoods: How collaborative project work fosters integration processes', *International Journal of Human-computer Studies*, 69 (10), 669–78.

Shediac-Rizkallah, Mona C. and Bone, Lee R. (1998), 'Planning for the sustainability of community-based health programs: Conceptual frameworks and future directions for research, practice and policy', *Health Education Research*, 13 (1), 87–108.

Shewarga-Hussen, Tigist, Bidwell, Nicola, Rey-Moreno, Carlos, and Tucker, William D. (2016), 'Gender and Participation: Critical Reflection on Zenzeleni Networks', AfriCHI '16: Proceedings of the 1st African Conference on Human Computer Interaction, 21–25 November 2016, Nairobi, Kenya, 12–23.

Silverstone, Roger and Haddon, Leslie (1996), 'Design and the domestication of ICTs: Technical change and everyday life', in Roger Silverstone (ed.), *Communicating by Design: The Politics of Information and Communication Technologies* (Oxford: Oxford University Press), 44–74.

Simone, Carla (2018), 'Everything is permitted unless stated otherwise: Models and representations in socio-technical (re) design', in Cecilia Rossignoli, Francesco Virili, and Stefano Za (eds), *Digital Technology and Organizational Change. Reshaping Technology, People, and Organizations Towards a Global Society* (LNISO; Cham, Switzerland: Springer), 49–59.

Simone, Carla, Locoro, Angela, and Cabitza, Federico (2019), 'Drift of a corporate social media: The design and outcomes of a longitudinal study', in Federico Cabitza, Carlo Batini, and Massimo Magni (eds), *Organizing for the Digital World* (Cham, Switzerland: Springer), 189–201.

Simonsen, Jesper and Hertzum, Morten (2012), 'Sustained participatory design: Extending the iterative approach', *Design Issues*, 28 (3), 10–21.

Smolina, Kate, Persaud, Nav, and Morgan, Steven (2016), 'Toward better prescription drug surveillance in Canada', *Canadian Medical Association Journal (CMAJ)*, 188 (11), E252–E253.

Sommer, Lutz (2015), 'Industrial revolution-industry 4.0: Are German manufacturing SMEs the first victims of this revolution?', *Journal of Industrial Engineering and Management*, 8 (5), 1512–32.

Song, Steve, Carlos Rey-Moreno, Anriette Esterhuysen, and Navarro, Mike Jensen and Leandro (2018), 'Introduction: The rise and fall and rise of community networks', in Global Information Society Watch (ed.), *Community Networks* (APC), 7–10.

Spinosa, Charles, Flores, Fernando, and Dreyfus, Hubert (1997), Disclosing New Worlds: Entrepreneurship, Democratic Action, and the Cultivation of Solidarity (Cambridge, MA: MIT Press).

Ssozi-Mugarura, Fiona, Blake, Edwin, and Rivett, Ulrike (2017), 'Codesigning with communities to support rural water management in Uganda', *CoDesign*, 13 (2), 110–26.

Star, Susan Leigh, and Ruhleder, Karen (1996), 'Steps toward an ecology of infrastructure: Design and access for large information spaces', *Information Systems Research*, 7 (1), 111–34.

Star, Susan Leigh, and Anselm Strauss (1999), 'Layers of silence, arenas of voice: The ecology of visible and invisible work', *Computer-supported Cooperative Work (CSCW)*, 8 (1), 9–30.

Stevens, Gunnar and Pipek, Volkmar (2018), 'Making use: understanding, studying, and supporting appropriation', in Volker Wulf, Volkmar Pipek, Dave Randall, Markus Rohde, Kjeld Schmidt, and Gunnar Stevens (eds), *Socio-informatics: A Practice-based Perspective on the Design and Use of IT Artifacts* (Oxford: Oxford University Press), 139–76.

Stevens, Gunnar, Pipek, Volkmar, and Wulf, Volker (2009), 'Appropriation infrastructure: supporting the design of usages', in W. Pipek, M.B. Rosson, and V. Wulf (eds), IS-EUD '09: Proceedings of the 2nd International Symposium on End-user Development, 2–4 March 2009, Siegen, Germany (Berlin/Heidelberg/New York: Springer), 50–69.

Stevens, Gunnar, Rohde, Markus, Korn, Matthias, and Wulf, Volker (2018), 'Grounded design: A research paradigm in practice-based computing', in Volker Wulf, Volkmar Pipek, Dave Randall, Markus Rohde, Kjeld Schmidt, and Gunnar Stevens (eds), *Socio-informatics: A Practice-based Perspective on the Design and Use of IT Artifacts* (Oxford: Oxford University Press), 23–46.

Stock, Tim and Seliger, Günther (2016), 'Opportunities of sustainable manufacturing in industry 4.0', Procedia CIRP, 40, 536–41.

Strauss, Anselm (1978), 'A social world perspective', *Studies In Symbolic Interaction*, 1 (1), 119–28.

Strauss, Anselm (1979), *Negotiations: Varieties, Contexts, Processes, And Social Order* (San Francisco, CA: Jossey-Bass).

Strauss, Anselm (1988), 'The articulation of project work: an organizational process', *The Sociological Quarterly*, 29 (2), 163–78.

Strauss, Anselm, Fagerhaugh, Shizuko, Suczek, Barbara, and Wiener, Carolyn (1985), *Social Organization of Medical Work* (Chicago: The University of Chicago Press).

Stumme, Gerd and Maedche, Alexander (2001), 'FCA-Merge: Bottom-up merging of ontologies', IJCAI '01: Proceedings of the 17th International Joint Conference on Artificial Intelligence, 4–10 August 2001, Seattle, Washington (1), 225–30.

Swan, Jack, Scarbrough, Harry, and Robertson, Maxine (2002), 'The construction of "Communities of Practice" in the management of innovation', *Management Learning*, 33 (4), 477–96.

Thoben, Klaus-Dieter, Wiesner, Stefan, and Wuest, Thorsten (2017), 'Industrie 4.0 and smart manufacturing: A review of research issues and application examples', *International Journal of Automation Technology*, 11 (1), 4–16.

Thomas-Hughes, Helen and Barke, Jenny (2018), *Community Researchers and Community Researcher Training: Reflections from the UK's Productive Margin's: Regulating for Engagement Programme*, Bristol Law Research Paper Series (Bristol, UK: School of Law, University of Bristol).

Tixier, Matthieu, and Lewkowicz, Myriam (2011), 'Supporting the knowledge sharing dimension of social support: The case of Aloa-aidants.fr', CTS '11: The 2011 International Conference on Collaboration Technologies and Systems, 23–7 May 2011, Philadelphia, PA.

Tjoa, A. and Tjoa, Simon (2016), 'The role of ICT to achieve the UN Sustainable Development Goals (SDG)', in Mata F. and Pont A. (eds), WITFOR '16: 6th IFIP World Information Technology Forum, September 2016, San José, Costa Rica (481; Cham: Springer), 3–13.

Toivanen, Hannes, Mutafungwa, Edward, Hyvönen, Jukka, and Ngogo, Elikana (2012), 'Pro-poor social and economic opportunities in the African ICT innovation ecosystem', (Espoo, Finland: VTT Technical Research Centre of Finland).

Trigg, Randall H. and Bødker, Susanne (1994), 'From implementation to design: tailoring and the emergence of systematization in CSCW', CSCW '94: Proceedings of the 1994 ACM Conference on Computer-supported Cooperative Work, 22–26 October 1994, Chapel Hill, NC (New York: ACM Press), 45–54.

Tucker, William, Blake, Edwin, Marsden, Gary, Pearson, Murray, and Westerveld, Rudi (2007), 'Reflection on three years of rural wireless Internet Protocol communication research and fieldwork', in D. Browne (ed.), Southern African Telecommunication Networks and Applications Conference (SATNAC) (n.p.: Telkom), 452–57.

Vassilakopoulou, Polyxeni, Pesaljevic, Aleksandra, Marmaras, Nicolas. and Aanestad, Margunn, 'Collective action in national e-health initiatives: Findings from a cross-analysis of the Norwegian and Greek e-prescription initiatives', Proceedings of the Scandinavian Conference on Health Informatics, 29–30 August 2017, Kristiansand, Norway (Linköping, Sweden: Linköping University Electronic Press).

Verganti, Roberto (2008), 'Design, meanings, and radical innovation: A meta model and a research agenda', *Journal of Product Innovation Management*, 25 (5), 436–56.

Verhaegh, Stefan, Van Oost, Ellen, and Oudshoorn, Nelly (2016), 'Innovation in civil society: The socio-material dynamics of a community innovation', in S. Hyysalo, T.E. Jensen, and N. Oudshoorn (eds), *The New Production of Users: Changing Innovation Collectives and Involvement Strategies* (New York/London: Routledge), 193–218.

Wagner, Ina (1994), 'Zur sozialen Verhandlung von Zeit. Das Beispiel computergestützten Zeitmanagements', *Soziale Welt, Sonderband*, 9, 241–55.

Wakamiya, Shunji and Yamauchi, Kazunobu (2009), 'What are the standard functions of electronic clinical pathways?', *International Journal of Medical Informatics*, 78 (8), 543–50.

Wakkary, Ron and Tanenbaum, Karen (2009), 'A sustainable identity: The creativity of an everyday designer', CHI '09: Proceedings of the 2009 SIGCHI Conference on Human Factors in Computing Systems, 4–9 April 2009, Boston, MA (New York: ACM Press), 365–74.

Walsham, Geoff (2017), 'ICT4D research: Reflections on history and future agenda', *Information Technology for Development*, 23 (1), 18–41.

Watch, Global Information Society (2018), *Community Networks*, International Development Research Centre (IDRC), Ottawa, Canada.

Wegge, Jürgen, Van Dick, Rolf, Fisher, Gary K., Wecking, Christiane, and Moltzen, Kai (2006), 'Work motivation, organisational identification, and well-being in call centre work', *Work & Stress*, 20 (1), 60–83.

Weibert, Anne, Krüger, Max, Aal, Konstantin, Salehee, Setareh Sadat, Khatib, Renad, Randall, Dave, and Wulf, Volker (2019), 'Finding language classes: Designing a digital language wizard with refugees and migrants', CSCW '19: Proceedings of the ACM on Human-Computer Interaction, 3.

Weibert, Anne, Randall, Dave, and Wulf, Volker (2017), 'Extending value sensitive design to off-the-shelf technology: Lessons learned from a local intercultural computer club', *Interacting with Computers*, 29 (5), 715–36.

Weibert, Anne and Schubert, Kai (2010), 'How the social structure of intercultural computer clubs fosters interactive storytelling', IDC '10: Proceedings of the 9th International Conference on Interaction Design and Children, 9–12 June 2010, Barcelona, Spain, 368–71.

Weibert, Anne and Wulf, Volker (2010), '"All of a sudden we had this dialogue...": Intercultural computer clubs' contribution to sustainable integration', ICIC '10: Proceedings of the 3rd International Conference on Intercultural Collaboration, 19–20 August 2010, Copenhagen, Denmark, 93–102.

Whitley, Richard and Gläser, Jochen (2014a), 'Editor's introduction', in *Organizational Transformation and Scientific Change: The Impact of Institutional Restructuring on Universities and Intellectual Innovation* (Bingley, UK: Emerald Group), 1–15.

Whitley, Richard, Gläser, Jochen, and Laudel, Grit (2018), 'The impact of changing funding and authority relationships on scientific innovations', *Minerva*, 56 (1), 109–34.

Winschiers-Theophilus, Heike, Winschiers-Goagoses, Naska, Rodil, Kasper, Blake, Edwin, Zaman, Tariq, Kapuire, Gereon Koch, and Kamukuenjandje, Richard (2013), 'Moving away from Erindi-roukambe: Transferability of a rural community-based co-design', Proceedings of the 12th International Conference on Social Implications of Computers in Developing Countries IFIIP WG 9, Ocho Rios, Jamaica, May 2013, 363–74.

Winschiers-Theophilus, Heike, Zaman, Tariq, and Stanley, Colin (2019), 'A classification of cultural engagements in community technology design: introducing a transcultural approach', *AI & Society: Journal of Culture, Communication & Knowledge*, 34 (3), 419–35.

Wolf, Christine and Blomberg, Jeanette (2019a), 'Explainability in context: Lessons from an intelligent system in the IT services domain', Joint Proceedings of the ACM IUI 2019 Workshops, 20 March 2019, Los Angeles, CA.

Wolf, Christine and Blomberg, Jeanette (2019b), 'Evaluating the promise of human-algorithm collaborations in everyday work practices', CSCW '19: Proceedings of the ACM on Human-Computer Interaction, 3, 1–23.

Wolf, Christine and Blomberg, Jeanette (2020), 'Ambitions and ambivalences in participatory design: Lessons from a smart workplace project', PDC '20: Proceedings of the 16th Participatory Design Conference, June 2020, Manzanales, Colombia (New York: ACM Press), 193–202.

Wu, Qguoru, Xu, Yuhua, Feng, Shuo, Du, Zhiyong, Wang, Jinlong, and Long, Keping (2014), 'Cognitive internet of things: A new paradigm beyond connection', *IEEE Internet of Things Journal*, 1 (2), 129–43.

Wulf, Volker (1999), 'Evolving cooperation when introducing groupware: A self-organization perspective', *Cybernetics & Human Knowing*, 6 (2), 55–74.

Wulf, Volker, Müller, Claudia, Pipek, Volkmar, Randall, Dave, Rohde, Marcus, and Stevens, Gunnar (2015), 'Practice-based computing: Empirically-grounded conceptualizations derived from design case studies', in Volker Wulf, Kjeld Schmidt, and David Randall (eds), *Designing Socially Embedded Technologies in the Real-world* (London: Springer), 111–50.

Wulf, Volker, Pipek, Volkmar and Won, Markus (2008), 'Component-based tailorability: Enabling highly flexible software applications', *International Journal of Human-Computer Studies*, 66 (1), 1–22.

Wulf, Volker, Pipek, Volkmar, Randall, Dave, Rohde, Markus, Schmidt, Kjeld, and Stevens, Gunnar (eds) (2018), *Socio-informatics: A Practice-based Perspective on the Design and Use of IT Artifacts* (Oxford: Oxford University Press).

Wulf, Volker, Rohde, Markus, Pipek, Volkmar, and Stevens, Gunnar (2011), 'Engaging with practices: Design case studies as a research framework in CSCW', CSCW '11: Proceedings of the ACM 2011 Conference on Computer-supported Cooperative Work, 19–23 March 2011, Hangzhou, China, 505–12.

Wyche, Susan, Dillahunt, Tawanna R., Simiyu, Nightingale, and Alaka, Sharon (2015), '"If God gives me the chance I will design my own phone": Exploring mobile phone repair and postcolonial approaches to design in rural Kenya', Proceedings of the 2015 ACM International Joint Conference on Pervasive and Ubiquitous Computing, 7–11 September 2015, Osaka, Japan, 463–73.

Yerousis, George, Aal, Konstantin, Von Rekowski, Thomas, Randall, Dave, Rohde, Marcus, and Wulf, Volker (2015), CHI '15: 'Computer-enabled project spaces: connecting with Palestinian refugees across camp boundaries', Proceedings of the 33rd Annual ACM Conference on Human Factors in Computing Systems, 18–23 April 2015, Seoul, Republic of Korea (New York: ACM Press), 3749–58.

Yin, Robert (1981), 'The case study crisis: Some answers', *Administrative Science Quarterly*, 26 (1), 58–65.

Yli-Huumo, Jesse, Ko, Ddeokyoon, Choi, Sujin, Park, Sooyong, and Smolander, Kari (2016), 'Where is current research on blockchain technology?: A systematic review', *PLoS ONE*, 11 (10), e0163477.

Yoo, Daisy, Kantengwa, Odeth, Logler, Nick, Interayamahanga, Reverien, Nkurunziza, Joseph, and Friedman, Batya (2018), 'Collaborative reflection: A practice for enriching research partnerships spanning culture, discipline, and time', CHI '18: Proceedings of the 2018 CHI Conference on Human Factors in Computing Systems, 21–26 April 2018, Montréal, Canada (New York: ACM Press), 11.

Zettl, Veronika, Ludwig, Thomas, Kotthaus, Christoph, and Skudelny, Sascha (2017), 'Embedding unaffiliated volunteers in crisis management systems: Deploying and supporting the concept of intermediary organizations', 2nd Proceedings of the International Conference on Information Systems for Crisis Response and Management, 24–7 May 2015, Krystiansand, Norway, 421–31.

Zuboff, Shoshana (1988), In the Age of the Smart Machine (New York: Basic Books).

Index